JEAN-BAPTISTE MORIN

ASTROLOGIA GALLICA
BOOK TWENTY-TWO
DIRECTIONS

Translated from the Latin

by

JAMES HERSCHEL HOLDEN, M.A.
Fellow of the American Federation of Astrologers

AMERICAN FEDERATION OF ASTROLOGERS, INC.
Tempe, Arizona
1994

First Printing 1994
ISBN: 0-86690-425-5

Published by:
American Federation of Astrologers, Inc.
6535 S. Rural Road
PO Box 22040
Tempe, AZ 85285-2040

Printed in the United States of America

This book is for

Gerhard Houwing

who wanted it

and for

Susan Horton

who made it possible.

TABLE OF CONTENTS

LIST OF ILLUSTRATIONS

LIST OF TABLES

ACKNOWLEDGMENT

My friend, Robert C. Donat, Ph.D., Editor of Research Publications of the A.F.A., very kindly offered to convert my word processor files for this book into a printed format. The typesetting of this book is the result of his labours. I am sure the reader will join me in thanking him for the considerable effort he expended in making the text easier to read.

J.H.H. 11 September 1991

TRANSLATOR'S PREFACE

This book contains a translation of an important treatise on primary directions by Jean-Baptiste Morin, M.D. (1583-1656), who was a native of Villefranche, France. Morin studied at Aix and later at Avignon, where he took his degree in 1613. He practiced medicine successfully for some fifteen years, numbering many important persons among his patients. In 1630 he was appointed Regius Professor of Mathematics at the Collège de France, and thereafter devoted most of his time to astrology. It would be fair to characterize him as a Court Astrologer.

Towards the end of his life Morin completed a massive astrological treatise which he called *Astrologia Gallica 'French Astrology'*. Unfortunately, he never saw it in print. It was published posthumously at The Hague in 1661: a thick folio volume of 850 pages. The main text occupies 784 double-columned pages and is divided into 26 books, of which the first nine are devoted to philosophy, religion, and science, and the remainder to astrology proper. The text is in the scholarly Latin of the 17th century. Not much of it has ever been translated into modern languages.

The author's autobiography, which forms one of the prefaces, is available in French.[1] Book 21 on determinations is available in both French and English,[2] Book 25 on mundane and meteorological astrology in French,[3] and the portion of Book 26 dealing with elections in French.[4] In addition, there is a German paraphrase of Book 21.[5] Aside from some short extracts from a few of the other books, that is the lot. Little more than 100 pages out of 850!

Actually, the situation is not so bad as it might seem, for the 21st Book contains the essence of Morin's astrological theory. And the present translation adds another 100 pages, consisting of Book 22 on directions, with some important chapters from Books 13, 15, 16, 17, 18, and 20, and two sets of precepts from Book 23 on revolutions (solar and lunar returns) and Book 24 on progressions and transits. Thus, a core subset of Morin's theory of natal astrology is now available in English.

Book 22, which is translated here, follows naturally after Book 21. I strongly advise those who take up this translation to prepare themselves by reading Book 21 first. Of the available English translations, I personally prefer the one by

---

1. *La vie devant les astres*, trans. by Jean Hièroz (Nice, 1943).
2. *La théorie des déterminations astrologiques*, trans. by Henri Selva (Paris, 1902); *Cornerstones of Astrology* (Dallas, 1972), trans. from the 1945 Spanish version of Friedrich Schwickert's and Adolph Weiss's *Bausteine der Astrologie*, vol. 2, *Die astrologische Synthese* (Leipzig, 1925-27), which contains a paraphrase of portions of Book 21 (apparently based upon Selva's translation) embedded in a text on the Morin method by Schwickert and Weiss; *Astrosynthesis*, trans. by Lucy Little (New York, 1974); and *The Morinus System of Horoscope Interpretation* trans. by Richard S. Baldwin (Washington, 1974).
3. *L'astrologie mondiale et météorologique*, trans. by Jean Hièroz (Paris, 1946).
4. *La doctrine des élections de Morin*, trans. by Jean Hièroz (Nice, 1941).
5. By Schwickert and Weiss. See note 2 above.

Richard S. Baldwin, *The Morinus System of Horoscope Interpretation*, published by the American Federation of Astrologers at Tempe, Arizona. French readers can use Selva's translation, which I believe is still in print.

But now to Book 22 itself.

It is not an easy book. Its language is often intricate, and it forces the reader to think. It cannot be skimmed. Many passages require rereading and pondering. There are frequent cross-references, some of which cannot be followed up because they refer to passages in the *Astrologia Gallica* or in the works of other authors that have not yet been translated. Some of the base-building in the earlier part of Book 22 is tedious. And the author occasionally digresses into theological considerations that are of less interest to 20th century readers than to those of the 17th century. He continually employs logical arguments to prove his points and uses axioms and illustrations that must have been familiar to his learned contemporaries but which are unfamiliar to us.

His method is that of a private tutor. He conducts a dialogue with the reader, often anticipating his questions and objections and answering them as he goes along. His goal is to teach the reader how to correlate the directions in a chart with definite timed events in the life of the native. Combined with the method of determinations, explained in Book 21 and reviewed in Book 22, it enables the reader to "read" the chart and make predictions. The method is straightforward but demanding, for its user must learn how to analyze the individual determinations and combine them. A tricky business.

The author provides a firm theoretical foundation for primary directions. He takes as his astrological basis the theory of accidental significators and determinations set forth in Book 21. His mathematical basis is the so-called *Rational System* of Regiomontanus. He does not simply hand these bases to the reader, but he explains why he believes they are correct. He cites previous astrologers who held other opinions and opponents of astrology who argued that the whole thing was false. He lists their arguments and refutes them systematically by a process of logic. He raises objections that might occur to a reader, along with some more subtle ones of his own, and refutes all of them. And last, but by no means least, he deals with the question of whether astrology is in conflict with religion.

Morin was a master astrologer. Anyone who has the patience to read what he has to say and who makes an honest effort to understand it will surely gain an insight into astrological theory that would be difficult to acquire elsewhere.

Our modern astrological tradition is a blending of the Arabian version of Greek astrology with the variants introduced by Claudius Ptolemy. Morin and his contemporaries did not know this. They supposed that the features of Arabian astrology that were not present in the *Tetrabiblos* were invented by the Arabs themselves. For example, Morin criticizes the Arabs for using the triplicity rulers as an important tool, not knowing that this was a standard feature of Greek astrology, already fully developed at least a century before Ptolemy.

Morin refers to the *Tetrabiblos* from time to time—sometimes citing Ptolemy's authority for something and sometimes disagreeing with him. Like Jerome Cardan (to whom Morin refers most frequently), he was too important as astrological figure to ignore.

One other point that should be emphasized is that Morin used the Regiomontanus system of houses and directions. The modern favourite is Placidus. They are different. They produce different timing—sometimes, especially in higher latitudes, considerably different. If the results Morin obtained from the Regiomontanus system were as good as he leads us to believe, this casts the Placidus system into doubt. On the other hand, Morin's younger contemporary, Placidus, and some of the latter's more recent followers claim excellent results from Placidian methods. Placidus leaned towards Ptolemy; Regiomontanus and Morin (without realizing it) leaned away from him. Who was right?

For the benefit of the reader who might like to try his hand at Regiomontanus primaries, I have given the necessary mathematical formulae in Appendix 5. I might mention that primary directions can be calculated for the zodiacal positions of the planets and their aspects, or they can be calculated for the *mundane* positions, i.e., for their actual positions on the celestial sphere rather than their projections onto the zodiacal circle. Morin preferred the mundane positions and criticizes his predecessors for using zodiacal positions. He even developed a means of determining the latitude of aspects by means of which the mundane positions of the aspects can be found. His techniques and results are thus at variance with those employed by the small number of twentieth century astrologers who use primary directions.

Finally, a few words about the present translation. I have tried to change Morin's Latin into English as faithfully as possible without writing English sentences that are totally unreadable. My main goal was to preserve the content of his text; my secondary goal was to preserve something of his style. Wherever possible I have avoided paraphrase. This has made the translation more faithful to the original but somewhat harder to read. Morin had a sizable vocabulary and seems to have been fond of using every particle in the lexicon. My translation uses a smaller vocabulary than the original; consequently, I have dulled his style to some extent. I have done this deliberately rather than stud the English sentences with seldom-used words.

It was considered stylish to write complicated sentences in Latin. Morin had learned this lesson well. He not infrequently launches into a sentence and turns it into a lengthy paragraph. I have sometimes broken these monsters up, but usually I have kept them together with a liberal use of commas and semicolons. Here and there I have inserted one or more words in square brackets to bring the thought into better focus. And I have added footnotes where I thought the reader might need some help.

I have generally retained Morin's technical terms, even though some of them are old-fashioned or obsolescent. Thus, I have retained "revolutions," "geniture," "figure," and "nativity" instead of rendering them as "solar return" or "horoscope." But *thema* 'theme' (horoscope) was too much. And I have altered his usage of *horoscopus* 'horoscope' (which he uses in its original sense) and *domus* 'house'. For *horoscopus* I have constantly written 'Ascendant', and I have translated *domus* as 'house' where it means celestial house, and as 'domicile' where it means 'sign' (a word he seldom uses). He occasionally uses the word *duodecatemoria* for 'signs'; I have rendered this as 'twelfths' with an explanatory footnote to avoid

xiii

confusion with the same word in its most common sense of 'twelfths (of a sign)'—the 2 1/2 degree subdivisions.

A few everyday words give trouble. The Latin *morbus* is a malady of undesignated type, severe enough to make the sufferer at least uncomfortable. I translate it uniformly as "sickness." (British readers may prefer to make the mental substitution "illness.") It is all the same thing: *morbus* 'sickness' can be a bad cold or a fatal illness. In French it is *maladie*, in German *Krankheit*, in Spanish *enfermedad*, and in Italian *malattia*. The word *filius* is sometimes "son" and sometimes simply "child." The word *lis* means "quarrel," "dispute," or "lawsuit." All are ruled by the 7th house. Sometimes the context offers a clue as to which one Morin had in mind, but more often not. I have generally favoured "lawsuit," but Morin's intent is not always apparent.

Other bothersome words occur in connection with the 2nd house, where it is not always clear whether his choice of words is intended to emphasize "wealth" as distinguished from "money," or whether he just got tired of using one word and switched to another for stylistic relief. The same thing is true of "dignities" in connection with the 10th house. It can mean simply a title of some sort, but more often it designates an office of some importance. The reader will have to sort this out for himself. Finally, for the sake of uniformity, I have used the same English equivalents for a few words as those Baldwin used in his translation of Book 21, e.g., *ingenium* 'mental qualities' and *mores* 'moral nature'.

Any translation is a crutch, but I hope this one takes the reader where he wants to go without too much pain.

James H. Holden
9 May 1990

JEAN-BAPTISTE MORIN

ASTROLOGIA GALLICA, BOOK 22, DIRECTIONS

James Herschel Holden

An English translation of Morin's treatise on Primary Directions, which constitutes Book 22 of his *Astrologia Gallica*, with appendices containing supplementary material relating to Book 22, and addenda containing fundamental astrological principles–in particular the Table of Universal Rulerships of the Planets from Book 13, the Universal Laws of Judgments of Solar and Lunar Returns from Book 23, and Aphorisms stating the Principal Laws of Transits along with Rules for the Prediction of future Events from Book 24.

This translation supplements Richard S. Baldwin's translation of Book 21 on Determinations (also published by the AFA). The two translations together provide a core subset of the theory of Natal Astrology set forth by J-B Morin (1583-1656), the leading figure of French astrology. Morin's theory is based upon the use of determinations and accidental significators,. Thus, it differs radically from the common theory that largely ignores derived houses and uses universal significators. Also, it is event-oriented rather than esoteric or psychological.

The translator is the Chief Research Coordinator of the American Federation of Astrologers and has been especially interested in the history of astrology

ISBN Number: 0-86690-425-5.

ASTROLOGIA GALLICA

BOOK TWENTY-TWO

DIRECTIONS

PREFACE

This is the principal and most divine book of all astrology. The one by means of which the times of the events that happen to a man after his birth are discovered, which is the supreme apex of natural prophecy, and the science that before all other physical sciences partakes of divinity. But the opinions of the old and the modern astrologers testify to how difficult and confused it has been hitherto, for they differ much among themselves, since the true principles of astrology were unknown to them. But we, to whom these principles have become known, are propounding this entire doctrine so very clearly from its proper and evident fundamentals, with contrary opinions and objections soundly refuted, that there will be no one hereafter who is able to call it back into doubt.

SECTION I

The Definition, Terms, and Division of Directions.

Chapt. 1. *What an Astrological Direction is; and what its Termini are; and how many Kinds of it there are.*

We are entering upon the principal matter of all astrology, but, Lord knows, the most difficult, shrouded in fog and frightening in its difficulties, which, unless I am deceived, so terrified the old astrologers, that their chief, Ptolemy,[1] however much he now and then philosophizes about the other things of this science, yet concerning directions seems to have been lacking in all calculation, content merely to expound two methods of directions, one following the succession of the signs and one against it, which we shall examine below.

---

1   Claudius Ptolemy (2nd Century), the most famous astronomer and science writer of classical antiquity. His astrological handbook, the *Tetrabiblos*, contains the fundamental instructions for calculating what are now called primary directions (in Book 3, Chapt. 10). His instructions were misunderstood by most of his readers (including Morin).

Nor did the rest of the old astrologers inquire into this matter any more deeply than Ptolemy, however eloquent they are in their distinguished ideas, but each one of them merely embraced the tradition of the predecessor that he chose to follow. Since the ancients handed down various modes of directions, which Junctinus[2] reviews in his *Commentary on Ptolemy*, Book 3, Chapt. 12, pp. 379 ff., a major confusion was introduced into astrology. But finally Lucius Bellantius[3] *Against Pico Mirandola*, Question 16; and Cardan,[4] in his book *Commentary on the Quadripartite*, Book 3, Chapt. 14, then in his *Book on the Judgment of Genitures* and other places, tried to discuss this subject with true philosophical reasons, so that at least in this one part they might defend faltering Astrology against the fiercer onslaughts of its adversaries. But they said too little about a matter of such moment, and what they did say was partly contrary to the truth, as will be plain in what follows, since indeed this treatise is the principal one of all astrology, not only in the breadth of its doctrine, but also in its necessity and its utility.

Since therefore so great a burden has been left to us: to look into this part of astrology more deeply, to untie its knots, to dissipate its fog, and to eradicate its difficulties, we shall try to the best of our ability, both with reasons and with cases, at least to open the road to those who come after us, to investigate more profoundly and to expound more clearly the truth of these matters, if anything which will be said in what follows may be less pleasing to them than to us. For in so arduous a subject I have striven chiefly to satisfy myself, because I am very fond of the truth, but not unaware that no one can please all, since Christ Himself with the infinite

---

2   Francesco Guintini, Th.D. (1522-1590?), a famous Florentine astrologer who spent the latter part of his life in Lyons, France, where his great *Speculum Astrologiae* [Mirror of Astrology] was published in 1573 and again in 1583. It contains the Greek text of Ptolemy's *Tetrabiblos* with a Latin translation and commentary, a systematic treatise of astrology based upon the Arabian tradition, and over 400 natal horoscopes used as exemplifications of the astrological rules.

3   Lucio Bellantio, A.D., M.D. (d. 1499), a native of Siena, who was in exile in Florence when Pico della Mirandola's book against astrology was published (1496). Bellantio composed a formal reply to Pico, *Responsiones in disputationes Johannis Pici adversus astrologicam veritatem*. [Reply to the Disputation of Giovanni Pico against the Truth of Astrology], and a more general treatise, *De astrologica veritate*, [The Truth of Astrology], which were published together at Florence in 1498.

4   Girolamo Cardano, M.D. (1501-1576), famous physician, mathematician, astrol-oger, and miscellaneous writer. Most of his astrological works appear in Vol. 5 of his *Opera*, published in 10 volumes at Lyons, France, in 1662. Morin refers here to Cardan's elaborate commentary on the *Tetrabiblos* or *Quadripartite*, as it is called in Latin. The reader should be aware that the division into chapters of the *Quadripartite* differs substantially from the division in F. E. Robbin's edition and tranlation of the *Tetrabiblos* in the Loeb Classical Library, which in turn differs slightly from the Teubner edition. However, those who have access to J. M. Ashmand's translation of Proclus's paraphrase of the *Tetrabiblos* will find that the division is nearly the same as that of the Latin *Quadripartite*.

wisdom of God the Father saw His own doctrine spurned by the Scribes and the Pharisees, and He bore it patiently. And so Cardan, in the "Peroration of the Work" at the end of his *Aphorisms*, says [p. 91]: "a direction is a reduction from that which is potential through the significator and the promittor to an action through the force of the Sun." But this definition states the effect of a direction rather than what a direction is: just as if someone defined a genethliacal figure of heaven to be the impression of the celestial influx upon the child being born. For as the celestial influx which is imprinted at the moment of birth is the effect of the genethliacal figure of heaven, so the reduction from potentiality to its act, which it signifies by a direction, is merely the effect of the direction properly said. Nor does this reduction begin from the moment of birth; otherwise, one who, because of a direction, is going to die from a burning fever in the 63rd year of his age, would begin to suffer from that sickness from birth and would grow steadily worse up to age 63; and consequently that native would never be healthy. Similarly, one who is going to be killed by a direction would begin to be killed from birth, which is plainly absurd, and so is the reasoning about the others. What in fact Cardan says, but does not prove, that the reduction from potentiality to action is through the force of the Sun, we shall subject to examination in its own place below. But here it is sufficient to know this much from what was said above: the definition given by Cardan is not legitimate, although it may agree in this with others, because there are two bounds or termini of a direction with a distance intermediate between them, of which one terminus is called the *significator*, and the other the *promittor*.

But all others think that an astrological direction is a certain reduction or progression, by which one terminus is transferred or is conceived to be transferred by the motion of the *primum mobile* to the location of the other to determine the years of the native's accidents. I add here what the function of directions [is] on account of the other progressions thought up by astrologers, designating months and days to their effects, which they usually call properly not directions but *progressions*,[5] of which we shall speak elsewhere. Moreover, the location of the second terminus is the circle of position passing through that same terminus by agreement of all the learned astrologers, who assert that "to direct" is nothing other than to find the arc of the equator that ascends above the circle of position of the significator, or the preceding terminus, when the following terminus is borne to this circle by the motion of the *primum mobile*.

Since therefore from the moment of birth, and during life, and even after the native's death, such directions of significators are accustomed to be made to their

---

5 By "progessions" Morin means what we would call "profections," i.e., symbolic directions that proceed at a fixed rate and are not dependent upon the actual motions of the planets. The most common type was the 12-year profection that begins wtih the Ascendant and moves forward in the zodiac one sign per year. This was used by the classical Greek astrologers and passed down to us through the Arabs. William Lilly explains it in his *Christian Astrology*, but it is virtually unknown to modern astrologers.

own promittors, so that the years of the accidents of this native are discovered by finding the abovesaid arcs, and since "to direct" is nothing else among all of them than to find that arc, it follows that among all astrologers up till now a direction is nothing else than finding that arc, by whatever way it may be sought, either through the revolution of a material sphere or through suitable tables.

But looking a little deeper into this doctrine in order to dispel its fog, we say here that a direction is in some respect the designation of an arc of the equator ascending above the circle of position of the significator when the promittor is borne to that circle by the motion of the *primum mobile*, or it is an arc of the equator intercepted between two circles of declination, of which one passes through the place of the promittor in its own location, and the other through the same place of the promittor when it has been transferred by the motion of the *primum mobile* to the circle of position of the significator. But in appearance a direction is twofold —one artificial, and the other natural; hence the twofold designation of the arc.

An *artificial* direction is the designation or finding of the said arc, either through the revolution of a material sphere or through suitable tables, which we shall first undertake to teach. But *natural* is the designation of the said arc by the reduction of the promittor to the circle of position of the significator through the natural primary revolution of the *primum caelum*, which begins at the moment of birth. And this is a direction, properly said, which will be explained more fully in Sect. 3, Chapt. 2.

Chapt. 2. *The Kinds of Future Events, both Universal and in the Human Species, arising from Celestial Causes; and what Future Events the Astrologer should Announce.*

Before we explain the doctrine of directions more fully, it seems to us that this chapter ought to be put first, because according to the definition given in Chapt. 1, the proper function of directions, at least of natural directions, is to presage future events to the native from the celestial bodies, and to discover the times of these, or the years, as will be taught in what follows. And consequently, with the suppositions already stated in Book 5, Sect. 3, Chapt. 1, concerning the possibility, the contingency, and the futurity of things; then, in Book 12, Sect. 3, Chapt. 24, about Divine Providence, fate, cause, and fortune, we have already said that of those future things arising from the celestial bodies some are inevitable, but others are contingent.

Inevitable future things are those that follow from natural necessity when their causes have been put in place, and they are of two kinds. Some in fact arise solely from the motion of the celestial bodies, such as equinoxes, solstices, conjunctions and configurations of the stars, eclipses, new Moons, full Moons, etc. Which motion, since it is regarded by all astronomers as being entirely regular and naturally inviolable, is certain because if its laws have become exactly known the true times of all these [phenomena] will be predicted with great certainty. But others are also [caused] by the active qualities of the celestial bodies, such as the various conditions of the year, the month, and the day—rains, winds, fair weather, comets, pestilences, floods, famines, and such like, which are caused by the stars according to their diverse location in the sky, and their diverse mutual configuration, and also by their diverse location on the globe of the earth or its parts. For since the celestial causes of these effects, namely great conjunctions, the annual revolutions of the Sun, eclipses, etc., act inevitably, they never lack an object on which to act, namely the globe of the earth; therefore, having postulated such causes, their effects may then be postulated as inevitable, unless they are involved in free causes, which are war, sects, and such like, about which [we will speak] below.

And that which we have said about the universal subject of the influence of the celestial bodies should likewise be understood about a particular subject, like a man, about whose generation when the *caelum* acts, his temperament, bodily form, mental qualities, and characteristics are necessarily [derived] from the stars, having taken into account the individual disposition of the seed and the womb. For in these things the *caelum* cannot be impeded, lest it act very like the disposition of the subject on which it acts. And although the effects of some particular celestial cause, such as Saturn, are said to be capable of being impeded by another cause of contrary virtue, such as the Sun; still, because the Sun will be conceded to be impeded just as much by Saturn as Saturn is by the Sun, it may more rightly be said that each planet does act, but in concert—one of them being either weakened or distorted by the other with respect to the effect that is necessarily produced in the passive subject by the concourse of both. The same thing is true of two or more other planets acting together in the same effect: they help or impede or distort each other with respect to their effect when they are determined toward the same thing.

But contingently future things are those which, even when their causes have been put in place, do not inevitably occur, at least in happening or being done, because the causes themselves can in fact be impeded. And such things are, for example, wars, sects, and such like, whose causes, even though they are in the *caelum* pouring out the seeds of such effects on those below, and indeed, even though they are rarely frustrated in their effect because of the greater propensity of man towards evil than towards good; yet, because they depend on the free will of men as the cause per se and the immediate cause, and because the will is the master of its own acts, consequently they can come to pass or not, according as the will determines itself either to compliance with the celestial influx or to prudently averting its effects; and therefore they can be predicted only conjecturally. Nevertheless, from a universal disposition of the *caelum* for wars, a war of some kind can safely be predicted, for a universal disposition will not everywhere be frustrated from taking effect, nor will there be lacking in some place at least princes or scoundrels prone to wars, especially when it produces such persons, or the disposition excites and sets into motion persons already produced; and a single man, even a common man, is sufficient [to start] a war, a schism, a sect, and such like in the whole world, or in the indicated part of it, as is plain from Mohammed, Luther, Calvin, Attila, and others. And the same reasoning applies to the rest of the dispositions of the *caelum* to other vices or virtues, that is, the depravity and perniciousness of human kind or its reformation and utility, which in this differ greatly, because the reformation of any kingdom or empire is not the undertaking of a common man but of a king or emperor divinely inspired to this end, whose authority helps his natural inclination. But very rarely is such a king or emperor born, who at least receives an education agreeable to his inclination, and who is not deceived or led astray by the evil arts of his counselors or assistants.

But in a particular subject, such as a man, future occurrences are contingent. First, those things that pertain to his moral nature, even those that mostly follow temperament and native propensity. For God said to Cain, "The desire for it will be under you, and you will rule it."[6] Then wealth, brothers, children, servants, spouse, journeys, religion, actions, profession, dignity, friends, enemies, imprisonment, sickness, for all these things are submissive to the will of man, as well as to prudence or imprudence. However, parents are not future things, since they precede, but future things happening to the native because of them or with them are signified. Finally, death, although it may be inevitable in the future, yet its quality is contingent and can be diverse. Nevertheless, whatever future things are signified by the stars for the man who is being born are most often accustomed to happen from two causes. First, because man most often yields to the natural propensity impressed upon him by the stars at birth. Second, because man lacking astrology [and therefore] ignorant of his own fate, especially of an unlucky fate, is not able to change it by forethought and prudence. Therefore, astrology is not only necessary, but very often also true in its predictions of future things for men, although among those men it is only conjectural, as [is the case] with medicine.

But having understood these things, we already say that the astrologer can predict some future things from celestial causes, but not in the same manner. For the things that are going to happen due only to the motion of the celestial bodies, he predicts with certainty through the laws of astronomy. But the things that are going to happen because of the active qualities of those same bodies he predicts with the laws of judicial [astrology] and not even in the same way. For general events emanating from the universal dispositions of the *caelum*, such as plagues, wars, floods, etc., are predicted in one way; and the particular effects that will happen after birth to any man who is being born, or will at least be signified for him, are predicted in another way. For in the latter case both the substance of the effect and also its time are predicted through directions; but how these things may be foretold—both their substance and also their time—will be explained in its own place.

---

6 Genesis 4:7. God was speaking of sin.

Furthermore, a particular event signified for a man after his birth is predicted with certainty so far as the time of its manifestation is signified; for the time itself depends on a certain and definite distance of the significator from the promittor; then by a certain motion of the stars in revolutions and transits of planets to the places of a geniture, [by] which [the revolutions and transits] agree with the direction for that event. But with respect to existence and substance that effect is predicted only conjecturally by human skill, even though by a conjecture that may very often be equated to certitude. But the substance itself of the effect, or its nature, can be predicted in three ways. First, very generally, as that a native will die a bad or harsh death. Second, more specifically, as that his death will be very violent. Third, most specifically, as that the native will be hung, or his head will be cut off, or he will be slain by the enemy, or he will be drowned, etc. And indeed the first prediction can be made from the first elements of astrology. The rest, however, deserve a greater glory, but they must not be undertaken by just anybody, especially the last, for in addition to an outstanding judgment illuminated by theory, they also require long and manifold exercise in their own field and in that of others; and the same reasoning applies to the rest. Therefore, having explained these things thus, we are now ready to discuss the significators and promittors of the effects that will take place for the man being born.

Chapt. 3. *The Significators of Things that will take place for a Man, and their General Definition and Number.*

There is nothing that is inherent in a man or will be inherent in him that is not signified by the stars in his natal horoscope. But those things that are inherent in him or will be inherent in him generally pertain either to his body or to his mind or to his fortune. And these kinds of things are separated into different categories. For things of the body comprise temperament, bodily appearance, life, strength, and health; then, the opposites of these—sicknesses, wounds, and death. The things of the mind: character, moral nature, mental qualities, religion, skills, knowledge. Finally, the things of fortune: parents, brothers, wealth, profession, dignities, servants, the wife, children, friends, enemies, journeys, freedom, imprisonment, exiles. Therefore it is necessary that the significators of these in the genethliacal figure be given, if the body, the mind, and the fortune (which no one active in astrology will deny) are affected by the stars. From which significators there is indicated not only what is inherent in the man being born in the matter of body and mind at the very moment of his nativity, but what [conditions] will accrue to him after birth in those things that pertain to the body, the mind, and to fortune. And this is why these significators are directed, so that the times of the events may be known in order to permit the exercise of prudence by their prevision.

Besides, among astrologers there is no little dissension with regard to the significators themselves. For Ptolemy, *Quadripartite*, Book 4, Chapt. 11, adopts only five significators to be directed for all the future accidents of the native, viz. the Ascendant for health and travel, the Part of Fortune for assets, the Moon for mental characteristics and conversation, the Sun for dignity and glory, and finally the Midheaven for the other actions of life and for the procreation of children. Moreover, Cardan in his *Commentary* not only adheres to this opinion, which he praises, saying that these five significators are sufficient bases for all the good and evil things that can happen to the native from the planets and the cusps of the sectors, but in that same place Haly[7] refutes [Ptolemy's theory] and assumes seven planets and twelve cusps for significators to be directed; and Schöner,[8] Book 3, and others follow Haly. But Cardan, not standing firm on his own custom, at the end of his *Commentary* to Book 3, throws over the opinion of Ptolemy, since for the state of mind he directs the Moon, the Sun, and Mercury, and for the state of the body, the Moon, the Sun, and the Ascendant. Moreover, in Book 3, Aphorism 39, he says to direct the planets and the fixed stars and also the rays of the planets to the 2nd house for wealth, making the cusp itself the significator of wealth; otherwise, the rays of the planets would be significators, against the opinion of all astrologers. Why then shouldn't all the other cusps be significators? Moreover, in his *Book on the Judgment of Genitures*, Chapt. 4, he directs Venus as a significator to the opposition of Jupiter for the time of his own marriage. And after that, in Chapt. 5, he counts 10 significators, viz. 7 planets, the Ascendant, the Midheaven, and the conjunction or opposition of the luminaries which most nearly preceded the birth. But in Chapts. 5 and 6 of the *Book of Revolutions,* and in Book 3, Aphorism 137, he recognizes the cusps of the twelve houses and the seven planets as significators, which he combines among themselves in various ways, and he rejects the preceding conjunction. What need is there for more [instances] to detect Cardan's inconsistency in this matter?

Moreover, although others have expressed an opinion about the significators to be directed and their number, yet the more common opinion among astrologers has hitherto been that of Ptolemy: just the five significators mentioned above, although Sixtus ab Hemminga,[9] the apostate astrologer, in his book *Astrology*

7   Presumably Haly Abenragel ['Ali ibn abi al-Rijal (d. after 1037)], author of *Praeclaris-simus liber completus de iudiciis astrorum* [The very famous Complete Book of the Judgments of the Stars] (Venice, 1485, etc.), or else Haly Abenrudian ['Ali ibn Ridwan (988-1061?)], author of a much read commentary on pseudo-Ptolemy's *Centiloquy* and some other astrological tracts.

8   Johann Schöner (1477-1547), German mathematician, astronomer, and astrol-oger who wrote *De iudiciis nativitatum libri tres* [Three Books on the Judgments of Nativities] (Nürnberg, 1545).

9   A Frisian physician who had studied astrology but had grown disenchanted with it to such an extent that he wrote a book against it, *Astrologiae ratione et experientia refutatae liber* [Astrology Refuted by Reason and Experience] (Antwerp, 1583).

Refuted by Reason, wants all the effects that are going to happen to the native to be due to only four significators, the Ascendant, the Midheaven, the Sun, and the Moon, the inferior ignorance of which is shown to be more obscure than the Moon itself, seeing that he wrongly directs these alone for all the native's accidents. Moreover, Origanus,[10] in Part 3, Member 4, thinks that the abovesaid five significators of Ptolemy are the principal ones, but that all the planets and the cusps of the houses ought to be directed. Therefore, this controversy over the number of significators has lasted down to us; nor has anyone brought forward any reasons for his opinion,except perhaps frivolous ones, such as Cardan set forth in his previously mentioned *Commentary on the Quadripartite*, Book 4, Chapt. 11 [p. 360], for the five significators of Ptolemy, saying:"For these are the bases of all the good things and parts of a house. For some are good things of the mind, some of the body, others of fortune. The good things of the mind are denoted by the Moon, those of the body moreover by the Ascendant, the most important things of fortune —glory and dignities—by the Sun, the moderately good things by the Lot [of Fortune], [and] the least good by the Midheaven. Again, in the case of relations, such as children and the wife, they are denoted by the Midheaven and the Moon. Therefore, since nothing is lacking, it is sufficient to direct these places." So, Cardan. But this reasoning proves nothing, except the same through the same, namely that good things of the mind are from the Moon because such good things are from the Moon, or they are properly signified by the Moon itself, as he says in that place, and so with the rest. Therefore, what wonder that these and similar ridiculous reasons have exposed astrology to mockery among philosophers?

Furthermore, this fivefold number of significators to be directed rests not just a little on a long-standing error of astrologers about the significators per se, or, (as Cardan says in his *Book of Revolutions*, Chapt. 5) *by essential nature*, which we have refuted in Book 21, Sect.1, Chapt. 3. For no more valid reason can be brought forward by Cardan why the Sun should be directed for life, glory, dignities, and the father, or the Moon for mental characteristics, the mother, and the wife, than that the Sun and the Moon are significators of these per se, or by essential nature, which however Cardan himself does not prove. Besides, if they are directed for these things for this reason, why shouldn't the twelve house cusps and the seven planets be directed, which Cardan himself, in the chapter just mentioned, makes significators by essential nature of the diverse accidents attributed to them— indeed, the rulers of these [accidents], [and consequently] significators by accident of these same events? For example then, if the Moon is directed for the wife because the Moon, Venus, and the cusp of the 7th are significators of the wife by nature, as he will have it in that same Chapt. 5, but the dispositors of these, or their

---

10 David Origanus (1558-1628) was professor of mathematics at Frankfurt. He was well known in astrological circles for his ephemerides and his treatise on astrology, *Astrologia naturalis sive tractatus de effectibus astrorum* [Natural Astrology or a Treatise on the Effects of the Stars] that was published posthumously at Marseilles in 1645.

rulers, significators by accident, why similarly shouldn't the cusps of the other houses be directed, and then the planets agreeing with the significations of the cusps, as the Sun and Saturn for the father or the 4th house, Jupiter for wealth or the 2nd? Therefore it is very clear from what was said above how uncertain, confused, and self-contradictory is Cardan's teaching about the significators to be directed, in which along with all the other astrologers he erred severely in this respect—that none of them hitherto has spoken of the significators that he calls "by accident." For example, the ruler of the Ascendant for life, health, etc., since it is the ruler of the Ascendant, the ruler of the Midheaven for actions and honours, since it is the ruler of the Midheaven, and so with the others. Nor similarly have they directed the planets found in the houses for the things signified by those houses, such as Venus posited in the 10th for actions or honours, Jupiter placed in the 7th for mental qualities, etc., even though experience proves that the directions of these are much more certain in their effects than those of the planets that are significators of the same effects by nature, unless they are determined in the figure by bodily position or rulership. And Junctinus certainly seems to have scented this in his *Commentary* on Book 3, Chapt. 12 of Ptolemy (p. 396), where, after he has put the significations by nature of the seven planets, he adds "The several planets signify these things per se in directions, and they are customarily directed for the events of these significations. But sometimes they assume accidental significations from the nature of the houses in which they are placed and from those which they rule, which can easily be inferred from the natures of the domiciles." Nevertheless, he never directs these planets because of their own accidental significations, for example, Jupiter in the 7th, or ruler of the 7th, for marriage, etc.

But in fact, in order to explain this difficulty, it seems necessary first to define in general what astrologers consider a significator to be. Cardan, cited above, says that significators are subjects of good and evil things that can happen to the native from the planets and the cusps of the houses, but he is deceived. For of the good and evil things that can happen to the native, there is nothing that is a subject [more] than the native himself to whom they happen. Moreover, since there are various kinds of good and evil things that happen to a man, and some refer to his life, some to actions, others to friends, etc., and these classes of events pertaining to the twelve houses are subjects susceptive of various kinds of accidents, such as those of life, health and sickness, actions, happiness and unhappiness; also, it is plain that the Ascendant as significator of life, is not a subject to which sickness or health happens, that is, it is not life itself, and so with the rest. Therefore, the Ascendant as significator of life is in no way the subject of those things which happen to the native. Then what is it?

Here surely shines forth the solid truth of the doctrine we have given in Book 21, Sect. 2, Chapt. 1, and elsewhere. Namely, that the Ascendant may be said for this reason to be the significator of life, since it signifies about the life of the native, which life can be said to be the subject of the first house because it is represented most efficaciously by the Ascendant. And the Midheaven may be said to be the significator of actions because it signifies about the native's actions, which can be said to be the subject of the 10th house, represented by the 10th house. And so with the rest of the significators. From which it is deduced that a significator in astrology is nothing other than a celestial substance, that is, a part of the *caelum* or a planet, signifying through itself, by reason of determination, about some class of things happening to the native; from which it is also said to be the significator of its own class or subject as far as affecting [the native] through a direction, by which definition certainly the universal significators that Cardan calls "by nature," but we call "by analogy," are excluded except insofar as they may have been determined in the celestial figure. Then the aspects, which do not[11] signify through themselves, since they do not exist in themselves, but [only] through the planets from which they emanate; and they have only a relative existence.

But it follows from this definition that there are as many significators in kind for directions as there are planets and celestial houses, i.e., the parts of the *primum caelum* occupying the spaces of the 12 figures, whose virtue is most potent in the cusps. Therefore, as Haly maintained, there will be 19 significators, although there are only 12 generalities signified by the 12 houses; to which, if with Ptolemy we add the Part of Fortune, there will be 20 significators. For just as the cusp of the tenth is directed separately for the things signified by the tenth house, and the Ascendant for the things signified by the first [house],[12] so the cusps of the other houses ought to be be directed principally for the things signified by their houses. And from that a true and natural mode of construction of the celestial figure can be proved, which, of whatever sort it is, the directions prove the first and the tenth houses at least to be rightly constituted.

Besides, references to the seven planets are not to be understood as references to the bodies of the planets themselves, but rather to their places fixed in the *primum mobile*, or the parts of the *primum mobile* determined to the nature of these planets at the moment of the nativity by reason of their celestial and terrestrial state, as was set forth very fully in Books 20 and 21. And the reason is that the planets are in perpetual motion, and from the moment of the nativity they move away from the places which they occupied at that moment. But in directing, the astrologer does not attend to the wandering planets' places, which are continually varied by their motion, but only to the places they occupy at the moment of the nativity, which are the fixed termini of the directions, and the parts of the *primum mobile* determined by the planets. So then the astrologer, making a judgment by means of the celestial influx on things past, present, or future that concern the native, contemplates the genethliacal figure, i.e., the constitution of the *caelum* at the moment of the nativity, as something [established] by God, or by nature, or rather by Divine Providence through natural causes—a fixed decree, in which through his natural characteristics the fate of the native is produced, recognizable only to astrologers. In each

---

11 The text has *nos* 'us' by mistake for *non* 'not'.
12 The text has 'the tenth', but plainly 'the first' is meant.

genethliacal constitution just as it is fixed and invariable, both with respect to the *caelum* and also to the Earth, but not to the movable bodies of the planets; he measures for directions the distances of the promittors from the significators, and these are also fixed. Therefore, in a genethliacal constitution he attends only to the fixed distances of the planets with respect to the *caelum* and the Earth, but not to the mobile bodies of the planets; consequently he directs the former, having taken into account their nature, as well as the celestial and terrestrial states that were allotted to them in their places at the moment of the nativity, and, by consequence, as the planets themselves were determined in the celestial figure. Therefore, he directs the Sun, the Moon, and the other planets merely as causes particularly determined, but not as the universal causes which Cardan calls "by nature," which directions of Cardan, Ptolemy, and the others are really chimerical and utterly absurd, and consequently always erroneous, unless a particular determination about that for which they are directed happens to agree with such universal causes. For what is more absurd than to want to direct the Sun in the twelfth house, badly afflicted by sign and by the rays of the malefics for the glory and dignities of the native, when, so afflicted, it plainly portends the contrary by its own determination and status—namely enemies, sicknesses, prison, exiles, etc.?

Besides, although we admit only 20 significators in general, that is the cusps of the twelve houses, the seven planets, and the Part of Fortune, nevertheless it must be known that any planet can be allotted a multiple signification in the same figure, for by however many ways it can be determined about the native, in that many also can its function as a significator be allotted. Moreover the same planet can be in one house of a figure, and ruler of one or more others; therefore, it will be at the same time the significator of diverse accidents pertaining to those diverse houses, and at the same time it is directed for all of these, as will be stated more fully below. But again, any kind of accident pertaining to the native, or the subject of any house, can have many significators at the same time; for example, life is signified by the Ascendant and its ruler, then by a planet in the first house and its ruler; honours by the Midheaven and its ruler, then by a planet in the tenth house and its ruler; consequently, the Midheaven and its ruler, a planet in the tenth and its ruler ought to be directed for honours and actions, each of course by a different computation, as will be explained in its own place; and the same reasoning applies to the others.

There is, moreover, a certain order that must be observed with all these significators. So in fact a sign occupying any house and its ruler are the principal significators of the accidents of that house, and the most principal is that part of the sign which occupies the cusp and begins the house, as is plain from the directions of the Ascendant and Midheaven. But a planet which is found in that house signifies the realization or the prevention of that accident, according to its nature, state, and determination; and if two or more planets are in the same house, the one nearer the cusp, especially if it has analogy and is strong, is preferred to the rest in that signification, and in the signified realization it designates the quality of it in accordance with its own nature. Moreover, the planets in aspect signify assistance to the realization or prevention, in accordance with their own nature and state and the kind of aspect; and the signification of the accidents must be pronounced from a combination of all these [factors].

Chapt. 4. *The Promittors of Future Things from the Stars for a Man; their Definition and Number.*

It seems to us that a promittor ought to be defined thus. Namely, that it is a part of the *primum mobile* determined with respect to some category of accidents for the native, or to the second terminus of a direction, according as it presages per se anything that is going to happen with respect to the subject represented by the significator, or to the native himself by reason of such a subject. Thus, Mars, represented with respect to life by the Ascendant, portends danger to life itself from sickness, a wound, death, or to the native himself by reason of life.

But by "a part of the *primum mobile*" is to be understood a part determined not only by reason of its own location in the figure, but in particular determined by the body of a planet or by an aspect; or, as I may say more concisely, such parts are understood to be the places of the bodies and the aspects of the planets in the *primum mobile*, according as they are determined in the genethliacal figure. And so, since there are seven planets, each of which has eleven aspects, namely two each of semisextiles, sextiles, squares, trines, quincunxes, along with the opposition, and in addition the antiscion; therefore, there will be 91 promittors, and with the Part of Fortune there will be 92.

Cardan, in his *Book on the Judgments of Genitures*, Chapt. 5, adds both of the nodes, or Caput, Cauda, [Sun], Moon, Saturn, Jupiter, Mars, Venus, and Mercury; but these points[13] are of no efficacy, even though astrologers hold that Caput is of the nature of Jupiter and Venus, and Cauda is of the nature of Saturn and Mars. For that virtue would be the same in all places; but already the point of the ecliptic which to us is Caput, or the Ascending Node of the Moon, is to those in the southern hemisphere the Descending Node; and the Node that is Descending to us is Ascending to them; therefore, there would be a different universal virtue of the same node at the same time, which is absurd. For any part of the *caelum*, or any planet, or its aspect, is of the same universal virtue, or insofar as it is seen in the *caelum*. But if it is said to be different with respect to different peoples, since the same point is at the same time ascending to some and descending to others, I ask what is the virtue of the head or the tail of the dragon of the Moon, when in the Torrid Zone those points are in its zenith, where they cannot be said either to ascend or descend, nor consequently to be distinguished by the name of Caput or Cauda. For they will not be of both virtues there, therefore both there and everywhere on

---

13 That is, the nodes.

earth they are of no virtue.[14] But because the planets are perceived to be more efficacious there, where they are closer to the ecliptic, and, moreover, when they are closer to their own or to the Moon's nodes, then they are nearer to the ecliptic, this has deceived astrologers, who have supposed that greater efficacy to be due to the nodes of the Moon or of the other planets.[15]

And as for the terms of the planets, 60 in number, that all astrologers admit to the number of their promittors with so much faith—as when Cardan, Junctinus, and others did not blush to predict or declare even a violent death from the direction of the Ascendant to the terms of Saturn or Mars, there is no need for us to tarry longer here in rebutting these things, since we have most adequately revealed the worthlessness of the terms in Book 15, Chapt. 13.

And finally, we shall discuss below whether the cusps of the houses can be promittors, as is pleasing to some astrologers, e.g. Origanus in Part 3, Member 4, Chapt. 1, who also directs the Ascendant to the cusps of the 2nd, 3rd, and 4th houses.

Chapt. 5. The Formal Difference between a Significator and a Promittor, and their other Differences.

A significator and a promittor agree in this respect, that each is a part of the *primum mobile*, determined about some kind of accidents for the native, but they differ among themselves in many respects.

Firstly, they differ formally in this respect, that a significator per se represents a subject affected by a direction, or about which the native is affected. But a promittor signifies the effect produced by itself. For an effect is always produced in accordance with the nature of the promittor. Moreover, another formal difference follows from this, namely that a significator concurs only subjectively with the effect that will be from the direction, but a promittor concurs efficiently, and as introducing the form at the time of completion of the direction. For it is proved by experience that the same significator, such as the Midheaven, or the Sun, concurring in the same way in directions with different promittors following [in sequence], causes different effects with them in the individual directions; moreover, that diversity is not efficiently from the significator, which is the same and concurs in the same way, but from the promittors, which are different in nature, in determination, and in their way of concurring. Which is confirmed by the fact that each individual effect is assimilated to its own promittor by reason of its nature and determination, just as the same wax is liquefied by heat and congealed by cold.

---

14 This isn't much of an argument, since logically it should also apply to the equinoxes of the ecliptic.

15 This seems to say that the planets are closer to the ecliptic not only when they are near their own nodes but also when they are near the Moon's nodes, which is of course not true. Morin certainly knew this, so his statement is puzzling.

But on the other hand, the same promittor, concurring in the same way with different preceding significators, still effects different things in the individual directions. Moreover that diversity is not efficiently from significators differing among themselves, because the effect is always in accordance with the nature and determination of the promittor; therefore, it is only subjectively from significators representing different subjects; just as the same Sun by its own heat hardens mud and liquefies wax,[16] but by its influx it effects one thing in a planet,[17] another thing in a brute animal, and something else in a man because the subjects are diverse in nature and disposition. Wherefore, it seems to us that Cardan ought to be refuted when he says, in *Aphorisms*, Book 3, Aphorism 26, "The place of the significator shows the nature of the event, the significator the form, the promittor the effective [agent], and the planets in aspect the helps and hindrances of the thing that is going to happen." Where, by "place of the significator" is understood the house of the figure which concerns the subject matter or the subject affected, by "significator" the planet posited in that house, which indeed from [its position in] the radix bestows some form or disposition upon the subject to which it is determined, or influences the native about it, but constantly throughout the whole course of his life. As for instance Venus in the first house bestows a Venerean moral nature upon the native that will last throughout his whole life; but through a direction of Venus to Saturn another form or mood happens to this nature—one of the nature of Saturn; consequently, the form in directions is not from the significator, but from the promittor, which is a planet or its ray.

Secondly, they differ because not every significator can be a promittor, as is plain from the cusps of the houses. For, that these only concur subjectively in directions and do not have any part in effecting [anything] will be proved below. In turn, not every promittor can be a significator, as is plain from aspects which otherwise would be directed to themselves mutually, against experience. For these do not signify anything through themselves, since by themselves they do not exist, but [only] through the aspecting planets. But every significator, by definition, signifies by itself; and so only the planets can be [both] significators and promittors. And in fact they signify the subject or the kind of accident to which they are determined by their bodily position, and the active impression from the radix on the native with respect to [the subject or accident] itself, and to this extent they are

---

16 This same illustration was used by Placidus in Book I of his *Quaestionum physiomathematicarum libri tres* [Three Books of Physiomathematical Ques-tions] (Milan: G.B. Malatesta, [1650]), as cited by John Cooper in his translation of Placidus's *Primum Mobile* (London: Davis and Dickson, 1814), p. 3 "The stars are indeed the universal cause, and indeterminate, as to their specific and individual effects; but are determined according to the variety of the passable subjects and nearest causes: as the Sun melts wax, dries up the mud, whitens it, blackens the human skin, with man generates man, a lion with a lion, etc." While neither Placidus nor Morin attributes this illustration to anyone, it seems likely to be from some earlier writer, perhaps Aristotle.

17 Or perhaps we should read *planta* 'plant' instead of *planeta* 'planet'.

significators. And besides, they presage anything that is going to happen with respect to the kind of accident represented by any antecedent significator, and so they are [also] promittors.

Thirdly, they differ because every significator signifies something that is present and existing in its action, namely a radical disposition of the native, received from some significator at birth, toward the kind of accident to which the significator itself is determined in accordance with its own nature and celestial and terrestrial state. But a promittor, as such, presages something that is absent, at least at birth, and only existing in potential, consequently something that is going to happen.

Chapt. 6. *Which Significator Ought to be Directed for Which Things.*

Astrologers very often talk wildly and err shamefully about this, being too much addicted to the doctrine of Ptolemy, Cardan, and the other older [astrologers], with their universal significators, which Cardan himself calls "by nature;" directing, for example, the Sun in every nativity for life, the father, honours, etc., without having any reason for [such] a determination of the Sun in the natal figure.

That the Sun should not be directed for this reason[18] is thus proved a priori. For whatever is directed ought only to be directed for those things of which it is a significator at birth, that is, of which it can be the cause from birth; moreover, every significator derives [its signification] solely from the houses of the figure because it is a significator at birth. For whatever is signified [by it] is from the essential signification of some house. And every planet has its [signification] through its determination in the figure by body, by rulership, or by aspect. And so it is a particular significator with respect to [one] native; and it does not cause everything in every nativity, but this thing in one, and something else in a second, just as it is determined in various ways by individual [circumstances]. Therefore, each planet is to be directed only for those things which it signifies particularly in a figure. For having taken away its particular signification, it can have no universal effect. Thus it is [the function] of a significator to determine the promittor for any kind of effect, which, however, a significator viewed universally cannot do. For the Sun, viewed in this way, does not signify the life any more than the father or dignities, but all of these, and others—riches, brothers, children, the spouse, etc.—indifferently. Whence it is no wonder that from such directions one thing is accustomed to be predicted, but very often something contrary happens; which imposes upon astrology and gives its adversaries an opportunity to scoff.

But the cusps of the houses are already determined particularly to the things signified by their own houses; in which, however, there now and then occurs a change. For the directions of the Midheaven very often bring marriages, imprison-

---

18 That is, as a general significator of life, the father, honours, etc.

ment, sicknesses, and death itself through notorious crimes, duels, battles, falls from a high place, and other things that originate from the action of man. For the Midheaven is the significator of actions, and consequently of a good or bad end to them. Similarly, the direction of the Ascendant to the Sun, the Moon, and the ruler of the Midheaven, when fortunate, causes honours, of which the Ascendant itself is not the significator per se, but [rather the significator] of the native himself. But we have said that the effect of a direction is from the promittor as well as from the significator, and each of them joins in this in accordance with its own determination, which must be carefully noted.

And indeed, planets are determined in many ways, viz. by bodily position, rulership, aspect, exaltation, and triplicity. And the bodily position of a planet in any house is stronger than its rulership in another, according to that common [rule], *the presence of a planet is more effective than the rulership of an absent [planet]*; and this is stronger in the case of an aspect, etc. And consequently, the directions of the planets for the particular things signified by them by reason of their corporal position and their rulership are very effective; but for things signified by reason of aspect, exaltation, and triplicity, the effects are scarcely perceptible, at least alone and through their own action. Yet it cannot be denied that Mars square the Ascendant or its ruler signifies about life, for it is proved by experience that the square of Mars to the Ascendant badly afflicts the things signified by the latter. Indeed, because Mars aspects all the houses, therefore it signifies about the subjects of all of them, more weakly to be sure where the weaker rays of the semisextile, sextile and quincunx fall, more strongly where the stronger rays of the opposition, trine, and square fall, and most strongly of all where in addition Mars itself is strong by reason of bodily presence or rulership. On which account, it ought only to be directed for those things that it signifies by bodily position or by rulership, but not for those that it only signifies by aspect, at least by a weak aspect. And there is no need to direct the square of Mars to the Ascendant for life, since the Ascendant itself is directed for life to the point where it is struck by the square of Mars, for the state of the significator is visible. But it will still be necessary to consider Mars in its own directions because that square must be considered, as inimical to life, and consequently its direction would be very dangerous to the ruler of the Ascendant following.

Furthermore, in the case of a significator, its own nature, its analogy with those things that it signifies, and its state must be looked at. For Leo in the Ascendant signifies something else about the life than does Scorpio or Gemini, and Scorpio something else than does Aries, although these two signs belong to the same planet. Similarly, the Sun as significator of honours signifies honours of a kind other than those signified by Saturn, and Saturn signifies honours other than those signified by Venus. Besides, the Sun is analogous to honours, but Saturn is contrary to them, especially when badly afflicted. Therefore, these and similar things must be noticed in significators, such as those things for which they are directed, and what effect is to be hoped for from them will be established more evidently.

The objection is raised: Every man's life is from the Sun, and this cannot be denied. Therefore it is the significator of life in every nativity, and consequently it ought to be directed for life in every one.

I reply firstly: The Sun, the Moon, and the other planets are the universal causes of life because they join universally in the generation of all living things, as do the four elements. But when in any nativity the cause of life is sought, the cause of a *particular* life, is understood, and the cause that is determined to life in that very nativity, but not the universal cause. Otherwise, the Moon, Saturn, Mars, etc., should all be directed equally for the life in individual figures along with the Sun, because they also, like the Sun, concur universally, but that would be a great confusion, which would provide nothing but errors.

I reply secondly: The Sun is the universal cause, merely through its active and perceptible heat, which alone it communicates here to inferior things, but not by its influence, which is communicated merely through a particular determination by location, rulership, aspect, etc.; as a result of which, the planet may be a particular cause. Moreover, the effects of directions derive only from the influences—hence, only from particular and determined causes.

But, having understood these things, we may now inquire about something else. Let the Sun be supposed to be in the 11th house, or the ruler of the 11th, so that it is determined about the native's friends. The question arises, For what things should it be directed? For friends, so that it may be known what will happen to them? Or, for the native [himself], so that it may become known what will happen in connection with his friends?

To which question I reply: The essential things signified by the houses, namely life, riches, brothers, etc., are established through their relation to the native, so far as he may affected by them or in connection with them, but not so far as that the things signified are to be affected in connection with themselves. For the native is the unique subject whom the celestial configuration primarily concerns, and all the accidents signified by the planets and the signs happen to him, according as they are determined in the figure. And consequently, when some yokel is born as the sole son of parents who are beggars, his riches, brothers, spouse, children, and servants are not affected by the *caelum*, but he himself receives a celestial impression, by which he is actively or passively determined and affected with respect to those things, and that either well or badly, according as planets agreeing or disagreeing with them by nature and state are found to be corporally present in the houses of these things or ruling them.

Therefore, from the direction of the Sun in the 11th house, or as ruler of the 11th, to the trine of Jupiter, the native will be well affected as regards his friends, but to the square of Saturn or Mars, badly affected. Yet, something good or evil can happen to his friends because as dignities may be lost, so it is with friends. However, they will not be lost, but generally something evil will happen to them in their life, fortune, etc., either through their own actions, or through ours, or through those of others. And the same reasoning applies to Saturn or Mars in the 3rd, which signifies the death of the brothers; but the signification and the direction primarily and essentially pertain to the native, to whom it portends that there will be misfortune in connection with his friends [and] brothers. Nevertheless, it is greatly worthy of admiration that the virtue of the native's figure also affects others in such a way that one who has Saturn or Mars or both in the third will see the death of his own brothers or sisters, whether he is the eldest or the youngest, or born in the middle, as is shown in my case, since I have Mars in the 3rd, and in that of the most noble Mr. Tronson,[19] who had Mars and Saturn in the 3rd. For while malefics in the 3rd portend to the native the loss of his brothers, at the very same time they threaten death to the brothers [and] survivorship to the native. And in the same way Saturn or Mars in the 7th presages the death of the spouse and the enemies before the native's own demise; from which it can be concluded that every significator, whether cusp or planet, should only be directed for those things that it particularly signifies by reason of its determination in the figure; and for this reason primarily only so far as the native is affected in them or by them or about them; and secondly, it can be directed for the status of things signified and for future accidents, especially if these things are persons, such as brothers, parents, children, the spouse, etc.

Similarly, let the Sun be in the 12th house. It may be asked, For what things should it be directed and what will be the effect of that direction?

I reply that it ought to be directed for the native's secret enemies, imprisonment, sicknesses, and other afflictions of the body. Not in so far as the native himself is affected primarily and essentially, but according as he is affected by these things. For, since the Sun in the 12th is a particular significator of such things, therefore, every promittor translated to its circle will produce an effect on the native from this category of things, both in accordance with the nature and state of the significator and also in accordance with the nature, state, and determination of the promittor. And consequently, the Ascendant, or its ruler, translated to that circle, threatens the native with sicknesses, imprisonment, and secret enemies. And the ruler of the 7th translated to that same circle also portends a bodily affliction to the native, but through the agency of his spouse, or a lawsuit, or an open enemy. And the reasoning is the same for the Sun in the 10th for actions undertaken and for dignities.

Again, let Mars be ruler of the 4th in the 6th, with the Moon in the 10th, whose square [falls] in the 7th. The question is asked, What will be the effect of the direction of Mars to the square of the Moon?

The Moon in the 10th is a significator of actions, and its square to the 7th portends lawsuits and disputes for the native. Moreover, Mars signifies parents and servants. Therefore, only the signification of the Moon's square in the 7th

---

19 Louis Tronson (b. 1576), whose horoscope is often cited by Morin.

should be combined with the signification of Mars; therefore, for the native lawsuits are predicted, or disputes with the parents or the servants or both, or because of animals, since of course the effect of the direction must be referred primarily to the native; and all prudence and the highest degree of knowledge is involved in making combinations of the significations of the significator and the promittor, as it should be. Moreover, many things can be combined in each direction; therefore, the several possible combinations should be predicted separately, unless it is plain from the figure of a revolution what future thing is mainly signified, for then this will be the main thing predicted.

Chapt. 7. *How many Kinds of Directions there are; whether Planets and the Cusps of Houses ought to be Directed against the Succession of the Signs; then, which of the Termini of a Direction is said to be the Significator and which the Promittor, and why.*

All astrologers expound a twofold [method of] direction. The first is said by them to be *direct*, or according to the succession of the signs, or *in the following direction*, by which they mean the preceding terminus, considered as the significator, is borne to the promittor, which follows. But they assert this wrongly, since, on the contrary, the promittor or the following terminus, is transferred by the motion of the *primum mobile* to the location or circle of position of the significator to get the arc of direction, which is nothing other than the difference in ascensions, whether right or oblique, of each terminus, taken in the circle of position of the *preceding* terminus, not the following; or, it is the arc of the equator or of a parallel to it, intercepted between the promittor which follows and the circle of position of the significator, the finding of which arc, is termed by us an *artificial direction*.

The second is called *converse*, or against the succession of the signs, or *in the preceding direction*, which they use for retrograde planets and for the Part of Fortune. And in this the significator, which follows, moves toward the promittor, which precedes, by the same motion of the *primum mobile* as the arc of direction exhibits, entirely as in the first direction. Thus in both cases, right or oblique ascensions are taken in the circle of position of the preceding terminus because the following [terminus] moves toward it by the prime motion, and not vice versa. And consequently, since in both there is the same motion of the *primum mobile* and the same method of finding the arc of direction, it seems that this should not be considered to be a twofold direction, but a single one.

And yet from another viewpoint it may be said to be twofold because the promittor or agent certainly follows the significator in direct [motion], but in the converse it precedes; and consequently in direct [motion] the preceding terminus assumes the function of the subject affected, but the following assumes the function of the agent or the one affecting; and in a converse [direction] it is the other way around.

20

But here there occurs no small difficulty in directing both the planets and the cusps of the houses; namely, whether the same terminus ought to be viewed now as the significator and then as the promittor with respect to the same other terminus following or preceding, and thus at the same time to assume the functions of both the subject and the agent, just as if at the same time two directions with diverse effects were being made, one direct from the preceding terminus to the following, and the other converse from the following terminus to the preceding itself.

And that this should not be allowed is proved by reason and experience. For since both directions happen at or are completed at the same moment of time, because the same arc is calculated in the same manner in either direction, if one effects something else than the other, then whenever any two planets or a planet and a cusp concur in direction, or whenever the time of the direction of one to the other is completed, the agents of such a concourse will always be twofold, as opposed to the customary manner in which concurrent causes act; consequently, two totally diverse effects will always happen at the same time, against experience. But if one does not effect something different from [the effect of] the other, it follows that the second of these is superfluous, which is also absurd and alien to nature. Therefore, the same terminus of a direction does not assume at the same time the function of the significator and the promittor with respect to the same other terminus following or preceding. And consequently, by a direct direction of Saturn in the 12th to the Ascendant or to Venus in the 1st, the effect will not be different from [the effect of] the converse direction of the Ascendant or of Venus in the 1st to Saturn in the 12th; but as it is one and the same concourse of causes, so, from it one and the same total effect will come forth, conformable and proportionate to the natures of these causes, to their state, and to the concourse itself.

You will object: Then take away the converse direction of the Part of Fortune and of the retrograde planets against [the teaching of] all astrologers.

I reply firstly: Astrologers have no cause why they only direct the Lot conversely; since by the passage of time it is moved in the following direction, i.e., it successively increases the number of its degrees in the ecliptic, just like the Ascendant, on which it depends; consequently, it should rather be directed to the following promittors, just like the Ascendant itself and the direct planets. But as for the retrograde planets, they indeed seem to be directed in the preceding direction —namely, to those promittors to which they were borne by their own apparent motion at the moment of the nativity; if indeed directions should be established by the apparent motion of their own planets and not rather by that common [motion] of the *primum mobile*. But the difficulty mentioned above always occurs, if the promittor is a direct planet, to which as to a significator the same direction in the following direction agrees by reason of motion; certainly because at the same time either the direction of these same termini to themselves is twofold with a twofold effect, which was rejected above, or because the direction is then individual with an individual effect, just as was established. But having postulated this, which one of the termini will be the significator and which one the promittor? Or which will be represent the affected subject and which the efficient cause? And what about a retrograde planet? Or a direct preceding planet? Here really we come up once more against a most difficult thing, seeing that there seems to be no reason favoring one terminus over the other. Nor can it be said that such a difficulty does not occur when a retrograde planet is directed to the preceding aspects of the planets, which are only promittors and not significators, as we have stated in Chapt. 4. For if a preceding *aspect* can be a promittor with respect to a following planet, why not all the more a preceding *planet*? But the latter is also a significator with respect to the following planet; therefore, there always remains the difficulty of the twofold significator and the twofold promittor in the same direction of the two termini.

Moreover, the difficulty is increased by the cusps of the houses: if they are directed conversely to preceding planets, or those directly to them, effects are produced in the subject of the cusp by the nature, the determination, and the state of the preceding planet, as I have learned from frequent and irksome experience from my own horoscope, which has Venus, the Sun, Jupiter, Saturn, and the Moon in the 12th house, whose individual directions to the Ascendant, or its directions to them, have always produced evil events in connection with my own person, which the Ascendant represents. And I have noticed the same thing in many other genitures, both with regard to the Ascendant and also with regard to the Midheaven; so that, just as in these directions, the cusps only assume the function of the significator, or the subject, or the native in the subject itself, or the [planet] affecting it, just as if they were directed to following promittors; and that will be shown more fully elsewhere with appropriate examples.

Therefore, it seems to us that such a difficulty from the things already mentioned above is terminated, so that we can state definitely: Firstly, that there is only a single way of directing, namely that in which the following terminus by the motion of the *primum mobile* is conceived to be carried to the circle of position of the preceding terminus, since this is done in every direction, and the ascensions of each terminus are taken in the circle of position of the preceding terminus. Moreover, the one that is moved is the only one that can properly be said to be directed, as opposed to the common way of speaking, from which, therefore, we think one should refrain hereafter.

Secondly, The effect of a direction is not from a single terminus but from the concourse of both [termini]. Just as if Mars in the 2nd is directed to the Ascendant, it will be a sickly or lethal direction; but the sickness will not be from the Ascendant alone, to which namely if Jupiter is directed, especially when lacking rulership in the 12th or the 8th, sickness will not be produced; nor from Mars alone, which, unless it is directed to the Ascendant, no sickness will be produced. Therefore, it is from the concourse of both. And the same reasoning applies to the rest.

Thirdly, Both termini do not efficiently concur in the production of the effect, but only the second, which of course designates the type of effect or determines it specifically. For the other [terminus] only influences the disposition in the subject or in the native himself to the effect; whether namely the subject itself or the native is going to experience such an effect or not. Moreover, the one that efficiently or actively concurs is called the promittor, whether it is a planet or an aspect or an antiscion. But the one that passively and subjectively concurs, i.e., the one whose subject is specifically determined by the second terminus, is called the significator, whether it is a cusp or a planet or the Part of Fortune, which, depending on the luminaries and the Ascendant, assumes a nature intermediate between the cusps and the planets.

Moreover, this is only to be understood with respect to the effect of a future direction, for strictly speaking both the promittor and the significator are efficient causes and signs, for from Book 21, Sect. 1, Chapt. 7, the significator is the efficient cause of the disposition of the subject in a direction; and the promittor is the sign or the significator of the form or type of effect that is going to be produced by the direction. For just as celestial causes are said to be signs of the effects that they produce, so are they the effectors of those things which they signify. For these are reciprocal according to that chapter.

Fourthly, The cusps of the houses, whether they are directed to preceding termini or the termini are directed to them following, are only significators, for they concur only subjectively, i.e., for the subjects to which they are determined, in as far as those subjects are going to be affected, or for the native in connection with those subjects. Nor does it hurt that the Sun in the 12th can be directed to Venus partilely posited in the Ascendant as to a promittor. For although Venus and the Ascendant are the same in position, they are not the same in nature, nor are they the same when they are together as they are when they are apart. For these three, the cusp of the 1st, the Ascendant, and Venus in the Ascendant differ in the following ways. First, the cusp is only an imaginary circle dividing the mundane space of the 12th house from the mundane space of the 1st house or the primary houses twelve and one. The Ascendant is a part of the *primum mobile*, or rather the beginning of the part of the *caelum* itself which is considered to be in the first space, which whole part has a force by reason of its determination for life; moreover, [that force] is greater in the Ascendant itself, or in its beginning, not in so far as it is a point, but in so far as it is the beginning of this part. Moreover, Venus in the Ascendant is the place of Venus very strongly determined to life, or it is the Ascendant itself infused with the Venusian virtue. And judge the same of the Part of Fortune, which only assumes the function of a significator or a subject. Moreover, aspects and antiscia are only promittors or agents.

But in the case where two planets are the termini of the same direction, it is more difficult to distinguish which of them is the significator and which is the promittor, whether they are in the same house of the figure or in different houses, since each of them can be a significator and a promittor in directions. And it seems to us that it ought to be determined in this way. If both of them are in the same house, it is certain that each planet is determined to the same subject or to the same kind of accidents for the native by its bodily position; and consequently, the future effect will be of that kind, at least from the bodily determination of the planets. But

23

the one that precedes is nearer to the cusp of that house; and consequently it will influence more strongly the subject itself, or the native with respect to the subject, for the preceding parts of a house are more efficacious than the following parts, and the cusp is the most efficacious of all. Therefore, other things being equal, the preceding [planet], as the one more efficaciously determined with respect to the subject, will represent it more efficaciously, or it will concur subjectively with it more efficaciously, since it is going to be affected by the following termini; and consequently it will be affected by a following terminus through direction, and not the other way around. And so, the preceding [terminus] will be the significator and the following [terminus] the promittor. Just as if the Sun and Mars ruler of the Ascendant were in the 10th house with Mars following; each of them is determined to honours by its bodily position, and each of them influences its disposition to honours in accordance with its own nature and state; but the Sun, being nearer to the cusp, is more efficacious; and consequently it will be the principal terminus of the direction, namely the significator, which signifies that the subject, i.e., honours of a Solar nature, will be affected or determined by the Sun. For otherwise the honours of a Solar nature that are signified would be affected or determined by Jupiter, or by Mars, or by Mercury, etc. Therefore, from the direction of the following Mars to the Sun preceding in the 10th, honours of a Solar nature, i.e., illustrious honours, will happen, not of just any nature, but martial or military from Mars itself. And it must be judged similarly with the rest. Thus, my Sun and Saturn are in the 12th, significators of sicknesses; and the Sun is closer to the cusp. Consequently, in the 8th year after birth a Saturnian sickness, namely a quartan fever, befell me from the direction of Saturn to the Sun: and of course the Sun, being nearer the cusp, signified the kind of sickness, namely a fever, but Saturn caused or contributed the specific type. And the reasoning is the same in other instances.

Moreover, I said above "at least from the bodily determination of the planets," for, from other determinations, such as rulership, the effect that is produced either differs in kind, or at least is modified in its kind by those other determinations. I also said "other things being equal," for if the following [planet] is ruler of that particular house or analogous to its particular signification, it might concur subjectively more efficaciously, as Saturn in the 12th for sicknesses or the other significations of the 12th to which it is analogous; although it seems to matter little or not at all whether we speak of sicknesses of a Saturnian nature subjectively represented by Saturn specified by the Sun through a difference in [the type of] fever, or sicknesses of a Solar nature, among which fevers are included, specified by Saturn through the difference of a quartan [type], since on the one hand a fever that is Saturnian is signified, but on the other a Saturnian fever (which is the same thing). Indeed it may seem that it ought rather to be asserted that the Sun in the 12th portends sicknesses of a Solar nature, and Saturn those that are Saturnian, and from their concourse in direction the sickness is made to be of the nature of the Sun and Saturn, which is a quartan fever.

Similarly, the Sun in the 10th presages dignities of a Solar nature, Mars ruler of the 1st in the 10th military ones; therefore, from their concourse in a direction, honours that are military, royal, or distinguished are certain to be presaged. And the same reasoning holds for the rest, when each planet, from its essential nature and its own state and determination signifies a future accident of the kind of that house which it occupies, for if Mars in the 10th is badly afflicted and is not the ruler of the Ascendant, it would rather portend the loss of honours; this would happen from that direction, because it makes even more clear that a following planet produces the changes characteristic of a promittor.

But if two planets are in different houses, and are therefore determined to subjects that differ in kind, and represent these subjects subjectively, there seems to be a greater difficulty in defining which will determine the other for the type of future accident [signified] by their direction, or which will function as promittor. But if to the Moon in the 12th is directed the square of Saturn from the 1st,[20] it will be square the promittor itself or the agent, since, from what has been said above, it cannot be the significator. Consequently, the Moon will be the significator or representative of the subject to be affected, with respect to the square of Saturn. Why not then with respect to Saturn itself, from which the force and effectiveness of that square derives, just as if Saturn itself had been in the 1st? Besides, if the Moon is posited in the 12th, it must not be said that Saturn directed to it either from the 12th or the 1st or the 2nd would produce effects of the same type, if indeed Saturn does not concur through its own nature alone, but also through its determination, which is different in different houses. And so, the effect of Mars will be different for a different determination. Similarly, if several planets are directed to the Moon in the 12th, one from the 12th, another from the 1st, and another from the 3rd, they will produce different effects from their individual directions, as experience proves. But the Moon is the same in all these, that is in its nature, determination, and state; therefore, the diversity of effects, i.e., the different forms of these, are brought about by the individual planets that follow, on account of their diverse natures and determinations, as is deduced from the elementary principles; and consequently, from what has been said above, the promittors will be called "concurring actively."

Nevertheless, it can also generally be said that in the concourse of any two termini, with which otherwise the name of significator can agree, it should be carefully noted which one of the different subjects that are otherwise signified by them is more likely to submit to or be determined by the other; or rather, through which of these subjects the native is more naturally and suitably affected by another subject; then [the judgment] should be declared about this [subject]. So that, if the Ascendant is directed to the Moon in the 12th, it is more appropriate for the subject of the Ascendant, i.e., the native's personality, life, temperament, moral nature,

---

20 That is, if the square of Saturn falls in the natal 1st and that aspect is directed to the Moon in the natal 12th.

mental qualities, to submit to, to be affected by, or to be changed by the subject of the 12th, i.e., sickness, imprisonment, exile, etc., than the other way around; and so for this reason the preceding terminus will be the promittor or the agent. And the same thing must be judged if Mercury ruler of the Ascendant in the 9th signifying by rulership the native's personality is directed to Mars in the 8th; for Mars signifying death will exercise the function of promittor and Mercury that of significator.

Fifthly, We say that the direction of planets and cusps should be admitted to be twofold: one direction, by which the following termini are conceived to be borne by the motion of the *primum mobile* to the circle of position of the preceding planet or cusp—and this direction is called direct or in the following direction because in fact the significator looks back at the following termini. And the other, by which the preceding terminus itself is borne to the circle of position of the other preceding terminus; and this is called converse or in the preceding direction. And both directions of the same cusp or planet to different termini before and after should be noted; not otherwise than if a planet is borne at the same time by any motion of direction to a preceding terminus when it should follow after a following one, because surely both directions are effective, as experience proves. However, it must always be noted in either direction, which of the different subjects of the termini would more suitably be affected by the other, as was said above. And if both termini are in the same house, it will have to be seen from the things said above which of these will more effectively be the subject for that house, so that it may be definitely established which terminus is the promittor and which the significator in that particular case.

Moreover, it is worthy of admiration that the same promittor, concurring in the same manner with different significators, still accomplishes different things in its individual directions. And that diversity is not effectively from the significators because the effect is always in accordance with the nature and determination of the promittor; hence, it is only subjectively from the significators; by which means the same Sun hardens mud and liquefies wax by its heat.[21] Similarly, the same significator, such as the Ascendant or the Midheaven or Jupiter in the 1st, concurring with different promittors in the same manner, causes different effects with them in the individual directions. And that diversity is not effectively from the significator, which is the same and concurring in the same manner, but from the promittors, which are diverse in their nature, determination, and way of concurring; which is confirmed by the fact that the individual effects are assimilated to their own prcmittor by reason of its nature or determination or both, just as the same wax is liquefied by heat and solidified by cold.

You will object: By allowing the direction of cusps in the preceding direction and in the following direction, the principal and more certain way of rectifying nativities by the native's accidents is taken away. For there is no more certain way

---

21 The same illustration used in Chapt. 5 above.

of rectifying nativities than by finding the true position of the angles of the figure; and this is found through the directions of the Ascendant or the Midheaven to significators corresponding to past accidents. But now, if a sickness happens equally from a direction of the Ascendant to Mars following in the 1st, and from the direction of this same Ascendant to Mars preceding in the 12th, it cannot be said whether Mars precedes or follows the Ascendant, nor therefore which degree of the ecliptic will be the Ascendant degree; and the directions of the Midheaven for honours or actions must be judged similarly. Therefore, a twofold direction cannot be assigned to the same significator. Moreover, the force of directions in the following direction[22] is the best known to all astrologers. Therefore, each significator can only be directed in the following direction.

I reply firstly, A sickness can certainly happen from either direction, because the Ascendant is the significator of life and health, and badly afflicted from either direction it is sickness; but different effects can also be produced from these same directions: in fact from Mars in the 1st, sickness or a wound or a burn; and from Mars in the 12th, sickness, imprisonment, or exile; in fact, because Mars in either direction acts in accordance with its proper nature and its own determination in the figure, but it is determined to one set of things in the 1st and to another set in the 12th. And thus, from [a direction of] the Midheaven to Jupiter in the 10th or the 11th, dignities of a secular nature happen, unless Jupiter is ruler of the 9th; but to Jupiter in the 9th, journeys, or an ecclesiastical position. From the Midheaven to Mars in the 11th, military honours through the aid of friends, especially if the state and determination of Mars agree; but to Mars in the 8th, dangers to life, or even a violent death.

I reply secondly, No nativity can be accurately rectified by a single accident pertaining to the Ascendant, e.g. a sickness, because of the objection already stated, but many accidents are required so that the rectification may be secure and certain; but if they correspond to their own causes according to the rectification of the direction of the Ascendant to Mars in the 12th, this will have to be judged to be more truthful, for they will not correspond closely to both. Therefore, the converse direction of a cusp does not remove or weaken the rectification of the nativity through many of the native's past accidents, especially because on the days of the accidents a transit of the planets is very often made through the cusps themselves, from which the certainty is then greater.

You will make a second objection: If the converse directions of the cusps and planets are just as valid as the direct directions, then when the Ascendant is conversely directed to Mars in the 12th in the 15th year from the nativity, a sickness, imprisonment, exile, or something like in kind to the signification of the 12th house will happen according to the nature and state of Mars; but in the 345th year, if the man shall have lived so long, as before the Flood, the same type of accident or another type will be produced again when the Ascendant is directed to Mars

---

22 That is, direct directions.

according to the succession of signs. But because Mars and the Ascendant are in the same mode in either direction, namely with the Ascendant as the subject and Mars as the agent or promittor, acting on either side with the same nature and determination, the same type of accident will be produced again, rather than another type. But both seem to be absurd, for the promittor will fulfill only once that which it signifies and promises it is going to do.

I reply: Neither is absurd or contrary to the actions of the celestial bodies. For when men used to live 800 or 900 years it was necessary that the Ascendant be directed to the same promittor several times according to the series of signs. Why then should two directions of it to Mars in the 12th not produce the same type of sickness, doubtless a tertian fever of some kind, or even something of a different type, since there are many types of Martian sicknesses, or a sickness in the first direction, but imprisonment in the second. Moreover, it is a false statement that the promittor fulfills only once that which it signifies it is going to do. For, as often as it repeatedly concurs with the other terminus, the significator, by direction in the preceding direction or in the following direction, always effects something new according to the diversity of that terminus and its own nature and determination. And consequently, even though in the 12th house it is only determined toward sicknesses, imprisonment, exiles, and secret enemies, yet in these it varies its effects by directions to different termini in a remarkable way. What then will it effect in addition if it is seen to follow its own rulerships in other houses? Similarly the Ascendant or any other significator; even though it may have only one and the same influence towards the subject that it represents generically by reason of house, or, in the case of the native, towards him himself; yet, this impressed force or disposition is something universal with respect to the different effects of that kind which can be produced by different promittors.

It is true that it may be said by some that from the direction of the Ascendant to a preceding Mars sickness is produced through the native's own fault, because the Ascendant is borne by the prime motion to the promittor. But from the direction of a following Mars to the Ascendant sickness is [also] produced without any action on the native's part, because the Ascendant will expect the promittor to be coming to it, or the latter will rush to the former. But from this it would follow that nothing good or evil happens to the native through directions of the Ascendant to following promittors, with the native himself concurring efficaciously or by his own action, which experience opposes. For even if the Ascendant, i.e., the native represented by it, maintains itself subjectively or passively in directions, yet this must only be understood, insofar as it is affected well or evilly according to the nature and determination of the promittors; but not because it can do nothing from which such an affection could happen to it.

You will object thirdly: The cusp of the 10th house is something immobile. Therefore it is not transferred to any preceding terminus; therefore it cannot be directed.

I reply: That although the cusp of the 10th house, or the 10th house [itself], is something immobile with regard to space, yet the part of the *caelum* that is culminating is mobile because of the prime motion; and consequently it is transferred by this to the location of a preceding promittor; and consequently it is directed, and the objection is refuted.

Chapt. 8. *In which the Various Methods of Artificial Directions Used by Astrologers are Set Forth, and the False ones Rejected.*

The diversity of directing has produced such confusion in astrology, that very many may still be in doubt as to the true method of establishing this operation —the principal one of the whole art.

Junctinus, in his *Commentary on the Quadripartite*, Book 3, Chapt. 12 (p. 381), explains the various opinions of the old [astrologers] about this matter, discordant among themselves and supported by no reasons, which it would be tedious and useless to repeat here. But the sum of all his discussion consists of this: that some direct by equal degrees, i.e., they take the longitudes of the significator and the promittor in the ecliptic without latitude, then they take the difference of their longitudes; for this, as they aver, is the arc of direction equivalent to as many years as there are degrees in that same arc. But others direct by ascensions of the degrees of the equator, and these are right [ascensions] both for the significator and the promittor if the significator is in the right circle or the meridian, but oblique [ascensions] if it is in the oblique [circle], i.e., the horizon or another intermediate circle of position passing through sections of the horizon and the meridian. The difference of these ascensions will be the arc of direction. Moreover, Junctinus says that it seems safer to him to direct according to both modes, viz. by equal degrees and also by ascensions of degrees of the equator; but because he offers no reason for his opinion, and because there can be only one method of directing that is true and natural, it is therefore plain that Junctinus is thrusting upon us here three [different] opinions on a matter of the greatest importance—two indeed of the old [astrologers] and one of his own. Which of these is truer has been a matter of controversy until now. But Junctinus's opinion overturns itself. For if the same direction is made by the equal method and by ascensions, whose individual arcs of direction will be different, as almost always happens, one of them must necessarily be false and erroneous in defining the time of a future event; therefore the astrologer would always be uncertain about the time of that event. And so it is superfluous to examine which of these two is true and natural, because the truth can only be defined by reason and experience.

And certainly in things unknown to the intellect experience must always be consulted first, since there is nothing in the intellect that was not first in the senses, and it is certain that false things do not coincide with experience except by chance and by accident; but those things which always or at least very many times agree with experience—those things are true. And they motivate the intellect to discover the reason behind this truth, so that it can therefore be said not inappropriately that reason is the daughter of experience. But indeed aside from the fact that direction by equal degrees is absolutely foreign to the intention of Ptolemy, who holds that in every direction the promittor and significator differ in location, i.e., in their circle of position, which, however, would not be the case where there are two planets differing in longitude in the ecliptic itself when it coincides with the horizon or another circle of position, as frequently happens beyond latitude 66°30', experience too proves that this is false. And this will readily be apparent if anyone wants to reduce to their proper causes all the accidents in the life of a 60-year old man buffeted by various events, for he will see that it is impossible. Nor should it be objected that some of the old [astrologers], such as Albumazur, Alchabitius, Messahala,[23] and others whom Junctinus reviews, used this method of directing. For it perhaps struck them that this mode is the easiest of all, while the other by ascensions is by far the more difficult,[24] especially when the significator is placed beyond the angles, undertaken either by Ptolemy's way—hitherto understood by few—or else by tables of ascensions that had not yet been published at that time. Whence it is not surprising that the majority, avoiding such labour or not knowing the true method of directing, has embraced the other method, since Cardan himself strayed very far from the truth in the three ways of directing that he explained, which differ among themselves and also differ from the intention of Ptolemy,[25] as Maginus[26] proves from Valentine Naibod,[27] at the end of his book on the legitimate use of astrology in medicine,[28] although in assigning the times of future effects they have very often been deceived, whenever they have increased the number of promittors by [adding] the terms of the planets.

Furthermore, it can also be stated that this way of directing is false, because of course a promittor cannot produce an effect on the subject represented by the significator solely through its own distance from the significator, taken in the

---

23 Three of the best known figures of Arabian astrology: Albumasar [Abu Ma'shar] (c.787-886), Alchabitius [al-Qabisi] (d.c.967), and Messahala [Masha'allah] (c.740-c.815).
24 Yet, these men were successful astrologers.
25 Actually, Cardan understood Ptolemy's method, which is what we would now call Placidian, while Regiomontanus and his faithful followers Naibod, Maginus, and Morin did not.
26 Giovanni Antonio Magini (1555-1617), Italian mathematician, astronomer, and astrologer.
27 Valentine Naibod or Nabod (b. 1527), German mathematician and astrologer, whose book *Enarratio elementorum astrologiae* [Explanation of the Elements of Astrology] (Cologne, 1560) discusses primary directions and contains the famous measure of time still called by his name. The "proof" cited from his book is invalid, as we shall see below.
28 De astrologica ratione ac usu dierum criticorum seu decretoriorum [Astrological Reason and the Use of Critical Days] (Venice, 1607).

ecliptic with the longitudes of both; but it is necessary that it be *determined* to such an effect, since the planets do not act on particular things except by reason of their own determination, as is set forth fully in Book 21. Moreover, because determination through its bodily position is necessary to a promittor, it may or may not be ruled by the place of the significator, because either a planet is a promittor, ruled by the place of the significator, or it isn't; from the promittor's direction to the latter, the effect itself is produced; therefore, by reason of the determination of the promittor itself through its bodily position, similar to the location of the significator with respect to the horizon,[29] by reason of which similarity the planet that is the promittor, when it is directed to the Ascendant, produces the same [effect] as if it were in the Ascendant. And yet the promittor cannot obtain that similar position unless it is transferred to it by the motion of the equator or the *primum mobile*; therefore, the arc of direction will have to be measured, not by degrees of the ecliptic, but by those of the equator; for the equator, not the ecliptic, transfers celestial bodies to the preceding spaces of the houses. And of all the celestial circles, only the circles of position are determinative of the virtue of celestial bodies, as is most evidently established from the circles of position of the houses, but not the ecliptic or the equator or the circles of latitude or declination; moreover, what is said about a planet acting as promittor is also to be understood about the aspects. And consequently, the method of directing by equal degrees must be rejected, both by reason and by experience, even though it may sometimes happen by accident that it agrees with experience, concerning which we shall speak at the beginning of the Second Section.

Chapt. 9. *That the Way of Directing by Ascensions given by Ptolemy is Natural and True, but Hitherto Understood by Few.*

Most astrologers follow the way of directing by ascensions, but although they hold that it is acceptable to Ptolemy, yet they are separated into various opinions about his intention. They have also introduced different methods of directing by ascensions, while some have tried to hunt down the arc of direction with the ascensions themselves, but others[30] with the equivalent horary times and the semidiurnal arcs familiar to Ptolemy himself.

Moreover, even though the method of directing by horary times is more involved than that by ascensions of degrees of the equator, nevertheless it would scarcely be of any importance by which of these two modes a direction was made, provided that it produced the same arc of direction either way, by which arc the time of the effect of the direction may be designated, which can be the same. But

---

29 Ptolemy, *Tetrabiblos* iii. 10, says that the promittor must be brought to a "similar place." But his definition of such a place does not agree with what follows here.
30 Most notably, Placidus.

when through different methods arcs emerge with many [different numbers of] degrees, i.e., differing by many years, it must be that either the true method was not handed down by Ptolemy through [the use of] horary times, or it has not been understood by all astrologers. And this is not surprising, since not only does that way involve no little obscurity, but also the examples of calculations given by the Prince of Astrology differ from his own doctrine, as Valentine Naibod learnedly notes in his *Commentary on the Quadripartite*, Book 3, Chapt. 15.[31] Furthermore, it is established in that chapter that Ptolemy was of this opinion about directions —that there is one single mode of directing, when Naibod says, "Surely, if anyone investigates this part of the doctrine according to nature, he will feel that from all [considerations] only one mode which he may follow is suggested to him, namely to ascertain by how many equinoctial times the [following] place—either the body or the point of aspect—is brought to the location of the preceding place in that geniture; and because the equinoctial times are carried across equally, both at the horizon and at the meridian, with respect to both of which similarities of places are taken." For the universal unity of this mode consists of that [very thing]. Firstly, that the significator is always in some circle of position; but the horizon and the meridian themselves are also circles of position, in fact passing through the same points, then all the others are passed through these. And the circle in which the significator is fixed is its horizon, either normal or oblique. Secondly, that the circle in which the significator is situated, that is, its horizon, may be conceived to have the same relation to its own proper meridian, as the horizon of the figure or region has to its own meridian. Thirdly, that the equator cuts across all circles of position equally or uniformly, i.e., no more degrees of the equator rise in one hour above one of the circles than they do above another; not otherwise than if the equator itself should revolve about common sections of the horizon and the meridian, just as Ptolemy says in that same Chapt. 15. Fourthly, that the degrees of the equator that pass through the circle in which the significator is fixed, until the following place or the promittor is borne by the motion of that same equator to that circle, are the desired arc of the direction, which is the equatorial distance of the promittor from the circle of position of the significator, and the distance from the significator itself is not single. Moreover, when it is conceived to have been borne [to that place], it is said to be in a similar position with the significator with respect to the horizon of the celestial figure, or in the same circle of position

Therefore, on account of these properties, common to whatever circle of position the significator occupies, Naibod says with Ptolemy that this general method of directions is *natural*. But I offer a truer reason, and a twofold one. The first is that by this means the method of directions may correspond with the

---

31 On the contrary, Ptolemy's precepts and examples are clear enough, but Naibod, like Regiomontanus, simply failed to understand them. This does not necessarily mean that the Regiomontanan method of directions and house division is wrong, but it does mean that it is not Ptolemaic.

construction of the houses, which is also made by circles of position. But the second and most important is that the promittor, transferred to the circle of the significator, will undergo the same determination from that position as does the significator itself, and consequently it ought to act and in fact does act on the subject of the house in which the significator itself is, not otherwise than if it were conjoined to the significator in that same circle, as experience proves. From all of which causes indeed, I declare this one mode to be natural, i.e., conformable to the natural principles of astrology, and consequently true.

Besides, among all the astronomers who have followed Ptolemy, Regiomontanus first understood perfectly this general way, and he composed tables suitable for its employment, namely tables of declination, right ascension, ascensional differences, oblique ascension at different elevations of the pole, and position, all of which he termed *Tables of Directions*.[32] And the last of these, as it was more difficult than the rest, but also more useful and of nobler use, by which namely is found the altitude of the pole above the circle of position, or the horizon of the significator, and from which are given the ascensions both of the significator and also of the promittor in that circle, the difference of which is the arc of direction. And as a matter of fact the arc of direction is in general nothing other than the difference of the ascensions of the significator and the promittor in the circle of the significator, when the significator is in the part of the *caelum* that is ascending, or the difference of the descensions if it is in the part that is descending. Moreover, the ascensions are understood to be *right ascensions* if the significator is in the meridian circle, but *oblique ascensions* if it is in a circle of position oblique to the equator. Therefore, let us explain here the method of Regiomontanus, so that this may be to us as some Lesbian rule[33] to which other things are compared.

First then, if the significator is in the Midheaven, he takes the right ascension of it and of the promittor, not having omitted their latitude if they have any. And, having subtracted the right ascension of the significator from the right ascension of the promittor, the remainder is the arc of direction. And the same is done if the significator is in the *imum caeli*.

Similarly, if the significator is rising in the horizon, he takes the oblique ascensions of it and of the promittor at the elevation of the pole above that horizon, not having omitted their latitude as [mentioned] above. And, having subtracted the oblique ascension of the significator from the oblique ascension of the promittor, whatever is left is the arc of direction.

But if the significator is in any circle of position between the horizon and the meridian, either above or below the horizon, he first finds the altitude of the pole above its circle of position; and this will always have to be found exactly. Then, if

---

32 *Tabulae directionum profectionumque in nativitatibus multum utiles.* [Tables of Directions and Profections very Useful in Nativities] (Augsburg, 1490).

33 I don't know what Morin means by "Lesbian rule." In the Greek language it would mean "second best," but this does not seem appropriate here.

the significator is in the ascending half of the *caelum*, he takes as above both its and the promittor's oblique ascensions at that altitude; and, having subtracted the oblique ascension of the significator from the oblique ascension of the promittor, whatever is left is the arc of direction.

But if the significator is in the descending half of the *caelum*, either in place of it he directs its opposite in the ascending half to the opposition of the promittor, just as above, and it produces the arc of direction; or, having found the altitude of the pole above the circle of the significator, he takes the oblique descensions of the significator and of the promittor at that altitude; and, having subtracted the oblique descension of the significator from the oblique descension of the promittor, the remainder is the same arc of direction.

Thus, therefore, from Regiomontanus it is plain that there is only one general method of directing according to the intention of Ptolemy. Let us then take up the examples given by Ptolemy himself, so that it may be plain whether he himself was consistent in his procedure.

He supposes, therefore, a region in which the longest day is 14 hours, i.e., in which the pole is elevated 31° above the horizon,[34] as is plain from his table of the length of the day, which region is that of Alexandria, Egypt. And, having put the beginning of Aries in the Ascendant as significator, and directing it entirely by horary times to the beginning of Gemini, or rather the latter to the former, he finds the arc of direction to be 45°, and this is found to be 45°02' in Regiomontanus's tables, for Ptolemy himself did not bother with a few minutes in these examples.[35]

And, having put the beginning of Aries in the Midheaven, and similarly directing the beginning of Gemini to it by right ascension, he says the arc of direction is 58°, which, however, from Regiomontanus's table is only 57°48', but this is of little importance.

But when he puts the beginning of Aries in the middle of the *caelum*, descending beyond the angles, so that the culmination of the *caelum* will occupy 18° Taurus, and directs the beginning of Gemini to this, then he falls into a scarcely tolerable error, stating the arc of direction to be 64°24', which, however, from the tables of Regiomontanus is found to be 66°52',[36] partly because he did not bother with an exact calculation to the minute, as when he says that 0 Gemini is 13° from

---

34 Actually, 30°22' according to Ptolemy, *Almagest*, ii. 9.

35 In fact, Ptolemy did not use minutes at all in his example calculations, but only whole degrees (see Robbins's edition and translation of the Greek text, and also Ashmand's translation of Proclus's *Paraphrase*). But the Greek edition and the Latin translation used by Morin (and Cardan) has degrees and minutes. However the minutes, while present in a few of the MSS, seem to be interpolations. Morin, of course, refers to them in good faith.

36 Ptolemy's example, as he clearly states, is based on proportional semi-arcs, or, as we would say today, the method of Placidus. A more precise calculation from the tables in the *Almagest* yields 64°07' for the arc of direction. Naturally it would not agree with a calculation from the tables of Regiomontanus.

18 Taurus in the Midheaven, although the distance is only 12°17', and partly because of the lack of tables of position for finding the altitude of the pole above the circle of position of the beginning of Aries,[37] [and] in this same example he gives another lengthy way [of making the calculation], confused, and not in accord with the universal mode of directing.[38] Many and learned men have spoken foolishly about the explanation of this [calculation of Ptolemy's].[39] But this direction can now be made by the tables of Regiomontanus, so that the error will become evident.

Therefore, let the Midheaven be 18 Taurus, with right ascension 45°31', the significator 0 Aries, the promittor 0 Gemini, and the latitude of the place 31°.

> The declination of 0 Aries is 0.
> Its right ascension is 0.
> Its Meridian Distance is 45°31'.

The altitude of the pole above its circle of position, as calculated from the spherical triangles, is 23°12'.

And because the significator is in the descending half of the *caelum*, we may, from what is said above, use the opposite point of the zodiac, that is 0 Libra, whose oblique ascension in the circle of position to which the pole is elevated 23°12' is 180°; and the oblique ascension of 0 Sagittarius, the opposite of 0 Gemini, in the same circle is 246°52'; from which, having subtracted 180°, there is left 66°52' for the arc of direction.

But so that the verity of this arc may be established more evidently, let us examine it afresh according to the method of Naibod, who, having thoroughly grasped the intention of Ptolemy, cleared it up, and, as is proper, explained it.[40] And because for Naibod's method the semidiurnal arcs of both the significator and the promittor are required, it will thus be found universally, whether the promittor or the significator have latitude or not.

With the longitude and latitude of a planet its declination is sought in the table of declinations in Regiomontanus or elsewhere, and through it from the table of

---

37 These two excuses are beside the point. The discrepancy is not due to lack of precision nor to the lack of an auxiliary table, but rather to the difference in method — Placidus vs. Regiomontanus.

38 Ptolemy was not confused, since his second way of making the calculation gives the same result as his first way.

39 With this statement Morin joins their ranks, as he mistakenly assumes that the method of Regiomontanus is in accord with "the intention of Ptolemy," which it isn't. But, having followed Regiomontanus up a blind alley, he proceeds to defend vigorously their joint mistake.

40 Actually, Naibod was so enchanted with Regiomontanus's method that he twisted Ptolemy's words around in an effort to provide Ptolemaic authorization for Regiomontanus.

ascensional differences for the altitude of the pole above the circle of position, for which the semidiurnal arc is sought, the ascensional difference is taken out, and this is added to a quadrant or 90° if the declination is north, but subtracted if it is south, and it becomes, or there is left, the semidiurnal arc of the aforesaid planet or point in the *caelum*. With this said, Naibod's procedure for directing the significator anywhere between the angles follows.

First. Find the altitude of the pole above the circle of position of the significator according to the 20th Problem of Regiomontanus.

Second. Take the semidiurnal arc of the significator at that elevation, and add it to the significator's right ascension if it is in the descending half of the *caelum*, or subtract it from the right ascension if it is in the ascending half; and in either case the result is the RAMC with respect to the given circle of position.

Third. Take the distance of the promittor in its own location from that RAMC; this is called the *primary distance*.

Fourth. Take the semidiurnal arc of the promittor also for the elevation of the pole above the aforesaid circle of position; and this is called the *secondary distance* of the promittor from that same Midheaven.

Fifth. Compare both of these distances of the promittor; then, if the significator is in the ascending half of the *caelum* at the time of the geniture, take the secondary distance away from the primary distance; but on the contrary, subtract the latter from the former if the significator is in the descending half, i.e., the preceding is always taken from the following, and [the difference] in either case is the arc of direction. As, in the example above, the altitude of the pole above the circle of position of the significator is 23°12'.

Its semidiurnal arc in the same circle is 90°.

The RAMC to which the circle of position is referred is 90°. The RA of the promittor is 57°48'.

The promittor's distance in its own location from that Midheaven—the primary distance—is 32°12'.

Its declination is 20°12' north.

Its ascensional difference in the circle of position of the significator is 9°04', which, with the addition of a quadrant or 90° (because it is north), makes 99°04' for the semidiurnal arc of the promittor in its own location or in the circle of the significator, which arc is the secondary distance of the promittor from the same abovesaid Midheaven. And because both distances are in the same half of the *caelum*, with respect to the Midheaven itself, the primary or lesser distance of 32°12' is taken away from the secondary or greater distance of 99°04'. And there will remain 66°52' for the arc of direction, exactly as above.

Moreover, Maginus, a man of the utmost skill in abbreviating calculations (who, in his book on the legitimate use of astrology in medicine, has communicated to us this statement of Naibod's, excerpted from his *Commentary on the Quadripartite of Ptolemy*, which has not yet been published), has thought out a very similar method of directing for significators between the angles in Canon 45 of his own *Tables of Directions*, and it is this:

First. Find, as above, the altitude of the pole above the circle of position of the significator.

Second. From the RAMC of the figure, which is 45°31', and the right ascension (RA) of the promittor, which is 57°48', he takes the primary distance of the promittor in its own location from the same Midheaven, which is 12°17'.

Third. He takes the secondary distance of the same promittor from the same Midheaven when it is understood to be transferred to the circle or the location of the significator, which distance is found to be 54°36'.[41]

Fourth. Since the significator and the promittor are in different halves of the *caelum*, he adds both distances, and they make 66°53', as was given from the other method above. But if the promittor and the significator had been in the same half of the *caelum*, the smaller distance would have been taken away from the greater to get the arc of direction. Moreover, the secondary distance is taken thus by Maginus without the semidiurnal arc from the table of positions for the latitude of the place of the figure. Since, having taken the declination of the promittor at the side of the table, and having taken the pole of the circle of position of the significator in the heading, he will have that distance in the common angle. And this way is easy and expeditious.

Therefore, these three modes agree with each other exactly, and they produce the same result. Whoever deviates from these is going to be considered wrong. And consequently, there are astrologers of no small reputation who are deceived in regard to the doctrine of directing promittors to significators that are not placed on the angles of the figure. And this is because they have either disregarded the latitudes of the significator and the promittor in directing, the omission of which causes error in the remainder of the calculation, or, not well comprehending the intention of Ptolemy with regard to the single general mode of directing, in the calculations of the example explained by him, which do not correspond to that single mode, have entangled themselves in various ways. Among whom are counted Cardan, who understood neither Ptolemy nor Regiomontanus on this doctrine, as Naibod proves in the place cited above;[42] then Origanus, who, as is apparent in the figure he gives in Part 2, p. 394, also, against his own opinion, wants the difference in RA between the significator and promittor to be the arc of direction, which, by a lengthy and greatly confused calculation not agreeing with the figure, he found to be 30°15', although in fact this difference is 43°44', and the true arc of direction from Regiomontanus's tables is only 25°, which difference of

---

41 This number is obtained by adding the ascensional difference of the promittor (0 Gemini) under the pole of the significator (0 Aries) to the meridian distance of the significator.

42 This statement is false, as mentioned in the preceding notes. See the pertinent sections of Cardan's *Commentary on the Quadripartite*, Book III.

some 5° from the abovesaid arc of 30°15' is altogether intolerable. We omit other astrologers of lesser fame.[43]

But now we should give this procedure for converse directions. Let the Part of Fortune or a retrograde planet be directed conversely, so that it may be known how far this direction extends in any year after birth. From the right ascension of the significator or the terminus to be directed take away the years elapsed from birth up to the the year [in question], converted into degrees of the equator; and find the distance of the remainder from the Midheaven or *imum caeli*, according as the same remainder falls above or below the earth (which the oblique ascension of the Ascendant will indicate), with which distance and the declination of the terminus itself above or below according to the location of the remainder, take the circle of position. Having taken the oblique ascension or descension of the terminus under the pole of that circle of position, according as the abovesaid remainder will fall into the oriental or occidental part of the *caelum*, and from this having subtracted the elapsed years, the arc of the ecliptic that corresponds to this remainder in the table of ascensions of the abovesaid pole will be the place of the direction by oblique ascension or descension.

For example, let Jupiter be in 27 Virgo 10 retrograde with 1°35' north latitude to be directed conversely, and let the years elapsed from birth and converted be 30°26'. Subtract 30°26' from the right ascension of Jupiter 178°01'; there will remain 147°35'. And this subtracted from the RAMC, which is calculated as 148°39', will leave 1°04' for the distance of the remainder from the Midheaven, which remainder will be above the earth in the occidental part of the *caelum*. With this distance and with the declination of Jupiter 2°36' north,take the altitude of the pole above the circle of position in the table of positions for the latitude of the place, which is 49°, and the altitude of the pole will be 1°. Therefore,since the remainder is in the occidental part, take in the table of oblique ascensions for the latitude of 1° the oblique ascension of the opposition of Jupiter, which is 357°49'. Then subtract 180°, and there will remain the orbital descension of Jupiter 177°49'. From which again take away 30°26' for the years elapsed, and there will remain 147°23'. By adding 180° to this last figure, it will become 327°23', which is the right ascension of about 25 Aquarius. Therefore, the converse direction of Jupiter is in about 25 Leo. This is in the Heart of the Lion,[44] having supposed the year of the nativity to be 1625.[45]

---

43 Perhaps a slap at Placidus.

44 The fixed star Regulus in about 24 Leo 36.

45 This discussion seems to be based upon an actual horoscope. According to Morin's version of *The Rudolphine Tables*, Jupiter would have been in the specified position on the evening of 5 March 1625. The time from the RAMC is then 10:59 LMT. Recalculation shows that none of the numbers are precise. The altitude of the pole above Jupiter's circle of position is 1°10' instead of 1°00'. The orbital ascension of the opposition is 358°04' (vs. 357°49'), etc.

Finally, it must be noted that since the true method of directing depends upon the same fundamentals as does the true method of constructing the celestial figure, namely circles of position drawn through the intersections of the horizon and the meridian;hence, let it be [noted] that the true method of directing has a place for the whole globe of the earth, with the exception of those two points on the earth which are placed exactly at the poles of the equator, where there is no meridian, and no intersection of the equator and the horizon, but where in fact they coincide. For which, see the universal method of dividing the *caelum* into astrological houses that we have given in Book 17, Sects. 2 and 3.[46]

---

46 The so-called Morinus system.

SECTION II

The Latitude of Significators and Promittors in Directions.

Chapt. 1. *Whether it is Right to use the Latitude as well as the Longitude of Significators and Promittors in Directions.*

Junctinus, in his *Commentary on the Quadripartite*, Book 3, Chapt. 12, p. 381 ff., exhibits a jumble of methods of directing from the older users, contrary to themselves, which display alike confusion in ability, since it is sufficiently plain per se that nothing is disproved by him, nor is it shown which of these methods is truer. Moreover, he does not have a procedure for using the planetary latitudes in any of these methods, but on the contrary he teaches how they should be projected by equal degrees in the ecliptic without latitude, according to Ptolemy, *Quadripartite*, Book 1, the last chapter, against which and against its commentator, Cardan, we have argued in Book 16, Sect. 1, Chapt. 6. And in Chapt. 8 we have said, against Origanus and Regiomontanus, that planets having latitude project their aspects into the same circle in which they have their latitude. And in Chapt. 9 we showed what circle that is.

Moreover, that in directions not only should the longitudes of the significator and the promittor be used, but also their latitudes, may be proved thus. For the circle of position ought to pass through the true place of the significator, since it is the true position of that place, which is not determined in the *caelum* simply by the longitude of the significator. Otherwise, the true places of two planets placed in the same circle of latitude would be the same, even though one was in the northern part of the *caelum* with respect to the ecliptic and the other was in the southern part, which is utterly absurd to suppose. Therefore, both the latitude and the longitude of the significator must be used.

Moreover, it may [also] be proved about the promittor. For whether a promittor is a planet or an aspect, it is certain that its true place in directions is conceived to be transferred to the circle of position of the significator. But that place is designated in the *caelum* not only by the longitude of the promittor itself, but also by its latitude, if it has any, as was said above. Therefore, in bringing the promittor to the circle of the significator, the longitude and the latitude of the promittor must be taken into account. Besides, as Cardan and the others will have it, if the significator and the promittor differ very much from each other in latitude, one in the south and one in the north, either little or no effect will be forthcoming from the direction.

Someone will object: The ecliptical places of planets having latitude are very often efficacious in directions. Which can be proved, not only from [the testimony of] many of the ancients, who had no [special] procedure for [using] the latitude in directions, but also from experience itself. And we have also experienced this now and then, with planets as well as with their aspects, and especially with the square. Therefore, either the latitude should be omitted, or it should be admitted that the way of directing is twofold, namely with latitude and without latitude; not of course with equal degrees, which we have rejected above, but with the ascensions of the ecliptical place of the promittor to the circle of position of the ecliptic place of the significator.

I reply. It is already sufficiently plain from Book 16, Sect. 1, Chapt. 6, and from Sect. 1, Chapt. 8 of the present book that Ptolemy and the rest of the ancients erred in omitting the latitude in directions. But as for experience, it must be said that when a planet or its aspect is in any sign, this is determined, since it is such a sign. Whence, the position of the Moon in Capricorn is said to be unfavorable because Capricorn is inimical to the Moon and its exile as has already been said elsewhere. Moreover, the ecliptic is the course or line of march most efficacious for [planetary] influence, as appears from the fact that the closer the planets are to the ecliptic, the more efficacious they are, and they are most efficacious of all in the ecliptic itself. Therefore, it is no wonder that after the point of the sign in which the true place of the Moon falls beyond the ecliptic, the point of its longitude in the ecliptic is more strongly determined to the nature of the Moon than the rest of the points of that same sign, since the ecliptic is the Sun's path, to which all the rest of the planets are subordinated in some manner, both with respect to their own motion and to their influences. But if that point on the ecliptic possesses the lunar virtue on account of the true place of the Moon beyond the ecliptic, it follows that the true place itself is of still greater virtue. For because "every single thing is such, and that is more," by an axiom of the philosophers.[47] Therefore, directions with latitude will always be more efficacious than directions without latitude, and consequently more certain; if, however, an annual revolution does coincide with a direction without latitude, by no means should the effect of the direction be rashly predicted from it. And consequently, since the direction without latitude will almost always differ in time from a direction with latitude, if the effect shall have begun with the direction which preceded in time, it will perhaps last until the [time of the] following [direction], especially if the following [direction] shall have been one with latitude, by the time of which the effect will also be extended; or, the effect will be perfected as it were by the more efficacious [direction], or at least it will be reinforced. Nevertheless, it can happen that a direction without latitude can produce an effect, and the [same] direction with latitude can produce another effect; therefore, each of them should always be considered, so that it can be compared

---

47 Unidentified.

with the solar revolution, for the one that agrees with the revolution will produce its effect. And these things may be said not only of the bodies of the planets, but also of their aspects, for the logic applies equally in both cases; but the direction with latitude, if there is one, is always more to be trusted than the one without latitude. And the joint effect will happen more certainly, the less the difference in time between them shall have been.[48]

Chapt. 2. *How the Aspects of the Planets may be Corrected for Directions both with Longitude and with Latitude.*

Although the places of the planets and the aspects can be referred to the equator, and can be defined in the *caelum* by their right ascensions and declinations; yet, all astronomers, led by the astrologers, have referred them to the ecliptic and designated them in the *caelum* by their longitudes and latitudes; because of course the ecliptic claims the rulership of the planets in the signs of the zodiac, from which astrologers judge the effects of the stars, and by which the influential force of the aspects is measured.[49]

Moreover, in Book 16, Sect. 1, Chapts. 6-8, we have reported the opinions of Ptolemy, Cardan, Bianchini, Schöner, Regiomontanus, Origanus, and Argol[50] about the celestial circle in which the aspects of the planets having latitude must be conceived; then, about their correction when they are referred to the ecliptic; and we rejected those opinions, and set forth our own in Chapt. 9, declaring that the aspects of any planet are conceived to be in that great circle, which from its appearance in the *caelum* deviates least from the path of the planet, and which we have called the *circle of aspects*;[51] and we have demonstrated the method geometrically, by means of which these aspects may be referred by longitude to the ecliptic with their own latitude. Which, along with some other things of the old

---

48 Morin says repeatedly that primary directions must be calculated *in mundo* to be valid. Here, he somewhat grudgingly allows the use of zodiacal primaries, but only as an extension in time of the corresponding mundane primaries.

49 Astronomical ephemerides continued to give the longitude and latitude of the celestial bodies until the early 19th century, when, to facilitate the comparison of theory with observations, they switched to right ascension and declination, with the exception of the Sun and Moon, which they continued to give both ways. Thereafter, astrologers were obliged to transform the coordinates in the national ephemerides or else calculate their own ephemerides.

50 Johann Schöner (1477-1547), German mathematician, astronomer, and astrologer; Giovanni Bianchini (15th cent.), Italian mathematician and astronomer; Andrea Argoli (1570-1651?), Italian astrologer.

51 This is approximately the great circle on the *caelum* on which the planet appears to be moving at the time for which the chart is drawn. But see the reference mentioned for an extended discussion of the concept

[astrologers], we have combined after long and repeated experience; and we have seen our [theory] excel all the rest both in reason and in experience itself, and to agree more accurately with the observed accidents of the natives. Now we assert that the aspects of the planets must be corrected for [use in] directions according to that same [theory], i.e., they must be reduced by it to the ecliptic by calculation of a longitude conformable with the latitude.

Chapt. 3. *In which a Table of Correction of Aspects of the Planets for Directions that we have Constructed is Set Forth and Explained.*

We have selected this table of aspects from the foundation that is established in Book 16, Sect. 1, Chapt. 9. And for its construction and arrangement three things must be known in advance: viz., the longitude and latitude of the planet at the given time, with the maximum northern or southern latitude which the planet itself can attain, from the calculation of the more correct ephemerides, according as with respect to the ecliptic it is in the northern or southern part of the world; which maximum latitude is the inclination of the circle of aspects to the ecliptic. From which is first discovered the true place of the node in which that circle itself and the ecliptic intersect, and then the true longitudes and latitudes of the single arcs of that circle, counted from the node, are found under that same inclination, as will be explained below. Moreover, in making the table we have used only the inclination of that same circle supplied by the astronomers for each planet and the individual arcs of the same circle by degrees, as is done for the table of declination of the degrees of the ecliptic.

Explanation of the Table

At the top of the table are placed the degrees of inclination to the ecliptic of the circle of aspects for the individual planets Saturn, Jupiter, Mars, Venus, Mercury, and the Moon from 1° to 8°. And in the first column on the left are put the degrees of the arcs of that same circle (which we designate by the name *excentric*), beginning from the node nearest to the planet. And in the space of the second column are put the latitudes of the several degrees of each arc corresponding to the inclination of 1° at the top of the column. And in the third column beside the groups of five degrees of the excentric are put the equation of the arcs of the ecliptic that are related to the excentric arcs, i.e., the arcs beginnning from the same node into which the circle of latitude falls. And it is this same equation by which the excentric arc or the arc of the circle of aspects is greater or lesser than the corresponding ecliptical arc. And in fact this equation increases from the node to 45°, then similarly it decreases down to 90°. But under the inclination of 1° is put only 0 for the equation because it does not amount to 1 minute of arc. And the arrangement is the same for the other columns of the inclination or maximum latitude of 2, 3, 4, 5, 6,7, and 8° placed at the top [of the table].[52]

Use of the Table

The use of this table can be one and the same for the Moon and for Saturn, Jupiter, Mars, Venus, and Mercury.

But for the Moon, because the ephemerides give its true longitude, latitude, and the place of its node, first the distance of the Moon is taken from its nearest node by subtracting the preceding place in signs, degrees, and minutes from the following place, so that the remainder is less than 90°.

Secondly, that distance, which is an arc of the ecliptic, is taken in the left part of the table in the column headed E_{xc}; but with the shortened *Equation* which corresponds to the latitude of that same planet taken from the same table to the right of that shortened distance; and so, through this shortened distance (which is the abovesaid arc of the ecliptic) and the true latitude of the Moon itself, there will be had in the first column on the left the corresponding arc of the excentric, namely by increasing the ecliptical arc itself by the equation, by which it is less than the corresponding arc of the excentric. And at the top [of the table] there will then be given the true inclination of the Moon's excentric to the ecliptic at that time by taking the proportional part where required, as is customary in other tables.

But for Saturn, Jupiter, Mars, Venus, and Mercury, the true place of whose north nodes is not known at the given time, their distance from the nearest node, and through it the place of the node itself in the ecliptic, will first have to be found. Moreover, that distance can be found just from a table, but not without effort if the minutes are close to the planet's maximum latitude, unless the table is constructed to every five or ten minutes of the maximum latitude of the planet, or of the

---

52 The table is actually twofold. First, it is a table of latitude as a function of the inclination of what Morin calls the *excentric* of the planet to the ecliptic and the distance of the planet from the node of the excentric on the ecliptic, measured in the plane of the excentric. The inclination, i, is given in integer degrees at the top of the table and the arc, E_{xc}, (Planet minus Node), is in the left-hand column. The numbers in the columns directly beneath the inclinations are the latitudes, b, calculated from the equation sin b = sin i sin E_{xc}. Second, the table serves to calculate the *equation* that Morin uses to correct the length of the aspect arcs. This quantity is another function of the arc, E_{xc}, and the inclination, i. It is in fact the difference between the *excentric arc* of a planet and the planet's distance from the nearest excentric node, measured in the ecliptic. Thus, it is like the *reduction to the ecliptic* of orbital astronomy. Or, in terms more familiar to astrologers, it is analogous to the difference between *ecliptic longitude* and *right ascension* if the obliquity of the ecliptic is replaced by a variable inclination, i. Therefore, it can be calculated from the equation $E_q = E_{xc} - E_{cl}$ where tan E_{cl} = (cos i)(tan E_{xc}), or more simply from $E_q = 3438' \cdot$ abs[-tan^2(i/2) sin 2(E_{xc}) +(1/2)tan^4(i/2) sin 4E_{xc}], where the second term is virtually negligible.

Jean-Baptiste Morin

TABLE OF CORRECTIONS OF THE PLANETARY ASPECTS

E_{xc}	1°	E_q	2°	E_q	3°	E_q	4°	E_q	5°	E_q	6°	E_q	7°	E_q	8°	E_q
1	0°01'	0	0°02'	0	0°03'	0	0°04'	0	0°05'	0	0°06'	0	0°07'	0	0°08'	0
2	02		04		06		08		10		13		15		17	
3	03		06		09		13		16		19		22		25	
4	04		08		13		17		22		25		30		33	
5	05		10		16		21	1	26	1	31	2	37	2	42	3
6	06	0	13	0	19		25		31		38		44		50	
7	07		15		22		29		36		44		51		59	
8	08		17		25		33		42		50		59		1 07	
9	09		19		29		37		47		56		1 06		16	
10	11		21		31	1	42	1	52	2	1 02	3	13	4	24	5
11	12	0	23	0	34		46		58		09		20		32	
12	12		25		37		50		1 02		15		28		40	
13	13		27		41		54		08		21		35		49	
14	15		29		44		58		13		27		42		57	
15	16		31	1	47	1	1 02	2	18	3	33	5	49	6	2 05	8
16	17	0	33		50		06		23		39		56		13	
17	18		35		53		11		28		45		2 03		21	
18	19		37		56		14		33		51		10		29	
19	20		39		59		18		38		58		17		37	
20	20		41	1	1 01	2	22	3	43	4	2 03	6	24	8	45	11
21	22	0	43		1 05		26		48		09		31		53	
22	22		45		07		30		53		15		39		3 01	
23	23		47		09		34		57		21		45		08	
24	25		49		13		38		2 02		27		51		16	
25	25		51	1	16	2	41	3	07	5	33	7	58	10	24	13
26	26	0	52		19		46		12		38		3 05		32	
27	27		55		22		49		17		44		11		39	
28	28		56		25		53		21		50		18		47	
29	29		58		27		56		26		56		24		54	
30	30		1 00	1	30	2	2 00	4	30	6	3 00	8	31	11	4 00	14
31	31	0	1 02		33		04		35		06		37		08	
32	32		04		35		07		39		11		43		16	
33	33		05		38		11		44		17		52		23	
34	34		07		41		14		48		22		56		30	
35	34		09	1	43	2	18	4	53	6	27	9	4 02	12	36	16
36	35	0	11		46		21		57		32		08		43	
37	36		12		48		25		3 01		37		14		50	
38	37		14		51		28		05		42		19		57	
39	38		15		54		31		09		47		25		5 03	
40	39		17	1	56	2	34	4	14	7	52	9	31	13	10	17
41	39	0	19		58		38		17		57		36		16	
42	40		20		2 00		41		21		4 02		42		22	
43	41		22		04		44		25		16		47		29	
44	42		23		05		47		29		11		53		34	
45	43		25	1	07	2	50	4	32	7	15	9	58	13	40	17

TABLE OF CORRECTIONS OF THE PLANETARY ASPECTS

E$_{xc}$	1°	E$_q$	2°	E$_q$	3°	E$_q$	4°	E$_q$	5°	E$_q$	6°	E$_q$	7°	E$_q$	8°	E$_q$
46	0°43'	0	1°26'	1	2°10'	2	2°53'	4	3°36'	7	4°19'	9	5°03'	13	5°46'	17
47	44		28		12		56		40		24		08		52	
48	45		29		14		58		43		28		13		58	
49	45		31		16		3 01		47		32		18		6 03	
50	46		32	1	18	2	04	4	50	7	36	9	22	13	09	17
51	47	0	33		20		07		53		40		27		14	
52	47		35		22		09		56		44		31		19	
53	48		36		24		12		4 00		47		36		24	
54	49		37		26		14		03		51		40		29	
55	49		38	1	27	2	17	4	06	6	55	9	45	12	34	16
56	50	0	39		30		19		09		59		49		39	
57	50		41		31		22		12		5 02		53		43	
58	51		42		33		24		14		06		57		48	
59	51		43		34		26		17		09		6 01		52	
60	52		44	1	36	2	28	3	20	6	12	8	04	11	56	14
61	52	0	45		38		30		23		15		08		7 00	
62	53		46		39		32		25		18		11		04	
63	53		47		40		34		27		21		15		08	
64	54		48		42		36		30		24		18		12	
65	54		49	1	43	2	38	3	32	5	27	7	21	10	16	13
66	55	0	50		45		39		34		29		24		19	
67	55		50		46		41		36		31		27		22	
68	56		51		47		43		38		34		30		25	
69	56		52		48		44		40		36		32		28	
70	56		53	1	49	2	46	3	42	4	38	6	35	8	31	11
71	57	0	53		50		47		44		41		37		33	
72	57		54		51		48		45		43		40		37	
73	57		55		52		50		47		44		42		39	
74	58		55		53		51		48		46		44		42	
75	58		56	1	54	1	52	3	50	3	48	5	46	6	44	8
76	59	0	56		55		53		51		49		48		46	
77	59		57		55		54		52		51		49		48	
78	1 00		57		56		55		53		52		51		50	
79	1 00		58		56		55		55		53		52		51	
80	1 00		58	0	57	1	56	2	56	2	55	3	54	4	53	6
81	1 00	0	58		58		57		56		56		55		54	
82	1 00		59		58		58		57		56		56		55	
83	1 00		59		59		58		58		57		57		57	
84	1 00		59		59		59		58		58		58		58	
85	1 00		2 00	0	59	1	59	1	59	1	59	2	59	2	58	3
86	1 00	0	00		59		4 00		59		59		59		59	
87	1 00		00		3 00		00		59		59		59		59	
88	1 00		00		00		00		5 00		59		7 00		59	
89	1 00		00		00		00		00		6 00		00		8 00	
90	1 00	0	00	0	00	0	00	0	00	0	00	0	00	0	00	0

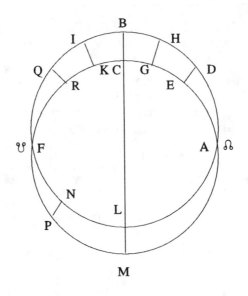

Figure 1

inclination of the excentric to the ecliptic. And I did not want to undertake the labor of such a lengthy calculation.

For example, in the following figure, let there be given Mars at E with longitude or true place 24°16' Leo and latitude ED 1°44' north ascending, which is [its position] on 4 November 1648 from the *Rudolphine Tables*, close to the *Ephemerides* of Durret[53] which are very often erroneous; moreover, let the maximum northerly latitude to which Mars arrives on 11 February 1649 be 4°15'. Then let it be found by the two columns of maximum latitude 4° and 5° that the true latitude of 1°44' only agrees with an excentric arc of 24°02' which lies between 24° and 25°; which proves the table to be true and in agreement with trignonometric calculation. But this cannot be found from the top row [of figures] of this table constructed only to integer degrees of the maximum latitude. Just as when the altitude of the pole having been given in degrees and minutes, along with the

---

53 Noel Durret (1590-c.1650), *Novae motuum caelestium Ephemerides Richelianae annorum 15, ab anno 1637 incipientes*. [New Richelian Ephemerides of Celestial Motions for 15 Years, Beginning with the Year 1637] (Paris, 1641). Owen Gingerich & Barbara Welther, *Planetary, Lunar, and Solar Positions A.D. 1650-1805* (Philadelphia, 1983), p. xv, say that Durret used his own tables, which, like Morin's, were based upon Kepler's *Rudolphine Tables*.

distance of the planet from the meridian, its declination cannot be found to degrees and minutes from the top row [of figures] of a table of positions.

Moreover, since the principal task of this art consists of finding the arc of the excentric exactly, if a table constructed to [intervals of] 5 or 10 [minutes of arc] of the maximum latitude of the planets is lacking, I recommend that this same arc, i.e., the distance of the true place of Mars in the ecliptic from the node that is nearer at the time, be found as is shown in Book 16, Chapt. 9. For quicker than the word this will be done to the desired precision, in fact merely by saying "as the tangent of the maximum latitude of Mars 4°15' is to the tangent of its true latitude 1°44', so the whole sine is to the sine of 24°02'," which is the desired distance. And because the greatest latitude was taken, it follows the true place of Mars.

Therefore, from that same place of Mars 24°16' Leo the distance of 24°02' is taken away, and 0°14' Leo is left for point A, which is the true apparent north node of Mars. But now this distance 24°02' of Mars from its node, which is the ecliptical arc AE, is reduced to the excentric arc by the addition of the corresponding equation, which is placed beside 24° of the excentric arc under the columns of maximum latitude 4° and 5°. And the value of this equation is a little more than 3', but not 4'. Therefore, having added 3' to 24°02', it makes 24°05' for the excentric arc AD, corresponding to the ecliptical arc AE, i.e., beginning from the same node, for the ecliptical arc is less than the corresponding excentric arc by [the amount of] that equation. Now the rest is very easy by the table. So, therefore, having first found the corresponding excentric arc for the Moon or Mars, all of the aspects must be counted from the derived terminus in the excentric [circle] itself according to the appropriate ratios, viz. by giving 30° of the excentric to the dodectile,[54] 60° to the sextile, 90° to the square, etc. And the final termini of the several [aspects] must be related to the node, either following or preceding, which is nearest to them, so that the increase or decrease of it will be apparent from them. So, therefore, the corresponding equation of the increase or decrease of it will be given in the table, always to be subtracted in coequating for the corresponding arc of the ecliptic, and then to be referred to the node nearest to [the aspect] itself by addition or subtraction, so that the true place in the ecliptic of the aspect itself, with its own latitude, may be had, to be taken [from the column to the right of] the column under the maximum latitude of the planet, from which the right ascension or oblique ascension of the aspect itself will be given in the tables of ascensions. And so, having found the sinister semisextile, sextile, square, trine, and quincunx aspects, the dexter aspects will be in the diametrically opposed longitudes, retaining the same latitudes but changing their designation,[55] as is said in Book 16, Sect. 1,

---

54 That is, the *semisextile*.

55 He means the latitudes are to be reversed, north for south, or vice versa. Also, the sinister and dexter aspects are to be taken in supplementary pairs: the sinister semisextile + 180° = the dexter quincunx, the sinister sextile + 180° = the dexter trine, etc.

Chapt. 9.[56] And therefore, with the [places of the] sinister [aspects] given in longitude and latitude, the [places of the] dexter [aspects], which are individually opposite them, are also known; or else, given the two semisextiles, the two sextiles, and one of the squares, the rest are given as their opposites.

Example

Moreover, so that the use of this table may be more evident, we shall find all of the aspects for Mars, both in the excentric or circle of aspects which we have explained, and also in the ecliptic, each with its appropriate latitude. Since therefore Mars is at point D, distant from A by 24°05', 30° is added to it for the sinister semisextile, and it makes 54°05'. This number being entered in column E_{xc}, [the columns] beneath maximum latitude 4°15' will give 3°26' north ascending latitude for that aspect, with an equation of 4'. Subtracting the latter from 54°05' or 1 sign 24°05', the remainder will be 54°01' or 1 sign 24°01' for the corresponding arc of the ecliptic. By adding to this the place of the node A, 4 signs 0°14', it will become 5 signs 24°15' for the longitude of the aspect or 24°15' Virgo, with the abovesaid north latitude of 3°26'. Similarly, to the abovesaid distance of Mars, 24°05', 60° are added for the sinister sextile; it makes 84°05' for the sinister sextile. Which number, found in column E_{xc} will give 4°14' [in the columns] under maximum latitude 4°15' for the north ascending latitude of this aspect, with an equation of 1'. Subtracting the latter from 84°05' will leave 84°04' or 2 signs 24°04' for the corresponding arc of the ecliptic. By adding to this the place of the node A, 4 signs 0°14', it will become 6 signs 24°18' for the longitude of this aspect or 24°18' Libra. Again, to the abovesaid distance of Mars, 24°05', 90° are added for the sinister square; it makes 114°05'. Which, having been subtracted from the semicircle ABF or 180°, will leave 65°55' for FI. Which number, found in column E_{xc}, will give 3°53' [in the columns] under maximum latitude 4°15' for the north descending latitude of that aspect, with an equation of 3'. Subtracting the latter from 65°55' will leave 65°52' for the arc of the ecliptic corresponding to FK, i.e., 2 signs 5°52'. By subtracting this from the place of the south node F, 10 signs 0°14', there is left 7 signs 24°22' or 24°22' Scorpio for the longitude of this aspect. In addition, since the place of the square in the excentric is I, and FI is 65°55' from what has been said about the square, therefore 30° are taken away from FI (which amounts to adding 30° to I itself for the sinister trine aspect), and the remainder will be 35°55' for FQ. Which number, found in column E_{xc} will give 2°30' [in the columns] under maximum latitude 4°15' for the north descending latitude of this trine aspect, with an equation of 4'. By subtracting this from 35°55', there will remain 35°51' for the arc of the ecliptic corresponding to FK, i.e., 1 sign 5°51'. By subtracting this from the place of the south node F, 10 signs 0°14', there will remain

---

56 See Appendix 2, which contains a translation of the method given in that place.

8 signs 24°23' for the longitude of this trine aspect, with its abovesaid latitude RQ. And so with the quincunx and any other one of the aspects mentioned above.

Experience

And the first notable experience of correcting aspects in this fashion was made by me in the nativity of the Queen of Poland, Marie Louise of Gonzaga,[57] whose endowments of body, mental ability, and spirit, superior to any praise, along with certain accidents of her life, merit a volume to themselves. For in the year 1645, on the 5th of November, at noon, she was married at Paris to Vladislav IV, King of Poland,[58] who, struck by the fame of her merits, wanted to marry her. For this most famous and outstanding accident, the wiser astrologers found no celestial cause, which having been adopted, other more outstanding accidents of life could be ascribed to genuine stellar causes. For when on 12 October 1626 she had fallen into a very grave sickness at Paris, in which she was also despaired of by the Paris physicians and handed over to an empiric physician, who restored her from a dying condition to the best of health by the use of antimony, of course, the astrologers conjectured that such an accident could only be referred to a direction of the Ascendant as the primary significator of life to the dexter square of the Moon badly disposed in the 4th house, with her exaltation of power in the 8th, and next applying to the trine of Mars ruler of the 8th in the 12th; and this was the true opinion of the wise men based on the given hour of the nativity. But because they took the square of the Moon in the common way in the ecliptic, as [recommended by] Bianchini and Regiomontanus, that sublime marriage with royal dignity had no celestial cause at its own time, which in this science seemed utterly absurd because of the importance of the accident, so that I need say nothing about the other lesser accidents passed through in the course of her life. I, therefore, having thought out then this correction of the time of aspects, found the dexter square of the Moon to be in 10°11' Libra with latitude 4°38' north, whose oblique ascension at the place of the figure is 190°34'.[59] From which, having subtracted 14°56' for the time of the abovesaid sickness according to Naibod's table, there remained 175°38' for the oblique ascension of the Ascendant. From which, having subtracted 90°, there remained 85°38' for the RAMC. To which, if 33°42' are added for the time from

---

57 She was the daughter of Charles I Gonzaga (1580-1637), Duke of Mantua.
58 Vladislav IV (*or* VII) (1595-1648) reigned 1632-1648. He was the son of Sigismund III by his first wife Anne of Austria. Vladislav's first wife was Renata Cecilia of Austria (d. 1644).
59 Assuming an inclination of 5° for the Moon's orbit, calculation from Morin's tables would seem to give 10 Lib 17 or perhaps 10 Lib 15 (depending on the value chosen for the "equation"), rather than the 10 Lib 11 he derived for the Moon's dexter square. The latitude 3N48, however, appears to be correct. This discrepancy is small, but his figure for the OA is further off. I calculate 190°56' (using his coordinates of the square).

The Horoscope of MARIE LOUISE
of Gonzaga, Queen of Poland

85°38'

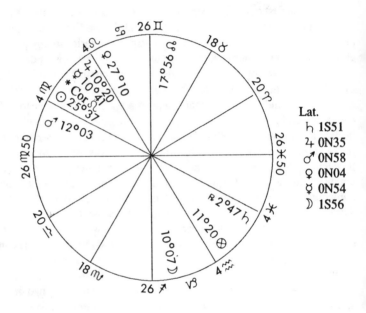

Lat.

♄	1S51
♃	0N35
♂	0N58
♀	0N04
☿	0N54
☽	1S56

Nevers, Nivernais Lat. 47°N
18 August 1611, 19:51 AT true (20:03 estimated)
From the Rudolphine Tables

Figure 2

birth to the day of marriage, it makes 119°20'. Moreover, the right ascension of Venus is 119°14'. And consequently marriage and royal dignity happened from the direction of the Midheaven, the primary significator of actions and dignities, to Venus ruler of the 1st in the 10th, sextile the Ascendant; and Venus is found in the domicile of the Moon and the exaltation of Jupiter ruler of the 7th, in which Venus also is strong by exaltation. And this is the cause of both accidents—at once elegant and genuine.[60]

---

60 The discrepancy in RAMC's rectified from these two events is only 6' by Morin's calculations. However, the recalculation widens this to 28' or more.

Moreover, trusting in the aforesaid rectification, the noble, distinguished in virtue, and most skilled in celestial sciences, Nicolas, Lord of La Mothe,[61] Chamberlain of the Most Serene Prince Gaston, Duke of Orleans,[62] whom I had taken as my only student in Paris up until that time, dared to write, while Vladislav was still alive, to Lord Des Noyers, his own personal friend, the private secretary of that Queen, very active in old astrology, that within a short time the Queen would be married to another King, because Jupiter ruler of the 7th and Mercury ruler of the Ascendant and the Midheaven, partilely conjoined in the 11th, would be directed in the year 1649 to Mars ruler of the 7th, with the direction of the Ascendant to the sextile of the Sun following closely, which is exalted in [the sign of] the 7th and is powerful in the 11th in its own domicile and partilely conjoined to the royal fixed star Cor Leonis,[63] but that she would suffer from a difficult sickness on account of Mars ruler of the 8th in the 12th. And so it happened, for with Vladislav dead in 1648, and she herself attacked by a long and difficult sickness, after having recovered her health this heroine was married to Casimir,[64] the brother of Vladislav, who had been elected King of Poland, and in whom her beauty and virtues had kindled a chaste love. The day of the wedding was 30 May 1649. From which prediction Goulas, Lord of La Motte, got outstanding praise along with the admiration of the Queen herself and an honorarium worthy of that Queen. And from this it is demonstrated not only that this nativity is outstandingly rectified, but also that the correction to the Moon's square made by us is absolutely true. And it is more amply confirmed by the fact that in the year 1629 Gaston of Bourbon, now the Duke of Orleans, had ardently desired to join himself in matrimony with the Princess Marie, and this was no light rumor and appearance. And then the Ascendant was precisely directed to the sextile of Jupiter ruler of the cusp of the 7th and the sextile of Mercury ruler of the Midheaven, but Marie de' Medici the Queen Mother and Cardinal Richelieu obstructed that marriage with as much authority as they could excercise. I had a second experience and one even more illustrious at the birth of the Most Christian King Louis XIV, which, by the altitude of the Sun taken by astrolabe at Saint Germain, occurred at 23:15 PM of 4 September 1638. And in the figure erected for this moment, previously published along with a prognostication addressed to Cardinal Richelieu; the RAMC is $152°47'$, and consequently the oblique ascension of the Ascendant is $242°47'$. And from this figure which we have corrected as will be said below, the birth took place

---

61 Nicolas Goulas (1603-1683), Lord of La Mothe, retired to his château after the death of the Duke of Orleans in 1660.

62 Prince Gaston of Bourbon (1608-1660), the younger brother of Louis XIII. He intrigued against Louis and particularly against Cardinal Richelieu.

63 Regulus, in about 24 Leo 25, is $1°12'$ from the Sun.

64 John II Casimir (1609-1672), son of Sigismund III by his second wife Constance of Austria, and a younger half-brother of Vladislav IV; he is sometimes called Casimir V.

at 23:11, at which time the horoscope was such as is shown below. So in fact he suffered two sicknesses, namely a fever on 9 March 1644, which was followed on the 12th day by erysipelas in the face. Then, an abundant and deadly outbreak of pustules with danger to his life, which began on 11 November 1647 with a swelling up of blood, erupting on the 13th.[65] Moreover, Jupiter ruler of the 1st in the 12th, which is [the house] of sicknesses, is besieged by the square of Saturn and [the square] of the Moon ruler of the 8th, and the Moon is injured by the opposition of Saturn; consequently, these two sicknesses arose from directions of the Ascendant, the primary significator of life, then of Jupiter ruler of the 1st,[66] to the sinister square of the Moon [falling] in the 12th, of which the former is converse and the latter is direct. For, having put down the estimate time of the nativity, no other genuine directions occur by which these sicknesses might be caused. But unless the square of the Moon is corrected by longitude and latitude, the pustules, which constituted the more dangerous of the sicknesses of the nature of Saturn, will have no cause, and the figure of the nativity cannot be rectified by these sicknesses. But in fact it can be done if that square is corrected according to our method. So, therefore, this figure must be rectified in accordance with [the method explained in] Book 18, Sect. 3, Chapt. 6.

First let the correct sinister square of the Moon be found by use of the table or the method given above. And it will be 5°42' Scorpio with 4°17' south latitude; and its declination will be 17°30' south, and its right ascension 211°54'.[67] Consequently, in the figure for the estimated time the distance of this square from the meridian will be 59°07', and the altitude of the pole above its circle of position will be 48°30'. The oblique ascension taken at this [polar altitude] will be 232°46'. If to this is added the time of the pustules reduced to degrees of the equator, which is 8°57',[68] it will make 241°43' for the oblique ascension of the Ascendant. But this from [the initial] hypothesis is 242°47'; therefore, the distance of the square of the Moon from the meridian is greater than 59°07'.[69]

---

65 Probably an acute attack of smallpox.

66 Mars is of course the ruler of the Scorpio Ascendant, but it is not in domicile, so Morin selects Jupiter, the dispositor of Mars, as the ruler. This is what he calls *the secondary ruler*. Cf. Book 21, Sect. 2, Chapt. 24 (p. 56 in Baldwin's translation). The ruler of the sign containing the ruler of the sign on the Ascendant is said to be especially significant when the ruler of the Ascendant is not in domicile, as in this case. (Jupiter is also co-ruler of the 1st house because the latter part of the 1st is in Sagittarius.)

67 These numbers are substantially correct, but those that follow have errors of several minutes—amounting in one case to 14'.

68 This is wrong. The unreduced arc of the event is 9°11' (Sep 1638 to Nov 1647), and consequently the reduced arc is 9°03'.

69 These numbers are all off slightly: the altitude of the pole should be 48°34', the OA 232°50', and the OA of the Ascendant 241°47'.

The Nativity of LOUIS XIV,
Most Christian King of France and Navarre.

151°44'

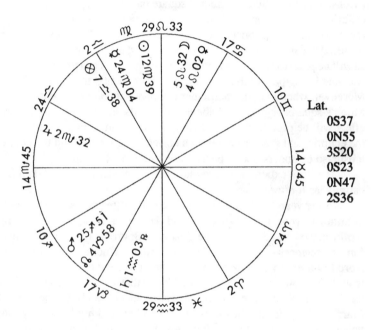

Lat.

0S37
0N55
3S20
0S23
0N47
2S36

4 September 1638, 23:11 AT true (23:15 AT estimated)
Latitude 49°N
From the Rudolphine Tables

Figure 3

Therefore, let it be supposed to be 60°10'. And consequently the RAMC will be 151°44', and the oblique ascension of the Ascendant will be 241°44'. Moreover, the altitude of the pole above the circle of position of the Moon's square will be 48°33' and the oblique ascension of that same square in that circle will be 232°48'. If to this is added the reduced time of the pustules, 8°57', it will make 241°45' for the oblique ascension of the Ascendant—namely, the value that arises from this meridian, which therefore is true. And consequently the figure given here is true, and the birth occurred at 23:11.[70]

Moreover, this can be confirmed. For, with the figure standing thus, the altitude of the pole above the circle of position of Jupiter will be 47°22', and Jupiter's oblique ascension will be 223°23'. If the time of the pustules, 8°52' as converted above,[71] is added to this, it will make 232°20'. Moreover, the oblique ascension of the Moon's corrected square taken in that circle amounts to 231°49', differing only 31' from 232°20'; and consequently the pustules were produced by these two directions concurring in the same year.[72] Moreover, the earlier sickness occurred because of the direction of Jupiter to the square of the Moon in the ecliptic, as will be plain to anyone calculating from this rectified [figure] on account of what was said in Chapt. 1 of this section; and consequently the sickness was less severe. Moreover, when in either particular or universal configurations of the *caelum* the Moon's square, as corrected above, falls in the ecliptic itself, then the maximum effect will be produced by it—that is, greater than from an uncorrected square in the ecliptic, and greater than from a corrected square beyond the ecliptic,[73] which must also be understood to be the case with the other aspects.

The third experience, also manifest and evident, will be taken from my own nativity, as follows.

In the year 1652, which I had predicted three years earlier would be a very unfortunate year, full of sickness and danger, as is plain from my many public writings, the Most Serene Prince Gaston of Bourbon, Duke of Orleans, a man very fond of sciences—and particularly, celestial sciences, ordered me on the 7th of April to observe with him in the Orleans Palace the major eclipse of the Sun that would occur on the 8th.[74] Moreover, I knew that at that time I would be endangered by sickness, as I had predicted to my astrological friends; but because at the end of March and [again] on the 4th of April I had purged my body very thoroughly by way of precaution, and thereafter I was feeling good, and it was not proper not to comply with the command of so great a prince, I therefore promised that I would

---

70 Again, recalculation gives the altitude of the pole as 48°40', the square's oblique ascension 232°54', and 241°51' for the OA Ascendant. Correcting Morin's 8°57' to 9°03' would yield 241°57' for the OA Ascendant, 151°57' for the RAMC, and a rectified birth time of 23:12.

71 This figure is evidently a misprint, since Morin used 8°57'above. However, as noted previously, it should really be 9°03'.

72 Recalculation gives the altitude of the pole as 47°32', Jupiter's OA 223°31', the rectified OA Ascendant 232°28', and OA of the Moon's square 232°03', and the final difference 35'.

73 That is, a square with latitude.

74 According to Oppolzer's *Canon of Eclipses* this was a total eclipse whose shadow path passed to the west of Ireland, across the northern tip of Scotland, and parallel to the coast of Norway. It was only partial at Paris.

do it. And so I went to Mr. Agarrat,[75] who had prepared instruments for this observation at his own home, and informed him of the prince's desire, warning him to see to it that the instruments were transferred to the Orleans Palace. But this was done in the evening; and the next morning, having constructed a darkroom in the open air in a suitable place, with curtains and other necessaries, only a quarter of an hour was left before the beginning of the eclipse. And then, when I had advised the Most Serene Prince of the imminent beginning of the eclipse, he, together with his dear wife the Most Serene Princess and many important personages, entered the room. Mr. Agarrat closed the door and displayed an image of the Sun cleverly projected with an optical tube onto a one-foot circle drawn on paper and divided for accurately measuring the digits of the eclipse. Another experienced man was taking altitudes of the Sun in the open air with a quadrant circle with a 3-foot radius beautifully made and accurately divided for measuring down to single minutes of a degree. But I was directing my attention now to the image and now to the altitude of the Sun, so that I might be more certain of the precision of this observation, which greatly delighted the prince and princess and the whole company. It was an eclipse of 10 digits 20', and it began at precisely 9:30 AM, and left off at precisely noon, as taken from the place of the Sun in Eichstadt's[76] Ephemeris. And all the ephemerides and tables were considerably in error with regard to it, the causes of which and the remedies we have given in our *Astronomy Restored from the Fundamentals*.[77] Moreover, the most erroneous of all were the *Tabulae Philolaicae* of Ismael Boulliau[78] and also his observation made at Paris, since he attributed to the Sun at the end of the eclipse only 48°40' of altitude, when in fact it was accurately observed with our quadrant to be 48°44', which difference of 4' is intolerable among masters of the art.[79] And he put the end of the eclipse at 11:50,

---

75 Antoine Agarrat, a 17th century French astronomer who was well-known in his own day.

76 The text has Euhstadt's, but this seems to be a typographical error. Lorenz Eichstadt (1596-1660) of Danzig (now, Gdansk) published three volumes of ephemerides covering the years 1636-1675. See Owen Gingerich & Barbara Welther, *Planetary, Lunar, and Solar Positions, A.D.1650-1805* (Philadelphia, 1983). If I understand Gingerich and Welther, Eichstadt's ephemerides were calculated from Kepler's *Rudolphine Tables* and constituted an extension of Kepler's own ephemerides (1617-1636).

77 Morin's *Astronomia jam a fundamentis integre et exacte restitua...* [Astronomy, now Completely and Exactly Restored from the Fundamentals...] (Paris, 1640).

78 Ismael Bouillau (1605-1694), a prominent French astronomer with a reputation as a careful observer. Some of his observations are still of value. His *Philolaic Tables*, based on Kepler's *Rudolphine Tables*, were published at Paris in 1645. However, Bouillau seems to have trusted his observations more than positions calculated from tables.

79 I have calculated the longitude of the Sun and the circumstances of the eclipse at Paris using modern elements. Assuming the place of observation to be at 48N51 and 2E20, the LAT of first contact was 9:29 AM, maximum eclipse 10:39 AM, and last contact 11:52 AM; the magnitude was 0.865 or 10 digits 22'48". The Sun's longitude at the last contact was 19°12.'1, the obliquity 23°29.'2, and the Sun's declination 7N31.'9. At ..

when in fact with the supposed altitude of the Sun 48°44', its place 19°20'55" Aries, declination 7°35' north, and with the altitude of the pole at Paris 48°51', having observed exactly with that quadrant the maximum altitudes of the Sun, the resolution of the spherical triangle has the Sun not a half minute of arc distant from the meridian circle.[80] But let us return to our subject.

Having taken a light lunch after the eclipse, I wanted to define the beginning and end of it in hours and minutes by calculation, so that the [time of] the middle [of the eclipse] might be known, for which [time] the astrological figure had to be erected. But either from the heat of the Sun, which I endured for 2 1/2 hours with a bare head, or from the malign influx of that eclipse particularly [acting] against me, or rather from both causes, a rigor and a fever with a fierce catarrh suddenly coming upon me, forced me to retire instantly to my lodging, where I was sick for almost a month with such a loss of strength and with an attack of deafness, that until now at the end of May neither the recovery of strength nor the lessening of the deafness is noticeably apparent to me after the 15th day [from the onset], although diet and medicine were duly adopted, and I fear a worsening unless I take precautions.[81]

Moreover, that this ecliptical conjunction of the luminaries in addition to the heat of the Sun was the cause of so great a sickness to me, is plain from the fact that in my nativity I have the Sun and the Moon in the 12th house, which is [the house] of sicknesses, in which this eclipse occurred with its own conjunction injuring my Ascendant, which is 28 Aries. And in this year's revolution [of my nativity] I have the Sun and the Moon rulers of the 8th, which is [the house] of death, with the Moon occupying that same house with Saturn, whose radical partile square falls upon the Ascendant [of the revolution]; and the sickness occurred when the Ascendant itself by annual direction came to the opposition of Saturn, from

Local Apparent Noon the Sun's altitude was 48°40'.9, which is closer to Boulliau's 48° 40' than to Morin and Agarrat's 48°44'. If Agarrat's assistant actually observed 48°44', then the quadrant was misoriented by 3' of arc. But the *Rudolphine Tables* have a sizable error in the solar longitude when the Sun is in Aries, and Morin gives the Sun's longitude as 19°20'.9 and its declination as 7N35, which yields a maximum solar altitude of 48°44'.3—exactly what Morin claimed they observed.

80 I think Morin has inferred Boulliau's time of 11:50 AM by comparing his reported solar altitude of 48°40' with Morin's 48°44'. If Morin's figure had been the true value at noon, then Boulliau's figure would in fact have corresponded to 11:50 AM. However, see Appendix 2 for a further discussion of this eclipse.

81 Morin was 69 years old and evidently not in the best of health. He seems to have spent part of the 2 1/2 hours inside the *camera obscura*, which was hot and undoubtedly reeking with the cloying scents of perfume and sweat emanating from the assembled aristocrats, and the rest outside in the sun. It is also possible that some of the food he ate at lunch was spoiled. Some of his symptoms sound like those of heat prostration, but we would not expect the effects of that ailment alone to linger for weeks after the event.

which the deafness seems to have arisen. But there was no radical direction of the common sort complete at this time, although the direction of Mars ruler of the Ascendant to the opposition of Saturn in the 6th was impending, which will be completed in the year 1653, 103 days from the beginning of the revolution, which also portends for me a dangerous sickness and many other evils.

But in this year of 1652, precisely at the time of the sickness, the direction of the radical Sun to the Moon's sinister square with latitude was completed, which direction along with the eclipse was very indicative of sickness because the Sun and the Moon were in the 12th house of the radix. For from the preceding table that square is in 17 Gemini with 1°02' north latitude,[82] whose oblique ascension under the pole of the Sun 41° is 53°08', from which, if 345°01' is taken away from the oblique ascension of the Sun, the remainder is 68°07', which is equivalent by Naibod's measure to 69 years and 41 days, which, added to the year of my birth 1583, gives the year 1652 A.D. with 41 days from the beginning of the revolution, leaving off on the 5th of April; and the sickness began on the 8th.[83] What better accuracy could be hoped for? I could offer here many other experiences, especially involving the Moon, but these should suffice.

Chapt. 4. *Whether the Aspects of the Planets ought to be Considered in the Equator as well as in the Ecliptic. And what should be Judged about the Direction of Aspects that are Distorted in the Equator by the Long or Short Ascensions of the Signs.*

Cardan says in his *Commentary on the Quadripartite*, Book 3, Chapt. 14, that Ptolemy conceived two aspects—one in the equator and the other in the zodiac — and never combined them; but in the ecliptic he takes the planets' aspects from a degree and minute to the same degree and minute [in another sign]; but in the equator he would consider the portion of the equator intercepted by the circles

---

82 Recalculation yields 17 Gem 14 with latitude 1N01.

83 These numbers are not very accurate. Accepting Morin's latitude of 45N25 for Villefranche, the altitude of the Sun's pole is 41°30', not 41°00'. And under this pole the OA of the Moon's square is 52°43', the Sun's OA is 345°08', and the difference is 67°35'. Converted into time, this is 173 days earlier than the date Morin derived, or about 15 Oct 1651. This discrepancy arises from Morin's having rounded off the altitude of the pole to an even 41° to avoid having to interpolate between the 41° and 42° columns. Easier, but less accurate. And to make matters worse, the latitude of Villefranche is actually 45N59 rather than 45N25. If the calculation were to be repeated for the true latitude of Villefranche, the pole would be nearly 42°, and the time of the event would be pushed even further back into 1651. On the other hand, Morin's apparent error in determining the zodiacal position of the Moon's square would increase the arc of the event by about a quarter of a degree, and would move the calendar date forward about three months, thus offsetting some of the error arising from his use of the wrong latitudes.

of position delimiting the arc of the ecliptic which comprised the exact aspect; and he considers it to be [the equivalent of] the ecliptic arc. And if both arcs are equal, the nature of the arc [as it is] established in the ecliptic will not be varied; and it will have an effect conformable to its own nature and virtue. But if they are unequal, Cardan holds from Ptolemy that the nature of the aspect is altered; and the sextile of [the signs of] long ascension and the trine of [the signs of] short ascension are altered and converted into the nature of a square; and consequently the judgment about the nature and effect of the aspect ought to be judged according to the prevailing aspect, namely in this way: that if an arc of the equator corresponding to the arc of a trine aspect lying in the ecliptic comes closer to a square than to a trine aspect, it should be said to be an ecliptical trine degenerated to the nature and effect of a square, and similarly with the rest. And astrologers commonly agree with this opinion.

Besides, except for what Cardan imposes upon Ptolemy, who does not take an arc of the equator intercepted by circles of position delimiting the exact aspect in the ecliptic, but the arc of the equator rising with that aspect, in the circle of position of the preceding terminus of that aspect, as is made plain in Book 18, Sect. 2, Chapt. 5, on the construction of the houses; this doctrine is self contradictory and seems to be devoid of reason. For an aspect in the ecliptic, since it is always exact according to Cardan's hypothesis, can never give way to an aspect less exact in the equator, especially since according to the opinion and testimony and experience of all astrologers partile aspects are more efficacious than platic aspects, and the circle of the ecliptic surpasses the equator by far as the circle of influential powers, manifestly from the fact that the Moon, Saturn, Jupiter, Mars, Venus, and Mercury have a more powerful influence in that point in which they are in their own nodes, i.e., it is the ecliptic they are nearer to and not the equator; consequently, the same thing should be judged about their aspects. But if an aspect in the ecliptic should be judged according to the nature which it is allotted in the equator as mentioned above, then it would certainly be proper to prefer the equator in influential powers to the ecliptic, to which the powers of the seven planets belong, on account of its determination at the beginning of the world, as has been mentioned elsewhere. But not to the equator, which has only a daily motion and those things which properly follow from that.

Besides, the aspects of the planets are projected upon the *caelum* (as is customarily said) by their own individual motion with their own path and speed, whether the planets are direct or retrograde. For when the Moon is moved forward by one degree by her own motion in the following direction, all her aspects are also moved in the following direction by one degree. And they are not projected nor do they emerge in the *caelum* because of the common or daily motion of the equator; therefore, they do not derive their own force from the equator, and consequently they should not be examined [with respect to their position] in it.

Moreover, if for selecting the nature of the aspect, both circles should be noticed, and their arcs are unequal; either the judgment will have to be made from the ecliptical arc alone, and so the equator will have no force for the aspects, against Ptolemy; or, it will have to be made from the equatorial arc alone, and so the aspects in the ecliptic will have no virtue as such, which will be even more unbefitting and absolutely contrary to experience; or [else], a mixture of the two — by saying that the sextile of [the signs of] long ascension does not have the nature of a pure sextile, nor of a pure square, but partly the benefic nature of the sextile and the malefic nature of the square; and consequently that it does not simply effect something good or evil by its occourse in directions, but according as the rest of the occurrences in a revolution and in transits. But actually the difficulty is not resolved by this expedient. For it will always be asked at what time the effect will occur from such a promittor. And according to Ptolemy it occurs when such an aspect in the ecliptic is transferred to the circle of position of the significator or of the preceding terminus, for he does not observe the latitude in aspects. Since then according to Ptolemy the effect gets its time from the aspect in the ecliptic, so from its own benefic or malefic nature it will get its own quality of evil or good, but not from the equator, in which, as was said above, there is no influential force.

Someone will object that Ptolemy, in the *Quadripartite*, Book 3, Chapt. 14, asserts that the sextile of the [signs of] slow or long ascension sometimes kills, as does the trine of [the signs of] short ascension; but the trine and the sextile are aspects of a benefic nature; therefore, from [signs of] short or long ascension they degenerate to the nature of a square, and consequently they ought to be examined [with respect to their position] in the equator. But I reply first that Ptolemy only directed five significators—namely, the Sun, the Moon, the Ascendant, the Midheaven, and the Part of Fortune. And indeed for life [he directed] either the Ascendant alone, or only the Sun or the Moon, according as he judged them to be aphetas, even though they were not determined toward signifying life in the nativity. But on the contrary he did not direct the Sun or the Moon in the 12th and 8th houses for life, even if they were particular significators of life by reason of their being rulers of the Ascendant, concerning which we may speak more fully in our *Astrological Prediction* if God extends life for us. And [Ptolemy] never directed the rest of the planets for life or health, even though ruling the Ascendant; and consequently it is no wonder that, with the true cause of death unknown, and with the fortuitous occurrence of a sextile of Mars or Saturn to his own apheta [in signs] of long ascension, he may have thought that this was the cause of death (even though it was harmless), and this at least *sometimes*, as he himself says; especially, when the true degree of the Ascendant had not been established, which he was accustomed to find, not by the native's previous accidents, but by the Animodar.[84]

I reply secondly, That the trines and sextiles of Saturn and Mars are also malefic if Saturn and Mars are determined to evil in the figure; i.e., if they are in the 12th or the 8th or if they are rulers of those houses, especially if they are badly disposed and dangerous to the significators of life by a hostile ray or elevated above

---

84 The method described in the *Tetrabiblos*, iii. 2, "Of the Degree of the Horoscopic Point."

them; but it has not yet been permitted to me even by long experience to detect that such aspects kill when there is no determined cause of death present except them.

Moreover, by the reason that they will have trines and sextiles in the ecliptic to degenerate, at least in quantity, into squares in the equator, by that same reasoning these squares in signs of short ascension will degenerate into sextiles, and in signs of long ascension they will be equivalent to trines. And so that it may be known whether or not any aspect of a planet degenerates (as they hold) to the nature of another, it will be made evident from this single example.

There is in my nativity a sinister sextile of Saturn, which from the table above falls in 12°22' Taurus with 3° south latitude. The altitude of the pole above the circle of position of Saturn is 42°50', in which the oblique ascension of Saturn itself is 352°38'; but the ascension of the sextile is 28°40'; from which subtracting the 352°38' the remainder is 36°02' for the arc of the equator coascending in the circle of position of Saturn. Therefore, since this arc is nearer to the dodectile than to the sextile, it may be said that the sextile of Saturn in the ecliptic degenerates to the nature of a dodectile in the equator, and consequently it is not distorted, as the sextile and dodectile are benefic aspects, but only the force of the sextile is diminished, as the dodectile is weaker than the sextile. And the reasoning is the same with the others.[85]

Chapt. 5. *Whether Directions to the Antiscions of the Planets and to the Nodes of the Moon are Efficacious.*

That the directions of the antiscions of the planets are efficacious may be proved by this reasoning: for every point in the *caelum* that is particularly determined to some planetary force is the efficient force of it by reason, as is established from the true places of the planets in the *caelum*, but such [also] are the antiscions of the planets according to Book 16, Chapt. 15. Therefore they are efficacious; and consequently, when in directions they come to significators, they produce effects in accordance with the nature, state, and determination of that planet of which they are the antiscions just like the aspects of the planets; and antiscions, like aspects, are only promittors and not significators. But experience proves this more evidently: either a planet is in the ecliptic where it is allotted a single antiscion, or it is beyond, in which case it can be allotted two antiscions in

---

85 Here Morin takes advantage of the fact that the aspect pair dodectile/sextile is uniformly benefic, while the pairs sextile/square and square/trine discussed above are mixed. He then shows that the word *degenerate* does not apply in the first case because it would be inappropriate to say that a sextile had degenerated into a dodectile. And therefore since the term *degenerate* is false in this instance, it must also be false in the case of the mixed pairs. Hence, the degeneration of one aspect into another is disproved.

the ecliptic, as is mentioned elsewhere.[86] And this experience will be made plain in its own place from the interpretation of genitures.

But with regard to the Moon's nodes, since in Sect. 1, Chapt. 4, it was shown that they have no virtue of their own, it follows from this that in directions they cannot have the function of a promittor or a significator—at least not an effective one. And consequently those astrologers who attribute to them the effective force of a promittor are much deceived; and they predict fortunate events from bringing Caput Draconis to the Ascendant or the Sun preceding, thinking it to be of the nature of Jupiter and Venus, but unfortunate events from bringing Cauda there, which they suppose to be of the nature of Saturn and Mars. And the same thing should be concluded about the rest of the nodes of the planets.

Chapt. 6. *Whether the Directions of the Fixed [Stars] and the Part of Fortune are Efficacious.*

That the directions of the fixed [stars] are efficacious may be proved in the first place by reason. For they are celestial bodies endowed with influential virtue, mobile under the twelfths,[87] and in a celestial theme determined entirely like the planets. Why then shouldn't they be directed as the planets are? Next, experience proves that directions of the fixed [stars] of the first magnitude produce notable and sudden effects, as will be plain from the genitures interpreted in their own place; therefore, they at least take the place of a promittor in directions, but whether also of a significator no one has observed until now. Why then will it be denied, since they are similar to planets?

But someone may say that if the fixed [stars] are admitted to directions, at least as promittors, their directions to some significator or other in the celestial figure will occur almost every day. Therefore, if great effects happen from fixed [stars]of great magnitude, why not moderate effects from those of moderate magnitude, and minor events from those of less magnitude, since no star is lacking in its own virtue, nor can it be said to be unnecessary in the world? See Book 20, Sect. 3, Chapt. 7, where this difficulty is discussed and resolved.

But with regard to the Part of Fortune, with which the Moon finds itself in the [same] ratio of ecliptical distance as the Sun is with the Ascendant of the

---

86 According to the cited passage, a planet with latitude has two antiscions, viz. the points in the ecliptic that (with zero latitude) have declination of the same magnitude and direction. An example is given of a point with declination +13°53': its antiscions will be 7 Tau 00 and 23 Leo 00 (assuming the obliquity of the ecliptic to be 23°30'). One of these will necessarily be close to the point's zodiacal longitude. Morin notes that the zodiacal longitude of the point itself may be to the right of both its antiscions, or to the left, or between them.

87 The signs of the zodiac.

figure,[88] or vice versa and alternately; it certainly seems to me to be worthy of admiration because both in the general judgment of a figure and particularly in directions it is perceived to be allotted a manifest force of advantage or loss according to the nature of the house that it occupies in the figure and according to its celestial state. Pontanus in Book 3 of his *De Rebus Coelestibus*,[89] in the chapter on the Part of Fortune, wishing to present some reason for this thing, says that the Sun and the Moon find themselves to be the authors of generation and parents as it were in these sublunary things as male and female, material and form in the beginnings of bodies, and day and night in time. For the Moon prepares the material and the Sun induces the form; the latter moderates the time of day, the former the time of night; the Moon provides the nourishment of the body, the Sun preserves the vitality. And this pertains to the Ascendant, which is subject to the jurisdiction of the Sun. Since, moreover, the Sun and the Moon have conjoined times, day and night; conjunctive actions, material and form; and conjoined domiciles, Leo and Cancer; it is proper that in the genitures of those being born, just as the Sun has its Ascendant, so the Moon similarly has its Ascendant, no more distant from the Ascendant of the figure than the Moon herself is from the Sun.[90]

I may add that since the Sun and the Moon are the only primary planets disposed about the Earth,[91] and for that reason the primary causes among the planets of sublunary effects, the origin of which into this mundane stage, since it pertains to the Ascendant; therefore, in individual generations the Ascendant along with the Sun and the Moon have so necessary a connection, that however great is the distance of the Sun from the Ascendant of the figure, just so great should be the observed distance of the Moon from another point in the ecliptic, which is called the *Part of Fortune* and the *Ascendant of the Moon*, and according as the Sun precedes or follows its own Ascendant, so also does the Moon precede or follow its [Ascendant]. Whatever there is about it, it is certain and verified by many experiences that its directions are efficacious, as will be shown by examples elsewhere; and the Part of Fortune itself is allotted the function of significator in directions as well as the function of promittor.

---

88 This is a roundabout statement of Ptolemy's definition of the Part of Fortune in *Tetra-biblos*, iii. 10, as being so placed that "that relation and configuration which the Sun has to the Ascendant, the Moon also has to the Lot of Fortune." This is a consequence of Ptolemy's formula for finding the Part of Fortune, Fortuna = Ascendant + Moon - Sun, which can be rearranged to read Fortuna - Moon = Ascendant - Sun or in words "Fortuna is as far from the Moon as the Ascendant is from the Sun."

89 Giovanni Gioviano Pontano (1426-1503), *De rebus coelestibus* (Basel, 1530).

90 Again Ptolemy, *loc. cit.*, "and it [Fortuna] may be as it were a lunar Ascendant."

91 Morin had adopted the Tychonian Hypothesis in which the Earth is the center of the universe. In orbit about it are the Moon and the Sun. And in orbit about the Sun are the other planets, Mercury, Venus, Mars, etc. This avoided difficulty with the Church and also offered most of the astronomical advantages of the Copernican universe.

You will object firstly that the Part of Fortune is a mere point in the *caelum*, greatly different from the point of the Ascendant, which at least has its own force, since it is the beginning of that part of the *caelum* that occupies the 1st house. But the point of the Part of Fortune is neither a part of the *caelum* nor the beginning of any part of the *caelum* which belongs to the celestial figure. Therefore the Part of Fortune can have no force.

I reply that the Part of Fortune does not have force because it is entirely a visual point or the beginning of a part of the *caelum* belonging to the celestial figure, but because it is a proportional connection of the Sun and the Moon with the Ascendant, by reason of which it can have force, or because it is a point in the *caelum* determined by the Sun and the Moon in a particular manner.

You will object secondly: Let the Part of Fortune be such a point and let it be of some virtue or other; why will it signify wealth, or why will it be determined to that, whatever house it may occupy, and whatever may be the nature, celestial state, and determination of its ruler in the figure?

I reply that even though the Sun and the Moon may be determined as the other planets are to the things signified by the houses in which they are placed and by the houses that they rule, yet because they are primary planets — indeed, by common consent, the parents or universal causes of all sublunar effects — with respect to which for that reason the consideration of orientality or occidentality of the other planets must be observed for their particular effects; in general it seems that it must be conceded that the Sun and the Moon at least from their own nature have a certain transcendental force for good, on account of which the Part of Fortune transcendentally determined by them or to their nature, also to utility or damage, is allotted a transcendental determination with the essential signification of the house to which it is particularly determined by its position in accordance with the nature and determination of its own ruler.

Chapt. 7. *That Judgment should not be Rendered on a Given Nativity without having Considered the Directions.*

Astrologers are frequently deceived in this respect: having been presented with the figure of a nativity, they throw down their judgments from a simple inspection of it, and from only the state of the houses and the planets and their determination they pronounce upon the fortune or misfortune of the nativity. But it often happens that that geniture which appears fortunate [when considered] in this way may be very unpropitious because of a series of directions. And conversely the one that appears unpropitious may be rendered very fortunate by a series of directions. For a single misfortune caused by directions, such as exile or prison, can frustrate the manifestation of many good things; and conversely a single fortunate event can weaken the manifestation of many evils. Why then [should there not be] more fortunate or unfortunate events signified by the directions that have not been consulted? And so, before an opinion is rendered on a given nativity, as astrological speculum should be constructed in which in the common manner a series of directions of individual significators is noted separately. But if such a speculum does not exhibit sufficient light for judgment, individual directions should be mixed together and arranged in a series by years, so that, from the series of accidents of life shown in this, a judgment on the happiness or unhappiness of the nativity may be rendered more wisely and more accurately.

SECTION III

The Motion or State of Rest of the Termini of a Direction; and the Measure of a Direction.

Chapt. 1. *Whether a Direction and its Effect are made by any Physical Motion of one Terminus to the Other.*

Lucius Bellantius affirms this in Question 16, Article 2 of his book against Pico Mirandola, and he says: "The force impressed on the parts of the *primum mobile* by the bodies of the planets at the moment of a nativity continually moves by its own proper motion and per se, so that it is found now in one degree of the *primum mobile* and now in another." Moreover, this statement is taken from the truth of directions and from experience, "which," he says, "most plainly demonstrates that that force operates through directions in every intermediate part where it hits upon a significator, and because if it were not mobile the impressed forces (*i.e., of the significator and the promittor*) could never come together, or one hit upon the other, so that they might produce an effect."

But truly, as we have now entered upon the innermost secrets of this doctrine, we should try to to make them plain to the best of our ability. We will say that Bellantius is deceived in many ways. In the first place, when he says that the force of the planets is formally impressed upon the parts of the *primum mobile*. For stars determine their own places in the *caelum* to their own nature with respect to us at the moment of the nativity, as Mars determines his own place in the *caelum* to the nature of Mars without any formal impression of virtue, as is more fully set forth in Book 20, Sect. 2, Chapt. 15.

Secondly, When he says that that force continually moves by its own motion and per se so that [it is] now in one point of the *caelum* and now in another. For if those forces impressed upon the *primum mobile* by the planets move with any motion of their own, then either they all move to the east, or they all move to the west, or some move to the east and others to the west at the same time, or only some of them move, but not the others. If this last is asserted, then let the reason be stated why the impressed force of the Sun moves, but not that of the Moon or Saturn. And since no reason can be asserted, since indeed this is contrary to experience, by which it is well-known that all the planets are directed with effect, it is plain that this last is false. But the third is impossible—about the motion per se that Bellantius assumes; hence [only] the first and second are left. But now if the forces of both the significator and the promittor are borne to the east, or both of them to the west, they will never be conjoined or meet each other to cause an effect. And if you say that one is borne to the east, as the force of the Sun, and the other to the west, as the force of the Moon following the Sun, then either there will be no directions of the Moon to promittors following towards the east, which is against experience, or else the lunar force will be moved simultaneously to the east for the following promittors and to the west for the Sun as significator, which we have already said to be impossible. Therefore the falsity of this opinion is plain. Besides, the force that is the accident would be moved locally by itself and not by the motion of the subject, or of the *primum caelum* on which it is said to be impressed; but among philosophers this is absurd. Finally, by the motion of the solar virtue to the rising and of the lunar virtue to the setting at the same time, both forces encounter each other at the midpoint of the distance of the promittor from the significator; and so the effects of the direction would happen twice as quickly as experience shows; therefore Bellantius's opinion has collapsed on all sides. Nor does the truth of directions prove such a motion, even though various effects happen from the same significator through the various promittors that follow, and which occur in order in accordance with the significator's own series, since this can occur from other causes, as will be proved below.

Regiomontanus in his *Tables of Directions*, Problem 25, says "A direction is nothing else than moving the sphere until the second place, i.e., the promittor, is brought to the position of the first [place] or the significator." And a little later, "A direction is the motion of the *primum mobile* by which the significator is brought to the position of the promittor, or vice versa" (which is more correct). And from this many have formed the opinion that a direction is made, i.e., its effect is produced, by some physical motion of the *primum mobile* which the effect itself terminates. But in fact a direction is only defined by Regiomontanus as the finding of the arc of direction, just as is mentioned below, i.e., as the *artificial direction* we defined in Sect. 1, Chapt. 1. And the truth of the matter is that the effect of a direction is not produced by any physical motion of the significator or promittor, namely one during which the effect is being made, and at the completion of which it has been made. For if the effect of the direction of Jupiter in the 11th house to the Sun in the 10th should happen through some motion of one of these planets to the other, then it would happen either on the day of the nativity itself, 2 or 3 hours after birth, when Jupiter by the motion of the *primum mobile* would come to the place or the circle of position of the Sun, or on the next day when the Sun by the same motion would come to the circle of Jupiter, [92] or between one or two months [later] when the Sun by its own motion would come to the place of Jupiter itself,[93] or in about 10 years when Jupiter by its own motion would come to the radical place of the Sun, for no other physical motion can be assigned by which one can be brought to the other that is not fictitious, from which there can be no real effect. Yet the effect of that direction does not happen at any of these times, but only after

92 That is, by having rotated through almost a complete circle and having thus come to Jupiter from the other side.
93 That is, the transiting Sun would conjoin the radical place of Jupiter.

30 or 40 years, which is defined by the arc or degrees of the equator intercepted by the two circles of declination, one of which passes through the place of Jupiter in its own position, and the other through the place of that same Jupiter in the circle of position of the Sun. And which arc is found, when, by the motion of the celestial globe to the setting, Jupiter is transferred to the circle of position of the Sun, as Regiomontanus held, following Ptolemy. Therefore, a direction is not made, i.e., the effect of the direction does not happen, through any physical motion, either of Jupiter to the Sun or of the Sun to Jupiter. Because, if anyone says that the effect is not produced by the motion of Jupiter to the Sun or conversely, but by the motion of the virtue of the Sun or of Jupiter impressed upon the *caelum*, it is plain that this is also false. For in addition to what was said above against Bellantius, the force of the Sun always remains in the place of the Sun, as the transits of the planets through the place of the Sun prove. Therefore, it is not moved from that place to another, otherwise at the same time and with respect to the same place it would be moved and it would remain at rest, which is impossible.

Andrew Argol,[94] a physician and a famous professor of Mathematics at the University of Padua, in the Introduction to his *Ephemerides*, Book 3, Astron. Chapt. 15, says that those who contend that the motion in directions is fictitious and not real are very much deceived, since it is real and the fastest motion of the *primum mobile* from the rising to the setting, accomplished at the time of the emersion of the native into the light of the world. "For (*he says*) at the native's origin, just as from the position and aspects of the planets, and the sign discovered on the horizon in the rotation then of time of the *primum mobile*, the active and passive qualities of the elements will remain impressed upon the native's body, as will some diverse dispositions produced by the stars that are rarely or never destroyed except after death; so also the motion of that origin and the downward rotation of the promittor to the place of the significator is actually discharged at the same time and remains impressed upon the native; [which] is going to produce the signified effect according to the distance of the degrees of the equator between the significator and the promittor and of the path of the *primum mobile* from one place to the other, assigning for each degree a certain space of time approved by experience."

Which words touch to some degree upon a natural direction as we have defined it in Sect. 1, Chapt. 1, but in a confused manner; and they do not resolve the difficulty. For, even though a natural direction may be made by the real and physical motion of the promittor to the circle of the significator, as was explained in Chapt. 1, yet the future effect is not produced by that direction or its motion, and even less so by an artificial direction. But astrologers so bind the real directions to the future effects on the native, that they do not wish these directions to be without

---

94   Andrea Argoli (1568-1657) of Tagliacozzo, a well-known astrological authority and ephemeris maker of the 17th century. Morin probably refers to his *Exactissimae caelestium motuum ephemerides...1641 ad 1700*. [The Most Exact Ephemerides of Celestial Motions...1641 to 1700] (Padua, 1648).

effects. And they say that a sickness or a wound happens in the year in which Mars is directed to the Ascendant. But concerning directions so conceived by astrologers, one may inquire whether they are made by any physical motion of one terminus to the other, as Bellantius contends, but not concerning the natural direction as we have defined it. And we have proved above that there is no motion of these termini by means of which a future effect might be reckoned by directions from the nativity.

You will object that if 4 or 5 promittors at unequal distances succeed to the Sun in the 10th house, the Sun will first produce an effect with the first and nearest promittor, then with the second, afterward with the third, etc. Therefore, either there is some motion of the Sun to them, or of them to the Sun; for both termini concur in the effect, and there can be no concourse without union, nor can there be an effect without a concourse, as Bellantius held against Pico.

I reply that it certainly seems to be that way, but in fact it isn't, for the reasons brought forward against Bellantius himself. Moreover, how and why the termini concur and produce an effect without these motions will be stated in the following chapter, for we have only undertaken [here] to show that the effect of a direction does not happen through the real motion of one terminus to the other.

Chapt. 2. *How by means of Termini that are Quiescent or Fixed in the* Caelum *their Effects may be Produced on Earth through their Concourse in Directions. And how their Effects, which Remain in Force for so Long, Finally Burst Forth into Action.*

This certainly seems to be miraculous in nature, for not even those ignorant of astrology can doubt the truth of this matter. And yet the method seems to escape human reason. Of course it is certain that the termini of the directions, namely the places of the significator and the promittor, are fixed in the *primum mobile*, just as was said in Chapt. 1. And it is likewise certain that the effect of a direction does not arise solely from the significator or solely from the promittor, but from their joint concurrence, [as explained] in Sect. 1, Chapt. 7. But a concourse cannnot be assigned to immobile termini. And this is the knot of the difficulty.

John Kepler, the celebrated Imperial Mathematician, who wanted to render an opinion on everything physical, asserts in his *Harmonies of the World*, Book 4,[95] "Fortuitous occurrences, as when a tile fallen from a roof strikes a passerby, [or] when this one, cut off by flames, perishes, etc. are to be attributed to each one's tutelary Genius. And if a natal horoscope contains indications of these occurrences, there must be a custodian or watchman such as this to bring forth impediments or harmful advancements from a natal star. And he does not see how the *caelum* can [accomplish] these things without [the aid of] Genii." By which words it is plain

---

95 Johannes Kepler (1571-1630), *Harmonices mundi* (Linz, 1619).

that Kepler was ignorant of [both] astrology and angelic nature to have boldly passed his judgment on these things. For he did not know that the celestial constitution only influences that which is produced by physical generation; and this it affects radically at the instant in which it is born, but it cannot say [anything] about good or evil angels. And besides he did not know the essential powers of the houses of the celestial figure, which are the determinants of the virtue of the planets, or the benefic or malefic nature of the planets themselves. From which it happens that if Mars or Saturn are in the eighth, or they are rulers of the eighth badly afflicting the significators of life, such deaths are accustomed to happen from the property of the house and the malefic nature of the planet; therefore, being ignorant of this, especially from experience, he could not see how the *caelum* could [inflict] such things on men without [the aid of] Genii, and he revealed what came into his mind about this matter.

But presently, not remaining steadfast [in this opinion], he says: "Those who perish by iron, by a fall, by drowning, and by other fortuitous events seem to have been abandoned by God and the Good Angel and delivered up to the tyranny of Satan, but those who predict cannot see such impiety of life in the stars. For divine assistance against depraved inclinations of behavior is not written in a celestial figure, and even less is it inscribed in the bluish hue of Saturn and the ruddiness of Mars, as are the kinds of punishment due for specific sins in the lawbooks. Nor is there any immediate natural connection between these things and the *caelum*." By which words it is plain, first that these accidents are not to be attributed to the tutelary Genius, nor to that Custodian or Watchman the impediments or contrary advancements coming forth from the natal star, as he held above. In addition, it would follow that it would happen that no upright man would perish by iron, by a fall, by drowning, or by any other fortuitous event; but whoever should die thus would be impious and delivered up to the tyranny of Satan; to assert which is impious and stupid. Besides, he is mistaken when he denies that astrologers can see impiety and other evil propensities of natives in the stars, for among astrologers this is all too common and clear from experience, although they cannot see divine assistance, about which they also do not judge, because of course it is above nature. In addition, the unlucky accidents of death are not inscribed in the bluish hue of Saturn or the ruddiness of Mars, as Kepler argues, but in their influence and determination in the figure of the nativity, which Kepler did not know. Finally, even though there is no immediate connection between these things and the *caelum*, there is an immediate connection of the *caelum* with the native through his nativity, and the *caelum* efficiently determines the native to these things. For just as the native actively determines the *caelum*, so does the *caelum* passively determine the native, as we have said elsewhere.

After this [Kepler] "doubts whether the Genii of men, i.e., the Guardian Angels, are impeded naturally by the stars, lest they should be able to resist the powers of the air lying in wait, and lest those impediments should be foreseen from the native's horoscope, which perhaps (*he says*) also influences the Genius no less than the mind of the one being born, and so the Guardian Angel might not be able to impede the imminent evil." By which words he again contradicts himself, since above he asserted without any doubt that if the natal horoscope contains indications of a violent death from a chance (as he says) occurrence, the Genius or Guardian of the native ought to be impeded by the stars, and so it ought to receive their influx, which it would not be able to resist, which was rejected above as being repugnant to the angelic nature, and absolutely unworthy of it and of its immutable beatitude, and absolutely inalterable by any causes, especially physical ones. Besides, Kepler says that a horoscope influences the mind of the one being born and his Genius; and thus again he asserts what he had denied above.

Having made these statements, he says then "that the foetus at birth conceives its own vital energetic faculty from the act of being separated from its mother, and the character of the *caelum* at that moment flows into it." But he more clearly opens his mind [on this subject] in his *Book on the Fire Triplicity*,[96] where "he denies that any force from the planets spreads into the signs or places of the zodiac, or through a real impression, as many hold" or through a determination unknown to Kepler and first discovered by me "but in the natural and animal faculty of the child being born it receives the constitution of the *caelum* which existed at the time of birth. And therefore that faculty is affected by all the transits of the planets through the principal places of the horoscope, as if images received in the mind were real stars coming together with the celestial ones and agreeing or disagreeing with them." By which words he also contradicts himself, for why would the faculty be affected by the daily transits of the planets through only those places in the *caelum* that are principal places in the horoscope, i.e., through the places of the planets, their aspects, and the cusps of the horoscope itself, and not by the transits through the other places in the *caelum*, empty with respect to that same horoscope, if in those same principal places no virtue from the horoscope remained with respect to the native, either through impression or through determination? To this question certainly I do not see anything solid that can be said in reply to support Kepler, nor for that matter another [question] that can be put: namely, why the faculty should be affected one way with Saturn transiting through the Midheaven and another way with it transiting through the Ascendant?

Finally, arriving at the mystery of directions, he says "That faculty not only perceives the transits of the planets, but also the successions of those parts of the *caelum* that held the planets at birth. Distributing its action throughout the whole life of a man by this proportion: so that by so much as a year is longer than a day, by that much slower an effect may follow its sign in a direction than the sign follows

---

96 Kepler's book on the conjunction of Jupiter and Saturn in 8 Leo on 26 July 1623 was translated into German *Discurs von der grossen Conjunction...* (Nürnberg, 1623) and into English by William Lilly in his *Prophesy of the White King...* (London, 1644).

in the direction of the parts,[97] so that this celestial impression may not only remain quiescent, but also while it remains may extend itself by an extension of its motion to a longer time of life. That is to say, this faculty is not only circular, but its motion is also circular and its time hypothetical, and you might say that the time of the motions of a horoscopic character grows along with the body of the native." And finally he concludes in this way: "No death in the stars, none in the horoscope, none in a direction: the substance of the body is that which, either flooding, snuffs out the flame of life, or running short, deserts it, while nature is stimulated at the time of directions to complete its own action." By which words he does not resolve the difficulties of such a mystery, but rather multiplies them when he says that the faculty marked with the celestial character is circular, is circular motion, and is a hypothetical time—which Kepler does not prove, nor if he did prove it would it remove those difficulties. Also, when he holds that all the accidents of a man are due to a faculty concerned with completing its own action; seeing that the accidents which are badly termed *fortuitous* or *casual* cannot be referred to that faculty intent upon its own action, since they are entirely beyond its action and concern, but in the directions of significators and the transits of planets they may shine forth greatly, and they may be caused by these; with the mind per se being ignorant of such fates, also with the radical constitution unformed. Then, in addition, not wishing the stars to cause death, he makes Nature, intent upon her own work, to be the destroyer of her own self and a homicide. And then he gives no reason why the faculty should observe the same ratio in time of a day to a year...

Moreover, I wanted to review here more fully Kepler's opinion of astrology and to show its defects, because in his *Harmonies of the World*, Book 4, Chapt. 7, "he thinks after the consensus of Haileseus, Rossini, and Philip Feselius, very famous (*as he says*) professors of philosophy and medicine,[98] that this new philosophy is the most true, and therefore this tender little plant ought to be fostered and reared with all care, so that it may put forth roots in the minds of philosophers." Thus in fact the truth of the matter is that Kepler was very ignorant of astrology, as is plain whenever he speaks of this science, as we have already shown elsewhere; and nothing is more improper than for an ignorant person to put forth an opinion. As for us, what then shall we too say about these things, lest we may seem to be completely silent with regard to so great a mystery of astrology? Let everyone be free to philosophize about it.

---

97 By 'parts' Kepler means degrees and by 'sign' he means 'indicator', i.e. a direction (which serves as a "sign" of some effect to come). This rather obscure sentence is intended to convey the idea that the ratio between a year and a day is equally applicable to the arc of a direction: so many years (of life) to so many degrees of arc.

98 Their fame, which Morin already seems to doubt, has faded. I suppose he refers to Eucharius Roeslin, M.D. (1544-1616), or his son of the same name, and to Philip Fessel, M.D. (fl. 1610), but I cannot identify Rossini, unless he means Gioseppe de Rossi (fl. 1576).

I say firstly, That the cusps of the houses and the planets and their aspects at the moment of birth are determined by that act to something with respect to the native, as is fully demonstrated in Sect. 1, and by their potential they are determined to other things. And so Saturn in the first house is determined by that act to the the native's temperament, health, moral characteristics, and mental capacity; but at the same time it is also determined by its potential to all the native's accidents represented by the preceding houses of the figure. For example, [it is determined] to causing sickness through its direction to the Sun in the 12th; and so Jupiter in the 11th is determined by that act to the natives's friends, but by its potential to honors, which it is perceived to cause by its direction to the Midheaven, when by act it stands in the 11th at the moment of birth. And the rest of the significators preceding Jupiter must be considered in similar fashion.

Secondly, That the influx of the celestial figure at the moment of birth is impressed upon a sensitive part of the native, not in fact diffusely, but distinctly and marvelously as it is in the figure of heaven, that is as the determination of the parts of the *caelum* and the planets are in that figure; and so there may be in that native the influential character of that figure, [with its various features] preserved in virtually the same location, the same order, and the same distances of the significators and promittors, just as they are found in the figure erected for the longitude and latitude of the place of birth. And therefore, just as the celestial figure[99] is the external beginning of the native's life, so is it also an efficient cause in the native, of a similar internal beginning through the impression of its own character upon the native, from which arises that manifest and wonderful consensus of the *caelum* and the native himself in acting and being acted upon.

Thirdly, That each significator in the celestial figure, i.e., a cusp or a planet, in accordance with its own virtue, both essential from its own nature and accidental from its determination in the figure, flourishes in the native through the impression of its own character: it is a sort of beginning of life, action, marriage, or suffering, to which all the following places of the figure are referred by a potential determination, whether they are planets or aspects of the planets, so that things related to that beginning may be such during the life of the native as those places are, both by reason of their nature per se and by reason of their accidental determination; and they will be in the same order of time as is the order of the distance of their places from such a beginning, so that of course the one that is less distant from that beginning is more quickly and sooner reduced from potential to action, i.e., it produces its own effect. Therefore, if Mercury ruler of the Ascendant, then the square to Mars ruler of the 8th, then the trine of Jupiter ruler of the 9th follow the Ascendant, the beginning of life, the native will first turn his attention to letters or to some other discipline from the direction of Mercury to the Ascendant, but then from the direction of the square of Mars to the same Ascendant, he will be dangerously ill, and finally, if he escapes [from that illness], he will devote his time

---

99 Reading *figura* instead of *figurae*.

to religion from the direction of the trine of Jupiter ruler of the 9th, for the determination of the promittor by body and rulership must always be taken into consideration, and not just the planet, as the old astrologers supposed, who handed down to us their own rules for directions.

Fourthly, Because since the figure of the *caelum* at the moment of birth is something permanent and stable, in which the whole life of the native along with his accidents flourishes both causally and implicitly, and that life and those accidents admit the succession and order of time, it is necessary that some cause of this succession and order be given in the *caelum*; and that cause is none other than the succession and order of the promittors potentially determined with respect to the preceding significators as was said above. For a potential determination proceeds from itself to an actual determination; and therefore those promittors, i.e., the planets and their aspects, are reduced from a potential determination to an action. But this is done by the first revolution of the *primum caelum*, which begins at the moment of the nativity; for when, by this revolution, some promittor is transferred to a circle of position that some significator occupied at that moment, and thus a natural direction of these is made as we defined it in Sect. 1, Chapt. 1, it is determined by that act to produce its effect at some time, according to the nature and location of that significator; and the virtue of such a direction for individual natural directions of the promittor itself to the preceding individual significators, is imprinted successively on the native by such a revolution, as a sort of supplement to the universal natal impression, which explains his particular fates, and efficaciously combines and puts them in order according to its own temporal series.

Furthermore, the effect of the direction cannnot be produced at the moment of the nativity because the promittor is not then actually in the location of the significator, but only potentially. Moreover, it is produced after the birth by virtue of its reduction from potentiality to actuality, which is accomplished by successive motion. And it is produced in about as many years from the birth as the promittor is distant in degrees of the equator from the circle of position of the significator according to Ptolemy's opinion, which will be carefully investigated in the next chapter. And the logic of this doctrine is fundamental because the determinative virtue of the houses or their cusps to different types of effects is very well known to astrologers through experience, and is therefore entirely certain; moreover, the cusps of the houses are circles of position. But the circle of position in which any planet or other significator falls at the moment of the nativity is allotted a particular force with respect to the native by that planet or significator by reason of the subjects pertaining to the house that that circle occupies in accordance with the nature and state of that planet; which force is impressed upon the native himself at the moment of his nativity. When, therefore, the promittor by that first revolution of the *primum caelum* is brought to that same circle, it is determined as was said above. And the force of that determination, since it is made by successive motion, is similarly impressed upon the native. And since the concourse and union of virtues of the promittor and the significator are thus made both in the *caelum* and in the native, when they are successively in that circle of position, it results from this that at the time designated by the arc of that motion something will happen to the native himself of the nature of the significator and the promittor in connection with the things essentially signified by the space or house of the figure in which that circle of position is found. And in sum, this is what I am able to say about such a mystery of Nature in accordance with the truth of experience based on lengthy investigation; and if it is not sufficient for anyone, he may give better [explanations] and disregard my opinion. Similarly, what does Galen have [to say] about sicknesses in Book 3 of his *On Critical Days*? Namely, that having erected the chart for the beginning of the sickness, an impression of that sickness is made upon the native by it, and the accidents of that impression appear through the motion of the Moon to her own square or opposition, or (as I also believe) through her own monthly directions to that square and opposition and other important places of the figure of sickness; moreover, it frequently happens that the direction and motion of the Moon take place at the same time on the same day. From which it is plain that the accidents either of the native or of his sicknesses are measured by the directions and motions of the planets transiting through places corresponding to the accidents.

Therefore I say fifthly, For this reason, since termini of the directions are quiescent or fixed in the *caelum*, their effects are produced on earth, namely in man, since by the radical influx of the celestial figure at the moment of the nativity, and the first revolution of the *caelum*, their concourse is made and impressed upon the native, [which will be] efficacious at a certain time, as has already been explained above.

Sixthly, That the impression of that concourse having been imposed by the first revolution of the *primum caelum* from the moment of the nativity, it follows that it will be continued and confirmed by those that follow, by which also each promittor is brought to the circle of position of the individual significators that precede it; and so it is often confirmed that the efficacy of a direction for an effect may finally then ripen and burst forth into its act; no wonder, after about as many annual revolutions of the Sun, as the arc of direction contains diurnal [motions] of the same Sun,[100] and consequently sooner or later, just as the termini are less or more distant from each other. Whence it is plain that the Sun by its own diurnal and annual motion concurs at least in the measure of time by which the effect of a direction is reduced from potentiality to actuality, but not by its own influx or influential force, as we saw in Sect. 1, Chapt. 1, that Cardan held. So therefore the effect of a direction may only smack of the nature and determination of the significator and the promittor, but not of the Sun except by accident, by reason of a determination of the Sun itself.

---

100 One "diurnal [motion]" equals approximately one degree, so Morin means that the number of annual revolutions of the Sun (years) will be approximately equal to the number of degrees in the arc of direction.

Finally, I contend seventhly, That the effect of a direction is produced not just by the impression received at the moement of the nativity, as Kepler thought, nor just from the *caelum*, as has been commonly credited hitherto, but from both of them working together: not, however, without an actual concourse of the revolutions of years and months, and of transits too, as is said in what follows, for here we shall only explain the mode of action of directions. You will object that from this it follows that after 365 years, corresponding to a complete diurnal [revolution] of the Sun, in which every promittor accomplishes its effects with [all the] individual significators of the entire zodiac, the force and efficacy of all its directions will be absorbed, and none of those effects will be left for those who live longer, such as were those men preceding the flood, who reached 500 or 600 years, using up the bulk of so long a life, and whom an astrologer might nevertheless declare to have been dead from the direction of some Anareta to some significator of life. Therefore, the preceding doctrine is false.

I reply that what is said does not follow [logically]. For just as through the second revolution of the *primum caelum* from birth the directions of the first [revolution] are confirmed, which correspond to the first 365 years of life, so through the third [revolution] are confirmed the directions of the second [revolution], which correspond to the next 365 years of life, and so on. And from this it results that after 365 years from birth effects similar to the previous ones [caused] by these same promittors will return, if the native shall have lived so long, as before the flood; having of course taken account of the native's age and other circumstances. It can also be said that since the force impressed upon the *caelum* by a determination will last as long as the native, that nothing prevents that after 365 years similar effects should still return through the recurrence of the directions, having taken account of his age and the disposition of things then existing. Finally, it can also be said that since the same direction may signify many things at the same time, by reason of the multiple determination of the significator as well as the promittor, in one revolution of 365 years it will produce one effect, and in another another, having taken account, etc. Therefore, the doctrine explained above is consistent and in accordance with experience without any confusion or ambiguities, and the simplest of all in approach and logic, which makes us cling to it. Therefore, enough has already been said about so difficult a subject.

Chapt. 3. *The Various Opinions of the Old and Modern [Astrologers] on Converting the Measure of the Arc of Direction into Time. And which of these seems Truer to Us.*

There is something in every branch of learning that testifies to the weakness of the human intellect, as in Theology, the Mystery of the Sacred Trinity; in Physics, the essence and production of forms; in Geometry, the quadrature of the circle; and in Mechanics, perpetual motion. If, then, the sharp edge of the intellect

Jean-Baptiste Morin

is dulled in scrutinizing these arcane matters, then it is not surprising if in Astrology, the highest and most divine of the physical sciences, there is also something sought that is conceded to be marveled at rather than understood. And such a thing is the measure by which an arc of direction is converted into time to determine the time of the future accidents of men. So, then, not without admiration it is established by experience that the arc of direction is equivalent to approximately as many years as it contains degrees of the equator. That is, the effect signified by a direction will happen in approximately as many years after birth as there are degrees in the arc of direction. And I said *approximately* because there is still a dispute among astrologers about precision. We shall, therefore, add here our opinion and the opinions of others about this measure.

Ptolemy, therefore, says in his *Quadripartite*, Book 3, Chapt. 15, "Moreover for each degree one should take consistently one year"[101] or as Naibod has it "and each of the times (i.e., *degrees of the equator, which Ptolemy here and there terms times*) is equivalent to one solar year." By which words it is plain that Ptolemy did not determine [this value] of the measurement with certainty, but only probably. But all astrologers down to our own time have followed his opinion, and some still hold to it. Moreover, Cardan in his commentary on this chapter, and after him, Naibod, thought that one year is not precisely equal to one degree of the equator, but [instead] to 59'08". Which is of course the mean diurnal motion of the Sun in the equator with a similar measure of time; but one degree [of this measure] is equivalent to 1 year 5 days and 8 hours; from which tables were constructed by Naibod and Magini which we will give below; and most astrologers have already subscribed to this opinion.

But the Most Noble Tycho Brahe, in his [treatise], *The New Star,*[102] Book 1, p. 113, having rejected these two opinions and having been taught by experience (as he says), thinks that the diurnal motion of the Sun, not in fact the mean motion, but the true or apparent motion on the very day of birth should be the true measure of the year for directions of the genethliacal figure and the true measure of the day for directions of the annual revolution. Moreover, the very well-known Mr. Longomontanus[103] wrote to me privately that Tycho Brahe meant the diurnal motion of the right ascension of the Sun and not the diurnal motion of its longitude. And I, who am unable to assign fictitious causes to the real times of effects, had long since conceived the same thing that had been conceived by Tycho [in his book

101 The reference is to *Tetrabiblos,* iii. 10 (Robbins's ed. p. 288, 7-8), or to Ashmand's translation of the *Paraphrase,* iii. 14.

102 The reference is to Tycho's book on the nova of November 1572. It was published in 1573 and dealt with both the astronomical and astrological significance of the "new star" that blazed up so brightly in the constellation Cassiopeia (Long. 6 Tau 52, Lat. 53 N 45).

103 Christian Severin Longomontanus (1562-1647), a Danish astronomer who worked as an assistant to Tycho Brahe for around ten years and thereafter was professor of mathematics at Copenhagen from 1607.

78

that] I had not yet seen, and that if the diurnal [motion] of the Sun was the measure of the year it was more fitting to attribute it to the true and real diurnal [motion] than to the mean [motion], which might be thought to be only fictitious, and rather to the diurnal [motion] in right ascension than to the [motion] in longitude, because it is not the ecliptic but the equator that is the natural and simplest measure of our time. Therefore, I had made tables on this premise for the equating of arcs of direction into time and vice versa.

But Kepler in his enclosure sent with nativities says "not having availed [himself] of experience, he thinks it reasonable to move the significators forward in the order of the signs towards the promittors by the natural proportion of a day to a year, if of course for any year the diurnal [motion] of the Sun is added to the places of the Sun and the Moon, departing by the same number of days from the natal day as the number of years departs from the natal year. And [as for] the reasons on account of which this should properly be efficacious—namely why that which was on the thirtieth day will signify for the 30th year—although the astrologers are not accustomed to give or to examine their reasons, being content with their own oracles, nevertheless the Samian philosophy[104] seems to promise [it], or if this doesn't disclose [it], [then] nothing does." This is Kepler, word for word. He wants then, if it is required to find where a direction of the Sun and Moon extends to 30 years after birth, to take from the ephemerides the places of the Sun at noon on the day of the nativity and then on the 30th day after the nativity, and subtract the former from the latter, and there will remain the arc of the ecliptic, which, added to the radical places of the Sun and the Moon, will show where the directions of the Sun and the Moon extend to in the ecliptic in that 30th year.

But Argol says in his treatise on astronomical measurements,[105] Book 3, Chapt. 23, "It is completely stupid to assert that Ptolemy seems to have been very exact in his knowledge of this [topic] in other minor matters, and [yet] did not explain the precise measure to us." And consequently he thinks that Ptolemy's measure ought to be retained, devoid of any reason appealing to experience. But if accidents do not happen exactly at [the moment of] contact of a direction, it may be because the places of the planets are not yet had exactly, or it may be from the strength or weakness of the significators and the promittors, which can accelerate or retard the individual times of the effects.

But to define which of these diverse opinions is truer belongs to reason or experience. And indeed, although reason is blind in this matter—namely why one day's [motion] of the Sun is more or less equivalent to one year—yet it seems to support this opinion of Tycho's and ours, namely that a real effect should be referred to a real cause but not to a fictitious one, as the causes of Cardan, Naibod, and Ptolemy seem to be. For, as Argol says, that which [is given] as Ptolemy's [opinion]

---

104 Apparently a reference to Pythagorean philosophy (Pythagoras was from Samos).
105 I do not know whether this reference is to Argol's *Tables of the Primum Mobile* (1610) or to one of his later books.

does not give satisfaction, first because Ptolemy himself did not assert that one degree is the precise measure of a year, then because we have already shown many times that he erred in his teaching of astrology, and finally because the opinions of the rest can be excused similarly, as Ptolemy's opinion is excused by Argol. Kepler in truth, even though he does assume a real cause—namely the true diurnal [motion] of the Sun in the ecliptic on the individual days from birth for the individual years, with the days corresponding to them in number—yet from other considerations reason is doubly opposed to this method. First, because in the direction of the Moon, and consequently of the other planets, he omits the latitude, contrary to that opinion which he rightly gave in the Preface of his *Ephemerides* from the year 1617, and against the opinion of Regiomontanus. Secondly, because it follows from this that through as many days from birth as the years the native is going to live the Sun would still have an influx upon the birth of the native by its own motion. But if by its motion, why not also by its celestial state, which varies from one day to another by reason of its conjunctions with other planets and its ingresses into signs? And why shouldn't the same thing be said about the other planets, and especially about the Moon, whose celestial state changes very rapidly? And yet the radical influx both by motion and by celestial state and the nature of the planets is only imprinted at the moment of the nativity, at which time that influx is the actual cause of those things that are in the native at the very moment of his nativity, but they are the potential cause of those things which will happen to him successively thereafter. Whence, those two aphorisms of Schöner, which he has in Book 1, Chapt. 15, should be exploded, where he says "That if the Moon on the third day after the nativity applies to Mars or to Mercury it will make many travels, etc." For the planets radically and primarily only have their influx [upon the native] at the moment of the nativity, although after birth they do have a secondary influx in two ways, i.e., by revolutions and by transits, but with respect to the primary influx and dependant upon it. But the inclination to travel belongs to the radical influx, as also every other kind of thing. And yet from Tycho and Kepler still another method can be put together: namely, by taking the diurnal [motions] of the Sun from birth, not in fact in longitude but rather in right ascension, and similarly applying them to the total number of years after birth, but from this also follow the two absurdities repudiated above.

Therefore, to put an end to this controversy, it only remains for us to consult the experience of things, a mistress neglected by Kepler, for this detects the method that is truer than the rest. But some [authors] in directing observe neither the latitudes of the planets nor the latitudes of the aspects, which is the greatest error. But others observe, and they all in fact make use of the latitude of the place of a planet and of its opposition, but in the longitude and latitude of the rest of the aspects they disagree, even though there is but one truth in this matter, and it can cause a notable difference in experience. Moreover, we have shown above how these aspects may be corrected in longitude and latitude. And to this end we have constructed the rational table given above, which we believe should be adhered to, because it is more conformable to experience for the rest of the aspects than a table agreeing with the method of Bianchini, because it substitutes the mean diurnal motion of the Sun in the equator, i.e., its mean diurnal [motion] in right ascension, 59'08", for each year in the reduction of the arc of direction into time in accordance with the opinion of Cardan and Naibod. For this measure is more accurate than that of Ptolemy and the old [astrologers], who ascribed one year to one degree, and rightly in Argol's opinion. Moreover, the Tychonic measure obviously deviates too much from the truth after the 30th year from birth when the Sun is around the beginning of Aries and Libra, where the diurnal [motion] in right ascension is only 54' or 55', and when it is around the beginning of Capricorn, where it reaches 67'. And similarly the Keplerian [measure] exceeds or comes up short too much when the Sun passes through those signs where it has its maximum or minimum diurnal [motion]. And I observed these things laboriously and as carefully as I could in many genitures, comparing by turns both the methods and the individual measures. But if anyone wants to test the same thing in the rectification of nativities, he should use first the accidents pertaining to the Ascendant or the Midheaven, whose true causes are the bodies of the planets or their oppositions, about whose latitude [all] astrologers agree; and through these accidents the Ascendant and the Midheaven may be rectified, having taken the measure of time according to one of the abovesaid authors. And then let him see whether other accidents caused by the squares of the planets directed to those same angles, with or without latitude, agree with their own times according to the measure assumed. For the mode which will more accurately and frequently agree in directions will probably be considered to be the truer. And I have found such a one as I explain here, as will be explained more clearly by examples in its own place.

Chapt. 4. *In which the Tables of Naibod and Magini are set forth for the Conversion of Time into Arc of the Equator and vice versa.*

The truth of the tables of this conversion will appear more evidently the farther away one goes from the moment of the nativity, such as the 50th or 60th year after birth. And because we discovered that the tables we had constructed for this same purpose according to Tycho's opinion deviated more from the truth, we consequently discarded them, and we have put below only the tables of Naibod and Magini.

Use of the Table

Take the years from the nativity in any of the four columns of years and in the column to the right you will find the degrees, minutes, and seconds equivalent to the year taken. Thus, 15 years are equivalent to 14°47'05", and so with the rest.

NAIBOD'S TABLE
For converting Years into Degrees of the Equator.

Yrs	0	'	"	Yrs	0	'	"	Yrs	0	'	"	Yrs	0	'	"
1	0	59	8	26	25	37	37	51	50	16	5	76	74	54	32
2	1	58	17	27	26	36	45	52	51	15	13	77	75	53	42
3	2	57	25	28	27	35	53	53	52	14	21	78	76	52	50
4	3	56	33	29	28	35	1	54	53	13	30	79	77	51	58
5	4	55	42	30	29	34	10	55	54	12	38	80	78	51	07
6	5	54	50	31	30	33	18	56	55	11	46	81	79	50	15
7	6	53	58	32	31	32	26	57	56	10	55	82	80	49	23
8	7	53	7	33	32	31	35	58	57	10	3	83	81	48	31
9	8	52	15	34	33	30	43	59	58	9	11	84	82	47	40
10	9	51	23	35	34	29	51	60	59	8	20	85	83	46	48
11	10	50	31	36	35	29	0	61	60	7	28	86	84	45	57
12	11	49	40	37	36	28	8	62	61	6	36	87	85	45	5
13	12	48	48	38	37	27	16	63	62	5	45	88	86	44	13
14	13	47	57	39	38	26	25	64	63	4	53	89	87	43	22
15	14	47	5	40	39	25	33	65	64	4	1	90	88	42	30
16	15	46	13	41	40	24	42	66	65	3	10	91	89	41	38
17	16	45	22	42	41	23	50	67	66	2	18	92	90	40	47
18	17	44	30	43	42	22	58	68	67	1	26	93	91	39	55
19	18	43	38	44	43	22	6	69	68	0	35	94	92	39	3
20	19	42	47	45	44	21	15	70	68	59	43	95	93	38	12
21	20	41	55	46	45	20	23	71	69	58	51	96	94	37	20
22	21	41	3	47	46	19	31	72	70	58	0	97	95	36	28
23	22	40	12	48	47	18	40	73	71	57	8	98	96	35	37
24	23	39	20	49	48	17	48	74	72	56	16	99	97	34	45
25	24	38	28	50	49	16	56	75	73	55	25	100	98	33	53

TABLE II

MAGINI'S TABLES
For converting Degrees of the Equator into Years.

Deg	Yrs	D	H	Deg	Yrs	D	H	Deg	Yrs	D	H	Deg	Yrs	D	H
1	1	5	8	26	26	139	4	51	51	273	0	76	77	41	14
2	2	10	17	27	27	144	13	52	52	278	8	77	78	46	22
3	3	16	1	28	28	149	21	53	53	283	17	78	79	52	7
4	4	21	10	29	29	155	6	54	54	289	1	79	80	57	15
5	5	26	18	30	30	160	14	55	55	294	10	80	81	63	0
6	6	32	3	31	31	165	23	56	56	299	18	81	82	68	8
7	7	37	11	32	32	171	7	57	57	305	3	82	83	73	17
8	8	42	20	33	33	176	16	58	58	310	11	83	84	79	1
9	9	48	4	34	34	182	0	59	59	315	20	84	85	84	10
10	10	53	13	35	35	187	8	60	60	321	4	85	86	89	18
11	11	58	21	36	36	192	17	61	61	326	13	86	87	95	3
12	12	64	6	37	37	198	1	62	62	331	21	87	88	100	11
13	13	69	14	38	38	203	9	63	63	337	6	88	89	105	20
14	14	74	23	39	39	208	18	64	64	342	14	89	90	111	4
15	15	80	7	40	40	214	3	65	65	347	23	90	91	116	13
16	16	85	16	41	41	219	11	66	66	353	7	91	92	121	21
17	17	91	0	42	42	224	20	67	67	358	16	92	93	127	5
18	18	96	8	43	43	230	4	68	68	364	0	93	94	132	14
19	19	101	17	44	44	235	13	69	70	4	3	94	95	137	22
20	20	107	1	45	45	240	21	70	71	9	11	95	96	143	7
21	21	112	10	46	46	246	6	71	72	14	20	96	97	148	15
22	22	117	18	47	47	251	14	72	73	20	4	97	98	154	0
23	23	123	3	48	48	256	23	73	74	25	13	98	99	159	8
24	24	128	11	49	49	262	7	74	75	30	21	99	100	164	17
25	25	133	20	50	50	267	16	75	76	36	5	100	101	170	1

TABLE III

MAGINI'S TABLE
For converting Minutes of the Equator into Time.

Min	Days H		Min	Days H		Min	Days H	
1	6	4	21	129	17	41	253	6
2	12	8	22	135	21	42	259	10
3	18	13	23	142	1	43	265	14
4	24	17	24	148	6	44	271	18
5	30	21	25	154	10	45	277	23
6	37	1	26	160	14	46	284	3
7	43	6	27	166	18	47	290	7
8	49	10	28	172	23	48	296	11
9	55	14	29	179	3	49	302	16
10	61	18	30	185	7	50	308	20
11	67	23	31	191	11	51	315	0
12	74	3	32	197	16	52	321	4
13	80	7	33	203	20	53	327	9
14	86	11	34	210	0	54	333	13
15	92	16	35	216	4	55	339	17
16	98	20	36	222	9	56	345	21
17	105	0	37	228	13	57	352	2
18	111	4	38	234	17	58	358	6
19	117	9	39	240	21	59	364	10
20	123	13	40	247	2	60	370	14

TABLE IV

The use of the two tables that follow is entirely similar. Someone will say that these tables calculate the mean daily [motion] of the Sun in Right Ascension as the measure of any year. But that mean daily [motion] is only artificial, or fictitious; and consequently it cannot be the true or real cause of a real effect, i.e., of the real time of effects, as it has also been assumed by us many times in similar circumstances in astrology.

But I reply: Between the maximum and minimum daily [motion] of the Sun in Right Ascension, necessarily the mean [motion] shown above is given by a part of the thing, for the transition from a real maximum to a real minimum is not made without passing through the mean, which consequently is not fictitious as he supposes. And therefore, since the maximum and minimum according to Tycho differ greatly from the truth, even if they occur on the natal day, it follows that of all these the mean [motion] differs the least, which indeed agrees with experience; and therefore it should be taken as the measure of the years in preference to the rest; but not exactly one degree, as Argol argues and as Ptolemy prescribed. And this mean daily [motion] for the measure of the arcs of direction is not like the mean motion of the planets that is put in the tables of arguments [of the planetary tables]. For those [mean motions] are merely artificial and only substituted for the true [places], which vary from day to day by the true motion of the planets.[106] But in directions there is no motion of the termini that is different in different years, as was shown in Chapt. 1 of this Section, but only the invariable arc of the equatorial distance of the promittor from the circle of position of the significator. And this arc, which corresponds to the years of the future event by the ratio of the daily [motion] of the Sun to a year, must be apportioned through this [particular] daily [motion] rather than through any other for the reason given above.

Chapt. 5. *Whether the Arcs of Direction of all Significators or Promittors Should have the Same Common Measure; and what the Logic of that Measure is.*

In his book *The Judgments of Genitures*, Chapt. 5,[107] Cardan distinguishes in the case of directions the effects that pertain to humans from those that refer to empires, kingdoms, cities, religions, and the rest of the more notable changes that take place in the world. And he holds that when planets are directed as promittors in figures erected for the beginnings of kingdoms, cities, sects, etc., or for the

---

106 Morin is thinking of such planetary arguments as the Mean Anomaly or the Mean Elongation from the Sun (in the older tables). These arguments are "artificial" in the sense that they do not have any such close relationship to the planets' geocentric motions as the Sun's Mean Daily Motion has to its Daily Motion in Longitude or Right Ascension.

107 "The Things Signified by Directions and their Mode [of Action]" (pp. 439-440 of the 1583 ed.).

moments of great conjunctions, whatever degrees of distance [there are] from the significator to the promittor, or the arc of direction, should be equivalent to the periodic time of the planet that is directed, which consequently must be understood of the aspects of that same planet. And therefore for Saturn as promittor the value, from Kepler's *Epitome of Astronomy*, Book 6, is 29 Egyptian years 174 days and 5 hours, for Jupiter 11 years 317 days and 15 hours, for Mars 1 year 322 days, for Venus 224 days and 18 hours, for Mercury 87 days and 23 hours, and for the Moon 27 days and 8 hours. Besides, although this dictum may resemble that of Ptolemy, who wanted one degree of that arc to be equivalent to one solar period, or one year, yet Cardan did not have any experience in empires, kingdoms cities, and religions with the abovesaid proportion, nor could he have had, since the beginnings of these things required for erecting the figures, as well as the moments of the great conjunctions, are unknown to men, and it would be pointless to construct the figures of cities, as we have said in Book 20, Sect. 4, Chapt. 4. But in the case of men the experience of the proportion is very well known.

Moreover, in human affairs it seems worthy of note that, although some of the significators are the points of the twelfths [of the *caelum*] simply and absolutely viewed, which are the Ascendant, the Midheaven, and the rest of the cusps of the houses simply determined only to the native, but others are said to be the Sun, the Moon, or another planet; and of the planets, some are primary, namely the Sun and the Moon [which revolve] around the center of the earth, but others are secondary or satellites, namely Saturn, Jupiter, Mars, Venus, and Mercury, which are arranged about the Sun as their primary; yet, experience proves that there is the same common measure for all these in directions, i.e., in the directions of all the significators each individual degree of the arc of direction is equivalent to 1 year 5 days and 8 hours, or 59'08" of the arc is equivalent to 1 year, in accordance with the tables above, even though the Moon, the Sun, and the *primum mobile* differ very greatly among themselves both in their nature and in their distance from the earth.

And reason seems to demand this. For all significators are points on the *primum mobile*, either complete in themselves, such as those that are in the Ascendant, the Midheaven, and the other cusps, or [those] particularly determined to the nature of the planets at the moment of the nativity, as has been said elsewhere, since they are the true places of the planets and of their aspects, but not the bodies of the planets themselves. Therefore, since all the significators and all the promittors too are in the same *caelum*, i.e., in the *primum mobile*, through whose motion each promittor is transferred in the same way to the circle of position of a significator, it is reasonable that all arcs of direction should also be measured in the same way, i.e., through the same measure common to all.

Moreover, what the reason or cause of this measure is, i.e., why the mean diurnal [motion] of the Sun in right ascension is equivalent to one year in directions was set forth for us above by Kepler from the *Samian Philosophy*, sc. of the *Munus Pythagoricum*, to which he was very much addicted; but this game of the intellect in numbers does not satisfy men who are more learned in physics, unless it is conceded that numbers are the prime ideas that effect all things;but that must first be proved, and it cannot be proved.

Cardan, at the end of the seventh of his *Books of Aphorisms*, in the peroration of the work, contributes this reason:[108]

> That since the Sun moves perpetually in the ecliptic, and runs through it in a year, also when it is situated in its individual degrees, it revolves in its diurnal motion once for each degree, in a circle that is parallel to the equator. Whence it happens, that if anyone conceives the equator as quiescent, as the theologians regard it, the degree revolved, by virtue of the Sun receives the universal force of the whole equator; and consequently, since the Sun in any degree of the ecliptic, goes around the whole equator in one day, and the whole ecliptic by its own motion in one year; hence it results that any degree of that same equator (which also receives the force of the revolutions of the 365 [circles] parallel [to the equator], and therefore also of the whole ecliptic) will represent one revolution of the ecliptic or one year.

But although this speculation may seem to be a refined one, it still does not satisfy me. For even if the Sun in any degree of the ecliptic should go around the whole equator every day and the whole ecliptic with its own motion in one year, it still does not follow from this what Cardan concludes without proof, namely that each degree of the equator receives the force of 365 revolutions in a year, and therefore represents a year, or an annual revolution of the Sun in the ecliptic, especially since the division of both the ecliptic and the equator into 360 degrees is artificial and not natural, even though the number 360 is a mean between the number of days 365 1/4 in which the Sun traverses the ecliptic and the number of days 354 3/4 in which it comes together with the Moon twelve times.[109] Besides the fact that Cardan says nothing about the Sun that cannot be said of any other planet, and especially Saturn, which revolves in circles [more nearly] parallel to the equator than those of the other planets, on account of its own motion's being the slowest among the planets.[110]

And consequently let him who will speculate about such an arcane matter and as much as he wants to. After my speculations I do not think any mortal is

---

108 This is a condensed paraphrase of Cardan's comment (*Opera*, p.91) rather than a direct quote.

109 Actually, 12 synodic months take place in 354 3/8 days; but this does not alter Morin's observation that 360 is very nearly the mean between 12 synodic months and a solar year.

110 Since a planet's declination usually changes during the course of 24 hours, the circle it describes is slightly tilted with respect to the equator.

going to return a cause of this thing that is entirely satisfying without a revelation; and this, it seems to me, is far more difficult that squaring the circle, so that here too in fact we ought to say something of what comes to mind. Indeed, the Angel revealed to the Prophet Ezekiel[111] 390 days from one side and 40 days from the other, about which he speaks to him, must be understood to be the same number of years; when he says in Chapt. 4 "A day for a year I have given to you," as astrologers employ the diurnal [motion] of the Sun for a year in directions; but he did not explain the cause. Similarly, in *Numbers* 14, 40 years are reckoned for 40 days.[112] I also see in nature that a day is exactly equivalent to a year, namely under the earth's pole, where the day and the year coincide and are the same, by taking a day for one revolution of the Sun above and below the horizon; and the diurnal [motion] of the Sun there is the same as a year. But in the first place this happens in a place where neither a celestial figure can be erected, nor can directions be set up, from the lack of a meridian circle. In the second place, astronomers do not take a day as one revolution of the Sun with respect to the horizon, but [rather] with respect to the meridian; by which convention the diurnal [motion] of the Sun is only around the 360th part of a year, and there is no astronomical day under the pole.

Therefore, we should admit the frailty of our talent in this matter, but we may admire and venerate God's infinite wisdom, Who made everything in weights, numbers, and measures, but in just such a way as pleased Him; and He wanted the least natural part of a year to correspond to a whole year in many things, as was set forth above in [the case of] revelations and nature.

Chapt. 6. *Whether the Effects of Directions are Brought Forth at the Precise Time when the Arc of Direction Corresponds Precisely to their own Measure.*

This question in the doctrine of directions is one of no little importance. Namely, whether from a direction, e.g. of the Ascendant to Mars posited in the second house severely afflicted with an arc of 30 degrees, which from Magini's Table above is equivalent to 30 years, 160 days, 14 hours, a sickness, a wound, or

---

111 Ezek. 4:4-6. "And you shall sleep on your left side, and you shall lay the iniquities of the House of Israel under it for the number of days that you shall sleep over it, and you will assume their iniquity. I moreover have given to you the years of their iniquity, in the number of days 390 days, and you shall bear the iniquity of the House of Israel. And when you have completed this, you shall sleep on your right side secondly, and you will assume the iniquity of the House of Juda for 40 days; a day for a year, a day, I say, for a year I have given to you." (translated from the Clementine *Vulgate*) This is the scriptural justification astrologers use for secondary progressions.

112 Num. 14:34. "according to the number of forty days, which you surveyed the land, a year will be reckoned for a day. And for forty years you shall get back your iniquities, and you shall know My vengeance..."

death will happen precisely at this time after birth; and so with the rest [of the directions].

And experience proves that this does not always happen, but the accident sometimes comes before the precise time of the direction, and sometimes follows it; not by one day only, or one month, but even by several, or rather now and then throughout the year, although this happens more rarely; and this [happens with] whatever may be taken as the measure of that arc and howsoever the aspects of the planets are corrected. For there is no nativity in which the effects of all the directions correspond exactly in time to their arcs; and very frequently it happens that if in any nativity two or three such directions are seen, the rest will in fact be found to precede or follow [the time of their effects] more or less.

Moreover, a fourfold cause can be assigned to this problem, and one valid for other reasons, and therefore more valid [from] the concourse of many reasons. First is the deficiency of the astronomical tables, on account of which the true places of the planets in longitude and latitude are not contained in the genethliacal figures; nor can [any improvement] be hoped for until the tables are remade in accordance with our principles and fundamentals of astronomy; since to this day a difference of around one degree is often found in the Moon's place between [the ephemerides of] Kepler and Argol

The second is that although the virtue of a direction is actually imprinted upon the native through the first revolution of the *caelum*, as is explained in Chapt. 2, nevertheless its virtue with respect to a future accident that it is going to produce, exists somewhat as a potential that must again be reduced to action at a time conformable to the arc of direction. But it cannot be reduced at that time from potentiality to action except by something actual: namely, a revolution conformable to the future event, and conformable transits of the planets by body or by aspect through suitable places in the geniture, which are first of all the places of the significator and the promittor, or places related in signification to them. And yet conformable revolutions and conformable transits do not always occur at that precise time, or if there is a conformable revolution for the year, there will not be a conformable transit for the day corresponding to the arc of direction, but either both, or the second, and especially a suitable transit will come before the precise time or after it.

The third, that the nature and state of the promittors or the significators may sometimes cause some irregularity. For Saturn from its own nature, and planets that are slow, retrograde, occidental, in cadent houses, and in short, debilitated, [indicate] a retardation of the effects; but Mars, Mercury, and the Moon, as well as planets that are swift, direct, oriental, in angles, and strong, presage anticipation. And not only should the promittor's state be noticed in this regard, but also whether it is in its own domicile or exaltation, or in those signs contrary to these, as well as whether it is favorably or unfavorably connected with the planets that are benefic or malefic by nature or by determination. For a promittor that is strong, either for good or for evil, produces an effect at the very time of the direction; indeed, if a planet precedes the promittor, or an aspect similar in signification to the promittor itself, it will anticipate the effects; but if the promittor is weak, and there is a planet or a powerful ray of contrary signification [configured] with it, that promittor will be frustrated in its effect; but if a planet or a ray of similar signification, follows that promittor, it will be able to retard its effects until a direction of the significator comes to them. And this must be very carefully taken into account in predicting the time of the effects of directions.

The fourth and last is that the sublunar causes that a celestial influx sets into motion, or at least excites, do not always comply with it equally, but they elude it either by the force of freedom, or they resist it by prudence when that influx has been recognized in advance, or from the obstinacy of the material they sometimes beget a slow disposition [of that influx]; or they are made altogether contrary to these [possibilities], with sublunary causes only slightly excited by revolutions and transits conformable to the times of the direction bursting forth into future events.

It will be objected that this doctrine overturns the rectification of nativities by the times of the native's previous accidents—that rectification on which the astrologers so pride themselves. For since a reliable rectification is not made from a single accident, but many are required; and the times of the individual accidents are not precisely equal to their arcs of direction, there seems to be no reason why one accident should be taken rather than another to whose time the arc of direction should be equated precisely; and so there will always be room for doubt about the truth of the Ascendant or the Midheaven.

I reply: Certainly, the astrologer needs to exercise great prudence in the rectification of nativities in order to determine the Ascendant and the Midheaven correctly, and this cannot be done by any artificial means. But first the given accidents must not be ascribed to any but their genuine causes, which he will be able to know from the natures of the houses and planets and their states. Then, for the foundation of the rectification of the Ascendant, he should select some accident that he conjectures is more likely to have arisen from a direction of the Ascendant to a suitable promittor, as if a quartan fever happened in the 5th year from birth, and Saturn is around 12 or 18 degrees of the equator distant from the estimated Ascendant in the following direction, he may boldly direct the Ascendant to Saturn for the time of that fever. After this, he should see whether the rest of the given accidents correspond by direction of their causes to the Ascendant so defined, and if they do, it will be a valid rectification; but if a difference of around one degree appears, and the nativity cannot be rectified otherwise by the given accidents, then the Oblique Ascension of the Ascendant will have to be increased or decreased by some minutes, until the arcs of all the directions correspond with their times as nearly as they can be made to do; meanwhile, diligently observing the years in which the revolutions and transits agree best with the given accidents, for a particularly conformable arc of direction will have to be assumed from the table for this time. The same [procedure] must be considered for a rectification based upon some direction of the Midheaven. And from a rectification so made, in which a series of accidents will agree in time with a series of suitable directions, there need be no doubt in any respect; certainly this alone can be the scientific way, and not any other. But it should be noted incidentally that astrologers can be deceived in this in rectifying genitures, because for the foundation of their rectification they are accustomed to calculate only a direction of the Ascendant for an accident pertaining to the 1st house or a direction of the Midheaven for an accident pertaining to the 10th house, although these accidents can be caused by directions of the rulers of the Ascendant or the Midheaven, as perhaps happens in those genitures that are said to be of very difficult or doubtful rectification. Therefore the astrologer's skill and prudence are especially necessary in such a case.

But from this it is plain how foolish Sixtus ab Hemminga's opinion is in his book, *Astrology Refuted*, where he holds that either all directions agree exactly in their effects as well as in their times in every geniture or else astrology is altogether false. But in Sect. 5, Chapts. 3 and 4, we shall make plain the lack of skill of this man, who has acquired so much authority among the haters of astrology.

Besides, it should also be noted here that when the direction of any significator to any promittor is completed, its effect can not only be retarded by one or two years, namely until a conformable revolution concurs [with it], but even if the effect is produced at the very time of the direction, still its force can endure until another promittor comes to the significator. For the effects of the significators are not changed except by the successive change of promittors. Moreover, the force of a direction may especially endure when one promittor is succeeded by another of similar nature or signification. If, therefore, the Ascendant is directed to Mars in the 2nd, with Saturn following 4 or 5 degrees later, the native will be prone to sicknesses and dangers to his life for several years from the time when the direction to Mars is completed until the direction to Saturn has been accomplished, or he will die from the direction of the Ascendant to Mars, whose force and malignity is extended by the following Saturn, or the latter will finally terminate with death the evil begun by Mars. And on the contrary, if Venus or Jupiter follows Mars, especially if one of them is ruler of the Ascendant, the force of the direction will produce its effect from the beginning, and it will not endure until the succession of the second promittor; which, on the contrary will suppress and temper the effect of Mars—if not altogether, at least in part.

At the same time too it was said above that the virtue of a natural direction impressed upon the native is something potential with respect to a future accident; yet that virtue at the time of the accident concurs actually with other causes subordinate to itself, namely with annual and monthly revolutions, as well as transits, whose virtue is only actual. And this can be proved, because a revolution alone, either of the Sun, or of the Moon, radically conformable to the accident signified, will not produce that accident in the absence of a direction or [if the direction] is not yet mature according to the time equated to the arc of direction, as was said previously; therefore the direction concurs actually with the effect, along with the revolution and the transit. And the same thing must be considered in the case of revolutions and their directions, which will be said in its own place. Besides, it must be noted that a planet or a point of the *caelum* in the Ascendant is in actuality in the Ascendant, and therefore it is determined in actuality to the things signified by the Ascendant; but a planet in the 2nd is only [determined] by power in the Ascendant and through the diurnal motion, and therefore only determined by power to the signification of the Ascendant. But a planet in the 12th is [so determined] neither by actuality nor by power in the Ascendant, at least by its diurnal motion, but only by its own motion, for it has crossed over beyond the Ascendant, or if it is in power in the Ascendant, that power can only become actual after 330 years, as many, namely, as are counted from the Ascendant to the Planet. Therefore, from the direction of the Ascendant to Mars in the 12th an effect will not appear before 330 years, which, you must understand, [is] from the reduction of Mars to the Ascendant by the prime motion.

Besides, if the Sun is in the 12th and Mars is in the Ascendant, and an effect can be produced from the direction of the Sun to Mars, why is it not produced from the direction of Mars in the 12th to the Ascendant, or from the Sun in the 12th to the Ascendant, since, as Mars or the place of Mars moves by the diurnal motion to the Sun's circle [of position] in the 12th, so does the Ascendant degree? I reply that Mars as a promittor has a means of effecting [something]. But the Ascendant degree, as such, can only have a means of being acted upon. It might be argued that if Mars and the Ascendant have the same degree, how can this degree be at the same time active and passive? But I reply that it will be effecting [something] by reason of Mars and the significator preceding in the 12th, but it will be passive by reason of [its being] a cusp, and with respect to the following promittor; and thus the difficulty is resolved, and the doctrine is self-consistent, in accordance with what was said above.

SECTION IV

The Effects of Directions.

Chapt. 1. *How Difficult it is for a Man to Predict the Kind of Effect Signified by any Direction.*

The action of the planets upon man is twofold. The first is radical in the nativity through its genethliacal constitution, which is impressed upon the native himself at the moment of birth. The second is accidental, coming on top of the first by directions, revolutions, and transits of the planets. Through the first, a planet acts with its total determination by reason of its own nature, its celestial state, and then its terrestrial state, explicitly to be sure for the things then present in the native, as for example life, temperament, bodily conformation, moral nature, mental qualities, etc.; and implicitly for future things, such as dignities, marriage, children, etc. And through the second a planet acts explicitly in accordance with the partial determinations of its own bodily position in the figure, its rulership, and aspects, for any of its given determinations in directions, revolutions, and transits.

But already in this doctrine of directions, it is a question of a summary of things. Namely, what effect any direction is going to define and predict. And I am not speaking of the particular forms of effects, which only he who is inspired by divinity [can] predict, [as is stated] in [Ptolemy's] *Centiloquy*, Aph. 1, as for example that John will be killed by Peter with such-and-such a sword, or will be drowned in the Seine, or that he will take Claudia as his wife, and such like; for this does not shine forth in the native's chart. But I speak only of that very specific kind of effect, such as whether John will be killed by an enemy, or drowned, or hung, or burned up, or decapitated, or whether he will marry, or obtain an ecclesiastical, political, or military dignity, and such like, which are only the most fundamental types of events. To hit upon these things by predicting from the native's chart alone, which combines such future events, is not indeed impossible for a man, but certainly very difficult, and it rightly produces exceptional praise for the astrologer [who can do it]. Moreover, the difficulty will be plain, and it will occasion no surprise, if we expose its principal causes, such as they appear to me.

The first, therefore, is that although the entire mundane space is divided into 12 parts, or primary houses, corresponding to the 12 kinds of accidents of man, still each kind is divided into various types; as, although the 12th house is in kind only about things adverse to the native during his life, yet these are of many types: namely, sicknesses, imprisonment, exile, servitude, secret enemies, and, through its opposition, servants and domestic animals. Similarly, although the first house is in kind only [the house] of life, nevertheless [the native's] temperament, bodily conformation,[113] health, moral nature, and mental qualities belong to it. The 7th is [the house] of matrimony, contracts (which are marriages of the negotiators), lawsuits, and open enemies; and so with the rest [of the houses]. And therefore when two termini concur in a direction, and one of them is determined in a certain manner by reason of the house it is in, or over which it predominates, so many types of effects occur[114] at the same time, that to discern which type may be produced, even by the shrewdest conjecture is [a matter] of no little difficulty. Just as, if the Ascendant is directed to Saturn in the 1st, ruler of the 12th. What will Saturn do or cause from being in the 1st and ruler of the 12th? Will it be sorrow? Will it be investigation of secret things? Will it be sicknesses? Will it be imprisonment? Will it be exile? And so with the rest.

The second reason perplexes the mind much more. For of the two termini that concur in a direction, one concurs by reason of its own nature, its bodily position, its rulership, and its celestial state; therefore, these individual things must be looked for in each terminus, and they must be combined to get a judgment about the kind of effect. For although a direction does not produce as many effects as combinations of these [termini] can be made; nevertheless, the effect that will be produced is always according to some one of these same combinations. And consequently, the skill of rightly combining or arriving at a true combination is the greatest secret, and the most difficult part of all judicial [astrology], to which most things concerning the subject and its celestial causes must be directed. So, for the sake of an example, let the Sun and the Moon be assumed as termini of a direction, involving a single house and therefore a single rulership; and these three things only can be combined—their nature, bodily position, and rulership—when the Sun is directed to the Moon, or the other way around, [yet] they will be found to be combined in 49 ways.

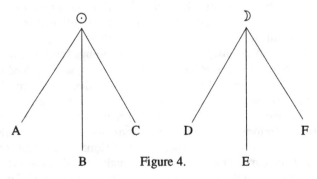

Figure 4.

---

113 Reading *temperamentum, corporis confirmatio* instead of *corporis temperamentum, confirmatio* 'bodily temperament, conformation'. Cf. the first paragraph of this chapter.

114 The Latin has *occurrunt* 'occur', but perhaps we should read *occurrant* 'may occur'.

For there are in the Sun, A its nature, B its bodily position, or the house of the figure that it occupies, and C its rulership, or the house of the figure over which it predominates; and in the case of the Moon, D is its nature, E its position, and F its rulership.

The individual items A,B, and C are combined reciprocally in 9 ways with the individual items D, E, and F. Pairs with individual items in 18 ways. Pairs with pairs, in 9 ways. Trios with individual items, in 6 ways. Trios with pairs, in 6 ways. Trios with trios, once. The sum of all of these is 49.

But in the case of the other planets, Saturn, Jupiter, Mars, Venus, and Mercury, which have a dual rulership, four items would have to be considered, and more than 300 combinations would occur.[115] For of these four, individual items with individual items would have to be combined first. Then pairs with individual items and with pairs; trios with individual items, pairs, and trios; then quartos with individual items, pairs, trios, and quartos; and this individually and reciprocally. But if to these are added the celestial states of the planets also to be considered, seeing that they act or do not act, or act differently, in accordance with their different celestial state, and the different kinds of effects also to be considered, into which the essential signification of each house of the figure is generally divided, then what each planet will signify in the house of the figure to which it is opposed, such a number of combinations will occur, that the human intellect would seem to be unequal to examining and pondering them for the kind of effect to be determined by a future direction, even if the necessary consideration of the fixed stars should be omitted.

The third reason is that future accidents, depending on the free will of man (of which sort are marriage, litigation, travel, dignities, etc.), are very often suppressed and eluded by the mastery of the will. Namely because the will per se is not subject to natural fate, which has authority per se only over the corporeal nature, but not over the rational spirit, which is of a spiritual order.

Still other causes might be brought forward, but these three principal ones should suffice to show how arduous it is to define whether and what type of effect any particular direction is going to produce. Since in addition the age of the native, and his sex, and lineage, and the law or customs of his native land must be taken into account, lest events should be predicted for an infant, or a girl, or a peasant that are only appropriate for men of the nobility, or that are alien to the customs of the native land. Therefore, this alone seems to be to be worthy of admiration: that human sagacity through a very intricate labyrinth of difficulties is nevertheless able to arrive at an idea of the type of effects, and [to do so] fairly often. And it seems to me that those who scorn and ridicule a learned astrologer, if he has strayed from the truth with regard to the kind and quantity of the effect he has predicted, are

---

115 I think the total number of combinations would actually be 225, but this is still a large number.

deserving of blame, rather than the astrologer himself, who chanced to err in this conjectural science.

Besides, since it must be determined first whether the direction under consideration is going to produce any affect, rather than what type it will produce; that, of course—the question of whether there will be an effect—should precede the question of what [kind] it may be and what sort it may be; and for that reason we shall unfold in the following chapter the means by which that may be known.

Chapt. 2. *How it may be Known Whether a Given Direction is Going to Produce any Effect, and what Kind it is Going to be.*

For this purpose, both termini of the direction should be considered, i.e., the significator and the promittor; for the effect is from the concourse of both [as we have shown] in Sect. 1, Chapt. 7, and the significator is a cusp or a planet, while the promittor is a planet, or its aspect or antiscion, or a fixed star. But in general, if the significator is a planet, the judgment should be made from the proper nature of that planet and from its celestial and terrestrial state. But if it is a cusp, the judgment should be made from the nature of the cusp and the state of its ruler—celestial as well as terrestrial. But as for the promittor—if it is a planet, judgment should also be made from its proper nature and from both its celestial and terrestrial state; but if it is an aspect, judge from the nature of the aspect and the planet aspecting, and from the state of both of these, and then from the ruler of the place of the aspect and the house in which the aspect falls.

But for the type [of accident], the significator should be looked at first. For upon its well-perceived signification the principal light of the prediction will depend. For since it is subjective in the effect, and the promittor is effective, and the efficient agent acts only in accordance with the nature and disposition of the subject, it follows that special account must be taken of this disposition in predicting the effect. And so it must be carefully investigated what the significator itself signifies with regard to that for which it is directed and adduced. Moreover, it is directed [first] for those things to which it is determined by its bodily position, and then for its rulership if it is a planet, or for the native in connection with these same things. Therefore, it must be carefully noted whether it signifies the same things by reason of its bodily position and its rulership, as the ruler of the 10th in the 10th, by which it will signify these things strongly; or whether it signifies contrary things, as the ruler of the 10th in the 12th, or of the 8th in the 1st. And whatever it presages more effectively will then be especially noteworthy, as also when it rules several houses. Therefore it should be seen whether a significator signifies good or evil for such things. Namely, in good houses a future good, or the deprivation or destruction of something good, or misfortune; but in evil houses, a future evil, or the deprivation, mitigation, or restoration of it; and this in accordance with Book 21, Sect. 2, Chapts. 2, 4, and 12, if the significator itself is a planet; or, if it is a cusp, by taking note of which ruler it is subject to, whether it is a benefic or a malefic and conformable in its effect, both by celestial state and by terrestrial determination, to the fortune or misfortune of the subject that this cusp represents.

After this, the promittor must be considered, whose function is to produce efficiently the effect of the direction, and on whom consequently that effect principally depends. And if it is a planet, it must be noted from its nature, analogy, celestial state, and determination whether or not it will agree with that significator in causing good or evil in connection with the subject for which the significator is directed. But if it is an aspect, it must first be seen whether it is benefic or malefic by nature; then of what planet it is, whether a benefic or a malefic; then what the state and determination of that planet is, in accordance with Book 21, Sect. 2, Chapts. 10 and 11; and finally, in which house that aspect falls; and from this, its concord or discord with the significator may be seen, as was just said for a planet as promittor. For, as an aspect falling in any house acts on its general subject by reason of the planet aspecting, and its celestial state and determination in the figure, then by reason of the proper nature of the aspect itself, so does that aspect, occurring to any significator, concur in the effect of the direction through its own force from the five things mentioned above. But the effects of the aspects are still to be distinguished in accordance with the house in which they fall and in accordance with the significators that they meet. For when Mars is posited in the 8th, its opposition effects one thing by falling into the 2nd house and another thing when it comes to the Ascendant by direction; thus, in fact, in the former case it dissipates the wealth, but in the latter it causes death or dangers to the life. But it can be said that each effect happens at the time of the direction; and the same is true of the rest.

Therefore, having carefully examined these things and weighed them on both sides with the proper amount of prudence, so that the concord or discord of the termini with regard to any subject may be plain—as, in the case of honours and dignities, if the significator is in the 10th house, now [examine] the termini themselves: either they will agree together in conferring honours, or they will agree together against those honours, or one will act for honours, and the other against, or both will be indifferent, i.e., each partly for honours and partly against, so that the victory is doubtful; or finally, one only is indifferent, and the other is for or against. In the first case, the honours will occur or some fortune in connection with honours, either in undertakings or in actions. Just as if the ruler of the Midheaven, well aspected and following, is directed to the Midheaven, also well aspected. In the second case, no honours will occur, but rather some misfortune in connection with them, either in undertakings or in actions. Just as if Saturn badly aspected is directed to the Midheaven or to the Sun badly aspected in the 10th. In the third case, although the victory of one over the other should be noted, yet the effect of the direction will follow the state of the promittor, for if the significator is for honours and the promittor against, nothing will be done, or only something evil in connection with honours; just as if Saturn badly aspected is directed to the Midheaven well aspected; for the action is from the promittor, but no one gives what he does not have. And if the significator is against something and the promittor for it, something at least moderately good will happen because the promittor by itself is able to confer that unless the disposition of the subject is altogether alien. Just as if, for an honourable soldier and one famous for his actions, Mars well aspected is directed to the Midheaven badly aspected: he will still attain a military honour, even though a middling one. In the fourth case, something good and something evil can happen, or something at the same time good and evil, at least successively, or something indifferent, or nothing; furthermore, if something does happen, it will always be small or middling. In the fifth and final case, if the significator is indifferent, and the promittor is for honours, some fortune will happen in honours, if against, some misfortune. But if the promittor is indifferent, and the significator is for, something good will happen; if against, nothing.

Further, in the concord or discord of the termini, it must be seen how great the strength of each terminus is for signifying about the subject of the direction. For the stronger or by the more numbers[116] they have signified either good or evil, the more certainly and abundantly the good or the evil will happen. Just as, if Taurus is in the Midheaven, and Mars is in Cancer in the 12th, injured by the square of Saturn, and Mars is directed to the Midheaven; Mars itself being powerful with more numbers will be susceptible to misfortune in connection with honours and actions, namely because it is malefic by nature, dejected in the 12th badly afflicted by the square of Saturn, and, in addition, inimical to the Midheaven. But if both termini signified only weakly, the direction will scarcely have any effect.

Besides, a more serious difficulty occurs here. For, since the 10th house in which the significator is placed is not only [the house] of honours but especially and primarily [the house] of the native's actions and undertakings, which are also comparable to honours, it must be discerned by some means whether the fortune or misfortune signified by its directions is going to be in connection with honours, or in connection with undertakings and actions, since it is known that even in the same geniture not all the directions of the Midheaven, or of the Sun in the 10th, confer honours, even though they are fortunate, as much by reason of the Midheaven itself or the Sun, as by reason of the individual promittors coming into configuration with them. And besides, honours do not always follow from famous deeds, do they?

I reply: That all the possible essential significations that pertain to the 10th house combine into one generic reason of immaterial mundane good to act upon the native in this connection; and in type this is either good fortune in actions, or simply glory and fame from outstanding actions, or the attainment of the dignity and profession [necessary] to act. And therefore, when the states of the significator and the promittor specified above are only looked at in a general way, only the highest kind of effect of a direction can be predicted, namely that there may be going to be something good or evil in connection with it to act upon the native; but

116 That is, by the number of good or evil testimonies the terminus has.

not whether it is going to be something fortunate or unfortunate in actions, or whether it will be an attainment or a loss of dignity, for misfortune in actions does not always destroy dignity.

Moreover, for this to be determined (which is at least to find a subtype), first, it must be seen whether the native's radical figure in itself diverts future dignities by directions, or presages their lack or destruction. For directions only deploy that which is innate in the radix, or, in their own time, they reduce to an act that which the radical figure contains in potential; and so they do nothing that is not presignified in the radix by the nature, state, and determination of the signs and planets; otherwise, the nature of the radical figure would make no difference for future accidents [arising] from directions; and the directions would be able to operate contrary to the radical constitution of the *caelum* and contrary to the native's disposition; and so the science of the stars would be absolutely contrary to itself, which is absolutely foreign to reason and experience. Therefore, when [the figure] is consistent with a lack of honours or with deprivation of honours, it is certain that a direction will not have any effect with regard to honours or dignities except perhaps frustrated endeavors; therefore the effect will rather be with regard to actions. But if either the future occurrence or the destruction of honours is signified, since nothing can be overturned that was not first there, then a direction will be able to strengthen the effect with regard to dignities, either that there will be [dignities] or that they will be destroyed, or at least favored or disfavored. And it will be possible to discern in another way and more closely whether there is going to be a good effect or an evil one in connection with actions or dignities by consideration of the significator and the promittor as follows.

If the significator itself is the cusp of the 10th house, which the Sun or the Moon, well disposed, rule by domicile or exaltation, or if the cusp itself is rendered fortunate by the presence of a planet that is benefic by nature or by determination and well disposed, but especially by exaltation, or by the presence of some royal fixed [star], or if it is in trine to the Sun or to the Moon, they being well disposed, or under the rulership of a planet that is exalted and angular, or at least in good aspect with it, and such like, the effect of the direction will be especially [determined] towards honours and dignities; and [these will be] more certain and outstanding, the more things are in concurrence with those testimonies, not however having excluded good fortune in actions.

Similarly, if the significator is a planet in the 10th house, or the ruler of the Midheaven, and especially if it is the Sun or the Moon, [or] primary planets, either Saturn or Jupiter, around which satellites are present[117] just as with the Sun—a

---

117 The reference is to the moons of Saturn and Jupiter, which had been discovered in Morin's lifetime. Galilei had discovered Jupiter's four large satellites in 1610, but Titan, the first satellite of Saturn to be discovered was only found by Huygens in March 1655. This would seem to show that Morin either wrote Book 22 not earlier than 1655 (the year before he died) or else revised this chapter in 1655 or 1656 to include Saturn with Jupiter as a "primary planet."

sign of excellence and dignity, and [the planet] is well disposed by sign, and especially by exaltation, or it is applying to the luminaries by aspect, especially by a good aspect, or to an exalted planet, or it is the ruler of the Ascendant in the 10th fortunately disposed, or with a royal fixed [star], or something else of excellence accompanies that significator, such as a doryphory of planets or of illustrious fixed [stars], the effect of the direction will also be especially in connection with dignities perhaps through fortunate future actions.

But if the planet is Mars, Venus,[118] or Mercury, which lack satellites,[119] and there are only single satellites of the Sun, and neither these nor the Midheaven has any excellent mode of signifying or any signification of excellence, it is more probable that the effect of the direction will be in connection with actions undertaken by the native, or in connection with arts and crafts.[120]

But as for the promittor, if it is a planet, and especially if it is the Sun, the Moon, Saturn, or Jupiter, well placed as [mentioned] above, and the ruler of its significator, or of the Midheaven, or even of the Ascendant is exalted or otherwise outstandingly well disposed, or also any other planet in excellent state, or with a royal fixed [star], the direction would be allotted its effect in connection with future honours. However, it must be carefully noted that if the promittor is a planet, the kind of event will have to be taken from the nature of the planet and the domicile in which it is placed rather than from that which it rules, namely because a planet is more efficaciously determined by its bodily position than by its rulership, unless the latter determination is very powerful from some other location, for if this is the case, the opposite can occur.

But if the promittor is the strong aspect of a strong planet, and especially the Sun, Saturn, or Jupiter, or another planet that is exalted, or the significator's ruler excellently disposed, the direction will tend more to honours.

But if the promittor is Mars, Venus, or Saturn, or their aspects, or those of other planets that do not have an excellent means of signifying, the direction will more likely operate in connection with honours. However, the annual revolution of the native and also his age suited or unsuited to honours or to labors will also help in distinguishing these.

However, it must be noted that a significator excellently disposed does not always or in all its directions cause honours, but only with conformable promittors. And the same things must be said about the promittor with respect to the significator. Whence it is no wonder that dignities rarely occur.

---

118 The Latin text has *Saturn*, but the context seems to indicate Venus.

119 Today, we know that Mars has satellites, but these were first announced in Swift's *Gulliver's Travels* (1726) as a discovery of the Lilliputians (confirmed by Hall in 1877) and were of course unknown to Morin.

120 According to the classical astrologers, the three terrestrial planets, Mars, Venus, and Mercury preside over occupations. See Ptolemy, *Tetrabiblos*, iv. 4 "The Quality of Action" and Firmicus, *Mathesis* iv. 21 "Actions."

Further, the things said above about the significator and the promittor espe-cially make known fortunate events in connection with honours, dignities, the profession, undertakings, and actions. But misfortunes are principally signified by promittors that are malefic by nature or by determination, such as Saturn and Mars, as well as the rulers of the 7th, 8th, and 12th badly disposed, as [when they are] in exile, fall, or otherwise, and in such a state joining in the direction either by body or by malefic rays, and also these same planets strong [and] joining with bad rays effect the same thing: for of course planets malefic by nature or determination, if they are strong, are very harmful with their malefic rays. Moreover Saturn, or a planet in the 12th, which is [the house] of secret enemies, imprisonment, and exile, or its ruler, especially a malefic, and evilly disposed, will bring misfortune more in connection with [the native's] honours, dignities, and his profession. But Mars, and then the rulers of the 1st, 5th, 7th, or 8th, and also of the 9th and the 11th, more in connection with actions. And it must be noted that Saturn badly disposed in the 10th not only portends evil in connection with actions or honours by its own directions to suitable following promittors, but also when as a promittor it comes by body or by bad aspect to the preceding Midheaven or its ruler, or to the Ascendant or its ruler, or to the Sun, the Moon, or the Lot [of Fortune]; and thus too with the other planets badly disposed in another house. For a planet causes that which it signifies by its bodily position and rulership in accordance with its own nature and state, not only as a significator, but also as a promittor, and in the latter mode of course effectively, but in the former subjectively through the influential disposition impressed radically, as has often been said.

So, therefore, the approximate kind [of event] or the subordinate type of effect can be known in advance from some future direction. However, for the greater surety and glory of astrology, in directions of the Midheaven or of a planet in the 10th house, when there is some doubt about the kind of event, it should not be determined uniquely towards what it is going to be, but it may be predicted that it is going to be in connection with dignities, or actions, or other things that pertain to the 10th house, inclining nevertheless towards what seems more likely to occur if any light appears; and thus the truth of a legitimate prediction will rarely be lacking in one kind [of event] or another. For from the many kinds [of possible events] no one's intellect is able to determine the one that is precisely true, although the science of astrology is capable of this. For the thing is inherently difficult, and [it is one] in which human intellect is often shrouded in fog, but the intellect of a Demon is much more perspicacious, and by this science he can predict many things with certainty that a man cannot attain to. Therefore, a wise astrologer, if he wants to look after his own reputation and that of astrology [itself], will only predict future things generically in the manner explained above, and he will not determine uniquely any minor detail unless there is an evident agreement of the testimonies and an evident disposition of the subject, or unless [he has had] frequent experience in connection with a particular type of thing, indicating that when a planet in a particular house is directed to another planet posited in another particular house, the effect sometimes happens in connection with the things signified by the houses that those planet rule, rather than the things signified by the houses in which they are situated. As will be testified by experience itself, in contradiction to the common axiom, that the presence of a planet is more powerful than the rulership of one that is absent.

Moreover, that which was set forth above about the things essentially signified by the 10th house must similarly be understood about the things essentially signified by all the other houses, for example about the things essentially signified by the 7th house, which are marriage, contracts, lawsuits, open enemies, etc. For it must always be seen to which of these the significator and the promittor are more disposed by nature, by analogy, and by celestial state and determination in the figure. For Venus is more disposed to marriage, Mercury to contracts, Mars to lawsuits, quarrels, and duels, especially if these planets are in the 7th or rule the 7th and the [native's] age is appropriate for these accidents. Similarly, the thing essentially signified by the 8th house is unique in kind to the highest degree, namely death, of which there are two subordinate types—natural death and violent death. And there are as many minor types of natural death as there are of sickness, but there are also very many types of violent death: by an enemy, by wild animals, by command of the prince, by falling from a height, by drowning, and such like, about which there is bound to be ample discussion in the practice of astrology; and so too with the rest of the houses.

Chapt. 3. *By what Means an Astrologer can Arrive at an Understanding of the Type of Effect from the Direction Producing it.*

If the kind of effect produced by a direction can by no means easily be determined by an astrologer, as was said in the previous chapter, then from this it is plain that to predict down to the finest detail is going to be much more difficult, especially in connection with the things signified by the 8th and 10th houses, which above all the rest abound in a diversity of types. Still, this can be proved to be possible from the fact that no other effects are produced than those that were potentially latent in their own causes; consequently, if anyone knows these causes exactly, he will be able to designate their effects specifically. For which purpose, it seems to me that the following method ought to be used.

Firstly, the approximate kind or the subordinate type of future effect should be sought from the previous chapter with as much prudence of mind as possible; as in the case of dignity or profession, whether a military one is signified by Mars, or a judiciary one by Jupiter, or a mechanical one, or an educational one from Venus or Mercury, having also looked at the rest of the things necessary for this [judgment]. In the case of death, whether a natural or a violent one is signified. And so with the rest.

Secondly, if dignity is signified, the custom of the country with regard to the distribution of dignities should be noted. For ecclesiastical status should be so separated from secular status that secular dignities would not accrue to ecclesiastics, nor ecclesiastical benefices to secular persons. Because *Caesar has divided the Empire with Jupiter,* and Christ said to Pilate,[121] "My Kingdom is not of this world," and "No one can serve God and Mammon."[122] And the Devil, the author of confusion, overturns that order in evil places, and benefices are conferred upon secular persons, the richer benefices especially upon magnates, who, permitting the title of priest to be borne by some ignorant or avaricious person when a fee has been paid, and not bothering with the divine service, unjustly take possession of the returns of the goods of Christ that He acquired with His Own passion for that service, and they impiously grow rich from these. But on the contrary very often abbots and bishops, having scorned God and the care of the souls entrusted to them, prostitute the sacred dignities, coveting secular things; and they become not only secular ministers of kings, but (horrible to say) also governors of fortresses and provinces, and sometimes even commanders and generalissimos of armies on the earth as well as on the sea. And this not against the Turk, pagans, or heretics, but rather [joining in league] with these against [other] Catholics; and so the people of Christ are oppressed with iron, flames, hunger, and terrible robberies, and through it all their blood is cruelly spilled for whatever these most unworthy pastors of souls maintain it is more worthy to be spilled for. But what astrologer will prophesy these monstrous things about a man distinguished by ecclesiastical dignities, from whose depraved will (which is not subject to the stars) and insatiable ambition these things come forth? For granted that they may also be inclined to such things by their natal stars, who will say that such ecclesiastics can be restrained neither by the fear of God, nor by respect for their own dignity, nor by everyday shame, and will be worse than secular men?

Besides, dignities are so called because they ought by the law of nature and were formerly accustomed to be conferred upon those more worthy; and this justice may still be observed among the barbarians of the New World, not yet infected by the poison of gold, who in fact elect leaders for their own wars, whose pre-eminence of talent and body, whose strength, eloquence, and outstanding deeds recommend them before all the rest [of their tribe], obviously because they judge it to be reasonable that those inferior in the gifts of nature should be under those who are superior, and because it is unjust and disgraceful to prefer idlers to those who are strong and noble. And among the Chinese, whose very great and populous kingdom is governed with the highest political skill, all dignities are conferred, free of charge, by the king, along with the most ample and appropriate stipends to every [recipient], and only on worthy men who also dispense the king's justice without charge. But among Christians (for shame!) this order of nature is inverted, and

---

121 John 18:36.
122 Matt. 5:24.

gold, which is said to be incorruptible, thus already corrupts everything, so that there is no dignity, secular, or judicial, or military, or political, or fiscal, and no office even so insignificant that it is not very disgracefully sold; indeed on account of such foul avarice, not only are the offices or dignities multiplied these days, but new ones without[123] any absolute necessity; indeed they are introduced for the destruction of the republic against [existing] laws, old customs, and liberty, and they are bought at an immense price, when on the contrary it should be most necessary to devote attention to suppressing the old ones or to decreasing their number. And so for the nobles, the learned, and for those who are most skilled in their own professions, as well as for men outstanding in virtue, the iron door to honours and dignities is shut unless the golden key to opening it is in their hands. Would that kings understood how disgraceful and pernicious this is!

Moreover, I am expounding these few things, and passing over much more in silence that should be carefully noted by an astrologer: lest on astral indications of outstanding character, or of eminence in some science or virtue, or of dignities promised by the stars, he should on that account pronounce dignities to a native in France, unless that native shall have been rich enough from his inheritance or otherwise to buy them. For even though all men born to dignities will be aroused by the stars at the time of suitable directions to seek them out or to qualify for them, yet very seldom will they be obtained in France, except by those who have the money available to buy them, and very often they are sold to those who are unworthy because of ignorance or offenses. And no one can doubt that such venality of offices is of all evils before God and man as detestable as bilge-water, and consequently it is tinder constantly [ready to excite] the burning wrath of God upon us, presaging the overthrow of the kingdom after stupendous and ruinous punishments are inflicted upon those who have introduced this venality and made it hereditary.[124]

Similarly, in France, violent death, at least from an open enemy, is more frequent than elsewhere because of the frequent duels and homicides, for which punishment is fairly rare on account of the infamous and pernicious venality of justice; whence, more impudently the boldness for killing, pillaging, and carrying out other crimes with impunity. But in Italy violent death is more to be feared from poison than from dueling. Furthermore, in the case of judicial death, there is one kind of punishment in France and another elsewhere, as well as one kind for a noble and another for a commoner. Therefore these and similar things must be known in advance by the astrologer in the part of the earth or in whatever kingdom [he is concerned with], so that he may pronounce more surely on future effects, since it is certain that the stars in acting follow the disposition of the subject to which the foregoing belong.

---

123 Reading *sine* 'without' instead of *sint* 'are'.
124 The pervasive corruption described by Morin did in fact ultimately lead to the French Revolution.

Third, the lineage of the native must be taken into account. For one dignity must be sought out from a direction of the same virtue for the son of a prince, another for the son of a baron, another for the son of a senator, another for the son of a merchant, and another for the son of a peasant. Nor should the native's age be omitted either, nor his kind of life, for the same things are not suitable for a boy, a man, and an old man, nor the same things for an ecclesiastic and a secular person, unless the order, as mentioned above, is perverted.

Having taken all this into account, he must now arrive at the more proximate cause of the type of future accident. Which is of course the significator and the promittor, of which the former, by its bodily position, rulership, or opposition aspect, on account of the mutual conformity in signifying of opposed houses, represents the subject that is going to be affected, while the latter signifies the future effect in these same ways.

Firstly, therefore, the strength of the termini of the direction must be noted, for the greater it is, the more noticeable is the effect that is signified. Which effect, thus from the smallest or from moderate things distinguished from the [appropriate] part of the *caelum*, and with the native's lineage, character, profession, state of health and reputation taken into account, will now begin to make known its own type to some extent at least.

Secondly, see whether the significator and the promittor agree in signification or disagree and in what, both from their own nature and from their accidental celestial state and terrestrial determination; for the effect will very often be in accord with that agreement or disagreement, for [when] Mars [is] principally the ruler of the 8th and the Ascendant, they greatly disagree for life, and the Midheaven and Saturn badly disposed [disagree] for honours; but the Sun, or Jupiter ruler of the Midheaven coming to the Midheaven itself, is the greatest agreement for honours; and the reasoning is the same in the rest.

Thirdly, since the promittor, according to Sect. 1, Chapt. 5, acts in the effect of the direction as the [terminus] acting and conferring the form of the future event, it must especially be inspected to determine the type of that event. And the promittor is either a planet or an aspect; consequently, if from the foregoing the kind of future event is conjectured to be a dignity, and the promittor is a planet, the sort of dignities that correspond to that planet as their cause may be seen in the Table of Universal Rulership of the Planets following Book 8, Sect. 3, Chapt. 3; then [it should be decided], which of these dignities agrees more with the lineage, character, age, and kind of life of the native. For Mars coming to the Midheaven causes military honours; Mercury, senatorial honours, or professions of learning, as in my case. But in addition, it must be seen in which house of the figure Mars is; for, coming to the Midheaven from the 11th, it will cause honours through the help of friends; from the 12th, it will harm honours through secret enemies; and finally, it is necessary to see which house Mars itself rules, for the ruler of the 2nd coming to the Midheaven will effect something other than if it were the ruler of the 12th. And having looked at all these things the type of effect can be judged. For the promittor brings to the effect of the direction all its own complete signification, even though it very often acts only according to some part [of that signification] in connection with the disposition of the subject. But if the promittor is an aspect, see what planet makes it, and what the nature of the aspect is, and in what house the aspecting planet is placed, and which [houses] it rules. And judge according to these. For a benefic aspect of a benefic planet will easily confer a dignity analogous to that planet [as shown] in the table previously mentioned. And if it is the Sun or the Moon, especially in its own exaltation, or with rulership in the 10th house, the dignity will be an illustrious one in consideration of the native's lineage and kind of life. But if it is a malefic aspect of a benefic, either the dignity will be a minor one, or oppositions and surmountable obstacles will occur in connection with it.

But if the event is conjectured to be contrary to dignity, it will be necessary to see what type of contrariety is signified. And the significator and promittor will indicate this. For if the significator, that is the Midheaven, or its ruler, or a planet in the 10th, is badly disposed by celestial and terrestrial state, and that planet is malefic by nature, that bad state of the significator portends a fall from a dignity. And if the promittor is a planet malefic by nature in the 6th, 8th, or 12th house, it will be a loss accompanied by death, or exile, or incarceration, and that on account of crimes or secret enemies. If the evils are minor, only a suspension of the dignity will occur, or a suppression of it, or some sort of misfortune or opposition in the exercise of it.

But since in this [kind of] variety it is very difficult for the human intellect to define exactly by the inspection of the natal figure alone the most minute detail of the future event, therefore in the prediction all the types of events should be expounded that can very likely arise from that direction, taking into consideration the native's lineage, age, and condition; and thus the honour of the science will be preserved. But if the figure of the revolution for that time is erected, it can be detected from it much more accurately and certainly whether the direction is going to produce an effect and what sort down to the least detail. For which the daily practice in connection with observations of the effects of the stars in these directions will especially make known, having taken into consideration the lineage and kind of life of the natives, according to Aphorism 1 of the *Centiloquy* "By you and by the science..."[125] For even though he is one who is knowledgeable (i.e., he judges from the science), he cannot declare the particular forms of things as this same

---

125 Pseudo-Ptolemy, *Centiloquy*, Aph. 1, "By you and by the science. For it is not possible that one who is knowledgeable can declare the particular forms of things, just as a sense cannot perceive a particular but only some general form of a thing it senses, and [so] the one discussing a thing must use conjectures about it. Moreover, only those inspired by a divinity can predict particulars." The point is that astrology can supply general information, but the astrologer must supply the details, based on his knowledge of the native and the native's circumstances, etc. Morin states this repeatedly.

aphorism states, because in fact the science is not concerned with particulars,[126] although he will also be able to predict the special form of the effect, as that the native will be the commander of an army, a counselor, a bishop, etc., but not that he will be commander of a particular army, or counselor of a particular parliament, or bishop of a particular church, etc. But doubtless with all these aids from annual revolutions and lengthy observations, he will always be safer if he stops with the subordinate kind [of effect], predicting only a military, judicial, or ecclesiastical dignity for men qualified by condition [for these dignities], or individual types of events pertaining to the proposed direction, and to expound the most appropriate ones to the native, at least when, without inspection of the revolutions, the prognostications of the directions are given out for the native's whole life. For thus his prediction will seldom be false, and its truth demands a sublime theoretical and practical notice of the causes, with notable prudence, or indeed wisdom, on account of the sublimity of this science.

But, for the greater elucidation of this doctrine, some examples should be added. Therefore, let it be supposed that the promittor Mars, ruler of the 12th, is directed from the 2nd house to the Ascendant, which signifies, or represents, the native's person, his life, health, moral nature, and mental qualities. It is sought, then, what the future effect will be. And firstly, it will be evil because Mars is naturally malefic, and therefore inimical to life. Secondly, since life, health, and moral nature are affected, so also by extension are either death, or sickness, or anger, or a quarrel; and this will be the more certain if the Ascendant is otherwise badly afflicted or Mars is inimical to it. Thirdly, because Mars is the ruler of the 12th, it also signifies sickness, imprisonment, or exile; but if it is also ruler of the 7th, namely if the Ascendant is in the sign Taurus, it will also signify quarrels and duels, and, because Mars is in the 2nd and it does not signify wealth there, but rather dissipation of wealth, then the native will not experience an increase in assets, but rather a dissipation of them, and, because it is opposite the 8th house, it signifies death or at least danger to his life. And from all this, to say precisely which of these things will happen is by no means so easy, but to this end two things in particular should be noted. First, which one of them is more strongly or more frequently signified, in the radical influx as well as by [the indications of] each terminus of the direction. Second, which of them is signified more in the revolution, in which the radical places of the significator and the promittor will have to be taken into account and also Mars, the promittor, and Venus, ruler of the Ascendant. Then, on which days of that revolution the transits of the planets become more appropriate for inferring evil, as will be taught in its own place. Moreover, it frequently happens that many things are signified at the same time by the same direction, things either distinct among themselves or connected by some subordination. Just as from the preceding direction there can be signified, in the same year or at the same time, sicknesses and quarrels, distinct among themselves, or anger, a quarrel, a duel, a

---

126 An important statement of principle.

wound, and death, or imprisonment—accidents connected by subordination. But whether one of the abovesaid accidents will be signified to happen from that direction, or several distinct accidents, or several subordinated accidents; and of what sort they are will have to be enunciated from the radical signification of the chart, which will contain either imprisonment, or violent death, or the absence of these, from what is more strongly signified in the direction, and from the agreement or disagreement of the revolution. Next, especially, from the native's state and his circumstances or business affairs in that same year. Also, if he has an open enemy, or if he will have gone to war, you will be able to predict wounds only or death, especially if the figure of the nativity inclines to violent death; and the same prudence will have to be exercised in the other cases.

Or, let Jupiter be in the 11th, directed to the Sun in the 10th, and the effect of the direction be sought. The Sun by its nature is analogous to honours, glory, and fame; and in the 10th it is determined to honours, dignities, and action; and consequently if it is fortunate in its celestial state, it presages illustrious actions, glory, and fame, as well as notable dignities. Moreover, Jupiter in the 11th is favorably determined to friends by its position, but potentially to honours; therefore the things signified by this significator and this promittor will be favorably combined, and that direction will therefore bring about honours for the native through the assistance of his friends, or the native's friends will themselves be the cause of his honours, which is the same thing. Or else, the native will win over to himself many friends through his profession or through outstanding actions and widespread fame, or those friends will be the cause of his outstanding actions and fame. But now, since the Sun concurs subjectively in this direction, and both by its position in the 10th and also by its nature it signifies great and regal honours as the kind [of the effect], and Jupiter effectively concurs; therefore the form or the type of honours at least will be [indicated] by Jupiter, taking into account Jupiter's rulership. For if it is ruler of the 7th, a dignity connected with warfare, such as governor of a fortress or a province, or command of an army, or something similar will be signified. If it is the ruler of the 9th, the dignity will be an ecclesiastical or ambassadorial one. If of the 10th, the dignity will be judicial rather than military or ecclesiastical, unless by chance the ruler of the 7th or the 9th is also the ruler of Jupiter, or is in strong and benefic aspect with it, or the ruler of Jupiter is in the 7th or the 9th. But the minor details of the effect, as that the native will be a captain, governor of a fortress, etc., or the pastor of a church, a bishop, or a counselor, or a chairman, etc., must be sought from the native's lineage, age, natural aptitude, and the strength or debility of the celestial causes in the radix and in the direction, since such is the strength of these causes at times, that they can lift a pauper up out of dung and set him down with princes, by God's will, Whose natural providence is dispensed principally through celestial causes.

So again, the Moon in the 10th house, ruler of that house, whose square aspect is directed into the 7th to Saturn, ruler of the 4th in the 6th. What, by probable reasoning, will be the effect of this direction? Since the effect of the direction is temporarily from the motion of the *primum mobile*, by which the promittor is borne to the significator, and since the promittor itself is determined by power (on account of that motion, which successively measures the time of future things) to that to which the significator[127] is determined by its position; therefore, since that square is in the 7th, it will signify misfortune in lawsuits, contracts, or in marriage; and because it is from the Moon, ruler of the 10th in the 10th, misfortunes will be caused either by a powerful woman or by the native's actions and profession. And because that square is carried to Saturn, ruler of the 4th in the 6th, that misfortune in lawsuits, contracts, or marriage will happen in connection with domestic servants, or subordinates, or animals, or in connection with parents or inheritances; and the reasoning is the same in other cases. For the entire prudence of this science is engaged to the highest degree in successfully establishing the combinations of those things that can be presaged by the promittor as well as by the significator. Which, since it is of itself very difficult if only the celestial causes are looked at, will always be increased [in difficulty] by the consideration of the disposition of the subject, namely the native, having taken into consideration his lineage, age, character, and kind of life, as has often been said. Finally too, [by a consideration] of his circumstances and business affairs, if the special effect of a present or imminent direction is sought. For the *caelum* acts in accordance with the present disposition of the subject, not only at the time of his nativity, as if the son of a prince and the son of a kitchen servant were born at the same time under the same roof, but also at the time of the directions, whose virtue is the same in both natives, but which will effect different things in the individuals by reason of the disposition of the subject, as the same Sun at the same time and in the same place hardens mud and liquefies wax.

Chapt. 4. *From what [Sources] the Certitude and Intensity of Effects may be Chosen through the Directions of the Significators.*

They are chosen from many considerations. For in the first place, if the significator is strong, either for good or evil — i.e., if for good it is a benefic planet and well disposed in celestial state, but for evil, a malefic badly disposed by sign, by conjunction, by aspect, etc.,—the direction will receive a more certain and intense effect, the latter being evil and the former good, provided that a similar promittor moves to it. And the same may be said about the cusps, for whose celestial state the nature of the sign must be noted, along with the conjunctions or aspects to that cusp. And the weaker the significator is, or the promittor, or both, the milder the direction will act, or it will do nothing at all.

But the following things come to mind that ought to be noted in connection with strength and debility:

---

127 Reading *significator* 'significator' instead of *significatur* 'is signified'.

1. A benefic planet well disposed by celestial state, is strong to do good and to ward off evil or to mitigate it according to its own determination, radical as well as directional, at least bodily and by its good rays. But badly disposed, it is weak, even with benefic rays, but it is stronger for evil, especially with malefic rays. But a malefic planet well disposed is strong to do good or to do evil according to its determination and the nature of its aspects. But evilly disposed, it is strong to do evil and to ward off good according to its determination, especially by body and malefic rays, for it cannot be helpful [even] with benefic [rays]. Finally, a planet that is peregrine and without any aspect from other planets, at least without a strong aspect, must properly be said to be weak for doing good as well as for doing evil. But it acts in accordance with its own nature and determination.

2. The stronger a promittor is, either for good or for evil, the greater and more certain the effect that must be expected, provided that its virtue[128] is transferred to a similar significator; and consequently the intensity and certitude of the effect will depend upon the strength of both termini.

3. A planet that is a significator or promittor and analogous, or configured with an analogous planet, is scarcely ever frustrated in the effect, and a notable one at that, which it also produces easily and quickly. And so, when the Sun in the 10th, especially when well disposed, is directed for honours, it presages outstanding honours when it meets a suitable promittor; or when that same Sun in the 11th comes to the Midheaven well disposed, or in which the Sun itself rules by domicile or exaltation; for in the prior mode as a significator and in the latter as a promittor it is analogous to honours; and the same thing should be judged if in the direction of Jupiter, ruler of the Midheaven, for dignities or undertakings, Jupiter itself or [another] planet [as] promittor is trine the Sun. And if the Sun is directed from the 12th to the Midheaven, which is ruled by Saturn in the 2nd, great secret enemies and great impediments in undertakings and actions will be signified, as [they were] to me in the year 1634 with Cardinal Richelieu in connection with the knowledge of longitudes that I had invented.[129] For then I obtained considerable fame but no dignity, and I suffered much from unfair judges and secret enemies.

4. If the significator and the promittor are in appropriate aspects with their rulers, that is in benefic aspect for a good action and in malefic aspect for an evil one, and both of them concur efficaciously in the effect, it will also make the effect greater. More or less the same should be judged if the significator aspects the ruler of the promittor, or the promittor aspects the ruler of the significator.

5. If the Ascendant, the significator of life, or its ruler is quite strong, a planet that is promittor will only kill if it is anaeretic by determination, i.e., one that is in the 8th or is ruler of the 8th, especially one that is malefic by nature. If it is of

---

128 Reading *eius virtus* 'its virtue' instead of *ad virtute*.

129 This refers to Morin's method of finding the longitude of ships at sea by astronomical observations. It is explained in his book *Longitudinum terrestrium nec non coelestium nova ac hactenus optata scientia...* (Paris: J. Libert, 1634).

moderate strength, the ruler of the place of that promittor will be able to kill. But if it is notably weak, any ray that is malefic by its nature or by a malefic determination will kill. Moreover, the significator is judged notably weak if its ruler is badly disposed by celestial state and determination, and especially if that significator is injured by malefics without any help from the benefics. Furthermore, that promittor may be judged to have the force for killing, which, especially malefic by nature, makes a hostile aspect to the apheta, not receiving [it], and not being received [by it] by domicile. Then, one that is contrary to the apheta, either by its own nature, as Saturn is to the Sun or the Moon, and Mars and Saturn to the Ascendant, or by its own determination, as the ruler of the 8th is to the Ascendant, or by its state, as Mars in Scorpio is a stronger enemy to the Ascendant in Libra. However, it must be noted that a strong apheta should be judged to be weak in [the native's] old age on account of the debility of his body. And so a strong significator of honours in boyhood should be considered to be of no virtue on account of the disposition of age to honours, unless the natural order is violated because of the native's lineage or the depraved customs of his native land.

6. A direction naturally signifying matrimony, as Venus ruler of the 7th house to the Ascendant or to the preceding Midheaven, will not be allotted any effect if by any other means the signification may be overthrown, either [because the native is] celibate or the entrance to religion is signified, as happened in my case from the direction of the Midheaven to Venus ruler of the 7th in the 12th combust along with Saturn and Jupiter ruler of the 9th; and the same reasoning applies to other cases.

7. Since directions are made by the revolution of the *primum mobile*, by which the promittor is transferred to the location of the significator, then when the significator and the promittor each have the same declination and of the same name,[130] from this they promise more certain and greater effects because they are thus united partilely in the circle of position; but, when they are disposed in the contrary mode and widely separated, they accomplish little or nothing.

8. From a weak or unfortunate significator, as the Ascendant, the Midheaven, or the Sun in the 10th, and a strong malefic promittor, a very bad and intense effect will follow—cutting off, overturning, or destroying the thing signified by the significator. For not every promittor cuts off in this manner, but only and especially one that is contrary in signification to the significator.

9. The significator of good things, whether it is a cusp or a planet, directed to its own benefic and strong ruler is very good, but to a planet that is in exile or in its fall in the place of the significator, it is bad; and it is worse if the planet that is the promittor is badly disposed.

10. If the Sun or its trine is directed to a planet in the 10th, or to the preceding ruler of the 10th, or to Jupiter, or to its trine to a planet in the 2nd, or to the ruler of the 2nd, in the latter case wealth and in the former honours are certainly signified, unless the state and determination of the promittors is contrary.

---

130 That is, north or south.

11. If a planet that is significator of good is strong and its ruler is weak, the thing will go well in the beginning and will bring hope, but it will not be able to be brought to perfection. But if the significator is weak and its ruler is strong, then the thing will seem difficult in the beginning, but finally it will be easily brought to perfection. But if the significator is strong and its ruler is strong, the thing will move forward easily and outstandingly from beginning to end; and it will be a great effect. But if both of them are weak, the thing can in no way be accomplished or begun; and this must be understood of radical positions as well as of directions of that significator in which consideration will still have to be given to the strength or weakness of the promittor according to Article 2 [above]. The same should be judged about a cusp as significator; and the same from a similar judgment in the case of an evil significator.

12. A benefic planet conjoined to benefic significators will increase their effects when they are directed to benefic promittors. For if the planet conjoined follows, it disposes the significator to the effect; if it precedes, it strengthens that same significator or increases it. But when a malefic promittor comes [to a benefic significator], it weakens its force, and it diminishes and guards[131] the significator or its subject. But a malefic planet conjoined to benefic significators diminishes and deters their effects: indeed, it frustrates the preceding [significator] in its effect, or overturns it, or otherwise disposes it to misfortune.

13. In every direction the kind, the type, the quality, the quantity and the time of the effect must be considered. And in fact the kind is taken from the property of the house of the figure that the significator occupies, or, if it is a cusp, as the Sun in the 10th signifies royal honours only in kind, according as the significator is in such a house. The type and the quality from the nature and state of the promittor, the quantity from the strength or debility of the promittor and the significator, and finally the time from the distance of both, as was explained previously.

14. In the direction of the Ascendant to the following Saturn, if Saturn itself is ruler of the Ascendant, and not a particular significator of sicknesses or of death, it will only signify sicknesses or danger to life in general on account of Saturn's malefic nature, and no sicknesses or danger of any great importance will happen, because Saturn rules the Ascendant. But if Saturn is inimical to the Ascendant, a greater sickness or a greater danger will be signified, also a more certain one, even though it is only general. But if Saturn is allotted no dignity in the Ascendant, or rather it is inimical to it, and in addition it is the particular significator of death or of sicknesses through its own determination by body, rulership, or opposition aspect, [then its indication] about sickness and danger to life cannot be doubted; and the same reasoning applies to other cases, whether to good or to evil; and this must be carefully noted. Consequently, if the Midheaven is in Virgo, the fall of

---

131 The word *tutatur* 'guards' or 'protects' seems inappropriate here. Perhaps we should read *frustrat* 'frustrates' as in the following sentence.

Venus, and it is directed to the trine of Venus, especially in Scorpio, the detriment of Venus, this direction will produce no good, as I know by experience.[132]

Chapt. 5. *Some things Universal as well as Particular that must be Noted in Connection with Directions.*

I have reckoned that it is better to put these things together in a single chapter rather than to explain each one in a different chapter, since from what has already been said the individual items can be easily understood. And first, in connection with the direction of any significator, such as the Midheaven for undertakings [and] dignities, the following may briefly be noted.

1. The Midheaven insofar as it is just a significator only signifies in connection with honours or actions, but not whether the honours are going to come to pass or whether the actions will turn out favorably.

2. A dignity happens from the motion of the promittor when it is transferred to the place or position of the significator; and consequently the promittor confers those dignities through its own action, as far as the type.

3. A dignity is not conferred by just any promittor that comes to the Midheaven, but only by one that is conformable and powerful by nature and by state or by affinity of signification; and even this one will not always confer [a dignity], namely if the Midheaven, or its ruler, or both are badly disposed and disposed towards something to which they are not suited. And from this it can be clearly deduced that the future occurrence of a dignity depends upon the suitability of the Midheaven and the efficacy of the promittors that come together with it.

4. The suitability of the Midheaven to dignities is taken from the nature of the sign, the nature and analogy of its ruler or from the planets posited in the 10th, and from their propitious state, both celestial and terrestrial, and especially from a favorable connection with the luminaries, or from the nature of the planets, or from the determination of the benefics with the Midheaven itself and its ruler. And similarly, the strength and efficacy of the promittor is taken from its own, its ruler's, and the aspecting planets' nature, state, position, and connection with favorable [planets]. But in the case of the unsuitability of the significator and the promittor, the reverse [of these configurations] will have to be considered. However, it is proved by ordinary experience that a dignity does not happen unless the promittor or those [planets] from which it takes its efficacy is connected with the Midheaven, or with those [planets] by which it is made suitable, either by rulership, or by aspect, or by similarity of signification, or by excellence of state. As happened to me from the direction of Mercury to the Midheaven, by which I was made Regius Professor of Mathematics, even though Mercury did not behold either the Midheaven or its

---

132 That is, when the Midheaven in Virgo comes to Scorpio and encounters a trine from Venus in Cancer or Pisces.

ruler, Saturn, nor did it rule [either of] them; but, from the fact that it was ruler of the 2nd, and consequently the significator of wealth, applying to its ruler, Venus, [which was] strong and in an important doryphory of the Sun, [while Mercury] itself was oriental and preceded all [the other planets]; and consequently it had an excellent state, and by reason of [its rulership over] wealth it had a similarity of signification with dignity and profession, from which those things necessary to livelihood are obtained. Besides, among the [various kinds of] dignities, Mercury, by its own nature or essentially, signifies mathematics. And a planet is never devoid of its own essential significations; and consequently it acts through its essential as well as through its accidental [significations] from its position or rulership in the houses of the figure, along with the nature or disposition of the significator to which the promittor moves; and the same thing must be judged about any other significator.

5. The native's lineage, bodily constitution, moral nature and mental qualities, must also be carefully contemplated in directions: for it sometimes happens that the first house is quite favorably constituted for the endowments of mind and body, and long life, so that from this are taken certainly the indications of future dignities, apart from any particular aptitude of the Midheaven, as in the nativity of the Blessed Charles de Condren,[133] whose 10th is occupied by Mars in exile; moreover, the Sun was in the 1st, and its ruler, Jupiter, in the 9th and trine its own ruler; consequently, he was made General of the Congregation of Oratory of Jesus, and was a man very well known for his knowledge and piety. But the 2nd house is also no less powerful for the same thing, as was shown above in my case with Mercury ruler of the second; then too the 9th for ecclesiastical and ambassadorial dignities and such like; for the one who has the 1st, 2nd, and 9th favorably disposed, or their rulers, will scarcely lack dignities. Therefore, it will have to be seen how the planets in these houses, or their rulers, are related to the planets in the 10th, or their rulers, so that what is going to be may be perceived from the occourse of the [pertinent] significators and promittors. And these things that are said here about the 10th house, must be understood similarly about the significations of the other houses.

Second. In any direction we shall note that it and frequently many [other] effects are signifying at the same time in the same year; and it is no wonder. For since every significator may signify many things at the same time, as the Ascendant signifies life, moral nature, and mental qualities, and the Midheaven dignities, undertakings, and actions; and each planet signifies those things to which it is determined by body, rulership, and aspect, and the planet that is the promittor also acts according to the significations of its own determination by body, rulership, and aspect, it almost always happens that the same direction produces many effects; from which it is plain that it is safer to predict all the effects that can be produced by the concourse of the significator and the promittor, having taken both of them

<hr>

133 Charles de Condren (1588-1641), French theologian and politician.

totally into account, rather than to predict just one effect. But one should always pay attention to the effect that is most strongly and principally signified, so that it is not overlooked and can be predicted more certainly; then pay attention to the revolution, so that one can note which signification it favors most.

Third, it sometimes happens that many new directions occur in the same year. And a more certain effect will have to be expected in that year if they concern the same signification, as directions of the Ascendant and its ruler for life, or of the Midheaven and its ruler for honours and actions, and if these directions agree among themselves as to good or evil. But if they disagree, the judgment will have to be made in accordance with the one that is evidently stronger, tempered nevertheless by reason of the contrary [indication]. And the exact time of both must be observed, for in this case quite often such an order of nature is observed, that from the effect of one the effect of another follows, as from a homicide [indicated] by one direction a public and shameful death [follows] from another; on which account the effect of the first direction must be prudently noted and predicted.

But when the directions that happen in the same year are of diverse significa-tion, as directions of the Ascendant and the Midheaven, it must be seen whether they can agree in anything, either for good or evil. And that thing must be predicted boldly, and the times must also be carefully sought out, so that it may be plain whether some subordination can be discovered in these effects, that are diverse in type, like that which exists in their times, and the judgment made accordingly; for some directions occasionally happen in the same year, subordinated in accordance with some total effect, such as directions of the Ascendant and the Midheaven for a depraved inclination, a bad crime, imprisonment, and death by judicial decree. And so with the others; but if no agreement in any total effect is found among them, then plainly they will signify different things.

Fourth, some of those things that happen after birth happen unexpectedly, such as a duel, drowning, a fall from a height, but others step-by-step, such as the highest dignities. For the former, a single suitable direction suffices; but for the latter, several are required, at least if the progress from the least through the middle to the greatest requires a notable length of time. But there is in human affairs some prime direction, from which many effects follow closely. As if there is a direction of Mercury to the Ascendant for the beginning of studies, there is no need for new directions for particular individual advances in the studies, such as passage from one class to a higher one. Similarly, if anyone perpetrates a homicide from the direction of the Midheaven to the square of Mars, ruler of the 12th, in the 8th, there is no need for new directions for his incarceration and violent death, which will follow that homicide, but that direction alone will suffice which portends all these effects; and in the same fashion, if anyone should be made Prime Minister of the Kingdom from a direction of the Midheaven to the Sun, since many good things and other dignities follow upon such a prime dignity without [any] new directions. Moreover, this [fact] must be noted in contradiction to those who wish to give particular directions to individual effects, and who do not perceive that from any prime direction many effects can follow, in which its force will appear after a concordant revolution or a concordant transit.

Fifth, when many planets are in the same house, and consequently determined to the same kind of signification, as in my case Venus, the Sun, Jupiter, Saturn, and the Moon are conjoined in the 12th, and the preceding [planets] are directed to the following, each promittor produces its own effect individually and in accordance with its own nature. And the same thing may be said for the other significators, whether they are cusps, or other planets that are directed either directly or conversely to the those planets posited in the same house, as I experienced in my nativity from the directions of the Midheaven and the Ascendant to the abovesaid planets.

Sixth, in future effects that are inevitably from the same fate, a particular direction is not required for each effect, e.g. for succession, which happens to a son or to a brother from the death of the father or brother, a suitable direction is not necessarily required in the nativity of a son or a surviving brother, but it suffices that the son or brother survives. For the law from which he receives the succession to the benefice is for him a fate of a lower order, equivalent to a particular direction. But in successions through selection by the will of another person, or depending upon chance, such as to an empire, the Papacy, a bishopric, the dignity of chancellor, and such like, a suitable direction is required. For such things happen to the native through superior fate, in which it is necessary that it should be the cause of the accident. And from this may be detected the notable error of those who wish to correct the nativities of the kings of France by means of the time of their coronation, and those who presage the death of the father from the directions of a future successor, when the kingdom has been received by the appropriate persons; for, as the death of the father principally depends upon his own fate and not on the fate of his son (unless he should be slain violently by his own son), so the succession from the father to the son is in fact assured to the son from the demise of his father, since aside from that nothing is necessary for the son to succeed; therefore no direction is required for this, although it can happen then with a suitable direction. Thus in fact the law by itself confers succession without any other consideration. And the same thing must be judged about the succession of children into the purchasable dignities belonging to their parents, by which the order of nature and justice is perverted in France, when a son who, from ignorance, offenses, or something else, is plainly unworthy of such a succession, is made a counselor, or a prefect, or some similar dignity.

Seventh, the proper, or determined significators of the father, the mother, or the spouse, etc., are directed for their accidents, not only [those that they have in] common with the native, such as love, hate, and contracts, but also their own, so that it may be known what should happen to them after the birth of the native from their fated connection with the native through his nativity, for otherwise this cannot be known from the native's chart. But it may be known far more certainly from the directions of the chart of the father, the mother, the brother, the spouse, etc.;

thus in fact the accidents of any man depend more upon his own natal constitution of the *caelum* than on someone else's or upon a common one, but this will be stated more fully below.

Eighth, in the directions of significators to the aspects of planets, see whether the nature of the aspect agrees with the nature and determination of the planet making such an aspect; that is, whether, when it is a benefic aspect, the aspecting planet is also benefic by nature and in a good house of the *caelum*, or whether on the contrary, when it is a malefic aspect, the aspecting planet is also malefic by nature in an evil house of the celestial figure; [for] if so, a notable effect will indeed follow in either case—in the first case, good; in the latter case, evil. And consequently, from the direction of the Ascendant to the opposition of Mars in the 8th, death will have to be predicted, as well as from the direction of the Midheaven to the square of Saturn in the 8th, on account of some criminal undertaking; and the effect will be more certain and worse if the celestial state of the planet is unfavorable; but from the direction of the Midheaven to the trine of the Sun in the 7th, it will be necessary to predict an excellent marriage for a woman, or a notable military dignity for a man.

Ninth, in an accident signified by the conjunction of one planet with another planet, or with the Midheaven, an accident must not be predicted from the direction of one of the conjoined planets to the other if they are mutually separated, unless account is taken of the age of the native and the nature of the accident, lest dignities or matrimony be predicted for an infant; and often no effect is produced by that direction, but by others, of which the termini conjoined are the significator or the promittor: for Venus, ruler of the 7th, following the Ascendant by two degrees, and signifying marriage, will not cause it two years after birth.

Tenth, when the Ascendant is directed for its own significations—temperament, health, life, moral nature, or mental qualities—the prediction must be made in accordance with the nature and state of the promittor. And the procedure is the same with the rest of the significators: when different promittors come to them successively, the promittor's state must be looked at, not only in the radix but also in the revolution; in fact, at the time when the direction is completed and the promittor itself takes up the rulership in the division of time—not having omitted the state of the significator too. And this must be carefully noted in all directions, as a secret of astrology.

Eleventh, those who have promittors in angles will experience their effects in the first part of life; those who have them in succedent houses, in the second part; and those who have them in cadent houses, in the third and last part.[134] However, understand this with relation to the things essentially signified by the significators

---

134 This aphorism follows naturally from taking the cusps of the Ascendant and the
     Midheaven as principal significators.

of the angle of the figure most closely preceding [the promittors], and with regard to those [natives] who will arrive at old age.

Twelfth, a direction of the Ascendant causes effects through an accident involving the things signified by the 10th, as when it is directed to the ruler of the Midheaven or a strong aspect with it, or when it is directed to a malefic, ruler of the 12th, whence [comes] imprisonment or exile, from which a loss of dignity follows; and similarly, the direction of the Midheaven causes effects through an accident involving life or death, as when it is directed to a malefic, ruler of the 8th, or its square or opposition. And thus Mr. de Chavigny[135] from the direction of Mars, ruler of the 12th, was incarcerated, exiled, and deprived of dignity. And the King of Sweden,[136] from the direction of the Midheaven to Saturn, badly disposed in the 8th, and at the same time to the body of Mars in the 12th, was killed. And the reasoning is the same with the rest.

Chapt. 6. *The Extraction of Figures from the Figure of the Native for other Persons Related to Him. Then, the Directions of Significators of these Persons, and their Effects.*

Persons related to the native from his own nativity are his parents, brothers, spouse, children, servants, friends, and enemies. And for these persons, Cardan, in his *Commentary on the Text of Ptolemy's* [*Quadripartite*], Book 3, Chapt. 4, Text 14,[137] teaches in it how to extract figures from the genethliacal figure of the native, through which the astrologer will be able to judge about the fate of these persons. And for the father he wants to take the place of the Sun by day and the place of Saturn by night. And for the mother, the place of the Moon by night and of Venus by day; similarly, for the wife, the place of the Moon by night and of Venus by day; but for the husband in a woman's figure, the place of the Sun by day and of Mars by night. And from these places, he wants to erect figures, always putting these places on the Ascendant of the [extracted] figure. As, for the father in a diurnal nativity he takes the place of the Sun, which he puts on the Ascendant in erecting the figure, from which and from the directions of the Sun itself he judges about the father's accidents or fate, no differently than one is accustomed to make judgment about the native's fate from his figure.[138]

---

135 Léon Bouthillier, Count of Chavigny (1608-1652), French official under Cardinal Richelieu (1585-1642).
136 Gustavus II Adolphus (1594-1632).
137 *Opera Omnia*, V, pp. 257-258, *et ff.*
138 That is, the extracted chart is read according to the same rules as a regular chart.

Furthermore, Ptolemy did not distinguish for which elevation of the pole the figure ought to be erected,[139] but Cardan always erects it for the latitude of the place of the nativity [regardless] of where the significator is located in the native's figure, whether it is the significator of the father, or the mother, or the spouse, etc.; but Junctinus in his comment on the same Book 4, Chapt. 3, asserting many times that this doctrine is marvelous and very true, erects individual figures for the elevation of the pole above the circle of position of each significator, whether father, or mother, etc. In which he at least errs less that Cardan [when the latter], whose nativity is nocturnal, puts for the figure of his father the place of Saturn on the horizon of his nativity, even though Saturn would still be under the horizon, namely in the 2nd house of his own natal figure; and he also puts the place of the Moon in the same horizon for the figure of his mother, even though the Moon was already above the horizon on the cusp of the 12th house. But now the *primum mobile* does not move back to the rising point, so that the Moon can be put on the horizon, and when by its continued motion through the meridian, the setting, and the *imum caelum* it restores the Moon to the horizon, then the Moon will be more than 10° distant from the place in the zodiac that it occupied at the moment of the nativity. But Cardan himself, thinking about it, says: *Someone will wonder how the significator of the father can be put in the Ascendant when it is not; and when it will be, or when it was, the places of the planets, at least of the Moon, are sensibly unchanged?* And he answers: *That just as material is placed in material, so both the forms and the causes of the native and of his parent are others placed in others without the succession of time.* But this reply is absurd. For in the first place Cardan says "where material is put in material," i.e., where material is subject to material, against the principles of philosophy? Second, even if the forms and causes of the native and of his parent were others placed in others, yet from this it does not follow that Saturn must be put on the horizon for the father and the Moon for the mother when they were not there at the moment of the nativity. Indeed, because they are others placed in others without any succession of time, as he will have it, it rather follows from this that they must be seen in the circles of position that they occupy at the moment of the nativity, which Junctinus at least observed. And Cardan, in his *Astronomical Aphorisms*, Segment II, Aph. 54, in fact prescribed this incidentally for children, but didn't use it.[140]

And yet Junctinus and Cardan, [following] after Ptolemy and the other old [astrologers], err especially in this: that they extract these figures from such

---

139 Naturally not, since Ptolemy evidently accepted the Equal House system of house division for charts, for which it is sufficient to know the Ascendant, and probably had nothing more in mind than a simple inspection of the extracted chart. By adopting quadrant systems, the latter-day astrologers created problems for themselves (such as the appropriate latitude to use in an extracted chart) that did not exist for Ptolemy.

140 *Opera Omnia*, p. 37. "When you extract a figure from another figure, you will put the Ascendant according to the elevation of the pole above the circle of position of the significator, and especially in the case of [charts extracted for] children."

universal significators, which Cardan calls "according to their essential nature," the worthlessness of which we have already shown many times. For the judgments taken from such figures and significators and their directions must necessarily be erroneous from what we have said in Book 21, Sect. 2, Chapt. 13, and because from this it would follow that for those individual men born on the same artificial day[141] at Paris (of whom there is no small number) the same things would in general have to be predicted about their mothers and wives from the extracted figures, of which (as they will have it) Venus is the universal significator, for the same things would be for every figure; and for the individual women born during the day, the same things would have to be predicted about their fathers and husbands, of whom the Sun is the significator. But these things are contrary to experience.[142]

Second, if these figures are valid for judging by the individual houses about things pertaining to the parents, such as about things pertaining to the native from the native's figure, and also if they can serve for judging about the mother, brothers, spouse, children, etc., as Cardan says in that place, then they will be valid for judging about the father's father, or the native's grandfather, and if in both the native's genethliacal figure and the extracted [figure] of the father, the Sun is under the earth (as happens in Cardan's figure), then the figure will be the same both for the father and the grandfather through Saturn in the Ascendant and in the same circle of position for both.[143] Wherefore, the same things had to be predicted about the father and the grandfather, as far as moral nature, the state of fortune, and the time of death. Indeed, the same things would have had to be predicted about the grandfather, the great-grandfather, the great-great-grandfather, and so on back to Adam, if they were still alive, because for all of them the figure with Saturn in the Ascendant would be one and the same, which is utterly absurd to contemplate. But on the contrary through this figure of the father, in judging about children, not only would a figure for children be extracted contrary to the native's own figure, as well as to the figure of children from the father's genethliacal figure, but also one which could be the same for the children of the children until the end of the world; and

---

141 By "artificial day" Morin means the day as distinguished from the night, rather than the time measure called "day" that includes the night and consists of 24 hours.

142 This is a valid argument against using universal significators to represent persons related to the native. For, as Morin says, if we adopt it, then everyone born on the same "artificial day" would have virtually the same extracted chart for each of the persons mentioned. Whereas, if we adopt his accidental significators, there would be six different types of each person, with some intermediate variations. This at least allows more individuality than the other way.

143 Here and in what follows Morin erects a straw man to belabor, since Cardan says nothing in the cited passage about extracting charts from extracted charts. In another place, in his *Book of Twelve Genitures*, Cardan does extract a chart (C 531A) for himself from his orphaned grandson's chart (C 531C) by putting Saturn on the Ascendant, since he says Saturn represents old persons, and finds that the extracted chart conforms in some respects to his own life. However, he gives no general rule for doing this sort of thing.

consequently, to presage the same things for them, which anyone can see is also absurd.[144]

Third, erecting the figure of the father from the native's figure, and from this figure of the father again the figure of a son, and from this again the figure of the father, would give a circular [procedure] that is absolutely worthless.[145]

Fourth, in the diurnal nativity of a woman, in the year in which her father will die from a direction of the Sun to Mars, in that same [year] her husband will also die; or at least, by whatever time after the woman's birth her father will die, by that same time after her marriage her husband will die; or they will experience sicknesses, wounds, etc., which is also contrary to experience. But if you say that the father's and husband's own genethliacal figures ought to be looked at to see whether these agree with those [extracted charts], it will be a worthless reply, for if they agree, then one set of them is seen to be superfluous. Will it be the father's own [chart] and the husband's? But if they disagree, will these extracted figures be credited rather than their own proper ones, through which the father and the husband received the impression of their own fates from the *caelum*, especially when this extraction of figures by means of universal significators is lacking in any fundamental rationality, as has already often been said.

And although Cardan tries to prove these figures, namely the figure of his own father, [and] by the direction of the Moon (which he wrongly holds to be the apheta in the figure) to the opposition of the Sun for the death of the father 23 years after the birth of Cardan himself, he abuses his incautious readers who are ignorant of these matters. Thus in fact the oblique ascension of Saturn in the latitude of the place of the nativity, 45°, is 57°33', that is if the latitude of Saturn is taken into account, which Cardan wrongly omits here. And having subtracted 90°, there remains 327°33' for the right ascension of the Midheaven, which, subtracted from the right ascension of the Moon with latitude, 344°49', leaves 17°16' for the distance of the Moon from the Midheaven, from which and from the declination of the Moon, 11°12',[146] the altitude of the pole above the circle of position of the Moon is found to be 20°. At which [latitude] the oblique ascension of the Moon is 348°57', and the oblique ascension of the opposition to the Sun is 368°12'. And,

---

144 Here again Morin is arguing against a straw man. And it is perhaps worth pointing out that his argument could be applied by analogy to prove that derived houses are of no value; for if the 4th house represents the native's father, then the 8th house represent's the father's children, of which the native is one; and, by Morin's reasoning, this means that the native is represented simultaneously by the 1st house and the 8th, which (as he would say) is absurd.

145 This is certainly true, but pointless, as noted above.

146 The Latin text has 11°21', but recalculation shows that the figures of the minutes have been transposed.

subtracting the former from the latter, there remains 19°15', not [even] equivalent to 20 years; therefore, Cardan is in error by more than 3 years.[147]

But in the figure extracted for his mother, Clara Micheria, he errs far more seriously on account of the Moon, which he places in the Ascendant with the latitude omitted, which latitude is 4°20' South.[148] For the Moon, i.e., the Ascendant, comes to the opposition of the Sun, or the Sun itself to the Descendant, in 9 years and not 20, as Cardan will have it,[149] for the nearly lethal hysterical passion of his mother. He will also direct the Sun to the opposition of Mars in 36 years from his own birth for the death of his mother, although it actually comes to the opposition in 43 years.[150] From which it is plainly evident what should be known about Cardan's doctrine and its verification.

And yet, it is certain that many things can be predicted about the father, the brothers, the spouse, the children, etc., from the natal figure alone. For experience proves that the malefics, Saturn and Mars, in the 3rd signify that the brothers and sisters will die before the native, in the 5th the children, in the 7th spouses, etc. In fact, the ruler of the 3rd in the 10th threatens the brothers with death and the ruler of the 5th in the 12th threatens the children, as I have often observed: namely, because the 10th is the 8th with respect to the 3rd, and the 12th is the 8th with respect to the 5th, which is [the house] of children; and the same thing is to be judged in similar fashion about other persons. Since the signs and planets involved in the individual significations of the natal figure related to the native are determined in the same general manner that we have set forth in detail in Book 21, therefore, as the Ascendant, its ruler, and a planet in the 1st are determined to the native's life, moral nature, and mental qualities, and signify about these things, and are also directed for them, and similarly in the case of the Midheaven, its ruler, and

147 The discrepancy between Cardan's calculation and Morin's is due to Cardan's having calculated what we would call a *zodiacal* primary direction, while Morin has calculated a *mundane* direction. Recalculation of both types of directions yields 22°38' for the zodiacal direction (which Cardan rounded to 23°) and 19°15' mundane. As Morin notes, the difference amounts to more than 3 years in the time of the event.

148 Here Morin assumes that the Moon should be in the Ascendant by *mundane* position, rather than by zodiacal position. Since the Moon has considerable latitude, it would rise with 22°44' Pisces instead of 11°42'. Morin neglects to mention that this would put the Moon in the 12th house instead of on the cusp of the Ascendant, in violation of the rule that says to put the significator on the Ascendant. And neither he nor Cardan judges a planet by its *mundane* position, but only by its zodiacal one. Hence, his argument is groundless.

149 Recalculation shows a zodiacal arc or direction of 15°09' and a mundane one of 9°18'. Cardan seems to have erred in calculating the direction, since he derived an arc of 20°.

150 Since Mars has only 36' of south latitude, the difference between the two modes of calculation is not so marked. I find 40°48' (versus Cardan's 36) for the zodiacal arc of direction and 41°37' for the mundane. Converted by Naibod's measure, this is equivalent to 42°31' or roughly 43 years. Here again Cardan seems to have made an error.

a planet in the 10th for honours and actions; therefore, the *imum caelum*, its ruler, and a planet in the 4th, determined in similar fashion towards the native's parents, will also signify about them; and if they should be directed, they should only be directed for them, and not for others to which they are not determined. And the reasoning is the same about brothers, the spouse, children, servants, and friends, always considering the three significators of each thing—the cusp, its ruler, and the planet in the house of the cusp, if the same number of distinct significators are found, with the observation put at the end of Sect. 1, Chapt. 3. For this general doctrine agrees closely with itself and with experience.

Further, when these significators are directed, whether they are cusps or planets, their circle of position is sought, as well as their own horizon and above it the altitude of the pole, just as if a new figure had been constructed for this horizon. And yet it must be known that these significators have a dual relationship. One to the native, by signifying for him any accidents [that occur] in connection with such persons, i.e., to them, from them, with them, or through their agency. The other, to those persons, by signifying their own accidents for them, such as honours, wealth, an early death, or the contrary of these. By reason of the first, the circle of position is only inquired into, so that the arc of direction interposed between the significator and the promittor may be known for the time of the accident for the native, and, from such a direction, future things concerning the parents, if it is the significator of parents, or concerning brothers if it is the significator of brothers, etc., judging about the accident according to the rules we have prescribed, without any consideration of fitting the houses of the figure to this circle or horizon. But by reason of the latter, the figure can be set to that horizon, so that from it the accidents that are peculiar to those persons will be apparent, as will be explained below.

But again it can be asked whether many figures should be erected and examined for a general judgment about the father's state—namely from the 4th cusp, from its rulership or the rulers of the 4th, also from the planets posited in the 4th, and each one of these put for an Ascendant in its own circle—or whether a single figure ought to be erected, and [if so], with which of these significators? For a plurality of figures would certainly beget confusion, since they could differ among themselves both by quadrant and by half of the *caelum*, but a single figure will signify the same thing for both the father and the mother, or for all the [native's] wives, or all his brothers, or for the native [himself] with these individual persons, which seems to be another inconvenience.

But looking at this difficulty attentively, it seems to me that a single figure should generally be erected to judge about the parents, or the brothers, or the wife, or the children; [151] and it should be erected from the cusp proper to those persons

---

151 Here, and in the discussion that follows, I have translated *filii* and its singular *filius* as 'children' and 'child' rather than 'sons' and 'son', since the topic under discussion is "parents and children" rather than the more specific "fathers and sons."

themselves and not from the planets that are rulers or from those that are posited in the appropriate house.

The reason is because the science of astrology ought to be uniform, and yet there is no general judgment about the native from a figure erected from a planet that was the ruler of the Ascendant at the moment of the nativity or that was in the 1st house, but only from a figure erected from the point of the ecliptic or of the equator that was ascending at the moment of the nativity, even though the ruler of the Ascendant and a planet in the 1st can be directed for the accidents of the native pertaining to the 1st house, and so they are valid not for a universal but for a particular judgment. Therefore, the same thing must be done for the figure of the father, which will be erected from the 4th cusp to judge generally about the state of the parents, but the ruler of that cusp, that is the Ascendant of the erected figure, will only be directed for the health and life of the parents. It is proved in the second place because the ruler of the cusp of the 4th does not have force in the matter of parents except by reason of that cusp or the degree of the ecliptic occupying it, therefore there is a greater force for parents in that degree. For *on account of that, every single one such, and that more.*[152] It is most efficaciously proved in the third place because a malefic in the 12th house of the native's figure portends death to his children, in the 11th to his parents, and in the 10th to his brothers, as I have often observed. And the reason for this is that the ruler of the native's 12th is the 8th with respect to the 5th, which is [the house] of his children, and consequently when you have erected a figure from the cusp of the 5th for the children, that malefic will fall in the 8th. And similarly, the native's 11th house is the 8th with respect to the 4th, and the 10th house is also the 8th with respect to the 3rd, which correctly demonstrates that the figures of those persons must be erected from the cusps to which those persons belong, and not from the planets that are rulers, for a like signification is not found in them.

But against this [we can repeat] what was objected to above: it is absurd for a single figure to signify the same things for individual persons of the same class, such as individual wives, children, brothers, and both parents. I reply: the figure does not signify separately or particularly for the individual persons, but jointly and universally for all of them. And this signification is universally determined by the individual natal constitutions of these persons, and by the sympathy or antipathy of each of these with the native's figure and the figure extracted for the parents, the brothers, etc. And if both figures of the father, namely his natal chart and the extracted figure are unfortunate, it is certain that the father will become more unfortunate because of that extracted figure, and so with the others. And yet the sex of the sign or the planet occupying the 4th house in the native's figure will, however, distinguish the sex of the parent principally signified.

And from this it follows that if the same father has many children, his fates following the generation of the children will be moved forward by the genitures of

---

152 An unidentified axiom.

the individual children, according as the individual figures of the father extracted from their genitures will be concordant or discordant with the natal figure of the father; and the same thing must be judged in the case of the mother. And then in the case of the native who is going to have many brothers or many wives.

Besides, it seems that this should put an end to the difficulty of all astrology unless I am greatly mistaken. Namely, whether the figure, or celestial constitution of the native, works in parents, brothers, the spouse, etc., which neither Lucio Bellantio [in his book] against Pico, nor Junctinus in the book cited above, were able to resolve. And it is still more difficult to define how the native's celestial constitution can act in brothers, the spouse, friends, and enemies, since between these persons and the native there is no natural subordination, which at least is found among parents and children. Junctinus, in the book cited above, holds that the natural constitution of the child is as a particular, and the natal constitution of the father as a universal, which converts a particular into itself. And he says that a father begetting a child imprints upon it something of his own celestial constitution, and this is recognized afterward in the nativity of the child. And therefore the nativity of the child brings us into some acquaintance with the father, not as a cause, but as a sign, for it does not bring about the father's fate, but it [merely] signifies it.

But in fact this heaps up difficulties, none of which it resolves. For in the first place the universal cause and the particular cause are not of the same order, but the former is superior and the latter inferior, just as the Sun is with respect to man in the generation of another man, the annual revolution of the world with respect to lunations, and the figure of the nativity with respect to its revolutions, but the celestial constitutions of the father and the child are of the same order; that is, neither is inferior to the other, although one is posterior to the other in time.

Second, What does Junctinus mean when he says that the father's constitution, as a universal, converts into itself the particular constitution of the child? For there is no conversion of one into the other, but each one remains as it is. But if by "converts" he means "determines," then it is particular or posterior to determine a universal or prior thing, but not the other way around, as is plain in the case of lunations with respect to the annual revolutions of the world, and the annual revolutions of nativities with respect to the natal figure.

Third, if Junctinus would assert that the father could be known through that which is imprinted upon the child, it would be a valid argument; for it is certainly true that the father imprints something upon the child as its efficient cause, but he wants to know the father through the celestial constitution of the child, in which nothing was made by the father, and [consequently] no impression can be made. Therefore he does not resolve the difficulties that he stirs up here.

Lucio Bellantio on the other hand wants the posterior figures, such as those of children, to determine, to help, to impede, or to modify prior figures, such as those of fathers. Not in connection with all the fates of the father, but in connection with some, i.e., those following birth; but Junctinus confesses that he doesn't understand how this can be done. And then this same Bellantio plainly asserts the opposite, and holds that the effects of following figures can be helped, impeded, increased, or diminished by prior figures.

But since neither [opinion] is satisfactory, we must try to loosen this knot as follows. The celestial constitution of the father is the cause of the father and his fate or accidents by common agreement of astrologers, and the father is the cause of the child; therefore, the celestial constitution of the father is the cause of the child, according to the common axiom, *that which is the cause of the cause, is the cause of the thing caused.* Therefore, the father's constitution passes to the children, though with the father as intermediary. And having done this, it will assimilate them to itself as much as it can, for this is common to all causes; and through this assimilation, as [it manifests itself] in the native, some obscure likeness to such a cause may be detected in the native. But the native himself has immediately from his own figure what sort [of person] he is, and he has an obvious similitude to that figure, as is known to astrologers; therefore, there must be between the figures of the father and the child either some similitude or some fated connection, from which also the true father of the native is recognized, and consequently among the effects of these [figures], which [effects] are the father and the child; and this [can be seen] in personal fate as well as in external fate. But for the child, his own proper constitution, from which he immediately received the impression of his own fate, is very much more powerful; therefore, this is not converted from the father's constitution or determined by it, but conversely. And so I think I am satisfied [with the resolution] of this difficulty, at least for subordinated constitutions and persons, such as father and child.

But in fact this does not suffice. For the question is not only about parents and children, but about brothers, the spouse, servants, friends, and enemies, between whom and the native there is no natural subordination, and yet true predictions about these [persons] are made from the native's figure. What then should be said about them? Certainly recourse must be had to something universal that is applicable or common to the native as well as to them.

It could be said by some that God, Whose Providence the heavens and all things serve, brought forth the native into light through natural causes at that moment of the diurnal rotation of the *caelum* which, from the position of the stars in the *caelum* as well as in the genethliacal figure, most agreed with the native's temperament [as regards his] moral nature and mental qualities [on the one hand] and his own proper fate and [that which he shares] in common with his father, mother, brothers, spouse, children, etc.; and by consequence such a constitution signifies for the native himself, for his parents, for his spouse, etc. But, having conceded Divine Providence, which none of those things that are made in the world evade, and [acknowledging that] God acts through natural causes or with them, one always asks, by what natural cause and by what means the native's own fate, and the fate that [he shares in] common with other persons, is caused? To which question a suitable response is lacking.

It may be said by others that the celestial constitution is the cause of this—that [the native] may have such parents, brothers, spouse, children, etc.—and it subjects him passively to such accidents. But insofar as that constitution is referred to other persons, it is only a sign that they are going to be [persons] of such a sort in moral nature, life, fortune, and agreement with the native, as his genethliacal constitution is a cause to the native for his marriage with a noble, rich, or beautiful woman, for it subjects the native passively to this accident; but the native's figure is not the cause that the woman herself is noble, rich, or beautiful, for it does not bring about such a woman, [who is] generally older than the native; therefore it is only a sign. Similarly, for this native the cause that he may have friends among kings and princes is his celestial constitution; but this constitution does not makes his friends kings; therefore, with respect to them it is not the cause, but only a sign; and the reasoning is the same with the rest. Therefore, in the case of the spouse, children, servants, and friends it seems that one should not inquire from the native's figure what sort [of persons] these are going to be in sex, form, character, fortune, and the rest of the accidents proper to them, but only what sort of [persons] they are going to be with respect to the native, such as whether servants or friends are going to be faithful or useful; but this is not altogether satisfactory. For if the native's figure is only a sign of such a future spouse or of future friends, but the signification itself, i.e., such a marriage, is some effect that cannot lack its own cause, what will be its effective cause? Besides, the father's natal figure is not only a sign with respect to children, namely that they may be of a certain sort in their life, moral nature, and fortune, but it is also their cause, as was said above—namely, that the father generates in accordance with his own constitution received from the stars; here then that universal that fits all cases is lacking up to this point. But having considered these things with as much attention as I could, I think that such a difficulty can be resolved as follows. Certainly, in the truth of the matter, the genethliacal constitution of the native subjects him first to his own proper fate, or the accidents of life, moral nature, mental qualities, actions, profession, assets, etc., then to that [which he shares] in common with other persons according to the strength and quality of his own figure. Moreover, the native's own fate is from his nativity first and per se, but there are two kinds of common fate—namely that which is properly common which is participated in equally by the native and by another person, such as a duel, a friendship, marriage, or quarrel, and that which is improperly common which is not participated in equally by the native and another person, such as those of brothers, parents, the wife, or the death of children before the native, or friends' misfortune. For these accidents are common to the native in this respect: that by the death of his parents, brothers, or spouse he loses something: namely, these persons that belong to him, as is related afterwards. But already, in common accidents of the first kind, such as that the native is going to marry a beautiful woman, three things must be noticed: namely, the native himself, the wife he is going to marry, and the marriage of both. The native's marriage to a beautiful wife is caused by the native's nativity subjecting him efficiently to that accident; but the figure, which is generally later in time, is not the cause of the wife's beauty but is only a sign of it; for her beauty comes from her own nativity, the cause per se. But that they should marry, whether freely or unwillingly, is the product of the astral consensus of their genethliacal figures to such an effect, as we have already said in Book 21, Sect. 2, Chapt. 13., and neither of the figures accomplishes this by itself, for just as such a wife is signified for the native, so in turn such a husband is signified for such a wife by her own nativity. Moreover, it is not apparent in his nativity, at least to human intelligence, that the native is going to marry a beautiful wife as number so-and-so [of his wives]. Consequently it is rightly said in the *Centiloquy that only those inspired by a divinity can predict particulars.* In fact demons know not only the native's chart, but also the chart of a beautiful woman whose nativity is more agreeable to his, and the circumstances of location, lineage, etc., yet they do not know for certain whether the native is going to marry this particular one because in fact the concourse of these individuals is subject to the secret Providence of God. But because demons diligently observe the practice, in natural things at least, of the ordinary Providence of God [acting] through second-ary causes, it happens from this that very often by a subtle conjecture they arrive at a preconception of individual effects; and so in a dream or in a mirror or otherwise they show virgins practicing certain superstitions for this purpose the true vision or image of a husband never before seen, as a certain duchess, outstanding in beauty and mental qualities, told me had happened to her. And the reasoning is the same with the rest.

But in common accidents of the second kind, such as that the wife, children, or brothers should die before [the native] or be elevated [in rank], of course the natal figure of the person to whom such good or evil happens is the principal cause per se of the accident, but the native's figure is only a sign, or at most an accidental cause, i.e., insofar as the native is passively subjected by his own figure to accidents of that sort, in which he either loses or gains something and is consequently disposed to fortune or misfortune in connection with such persons—of which passive subjection and disposition in the native, his own figure is the cause per se for him. Therefore, the effect is also, as [mentioned] above, from the common consensus of the figures, by which these make their influx into it; and consequently all accidents that the native has in common with other persons are efficiently [produced] by the common consent of the figures to those accidents. In fact it is apparent from this, because the more strongly these things are signified in the native's figure, the more certain it is that they will happen to those persons; which certainly argues that the native's figure brings some influx to the common effect. Besides, since the effect is made by the common signification and consensus of the figures, it is necessary for both of them to have an influx upon it. From which it is plain that the native's figure acts as a significator and a universal cause of all those things that pertain to the native himself, whether they are proper to him, or whether they are in common with other persons; but in common [accidents] the [cause] is determined by the figures of the other persons in the manner of universal causes.

And this is my opinion about this difficulty, but if anyone offers a better one, I shall willingly embrace it.

But it can be asked whether those things that are signified for the native concerning his parents, spouse, children, servants, etc., either in them, or by them, or, on the contrary, those things that are signified for those persons by the native's figure will always happen?

I reply first that the more strongly they are signified in the native's figure, the more certain they will be; and the more weakly they are signified, the more uncertain they will be. Second, they will not always and inevitably occur, but only as [we might say] usually and contingently. For the things signified do not happen unless they are given to that person and unless they concur actively or passively in the effect. But there is no necessary cause that they should be given, but only a contingent one; and consequently they are not inevitable, but only a hypothetical and conjectural prediction can be made about them. For example, if misfortunes are strongly signified for someone from his wife, he will, if he marries, very probably experience such things. And so with the rest. Moreover, the concourse of contingencies is from the secret Providence of God, also through secondary causes, and especially through universal ones; [and] the celestial causes that subject particular sublunar events to themselves are of this sort.

Having settled [these matters] thus, now the following general rules may be noted.

First, since it was said above that the 4th cusp, its ruler, and then the planets that are in the 4th are significators of the parents, therefore if the ruler of the cusp or another planet is on that cusp, there will arise from this a much more effective significator, whether for directions for the native or for a new figure for those persons themselves, than would be the case if the cusp and its ruler were separated and seen in different places: *For a united virtue is stronger than a divided one.*

Second, if the significators are separated for the parents, or the wife, or someone else, the circle of position will have to be found for each of them and individual directions established for the native. For from these and from an astrological speculum of the aspects, the particular accidents of the native involving these persons, and hence involving their own fates will be more abundantly and evidently apparent; but in figures erected from cusps [alone], the proper accidents of these persons may be known, at least in a general way, [as they are] contained in the native's figure.

Third, since the Sun and Saturn are analogous to fathers and husbands, and the Moon and Venus to mothers and wives, Jupiter and Venus to brothers and children, Saturn and Mars to enemies, etc. (for each planet is said to be analogous to those things that it brings, not to those that it takes away), for this reason the proper significators of parents, brothers, etc.—significators by determination— when they are [also] analogous to those things [they signify], will be especially significative of those same persons. From which it perhaps happened that they were once taken to be the primary and true significators [of those persons], especially since analogous [planets], if they are also determined, produce effects in connection with those persons that are much greater than [those produced by] the others.

Fourth, when several planets are in the same 4th house, or in the 7th, etc., notice which of them is the strongest in that house, or the closest to the cusp, or which is analogous in its signification, and choose that one for the principal significator among the planets; but do not despise the ruler of the house, for it is more powerful than the rest [of the planets in the house].

Fifth, the individual significators of the parents, the spouse, the children, etc. signify only generally for those persons, and not every significator for every person. For the native has only one father and one mother with whom he can have a natural connection, and yet there can be 5 or 6 significators of parents, namely the cusp of the 4th, two or three rulers of the 4th, and 3 or 4 planets in the 4th. But on the contrary there can be 15 or 20 brothers or children, and there cannot be that many significators of children or brothers; therefore, whether there is one significator of parents or several, they can only signify generally, both for the native about his parents, and for the parents themselves, at least insofar as they refer to the proper fates of those persons. But the more significators there are, the more things they will signify about the parents, brothers, etc. And yet a planet which by sex and analogy agrees more with the father will signify more particularly for the father, and one that agrees more with the mother will signify more particularly for the mother. And the reasoning is the same in the case of brothers, children, servants, etc. in which the sex of the planets and the signs will have to be admitted for discerning the sex of the persons.

Sixth, in a figure erected for the parents, proper fates should not be sought for the father and the mother in connection with the individual houses—riches, brothers, parents, children, etc., although Cardan wants to do this. For this figure is not that of one person only, but of more than one, namely of the father and the mother, and therefore common to both and proper to neither; therefore, one will have to pronounce only universally and indiscriminately about their fates from this figure. And the Ascendant and its ruler will have to be especially noted. Namely, whether the ruler is in the 7th, 8th, 10th, etc. of that figure; and according to this one will judge about parents in a general way as if in the native's figure, for if in that figure the ruler of the Ascendant is in the 5th, the parents, or one of them, will have other children; if in the 7th, they will have lawsuits, or one of them will marry again; if in the 8th, they will die before the native, etc. And in this figure directions cannot be made for the particular accidents of one of these parents, such as marriage, children, dignities, death, etc., as in the native's figure; for that would be extracting proper and particular fates from a common figure, which was rejected above. And the same thing must be said about [figures for] the spouse, the brothers, etc.; therefore, directions of these significators are only made for the native's particular accidents in connection with these persons, from which some general conjecture can be made as to what is going to come to light for them in the future, as was said above, or, in sum, for the accidents of these persons only indiscriminately and universally, unless some means of distinguishing them becomes known from some other source, as from the sex of the sign or the planet occupying the cusp.

Seventh, among the significators of persons, i.e., of parents, the spouse, brothers, etc. the cusp is the primary significator, as is also plain in the case of the native, for whom the Ascendant is the primary significator. And yet it cannot be said that judgment should be made about individual persons of the same order (as of individual brothers) from a single significator, whether it is a cusp or a planet. For otherwise the same thing would have to be predicted for the native from each of his children or brothers, or if from extracted figures the fates of persons were predicted, they would be the same for the individual brothers, or children, or for the father and the mother, or for individual wives, because the significators of these persons in the native's nativity are not changed. Moreover, this is contrary to experience. Since, therefore, a plurality of figures extracted for parents has been rejected by us above, it is sufficient to say that the individual significators of the parents signify only generally and indiscriminately for both parents; and that the native's figure and those things which are deduced from it are like a material or something universal with respect to other persons, but their own figures are like a particular form. For the native's figure signifies only generally good or evil for the parents, the spouse, the children, etc. by reason of the state of the significators, and this general signification will be confirmed or refuted by the natal horoscope of each one, and it overcomes them if they are contrary to itself. But for the native himself it signifies particularly those things which are going to happen to him in connection with those persons, as was said above.

Eight, all directions of the significators begin from the native's birth, and not the directions for the spouse from the time when he marries, or the directions for children from the time when he begins to have children; for the force of the directions is not imprinted upon the father, the spouse, the children, the brothers, etc., but upon the native through the first natural and successive revolution which is made from the moment of the nativity. And by reason of this impression, all the effects of the directions pertain and are referred to the native first and per se, as particular effects happening to him in connection with the subjects of each of the significators of those [persons], whether it is the father, the brothers, the spouse, etc. And therefore when the 7th cusp is directed before marriage for a native not yet of marriageable age, it only signifies about enemies and lawsuits or about contracts; but for a native of marriageable age it signifies whether he will marry or not, then it signifies about a wife, lawsuits, enemies, contracts, and, through its opposition, about life. But after marriage it is directed for accidents involving the wife, lawsuits, enemies, and contracts; and after the wife's death it can be directed for a new wife; but always moving forward the cusp of the 7th or its ruler by directions to other promittors; otherwise the same accidents would be signified with [each of] the individual wives and with equal intervals of time from the moment of each marriage, if for the individual [wives] the cusp of the 7th or its ruler were to be directed to the promittors next following itself.

Ninth, for every person it is especially necessary to know the natal figures of those with whom he is associated by any connection, whether they are parents, or brothers, or spouse, or children, or servants, or friends, or enemies, so that he may understand the consensus or disagreement of these with his own figure for good or evil, and consequently be able to foresee whom he should trust and from whom he may have hopes or whom he should fear for his own safety and advantage.

It can be objected about the things predicted that the directions of the significators of the father, the spouse, the brothers, etc. made for particular accidents of the native involving these persons ought to be as certain as the directions of the Midheaven for the things signified by the 10th house in the natal figure, or of the ruler of the 2nd for riches, etc. For the general procedure is the same for [all] the individual significators of the natal chart. But the directions of the Midheaven are certain in these effects, so why shouldn't the particular fates of these persons be known with equal certainty? For they are common to them and to the native, for when the native's wife dies, the native himself loses his own wife; therefore, the particular fates of these persons can be known through the directions.

But I reply that it is false that directions of the significators of the father, the spouse, etc. are as certain in their effects, insofar as those persons are particularly or commonly involved, as the directions of the Midheaven for the things signified by the 10th house. For the parents have their own genethliacal figures, to which they are more subject than to the native's figure; but the things signified by the 10th house do not have their own proper figure different from the native's figure; and consequently they are more subject to the latter than are the parents, the spouse, etc., and especially for accidents that are not properly common to the native himself, such as for the death of the wife or the father.

Moreover, it must be carefully noted that when we speak here about the fate of the native and the fates of other persons closely related to him, such as his father, brother, spouse, enemies, etc., we are speaking only about fates to be predicted from the directions of those significators or from extracted figures; but not about other things that are generally predicted from the planets that are significators of persons, from the fact that they are in this or that house of the native's figure, according as the signification of the house is referred to the native. For example, the ruler of the 4th in the 11th will signify that a parent is a friend to the native before all others; but because the 11th is the 8th from the cusp of the 4th, for which cusp, if the figure of the father is extracted, the ruler itself will be found in the 8th, consequently it presages a short life for the father. Moreover, it must be distinguished what the planets that are significators of persons signify, both as they are determined in the native's figure and in the figure that is extracted for parents, the spouse, etc. Yet it can be said that when these planets are directed in the natal figure, they are directed for those things that they signify for the native, both by reason of their bodily position and by their rulership; therefore, in directions one must take nto account the scheme of all those things that they can signify particularly for the native himself and also those that they can signify for these persons by reason of their own determination in the extracted figure.

But, so that the truth of the doctrine we have given above may be set forth more plainly, we shall append some examples of nativities taken from Junctinus in which he judges falsely about the quality of the parents, fortune, and death from the universal significators Saturn and the Sun, but in which we judge much more correctly from particular significators[153] or determinations. His figures and judgments may be seen in the chapter of his book cited above,[154] but the following [judgments] are ours.

In the nativity of Pietro de' Medici (p. 154) Venus is ruler of the 4th in Aquarius, a masculine sign,[155] and its ruler Saturn, analogous to the father and masculine, was in the masculine sign Gemini. And consequently the father was signified by these [positions] rather than the mother, and he was [a man] of outstanding moral nature and famous because of Venus, which applied to Saturn by trine. But because Saturn was with the Eye of Taurus,[156] a violent fixed [star], and square the Sun, it therefore signified a short life for the father.[157]

In the nativity of Giuliano de' Medici on the same page, The Sun, Mercury, and the Part of Fortune are in Aries in the 4th house, and the Sun, masculine and analogous, occupies the cusp exalted. And indeed from this a truly illustrious father was signified, especially because the Sun was in partile trine to the Moon. But because Mars, ruler of the Sun and the 4th was also ruler of the 11th, which is the 8th from the 4th, and consequently the ruler of the 8th in the figure extracted from the cusp of the 4th in the right sphere,[158] and Mars is in the antiscion of Saturn;

---

153 That is, from *accidental* significators.

154 Morin does not give the charts, but I have put them in Appendix 3 as they are cited from Junctinus's *Speculum astrologiae* in Alan Leo's *Notable Nativities*. They contain a number of errors, a few of which I have noted in the Appendix, but Morin evidently used them as he found them. *NN* does not give the birth times, so I have had to establish them from the house cusps. They may, therefore, differ by a few minutes from the times given by Junctinus.

155 Giuntini's chart shows Venus in 1 Aquarius, but actually it was in 29 Capricorn, a feminine sign, which somewhat reduces the validity of Morin's argument.

156 Aldebaran or Alpha Tauri, which was in 3 Gemini in 1472.

157 Pietro II's father was Lorenzo the Magnificent (1449-1492), who died of gout at the age of 43.

158 As Morin directed above, an extracted chart should be erected for the pole of the house from which it is extracted, not for the pole of the place (the latitude of the place). The pole of the 4th house is zero, so a chart extracted from it will have cusps as shown in a table of houses for $0°$ latitude (the *right sphere* in the older terminology). Note that this is contrary to the usual procedure in horary astrology, where the houses are simply renumbered and the original cusps remain unchanged.

consequently a short life was signified for the father; and these two were broth-ers.[159]

In the nativity of Lorenzo de' Medici, Duke of Urbino,[160] Mars ruler of the 4th was conjoined to Jupiter in Leo, which signified an illustrious father; besides, the Sun and the Moon had their exaltations in the 4th, and they were in mutual trine. But because Mars was also ruler of the 11th as above, that is of the 8th in the figure extracted from the 4th cusp in the right sphere, which is the principal significator of parents, and it was opposed to Saturn, a short life was consequently portended for the father—I say the father, rather than the mother, because Aries in the 4th and Mars, its ruler, are masculine.

In the nativity of Catherine de Medici (daughter of the abovesaid Lorenzo), who married Henry II, King of France, the Moon and Jupiter, rulers of the 4th, were conjunct, and their ruler, Venus, is in Taurus with the Sun; and consequently the nobility of the parents will be indicated. But because Mars was in its fall in the 4th, square the Moon and Jupiter, and opposed to Saturn, ruler of the 11th, her mother survived her [birth] by only one day, and her father by two days, as if paying a penalty for the birth of his offspring;[161] for this woman was of bad morals, as her figure indicates, notwithstanding the touch of Venus in the Ascendant and in Taurus with the Sun, which made her very famous; and she was also very pernicious. Would that before the King of France had married he had consulted a learned astrologer about her nativity and his; for he would have seen that a violent death was strongly portended—both from his own nativity, in which the Sun in the 1st is afflicted by the squares of Saturn and Mars, then by the opposition of Jupiter, ruler of the 8th, but also in the nativity of this woman, in which Mars, ruler of the 7th and consequently significator of her husband, was afflicted by the opposition of Saturn and the squares of Jupiter and the Moon, then the square of Mercury, which was ruler of the 2nd, i.e., ruler of the 8th of the figure extracted for the husband from the cusp of the 7th. Certainly, that figure of Catherine de Medici is frightful, whence it is no wonder that it was unfavorable for the parents and the husband; and such a consensus of the figures of Henry and Catherine herself caused Henry's death in accordance with the doctrine set forth above. Therefore, let these kings and princes consult astrologers when contracting matrimony, undertaking wars, entering battles, and things of similar moment—not ignorant astrologers to be sure, but those distinguished by their learning and experience, and experts in fate,

159 Giuliano II was a younger brother of Pietro II de' Medici.
160 The son of Pietro II de' Medici and a grandson of Lorenzo the Magnificent.
161 These intervals are not quite correct: Catherine's mother, Madeleine de la Tour d'Auvergne, died on 29 April; and her father, Lorenzo II de' Medici, died on 5 May. Shortly after Lorenzo's death, his mother, Alfonsina Orsini, and his aunt, Maddalena de' Medici Cibò, died. In fact, Catherine's only remaining close relation was her father's sister, Clarice, the wife of Filippo Strozzi. At the age of 6 months Catherine was entrusted to this aunt, who raised her until she was 6 years old.

without the knowledge of which the greatest errors are wont to occur in royal councils and in the administration of the kingdom, so that on this account the Secret Council of the most powerful King of the Chinese should be greatly praised, since no one is admitted to it who is not an astrologer—but this is only mentioned incidentally.

In the nativity of Ottavio Farnese on p. 156 the Moon was ruler of the 4th, and its ruler, Jupiter, in the Ascendant and in Aries, and Venus, ruler of the Sun, in partile trine to the cusp of the 4th; and consequently, illustrious parents were signified. But because the Moon was conjunct Saturn, ruler of the 11th, i.e., of the 8th in the figure extracted from the 4th cusp; a premature death, which was also violent, was consequently presaged for him.[162]

In the nativity of Francis, Grand Duke of Florence, the Moon is the ruler of the 4th, conjunct Venus in Pisces, afflicted by Mars and Saturn,[163] ruler of the 11th. And the Sun was exalted in the 1st, which is the 10th of the figure extracted from the cusp of the 4th. Therefore, this nativity signified the glory and princely status of the father.[164]

Whoever wishes to do so can apply the doctrine given above to other genitures, and he will find it agreeing with the truth. And from the genitures explained here and the abovesaid general doctrine the following particular rules can be deduced.

1. If the Sun and Saturn, analogous to fathers, or the Moon and Venus, analogous to mothers, are in the 4th, or are rulers of the 4th, they strongly signify parents before all other [planets].

2. If the 4th or its ruler is well disposed, it will be good for the parents; if evilly disposed, it will be evil for their life and fortune.

3. Planets in the 4th or rulers of the 4th exalted, and especially the Sun and the Moon, signify the parents' nobility; but if, on the contrary, they are in their fall, it is very bad, and they give at least fathers-in-law[165] of inferior condition.

4. If Saturn or the Sun is ruler of the 4th, or is well disposed and in aspect to the 4th and applying to an exalted planet, it will be fortunate for the parents, especially if that planet is ruler of the 4th house.

5. The same [planet] ruler of the 4th and the 11th, or the 8th in the extracted figure, or the ruler of the 4th with the ruler of the 11th, especially configured with

---

162 That is, for his father, Pierluigi (1503-1547), Duke of Parma and Piacenza, who was murdered in his bed on 10 September 1547 by political enemies acting under orders of the Emperor Charles V. Interestingly, Duke Ottavio's wife was Margherita, an illegitimate daughter of Charles V, and Duke Pierluigi was the son of Pope Paul III (1468-1549).

163 I fail to see how the Moon in 18 Pisces or Venus in 12 Pisces is afflicted by Mars in 27 Aries opposite Saturn in 25 Libra.

164 His father was Cosimo I de' Medici (1519-1574), Grand Duke of Tuscany.

165 See Rule 7 below.

a malefic, either by body or by malefic aspect, shortens the life of the parents. And the ruler of the 4th in the 11th, or the ruler of the 11th in the fourth, does the same thing.

6. The ruler of the 4th in the 1st, which is the 10th in the extracted figure, or the ruler of the 1st in the 4th, especially well disposed, exalted, and analogous, presages an illustrious fortune for and the elevation of the parents.

7. What is said here about parents should similarly be understood about brothers, the spouse, children, etc. And if the native rejects marriage, or has only one brother, or one wife, or one child, the fate of his progenitors, or his brother, or his wife,[166] or his children will appear more evidently and distinctly from his natal figure than if he has many such persons of the same order. And I call "persons of the same order" those who belong to the same house, such as the father, grandfather, father-in-law, and uncle to the 4th; brothers and relations[167] to the 3rd; children and grandchildren to the 5th. In fact, I believe that all these persons should be divided into only three orders, viz. those who are superior, equal, and inferior to the native. Of the first order are the father, grandfather, father-in-law, and uncle; of the second, brothers and relations; and of the third, children and grandchildren. And it must be noted that accidents that are signified by the natal figure to happen to the father-in-law or the spouse must only be understood to be going to happen after they have actually become [the native's] father-in-law or wife; and so with the other relatives by marriage.

8. By way of conclusion, it must be noted here that when a figure for the father has been erected in the manner we have specified, a figure for the grandfather must not be erected from it. Nor from a figure for the grandfather, another for the great-grandfather. Both because the father, grandfather, great-grandfather belong to the same 4th house of the native's figure, and also because there is a common influx of the *caelum* upon the native for these persons, it [consequently] touches only the closest ones effectively or noticeably, but in the remoter ones it fades out.

Chapt. 7. *Whether at the Native's Death there is a Cessation of the Celestial Influx from his Natal Figure upon his Parents, Brothers, Spouse, Children, and other Persons Belonging to him and Surviving him.*

This question, it seems to me, is the most subtle in all astrology, and one of no little importance, especially in connection with astrological interrogations.[168]

---

166 The Latin text has *fratris uxoris* 'brother's wife', but this is a blunder for *fratris, aut uxoris* 'brother, or wife'.

167 Principally, cousins.

168 Horary questions, treated in Book 26.

Indeed, it seems that it ought to be asserted that that influx ceases. For at the moment of the native's geniture his children are not yet [born], nor possibly his wife [or] brothers, and his father can [already] be dead; consequently, these persons have not received the celestial influx relating to themselves, but only the native has received the influx [that indicates] that he is going to have parents, brothers, a spouse, etc., of a certain sort; consequently, this influx is inherent only in the native; from which it follows that, with the native dead, that influx is extinguished, or leaves off.

But on the other hand it seems that it must be denied that it ceases. For if from the native's figure a violent death is signified for the wife whom he is going to marry, and, with her husband dead, she has no further risk of a violent death or other presages of her own figure extracted from the husband's nativity, it is plain that those presages were groundless both before and after the native's death, which, however, must not be asserted, since it is certain that the native's figure does signify for such persons, because otherwise the effects of the houses of parents, brothers, the spouse, etc., would be groundless.

So then this question seems to me capable of being resolved with a few [considerations] from what was already said in Chapt. 6. [For] when the native dies, that influx certainly ceases to be or leaves off that was impressed on him by the *caelum* in his nativity with regard to accidents that are particularly his or that he shares in common with such persons. But the source of that influx, i.e., the virtue of the celestial figure, remaining in the *primum mobile* through determination, and acting upon the native during his life through the correspondence with the similar figure impressed upon that same native, although it may cease to act upon the deceased native, nevertheless does not then lose its force upon those persons, insofar as they were [related] to that native, but [in fact] retains it for so long as all these persons live—relics, as it were, of the native himself [and] participants in his fate. And although this virtue may be very slight in comparison with the virtue of the proper geniture of each of these persons, as if [when] the wife's figure is lacking in the signs of violent death, but the husband's figure presages the contrary, she will not die violently on this account, because of course everyone depends more upon his own fate than on someone else's; yet, if both the wife's own figure and her figure extracted from the nativity of her husband should signify a violent death, then she will all the more certainly perish by a violent death. And if this is still signified for her by a figure extracted from the figure of her own brother, or from that of some one of her children, it will be a presage even more to be feared. And this solution, in addition to the fact that it is agreeable to reason, also confirms its truth by experience.

SECTION V

In Which Objections against the Doctrine of Directions are Considered and Disproved.

Chapt. 1. *Pico Mirandola's Objections to Astrological Directions and the Refutation of those Objections.*

Since nothing in astrology is more worthy of admiration than the evident effects of directions, nothing has hitherto been more obscure or confused in the explanation of its causes and in the variety of opinions. It would certainly by surprising if the haters of this divine science had left this part of it untouched by their teeth—this part by which both the types and the times of future events are predicted, which for that reason must be considered to be the crown of all astrology. And if many of the leading astrologers have been deceived with regard to the the doctrine of directions, what must we expect from those ignorant of it, such as Pico della Mirandola, Alessandro de Angelis, Sixtus ab Hemminga, and such like persons when they subject and condemn it to their own examination? Nothing more than the absurd things that we have already refuted here.

And so Pico della Mirandola,[169] in Book 7, Chapt. 7, supposes *That if the Ascendant is in 15 Leo, and Saturn is in 6 Virgo, that since the Ascendant is distant from Saturn by 21 degrees, the astrologers contend that the first degree of its distance from the Ascendant ought to be the first year; the second degree, the second year; and so on; then it would be that the 21st year would be dangerous from the rays of Saturn and would threaten the danger of death to the native. This is (he says) the position astrologers take on directions. From which Ptolemy pronounces on the length of life and the whole crowd of astrologers pronounce all the accidents and changes of fortune.*

But with this, Pico already imposes upon astrologers, and especially on Ptolemy. For that position on directions is by equal degrees of the ecliptic without latitude, contrary to the opinion of Ptolemy and the wiser astrologers, as we have taught previously. Besides, it is false that they attribute the first degree of the distance to the first year, and from this judge about that, as Pico will have it, and then about the second year from the second degree; but [the astrologers] only measure the equatorial distance between the circles of position of the significator

---

169 Giovanni II Pico (1463-1494), Lord of Mirandola (usually called Pico della Mirandola), Italian humanist. His book *Disputations Against Astrology* was published posthumously at Bologna in 1496. It is divided into twelve books whose contents are summarized by Lynn Thorndike, *History of Magic and Experimental Science* 4, Chapt. LXI (pp. 529-543).

and the promittor, and if this is 21 degrees, they say that in his 21st year or thereabouts the native will be seized with a sickness, with no account taken of the intermediate degrees between the two termini, whose effect will only happen in the 21st year. But Pico didn't understand this.[170]

But then against the doctrine of directions Pico rises up thus in his own manner with exclamations devoid of reason. *What can be thought to be more frivolous, more irrational? For in the first place, this distribution of the degrees to the years—is it not made rather arbitrarily, especially since the division of the signs into 30 degrees depends entirely upon the judgment of the mathematicians that that number is more convenient for arithmetical divisions?*

To this, I reply that the division of the *caelum* into 12 signs is not fictitious, but natural, as we have shown in Book 12, Sect. 1, Chapt. 4, but a division of the signs into 30 degrees or the whole of the ecliptic or the equator into 360 degrees is in fact artificial for convenience in calculation, since if a natural division [taken] from the Sun with its 365 and 1/4 days had been instituted for the zodiac or the equator, it would have been too inconvenient.[171] But in Sect. 3, Chapt. 3, we said that the measure of a year is not a whole degree, but only the mean diurnal [motion] of the Sun, which we proved there to be real and to have a value of only 59'08", 365 1/4 of which are equivalent to 360 degrees, into which the circumference of the *caelum* is divided. Consequently, the division of the arc of direction into years in this manner is not fictitious. But if one questions even further as to why the diurnal [motion] of the Sun is equivalent to one year, let him see Chapt. 5 of that same section.

But then he exclaims thus again and asks, *How can Saturn placed in 6 Scorpio when I was born harm me, even if we grant to the astrologers that its influx in the 21st year pertains to me? For at the time when it will pertain to me, Saturn will not be there.[172] And when Saturn will be there, that degree will not pertain to me.*

But I reply that it is no wonder that Pico was unable to conceive how Saturn in the abovesaid hypothesis could bring harm in the 21st year from the nativity, for he has completely ignored the mode of action of the stars, in the nativity as well as in directions, which we explained in detail above. For it is not necessary that it remain in the same place that it occupied at birth, so that the place itself might make

---

170 Pico may have erred only in putting the cart before the horse: by giving a specific instance first (Ascendant to the conjunction of Saturn), followed by a general statement (the first degree following the Ascendant corresponds to the first year of life). If so, then both of his statments are true. But Morin assumes (perhaps merely to disagree with him) that he meant that the specific influence of the direction to Saturn begins in the native's first year and continues until his 21st year, which is of course contrary to the theory of directions.

171 It was in fact tried by the Chinese, but eventually abandoned.

172 Since Saturn's period is 29 1/2 years, at age 21 it would be in dexter trine or square to its natal position, rather than in conjunction with it.

its influx upon the native, but only that in the nativity that part[173] of the *caelum* was determined by Saturn to its nature with respect to the native, having taken into consideration its own celestial and terrestrial state. This being the case, the Saturnine influx of that part [of the *caelum*] will pertain to the native, not only in the 21st year from his birth, but throughout the whole course of his life, as is demonstrated by the transits of the planets over that place or part. Nor is it necessary that in the 21st year, when the effect of the direction of the Ascendant to the radical place of Saturn is produced, Saturn should be there in substance (although this would be efficacious), but only virtually through its previously mentioned determination. But when he says "when Saturn will be there, that part will not pertain to me," Pico himself doesn't know why he says that. For by the transits of the planets over it that part is proved to pertain to the native throughout his whole life. But perhaps he understood that then there will not be a 21st year from the native's birth, to enable effect of the direction to be produced through the influx of this part and Saturn. But the effect of the direction is not produced by Saturn's transit through that part, but by the concourse of the Ascendant as significator and that part as promittor, whether Saturn is in that part or whether it is not, as we have explained in detail previously.

After this he says, *If the astrologers should say that just as clothes infected by a pestilence do not lose[174] their poison at some particular time, so also it may happen in the case of the parts of the* caelum *that they may retain for a long time the contagion received from an evil star.* Pico replies *that if the philosophers had this saying, it would order them to remember that the affection of light does not remain in the subject, but departs with the body from which it emanated. And light is the vehicle and the fomentation of all these celestial impressions, as Avicenna says in his [account] of meteors.*

But I reply. Pico and Avicenna[175] were ignorant of this celestial philosophy. For it is not by [the action of] Saturn that the force is impressed upon those parts of the *caelum* in which it formally inheres, as a pestilence impresses its poison upon the clothes. But only the part of the *caelum* in which Saturn is present at the moment of the nativity is determined to the nature of Saturn with respect to the native for as long as he may live subject to the influences of the stars. But consequently that force of Saturn is only virtually present in that part through its determination, as has been very often said and proved elsewhere. But [as for] Pico's statement that "light is the vehicle and fomentation of all the impressions" or celestial influxes,

---

173 Here, and in what follows, both Pico and Morin use *pars* 'part' as well as *gradus* (literally, 'step') for "degree." I have preserved the distinction, since the word 'part' seems to emphasize the idea that a degree is a part of the *caelum*, although (at least in Pico's case) it may be merely a classicism (the Greek word for degree is *moira* 'part', and both Manilius and Firmicus use it's Latin equivalent *pars*.)

174 *Amittunt* 'lose' instead of *admittunt* 'admit'.

175 Ibn Sina (c. 979-1037) was primarily a philosopher and physician.

we have plainly proved this to be false in Book 11, Chapt. 13, where we have discussed light in opposition to Pico. And its falsity is plainly evident from the fact that planets and stars when they are under the earth—indeed the Sun and the Moon when they are above the horizon—experience total eclipses and with [some] duration[176] and yet they powerfully influence the earth and men being born in accordance with their own formal forces and their proper natures, no less than when they shine above the horizon, as should be well known to everyone, even to an astrological tyro. Besides, the planets, the Sun excepted, do not shine with their own light but only reflect the light of the Sun.

Pico continues in this fashion, *The astrologers say in reply that when it comes to the same degree* (i.e., Saturn's place mentioned above) *there is an advent of the other planets in the same number of intervening years* (viz., 21); *do they think that that virus can be abolished or lessened by the arrival of salutary lights?*

I reply that the force of Saturn, which is present by determination in the abovesaid part, can neither be diminished nor abolished by the transit of the other planets over that part so long as [Saturn's] efficacious determination lasts, and it will last as long as the subject with respect to which it was allotted a determination, that is as long as the native remains in the nature of things, subject to that determination and to the influences of the stars. And when Mars, during the life of the native, transits over the abovesaid place of Saturn, the native will suffer from [the effects of] Mars by reason of its own nature and its determination in the native's figure, according to the force of Saturn's place which it is crossing, as will be related in more detail when we take up the subject of transits specifically. And the same reasoning applies to the rest of the planets when they make a transit—always with the virtue of Saturn in that part surviving by determination throughout the whole life of the native.

Again Pico rises [to the issue] thus: *If the qualities accepted and received from the stars do endure in the regions of the* caelum *and are not confined to a narrow space of time, it will not only have to be observed in fates what planet is found in what place of the* caelum *either in the current year or in the hour of the geniture, but also which [planets] have passed over these same places in the preceding years.*

But I reply that this is not necessary, and in fact it is absolutely contrary to the principles of astrology. For the places of the planets preceding the nativity were not determined with respect to the native, as the abovesaid place of Saturn; thus indeed such a determination of the parts of the *caelum* is made only at the moment of the nativity for the individual places of the planets and their aspects and the cusps of the figure. And Pico's scheme would be valid if the virtues of the planets were

---

176 I suppose Morin is referring to the duration of totality in eclipses. The maximum duration of a total lunar eclipse is about 1 hour and 40 minutes, but of a total solar eclipse only about 7 minutes and 30 seconds. His point is that, if the influence of a planet depends upon its light, planets and stars would have no influence while they were under the earth (roughly 50 percent of the time), and to make matters worse the Sun and Moon would lose their influence when eclipsed above the earth.

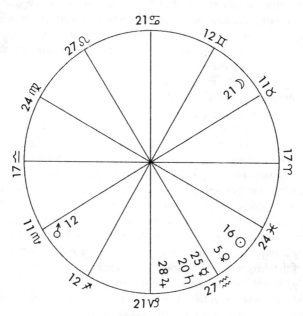

Giovanni Pico della Mirandola
Mirandola 45°N
24 Feb 1463, 8:22 PM – 17 Nov 1494
Firenze
NN 462

Figure 5

impressed upon the parts of the *caelum* and became formally inherent in them, but this is hardly the case, as we have explained before.

Finally, (he says) *this invention of directing is nothing other than to subject things not only to the constellations which are* (supply: 'at the time of the geniture'), *but also to those which will be. For what else is it to say that the Moon, which at my birth was moving away from the sextile rays of the Sun,*[177] *is, however, going to produce a misfortune at some time then from the square aspect of the Sun, which [the Moon] was not in fact under when I was born; but it would have been if it had stood more distant from the Sun with more parts interjected; which parts* (namely, those by which it was distant from the square radiation), *when it passes over [them] after a certain number of years from it, will that calamity be inflicted?*

---

177 An actual reference to his own chart (see below).

But that constellation was not [in effect] at the time of my origin; and if it is going to be [in effect] at some time afterwards, [it will] nevertheless [mean] nothing to me; for whom, if there is any fate, the previous disposition of the caelum *gave it. It is plain, therefore, how absurd, how false, how unsuitable the proposition of directing is, which the astrologers use daily.*[178]

But I reply that Pico, because of his lack of understanding of astrology, has involved himself more and more in the entanglements of falsity. In the first place, because he supposes that in a direction the Moon, the significator, or the force of its radical place, is moved to the promittor, the square of the Sun. But we have shown this to be false in Sect. 3, Chapt. 1. Second, because it is false that astrologers, by directions, subject things or the native to constellations that are not [in effect at the time of birth], but can be [in the future], since [in actuality] they will only subject him by directions to the constellations or celestial causes that are [present] at the moment of his nativity. For if the Moon is then in sinister sextile to the Sun, a square to the Sun may follow that, which square is given at the moment of the nativity and its distance from the Moon itself; which distance, the Moon's force that was impressed virtually on the Moon's place does not traverse, so that the effect of the direction of the Moon to the square of the Sun may be produced, as Pico thought, but it is only necessary that the promittor, or the Sun's square, be transferred to the position of the Moon's place through the prime revolution of the *caelum* after [the native's] birth; and the formal impression of that natural direction having thus been made upon the native, its effect can be produced in as many years from his birth as the number of degrees of the equator by which the promittor is distant from the circle of position of the Moon, just as is explained in detail in Sect. 3, Chapt. 2, which see.

Thus far, then, it has been evident how absurd, how false, and how inappropriate Pico's reasons against astrological directions are; the truth of which he himself experienced very bitterly, when, in the 33rd year of his age,[179] immediately after he had written his twelve books against astrologers, he had to die from the

---

178 This is the sort of Latin eloquence that excited admiration in Italy in the 1490's. Both Morin and I have added words and explanations to it to try to make it understandable, but it would be necessary to abandon the original format altogether and write a paraphrase to put it into acceptable English.

179 Pico was born on 24 Feb 1463 and died on 17 Nov 1494 at the age of 31 years and not quite 9 months, that is to say in his 32nd year. However, the statement that he died in his 33rd year may have resulted from the calendar used by the two writers cited below. Bellantio was from Florence and Syrigato from Siena, both of which towns used the style of the Incarnation, i.e., New Year's Day was 25 March rather than 1 January. Pico's birthdate would have been considered to be 24 Feb 1462 in that version of the calendar, which by simple subtraction from the death date, 17 Nov 1494, would have made his age at death 32 years and not quite nine months, which would have been his 33rd year.

direction of his Ascendant to the body of Mars in the 2nd,[180] opposed to the Moon in the 8th, and square Saturn and Mars, as had been predicted to him by Lucio Bellantio, a physician of Siena, Antonio Syrigato of Florence, and Angelo de Catastini,[181] a Carmelite, as is reported by Giuntini on p. 540, where he puts [Pico's] celestial figure.[182] And how uncommonly well and easily Pico's objections can be resolved by the self-consistent doctrine we have set forth.

Chapt. 2. *In which Alessandro de Angelis's Reasons against Directions are Proposed and Refuted.*

D e Angelis,[183] in Book 4, Chapt. 20, rises up strongly against directions. And I omit that afterwards in imitation of Pico he supposed the place of the significator to be moved to the place of the promittor according to some astrologers; then, from Cardan's *Book on the Judgments of Genitures*, Chapt. 6, he selects for rebuttal many things about directions that Cardan himself only intended to apply to revolutions—which De Angelis did not know enough to discern. And [so at length] I come to the arguments of his that follow.

First he says that *He cannot conceive what a "place" is to the astrologers, and he argues against it from the properties of a place as defined by Aristotle, and he does this with many words and passages that are plainly of no importance for this matter.*

I reply then that Alessandro de Angelis had not thought that the place of a star is one thing to physicists and another to astrologers. For the physical place of a star is the surface of a body immediately encircling the star, as Aristotle holds, [and] against which we have written in Book 5, Chapt. 4. But the astrological place is a

---

180 Recalculation shows that 12 Scorpio, the reported longitude of Mars, would have come to the Ascendant (17°12' Libra) with an arc of direction of 32°56' or very nearly 33°, as the Italian astrologers recorded. However, Mars was actually in 13°48' Scorpio with latitude 1N55, so its zodiacal rising would have yielded an arc of direction of 35°21' and its mundane rising an arc of 33°54'. In the true latitude of Mirandola, 44°53', the arcs of the recalculated place would have been: zodiacal, 35°17' and mundane, 33°50'.

181 John Gadbury, *Collectio Geniturarum* (London: James Cottrel, 1662), p. 51, has *Catastivi*. Not having Junctinus's original at hand, I do not know which spelling is correct.

182 I have added Pico's chart from NN 462 (presumably cited from Junctinus). It has Ascendant 18 Libra, while Cardan's chart (C 490C) has Ascendant 6 Libra, but the latter was perhaps drawn incorrectly, as it apparently gave the same birth time (it actually has "ho. 1.min.42.post.merid.," but this must be a blunder for "ho. 2.min.42.post.oc-casum.").

183 Alessandro Angeli (1562-1620), a Jesuit from Spoleto, was the author of a book *Against the Astrologers* published in 1604.

part of the *primum mobile* under which that star is seen from the earth, and which determines that star to its own virtue with respect to the earth, [as we have explained] in Book 4, Chapt. 7.

But he argues, *It is insane to say that the signs of the zodiac are places of the planets, which are seen in them because of an error of the eye; and no less insane than if someone should say that the Moon or its orb is the place of a mountain which is seen in the direction of the Moon.*

But I reply that there is a great difference between the two. First because that mountain, seen from any direction—from the east, from the west, from the north, from the south, and from regions in between—will not be seen in the direction of the Moon, while a planet, especially one not liable to [be affected by] parallax, [184] and any fixed star, can be seen in the same part of the *caelum* from anywhere on earth. Second, because the place of the stars in the *caelum* is independent of the eye and only depends upon nature, which God himself made. For even if all men were born blind, as some are born, nevertheless the places of the planets in the *caelum* would be given with respect to those born; that is, the parts of the *caelum* would be determined by the planets with respect to those born. Third, because the place of a mountain imagined to be in the [the place of the] orb of the Moon is of no virtue. But the place of a planet in the zodiac is of great virtue, as experience testifies.

After this he asks, *where does this vicarious power of a star reside, seeing that the star does not remain in the place it occupied at the moment of the geniture.* But then he cites the authority of Cardan, who says in his [*Seven Segments of Astronomical Aphorisms*], Seg. 1, Aph. 38, *Those impressions from the geniture, which remain in place up until the time in which they are perfected, are partly in the place and partly in the material* De Angelis exclaims, *Therefore, does the* caelum, *impervious to contrary qualities, contract this disease? How does this contagion lurk for so many years? Why, or by what, is it called forth after 20 years?*

I reply first that Cardan, Bellantio, and some others have been deceived in thinking that the force of a star is formally impressed upon the *caelum* and that it remains in that place only up to the time when the effect of the direction is produced, since no formal impression upon the *caelum* can be made by the stars, but the place of a star in the *caelum* is determined with respect to the native, in whom there is a formal impression of the whole celestial constitution at the moment of his nativity, [which lasts] for the native's whole life, as we have quite often stated. I reply secondly that De Angelis is mistaken when he supposes that the force of the celestial bodies, which is the source of the effects of a direction, is of some kind of contrary qualities, i.e., in his mountain of elements, since he denies and rejects their influences. And that force does not "lurk," but flourishes continually with respect

---

184 By "one not liable to parallax" he presumably means Mars, Jupiter, or Saturn, for which Kepler had been unable to detect any parallax in Tyco's observations.

to the native until, at the time of his death, he is released from the influx of the stars and the domination of the *caelum*, as is proved by the transits of the planets over the principal places of the horoscope before and after the exact time of a direction. And these transits are in fact effective on the native even though they are far weaker than the directions, especially solitary ones that are not reinforced by directions or revolutions. And why and by what the abovesaid force is brought forth after 20 years may be read in Sect. 3, Chapt. 6.

Then he asks, *why doesn't Saturn exude a force of this sort continuously? Or why doesn't it infect the whole* caelum *through which it passes, but only that certain part of the circle that it occupies, or seems to occupy, at the time of birth and conception? Since men are born at every time and every moment of time, it is necessary for Saturn to exude its force continuously; therefore, when the Ascendant finds the whole* caelum *drenched with Saturn's poison, there is no reason why its efficacy should be called forth in the 21st year, rather than in those following or preceding.*

But I reply that Saturn does continuously exude its force on these inferior things, and the whole path of Saturn in the *caelum* is similarly infected with the determinative virtue of Saturn mentioned above, but not with respect to each native. But only that part of the *caelum* is determined with respect to a native, under which it is or can be discerned at the moment of that native's nativity; and consequently only it can produce the effect of a direction from the concourse of the Ascendant with that part [of the *caelum*] and not with any other.

He objects further *That that part of the zodiac that was the place of Saturn in the nativity of one person, is very often the place of Jupiter, Mars, or another [planet] in the natal [figure] of another person; and it must be acknowledged by these [interpreters] of the planets if they wish to be consistent, that that [part] at the same time obtains the powers of Saturn, Jupiter, and Mars. Why then Saturn discharges its effect, when the Ascendant approaches, rather than another planet, is difficult to explain.*

I reply that it would certainly be difficult for Alessandro de Angelis, who is absolutely ignorant of these matters, but very easy for us from the principles that we have expounded. For we say that the *caelum* is the first cause in nature, eminently embracing the forces of the causes of the inferior celestial [bodies]; and therefore from the individual ones of these [causes] determinable in accordance with the nature of each. And in consequence the same part of the *primum caelum* can be determined with respect to one native to the nature of Saturn, with respect to another to the nature of Jupiter at a different time, with respect to still another to the nature of Mars, etc. And consequently that part can act in different ways in each individual by reason of its own determination with respect to each of them without any confusion whatsoever, because, of course, determinations are formally different.[185] And from this it happens that when in one native's figure the direction of the Ascendant to the following place of Saturn is completed, an effect of Saturn is produced, but not an effect of Jupiter or Mars. And it is much more remarkable that at the same time the same part of the *caelum* is determined to the nature of Saturn or Jupiter with respect to those who are born under different meridians: to one it becomes the cause of life, to another, of riches, to another, of brothers, parents, children, etc., by reason of the different position of that part with respect to each individual native, since here a twofold determination of that part appears: first, to the nature of Saturn, which can be common to many, and then to this type of accident rather than to another, by reason of its particular position in the figure with respect to each native. And still, nothing in astrology is clearer, not of course to those who are ignorant of the science, but rather to those who are skilled in it, from which it is plain how marvelous is the force of action of the celestial bodies, displaying in this regard the most excellent character of divine virtue and omnipotence.

Therefore, when Alessandro de Angelis concludes in this manner: *What therefore, could be fashioned that is more insane than directions? What could be thought up that is crazier? [For] every "place" of the planets is fictitious, the motion by which the contrived division of degrees approaches to it is fabulous, and the force that a planet is said to bestow upon a place is imaginary. And shall we believe that the length of life, the time of death, the causes of sicknesses, and all the important affairs of human activity depend upon all these ridiculous occurrences and upon the "forces" of things? Oh happy minds that had the good fortune to contrive such things! Oh fertile fields of ridiculous things in which the principles of all things that are made on sea or land are contained!*

We may only say that it is absolutely insane to judge openly about things one knows nothing about and to exhibit with a fecundity of ridiculous exclamations a sterility of reasons and one's own stupidity. But our doctrine of directions is fixed on very sound fundamentals, so that nothing can be objected against directions that cannot be resolved through it easily and clearly, as was shown above.

Chapt. 3. *In which Sixtus ab Hemminga's Reasons against Astrology, and especially against Directions are Refuted.*

Origen, St. Ambrose, St. Augustine, and other fathers of religion, excited by zeal, especially in a time in which the distortion and abuse of astrology was greater, must, I think, be excused for having written about this science, which was not sufficiently well known to them; for God did not give them to us as doctors of physical things, but of everyday affairs; and in this role they at least had good

---

185 That is, each determination is specific for the individual for whom it is made; hence, it is necessarily different from every other determination.

ntentions. But in the case of others [equally] unskilled, who undertake with utter arrogance to overthrow the same thing either with writings or with public speeches, their madness is really immoderate, since it is nothing else than spouting into the *caelum*, to attest publicly to their own ignorance, and to wish to deceive God of the glory due Him on account of the marvelous gifts granted by the celestial bodies, when, labouring vainly in a talent not entrusted to them, they think themselves capable of doing great things.

But in the case of Sixtus ab Hemminga,[186] M.D., of Frisia, who, in his knowledge of astronomy and astrology, far surpassed Pico Mirandola, Alessandro de Angelis, and the rest of the haters of astrology, both old and new, he has erected a number of natal figures, judged them, and discussed the mysteries of directions and revolutions, based on lengthy reading and comparison of the [astrological] authors' [works], and yet he writes very vehemently against astrologers, so that now he is a shield for De Angelis himself, and now a spear to stab into astrology. What else shall we say of him other than that he has sinned more from malice than from ignorance; and, having become a spontaneous apostate, the most impudent of all, he has nevertheless laboured under a dense ignorance; but malice predominated in this, as shows here and there in his book, *Astrology Refuted.*[187] For that reason he is called by Alessandro de Angelis, in the last chapter of Book 5, *a man by far the most eminent in astrological principles*, and so he is introduced, speaking of himself in Geniture 22. *But* (says ab Hemminga), *since I took up the practice of astrology, [and] acquired it by long use and constant practice, I think I have experience absolutely contrary to the experience of the astrologers—not fallacious and doubtful, but true and consistent, by which the counterfeit truth of all this doctrine of theirs is convicted of the most open falsity. For I have learned from innumerable experiments with genitures that nothing at all can be apprehended from the position of the stars.* And in the geniture of [the Emperor] Charles V: *Moreover, since I have inspected the matter thoroughly—having been taught by long use and much experience—I have found the doctrine of astrology, which I favored earlier before it was well known [to me], to be impossible, not worthy of faith, and useless.* But since it would have been stupid for a philosopher and physician to have favored this science very much without any persuading cause, it is credible that the same thing happened to Sixtus ab Hemminga that once happened to me. Namely that, misled by the evidence of many, even marvelous, experiences, he wanted to scrutinize the innermost parts of this science, i.e., the

---

186 A Dutch physician who lived from 1533 to 1586.

187 *Astrologiae ratione et experientia refutatae liber...nunc primum...editus contra C. Leovitium*, H. Cardanum et L. Gauricum. [Astrology Refuted by Reason and Experience...now Published for the first time...against C(yprian) Leovitius, J(erome) Cardan, and L(uca) Gaurico] (Antwerp, 1583). Sixtus took Leovitius as his principal target. See Lynn Thorndike, HMES 6, pp. 193-196, for a summary of the contents of Sixtus's book.

principles, reasons, and fundamentals with whatever skill he possessed; and in [doing] this he was astounded because this very celebrated science was seen to depend more on trifles and figments than on genuine reasons. And not being able to discern the true from the false to unlock the sanctuary of nature and to build for himself a suitable foundation for knowledge, he seized an opportunity from the trivialities of the Arabs and the other old [astrologers] that defile this very noble science and resolved to write against it and to render it infamous to posterity. But really from his principal reasons against astrology, now referring, and now rebutting by means of argumentation, one concludes with little doubt that he had only affected the practice of this discipline to the end that he would be able to rage with atrocious fury against the science with a greater evidence of probability. But in truth he was quite ignorant of the fundamentals of this science, a fallacious writer and a deceiver of the inexperienced, even though he occasionally rises up rightly and neatly against the trifles of the Arabs and the false dogmatic statements of some of the other old [astrologers].

But since our task here is [to deal] with the least sensible of all the enemies of astrology, and since his whole book[188] cannot be discussed in detail and disproved with less effort than by [writing] a volume that would be more or less equal in size to Junctinus's volume on astrology on account of the multitude of genitures that he cites in addition to the thirty he has explained [in detail], as well as the aphorisms handed down by the astrologers, which he rises up against; for this reason, it seems to us to be right to reveal the lion by his claws—to expose his principal reasons, both the ones against astrology in general and those against directions in particular; for all the other objections that he raises can easily be refuted by the doctrine we have set forth.

And so in the first place he holds in his demonstration *that if any things are done or signified by the stars, they ought also to be comprehended with certainty and known in advance, not by some obscure conjectures.*

But I reply that this is plainly stupid; since by this very reason not only would medicine have to be removed from the number of the sciences, but also, like astrology, it would plainly have to be rejected as being false and useless. Doesn't ab Hemminga know that his own medicine is conjectural—at least in practice? Moreover, that it should not be rejected is proved, not only by authority of *Ecclesiasticus*, Chapt. 38, *Honour the physician because in fact the most High created him, etc.,*[189] but also by the public need [for it]. For astrology and medicine agree absolutely in this [respect]: that the theory of both is certain, and founded on valid principles, even though these principles are not perfectly known by men; but the practice of both requires conjecture on account of the concourse of various causes, the diversity of the subjects, and the mutability arising from the various concurrent causes. And from this it is easy to conjecture that Sixtus ab Hemminga

188 A quarto volume of some three hundred pages.
189 Ecclus. 38:1.

was no better a physician than he was an astrologer, since he neglected the science, which, Hippocrates, in many places, and Galen, in the whole of Book 3 of his *Critical Days*, recommended as being very necessary to a physician.[190]

Secondly, he wants *astrologers to demonstrate that, just as everyone understands and feels the efficacy of the Sun and the Moon, so he may [also] pronounce things that are [equally] certain about the rest of the stars.* And by "the rest of the stars" he means even the smallest fixed [stars].[191]

I reply that an astrologer pronounces no less true things about the 12 twelfths[192] and the 5 lesser planets, Saturn, Jupiter, Mars, Venus, and Mercury, than he does about the Sun and the Moon, since he will only pronounce about all of these in connection with their celestial state and their determination with respect to the native; and these are the principal celestial causes that change this inferior world,[193] and ab Hemminga is deceived if he thinks that the influence of the Sun is better known than the influence of Saturn or Mars, although its light and heat are better known than their light and heat and cold. But many true things may also be pronounced about the principal fixed stars, such as Spica Virginis, Caput Medusae, the Eye of Taurus,[194] and other similar stars. But as for the smallest [fixed stars], their force is insensible, at least on humans. See what we have said about this matter in Book 8, Sect. 3, Chapt. 4.

Thirdly, he holds *it to be necessary in the judgment of future things to know absolutely all of the fixed stars, even the smallest, and their forces, also, the variation of their forces for different motion and different position; from which he asserts that astrological judgments must necessarily be false because of the continuous alteration of the position and configuration of the fixed stars, which is incomprehensible to the astrologer, who also cannot demonstrate that the smallest of the fixed [stars] is useless in this regard, since the smallest fixed [star] is 702 times greater than the Moon.*[195] But I reply: 1) That ab Hemminga cannot

---

190 Astrological works are ascribed to both Hippocrates (c.460-c.370) and Galen (129-199). Hippocrates lived two centuries before the invention of horoscopic astrology, so his use of astrology, if any, would have been limited to Moon phases or something similar. Galen wrote or is said to have written a book on Critical Days (No. 14 of the "Sixteen Books of Galen" compiled by John of Alexandria in the seventh century. See George Sarton, *Introduction to the History of Science* [Baltimore, 1927], I: 480, and Lynn Thorndike, HMES 1, 178-179.

191 The last sentence is also italicized in the Latin text, but it seems to be Morin's comment rather than a continuation of the citation from ab Hemminga.

192 That is, the signs of the zodiac.

193 That is, the world below the stars.

194 These stars are Spica, or Alpha Virginis; Algol, or Beta Persei; and Aldebaran, or Alpha Tauri.

195 If he was comparing diameters, ab Hemminga had the right order of magnitude. Our Sun is said to be rather smaller than average as stars go, and it is about 400 times the diameter of the Moon. In volume, of course, it is 64,000,000 times greater than the ..

demonstrate the necessity he has supposed [to exist], since it is plainly false. And we have proved this in most evident fashion, because if astrologers do not in fact judge about any accident, such as life, honours, marriage, etc. from all 7 planets and all 12 signs, but only from those which are determined to that accident in accordance with the true principles of this science that we have stated—and whoever would judge otherwise would be altogether confused and deceived—how much less will they judge about life, honours, or other things from the concourse of all the fixed [stars], even the smallest; 2) But this error, common to Pico Mirandola, Sixtus ab Hemminga, and Alessandro de Angelis, as if by tradition, has taken its origin from the fact that they have wrongly supposed that every accident of the native depends upon the whole (as they say) substance of the decree, i.e., from the entire natal constitution, which, however, we have shown to be false in Book 10 in opposition to [the opinions of] Pico and de Angelis.

I reply secondly that astrologers do not deny that the smallest fixed [star], i.e., at least of the 6th magnitude, is far greater than the Moon, but they only deny that their force is perceptible to us like the Moon's virtue is on account of the stupendous distance of these [stars] from the earth—[one so great that] if the Moon were removed [from the earth by] a hundredth part of it, it could not be seen, and it would act upon us much less perceptibly. For in similar fashion, a great fire 1,000 paces distant from us does not warm us at all, while the flame of a candle two inches away from the hand will warm it. And it is not because of this that the astrologers say that these [stars] are unnecessary or useless, for God, who calls them by their names, knows their use. But in fact their distance from us is so great that only the force of the more notable [stars] is strong enough to be perceived and discerned by us; whence, the imperceptible effects of the others are rightly held to be naught by the astrologers. But as regards the change of configuration and position of the more notable [stars], the configuration can be viewed with respect to the fixed [stars] and the planets. The configuration is not changed with respect to the fixed [stars], else they would not be fixed and always at the same distances among themselves, [196] but it is changed with respect to the planets; however, aside from their conjunctions with the planets, they are not perceived to have any efficacious connections with them in the *caelum*, [197] although with respect to the earth they have their own risings and settings that are potent and not unknown to astrologers. Moreover, their positions are varied with respect to the *caelum* and the earth: with respect to the

Moon; and in mass, about 27,000,000 times greater. Thus, a star is much greater than the Moon, and this is ab Hemminga's point. But he did not know that the distance of the nearest star is something like 25,000,000,000,000 miles, while the Moon is only 240,000 miles distant.

196 Their changes with respect to each other (called *proper motion*) are so slow that they had not yet been recognized in Morin's day.

197 He means that the planets' conjunctions with the more notable fixed stars have a perceptible influence, but their aspects to them do not.

caelum by reason of the motion of the fixed [stars] through the twelfths, [198] through which circumstance they are subjected to the rulership of the planets in whose domiciles they are placed, just as the planets themselves; but their motion is very slow, so that in 2,000 years they may not change their rulership. [199] And with respect to the earth, so far as through that motion, with a similar slowness, they are raised or lowered insensibly in the meridian circle, which is of no sensible efficacy, seeing that a greater or lesser declination of the planets, causing a greater or lesser altitude in the meridian circle, is perceived to introduce no sensible variation of effects—in particular, none peculiar to itself. And the universal immutability of the fixed stars in their configuration and position, which was incomprehensible to Sixtus ab Hemminga, is reduced to this. However, we do not deny that research in the astrology of the fixed stars and the understanding of the constellations is needful, as far as their proper and formal virtues; but how many and how great are the desiderata in medicine, the whole of physics, theology, and pure mathematics? Should, therefore, so many noble sciences be rejected as useless? A perfect knowledge of any science does not belong to this wretched life, especially since Adam's sin, which infected all men with ignorance and malice, but to the blessed and eternal life in which we shall see God just as He is, and in this simplest truth every possible verity with the clearest view. Meanwhile, we all labour with the search for truth in a manner suitable to our lot; and it should be sufficient for us that at least the primary celestial causes and their forces—the principal modes of acting—should finally become known to us, as they are established in this work; concerning which, posterity will pass judgment upon what we have provided for it.

Fourth. *He laughs at astrologers because after comets, eclipses, and similar universal configurations, they attach some succeeding effects, such as wars, pestilences, and the deaths of princes to those causes; and they do not predict such things from these [configurations] in particular—at least, not without falsehood, such as that such-and-such a prince will die, or the plague will rage in such-and-such a city.*

I reply that from the places of comets, eclipses, and the rest of the universal configurations, only universal predictions can be had, but not particular ones for princes or others, unless their exactly rectified natal figures are available. And an error can occur in such [universal configurations] from two causes. First, since the motions of the luminaries are not yet exactly determined, the true hour of an ecliptic configuration cannot be had, and the hour of the generation of a comet [200] is known with even less accuracy. Second, because the accurately rectified figures of princes

---

198 The signs of the zodiac.

199 He means that if a star, at some epoch, were at the beginning of a sign, it would stay in that same sign for 2,000 years. In fact, it would take about 2,150 years for the star to move into the next sign.

200 Presumably, he means the time when a comet first becomes visible.

are not available, for this [accuracy of rectification] is not [within the capability] of every astrologer, but only of one who is highly skilled. But that a plague should invade this city rather than that one depends not only upon the universal configuration of the *caelum*, which by itself can signify a pestilence, but also upon the situation and position of the city [in question]. And all these things are not known to every astrologer; but it cannot be proved that they are impossible to know. For if princes would bring together men capable of [investigating] this matter, or if by the help of these princes [so that they would] not be indigent,[201] they would devote themselves to this task, marvelous things would be done in this regard; and there would not be attributed to the science [itself] what is solely caused by the lack of human curiosity.

Fifth. He holds *that judgment about the native depends upon the celestial configuration of conception, quickening, birth, and other intermediate [phases of the birth process], whose beginnings, he says, are unknown to the astrologer; and the [native's] temperament and moral nature is varied by his rearing, excercise, way of life, etc.*

I reply that these objections, which have no weight, have already been abundantly satisfied in Book 21, Sect. 2, especially in Chapts. 15, 16, and 19 in opposition to [the objections of] Alessandro de Angelis, who offers the same song as Sixtus ab Hemminga in connection with this matter. See those chapters.

Sixth. He argues from Marsilio Ficino's [book] on Plotinus,[202] *that if from the coming together of two rays anything more may be done than by a single ray, then much more [still may be done] with the coming together of all the planets and all the fixed [stars]; but, the more causes that flow together, the more difficult the judgment [becomes], because all the perfected causes are not known individually, nor, if all are known, would it be immediately known what new things would be effected [by their combination], especially if the sublunar causes[203] are taken into account. Therefore, the knowledge [of these things] is impossible.*

I reply that Hemminga always clings to this confusion—that all the planets and fixed [stars] concur with whatever type of accident the native is going to have, which is rejected above at Objection 3. And so we have conceded that the more causes are determined by body, by aspect, and by rulership to the same type of accident, the more difficult it is to judge about it. Moreover, it would be impossible, and no less false, to render an opinion about a sickness from a combination of many

---

201 In other words, if astrologers could get government grants to pay for their research and provide them with a reasonable stipend at the same time—the goal of every modern scientist.

202 Marsilio Ficino (1433-1499) was an Italian humanist scholar and philosopher, famed for his translations of Plato and Plotinus. The reference is probably to his commentary on Plotinus, published in 1491.

203 The non-astrological causes.

[different] causes of sickness. And these are the more potent arguments, but [still] of no importance, raised by Sixtus ab Hemminga against universal astrology.

Now we may see in how many different ways he errs in [his discussion of] directions, which comprise the principal argument for the verity of astrology, but in which he professes to have perceived no verity at all, but only perpetual falsity, having displayed for this [purpose] 30 nativities notable for a variety of events, which he examines in his own fashion through the decrees and directions of the astrologers.

And so first he judges about this science from nativities, either not rectified by any method, or only by one or two accidents. Which, however, is not sufficient to give one faith in the rectification if many accidents that are important have preceded, as they have in the nativities that he explains. And from this to predict future [accidents] at their own time through their own proper causes, or to refer the rest of the accidents to their own proper causes according to their time, is absolutely impossible if one should have erred in the rectification from a single accident. In fact, ab Hemminga judges from figures that differ in [the longitude of] the Ascendant by 10, 15, or 20 degrees and more from [those given by] Junctinus. And it is more likely that Junctinus, a famous astrologer and very diligent in the collection of nativities, has given the figures which he displayed in good faith [than that ab Hemminga has done so].

Second. If, in the figures he has selected, 2 or 3 accidents are found to agree as far as the time and the type of effect with his own causes of direction, but not to the minute of the arc of direction or of the time, he thinks the doctrine of directions ought to be rejected, and he gives vent to useless questions as to why one direction anticipates its effect by 4 or 5 minutes of the equator or about one month, or another one follows its effect by the same amount. Concerning which futile reasoning, we have said enough in Sect. 3, Chapt. 3, which see.

Third. He has not used any directions other than those of the Sun, the Moon, the Ascendant, and the Midheaven for all the native's accidents. Which is mere ignorance, even though prescribed by Ptolemy; who, however, adds the Lot [of Fortune], rejected by Sixtus without [having given] any reason. For the Sun, the Moon, the Ascendant and the Midheaven are not significators determined to all the native's accidents, but only to some of them: namely, the Ascendant to accidents of the 1st house, the Midheaven to accidents of the 10th, and the Sun and the Moon to the accidents of those houses in which they are [posited] and those which they rule. But the other planets, Saturn, Jupiter, Mars, Venus, and Mercury, and the other cusps are no less determined to the native than the Sun, the Moon, the Ascendant, and the Midheaven; therefore, they must be directed for those things to which they are determined by position or rulership, which we have very plainly stated in Sect. 7, Chapts. 4, 5, and 6, against [the opinions of] Ptolemy, Cardan, and the other old [astrologers], so that there is no need of any other response here.

Fourth. In the directions which he selects and calculates to refute astrology, he does not refer the effects to the proper causes, but [he assumes] foreign [causes] from the effects, and similarly [he assigns] causes to foreign effects. For what else could he do, since he only directs 4 significators and does not pay any attention either to their determinations or to the determinations of those that he omits?

Fifth. The greater part of the directions he proposes are to the terms of the planets, which we have proved in Book 13, Chapt. 13, to be mere figments and of no virtue. How then could he establish true directions with them? But since he omitted the greater part of the significators in the geniture, it was necessary to increase the number of promittors by figments.

Sixth. If, for example, the direction of the Moon to the square of Mars in [the chart of] one native is said to have produced some effect, he wants it to produce the same effect in every chart, without taking any account of the determinations of the significator and the promittor in these diverse genitures, nor of the lineage, sex, condition, or any other dispositions of the subject native. And if he can show the contrary in any nativity, he denies that the abovesaid effect was produced by such a cause. And in addition he asks why the same effect or a similar one could not be produced by celestial causes other than those which he refers to, without any consideration of their determination? And what else is this than to be swayed by ignorance, to totter, and to fall into the greatest absurdities through the lack of [consideration of] the determination of the true significators and promittors in individual genitures, observed and applied to judgment; and consequently to commend outstandingly the very great force of that determination in astrology?

Seventh. In the universal judgment of life, riches, the wife, honours, etc., the judgments are not argued from the true and genuine causes of these accidents through determinations to such things, but principally and indiscriminately from causes universally analagous, which Cardan calls significators "according to substance." We have shown in Sect. 1, Chapts. 3, 4, 5, and 6, how great a mental aberration this is. Therefore, why is it surprising if Sixtus ab Hemminga, entangled in so many errors, was unable to apprehend the verity of astrology either in the charts of others or in his own, especially when he was mostly proving wrong the dogmatic statements of Ptolemy, Cardan, Leovitius, and others and no few of their aphorisms of manifest falsity?

Besides, for the greater confounding of this writer, we may expound here his geniture and accidents, the causes of which he could never find from his own figure rectified by himself.

Chapt. 4. *In which the Truth of the Doctrine of Directions is Demonstrated in the Chart of Sixtus ab Hemminga.*

The exact figure of the nativity is the cause of future accidents for the native, as far as their type and time; and in turn, these accidents are due to this cause; and consequently, given this [figure], the accidents can be found as far as the type and the time. And in turn, with these given as far as the type and the time, the exact figure of the nativity can be determined from some other [figure] that is close to it, i.e., one preceding or following the exact one by some minutes of an hour, indeed by some hours. But this is not [within the capability] of every artist, but only of one very skilled in the recognition of the celestial causes, who of course knows how to connect the effects rightly with their own true causes. And the entire effort consists of this: to take some accident, and through directions connect it with its causes, that is its significator and promittor, capable of producing it from their own nature and determination. For if, with this connection made, the rest of the accidents as far as their type and time may be found by directions similarly connected to causes capable of producing those things, the exact figure of the nativity will have been found; but if not, the hypothesis of the first connection is false, in which the significator should always be the Ascendant or the Midheaven, since these are what is sought.[204]

Therefore, Sixtus ab Hemminga, for the rectification of his own geniture, takes a sickness in the year 1559 on the 8th of December at 5 A.M., which was a very acute fever, with pleurisy and inflammation of the liver, and in which his life was almost despaired of; which, according to astrological opinion, supposes that it was caused by the direction of the Ascendant to the antiscion of Mars, whose oblique ascension under the pole of the figure was $284°02'$. And the time of the accident converted into degrees of the equator according to Ptolemy, $26°50'$. Therefore, having subtracted this from $284°02'$, there remains $257°12'$ for the oblique ascension of the Ascendant; from which the true time of the nativity comes out as 13 hours 6'30". But in order to confirm this Ascendant, again he directs it for a sudden sickness with lack of breath and a sudden discharge of poison, which began on 2 December 1566 at 7 o'clock, followed by a quotidian fever, to the square of Mercury, whose oblique ascension was $290°25'$; and the converted time of the accident, $33°50'$. And having made the subtraction of the latter arc from the former, there remains $257°35'$ for the oblique ascension of the Ascendant, but not precisely $257°12'$, as above. Therefore, he rejects both directions because he wants both of them to agree to the minute; otherwise, he denies that such effects are from such causes and that there is any truth to be had in astrology. Besides, he cannot find any causes by directions for the rest of his accidents.

---

204 That is, the chart should be rectified by accidents arising from directions of the angles, since the time of such directions is directly dependent upon the birth time, while the time of interplanetary directions is only indirectly dependent on the birth time and is consequently much less sensitive to a change in that time. For example, in ab Hemminga's chart Mercury comes to the conjunction of Mars with an (unadjusted) arc of $38°46'$; but if we add $15°$ to the RAMC and recalculate the direction, the arc is reduced to $34°48'$—a difference of only $3°58'$. And the Moon comes to the conjunction of Saturn in the original chart with an arc of $16°58'$; but if $15°$ is added to the RAMC and the direction is recalculated, the arc is reduced to $15°48'$ — a difference of only $1°10'$.

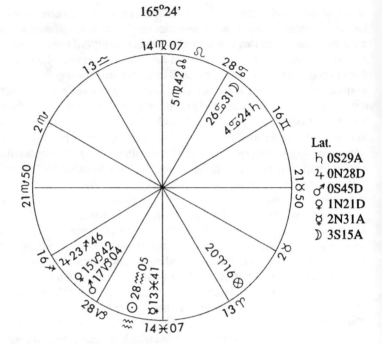

Sixtus ab Hemminga
Bellocomi in Frisia 53N00
6 February 1533, 13:01 True Time
from the Rudolphine Tables

Figure 6

Moreover, Sixtus ab Hemminga is deceived in many places in his own figure and the others. First, because he has quite a few erroneous places for the planets. For he has Mars in 17°33' Capricorn, when in the *Rudolphine Tables* it is only 17°09'; and he has Mercury in 17°25' Pisces, when from the *Rudolphine Tables* it is only 13°41'. Second, because he omits the required correction of the aspects. Third, because the conversion of time into degrees of the equator taken from Ptolemy is not legitimate, as we have said in Sect. 3, Chapt. 3. Fourth, because he only directs four significators: the Ascendant, the Midheaven, the Sun, and the Moon. Fifth, because he uses fictitious promittors, such as the terms of the planets. Sixth, because he absolutely did not know how to determine the true causes of effects,[205] so that he could connect the one with the other.

---

205 Reading *effectuum* 'effects' for *affectuum* 'dispositions'.

But, having taken his accidents and their times from ab Hemminga himself, I find their proper causes, and thus I show the truth of astrology.[206] For the basis of the rectification I take his marriage, celebrated on 2 August 1563, which accident simply and per se is a kind of action, and therefore it pertains to the Midheaven, even though by inclination it may pertain to the Ascendant. And Venus, ruler of the 7th, was the analogous significator of the wife, and conjoined to Mars, ruler of the Ascendant, i.e., to the significator of inclinations, evidently promised marriage. Therefore, for the time of the marriage I direct the square of Venus to the Midheaven thus:

Right Ascension of the square to Venus corrected by our table	195°04'
Naibod's Table	30°03'
Right Ascension of the Midheaven	165°01'

And consequently the true time of the nativity was 12:59; this is only 7'30" earlier than ab Hemminga puts it.[207] And I take his marriage because in a man of 30 years it cannot be said that it was not spontaneous and from the inclination that Mars, ruler of the Ascendant, strong and conjunct Venus, ruler of the 7th house, had impressed. Now we may see whether the rest of his accidents have celestial causes that are no less in agreement with their own times.

And so in the year 1542, at the end of April, he was first attacked by a sickness of 12 days arising from indigestion. And this was from the direction of the Ascendant to the square of the Sun in the domicile of Saturn, which, through its antiscion, is on the cusp of the 12th, which is intrinsically [the house] of sicknesses.

Oblique Ascension of the square to the Sun	264°18'	264°20'
Oblique Ascension of the Ascendant	255°01'	255°01'
Difference	9°17'	9°19'
Converted Time of the Accident	9°05'	

In the year 1544, on the 10th of December, at the 3rd hour, [he had] pleuritis with delirium and danger. And it was from two causes. One is the direction of

---

206 Recalculation shows that a few of the planetary parameters that follow are correct (i.e., within 1' of the stated value), but the majority display errors of 10' or 15'. And the recalculated arcs of direction are generally 10' to 15' further away from matching the arcs of the event. To facilitate comparison, I have placed Morin's figures on the left and my recalculation on the right.

207 Since I do not know what value Morin took for the maximum inclination of Venus, I am unable to verify his calculation of the right ascension of the corrected square. Modern tables give the succeeding maximum as 1°40'. This would yield a corrected dexter square at 15°40' Libra and 0N59, which would have RA 194°48'—16' less than Morin's figure.

Jupiter, ruler of the 1st house and consequently the significator of life, to the opposition of Saturn posited in the 8th house.

Oblique Ascension of the opposition to Saturn		
in the circle of position of Jupiter	301°35'	302°08'
Oblique Ascension of Jupiter	290°06'	290°30'
Difference	11°29'	11°38'
Converted Time of the Accident	11°35'	

And the other [cause] is the Sun, significator of sicknesses on account of its antiscion [falling] on the cusp of the 12th and its square to the Ascendant, [directed] to Mercury, ruler of the 8th; and this caused the delirium and the danger to life; but first also the danger to life on account of Saturn's being in the 8th.

Oblique Ascension of Mercury in the		
circle of position of the Sun	345°06'	345°07'
Oblique Ascension of the Sun	333°36'	333°37'
Difference	11°30'	11°30'

And because the effects of Saturn are usually longer lasting than the effects of the rest of the planets, another but less serious pleuritis happened again from the concurrence of these two directions by the virtue still subsisting on 14 January 1546, of which the converted time was 12°48'.

In the year 1551, in the month of August, he had a tumor of the foot that hindered his walking and lasted for two years. And the direction of Saturn to the Moon made this long sickness, Saturn being badly disposed in a water sign in the 8th, with the Moon also in the same sign and in the 8th house, and Mars, ruler of the Ascendant and the 12th, opposed to them. And Saturn, as it often does, delayed its effect by almost a year, but it compensated for its delay by the long duration of its evil, as is its characteristic.

Oblique Descension of the Moon in the		
circle of position of Saturn	135°51'	135°49'
Oblique Descension of Saturn	118°44'	118°51'
Difference	17°07'	16°58'
Converted time of the accident	18°00'	

In the year 1555, on the 15th of April, he suffered a colic or diarrhea lasting a month with danger to his life; which was followed by bulimia lasting for two years. And this sickness was from the direction of Jupiter, ruler of the 1st and therefore significator of life, to Venus, in the 2nd house and in a sign of Saturn, conjoined to Mars, ruler of the 12th, in opposition to Saturn in exile in the 8th, with

Mars closely following Venus, whence Venus itself, also inimical to the Ascendant, was very contrary to life, especially since it was opposite the 8th.

Oblique Ascension of Venus in the circle of position of Jupiter	312°05'	311°49'
Oblique Ascension of Jupiter	290°06'	290°30'
Difference	21°59'	21°19'
Converted time	21°51'	

And the bulimia lasting for two years certainly happened on account of some error in the things undertaken and done for the recovery of his health, or in exercises, in which things ab Hemminga, as a physician was unlucky, on account of the direction of the Midheaven, the primary significator of actions, to the square of Saturn in the 8th, corrected by our method. The arc of this direction was 21°33'.

In the year 1559, on the 8th of December at the 5th hour of the morning, a very severe fever occurred with pleuritis and inflammation of the liver, in which his life was almost despaired of. And this sickness was from the direction of Jupiter, ruler of the 1st, to Mars in the 2nd, ruler of the 12th. But not from the direction of the Ascendant to the antiscion of Mars, as ab Hemminga supposed; for Jupiter rules the liver, and the former cause is unequal to the effect.

Oblique Ascension of Mars in the circle of position of Jupiter	316°52'	316°16'
Oblique Ascension of Jupiter	290°06'	290°30'
Difference	26°46'	25°46'
Converted time of the accident	26°28'	

In the year 1566, on the 2nd of December, there occurred a sudden sickness with lack of breath and a sudden discharge of poison, which ended in a quotidian fever. And how specially this sickness squares with the direction of Mars, ruler of the Ascendant and the 12th, to the Sun, which essentially rules the heart and the vital faculty, is plain to all who are skilled in astrology. But because both of them are under the rulership of Saturn in exile in the 8th and in the domicile of the Moon, which is also in the 8th, it is no wonder that their effect was delayed until the year in which a revolution corresponding to this sickness occurred—namely, one in which Saturn was in partile opposition to the Sun and square the Moon, and Mars was on the cusp of the radical 8th; For the state of the planets in the preceding revolution was not indicative of sickness. Indeed, it was delayed thus until the 2nd of December, on which the Sun, Mars, and Mercury were conjoined by transit in opposition to the cusp of the radical 8th, and Saturn was with the Moon squaring those [planets] and the Midheaven.

Oblique Ascension of the Sun in the
circle of position of Mars   340°00'   340°09'
Oblique Ascension of Mars   308°13'   308°31'
Difference   31°47'   31°38'
Converted time of the accident   33°17'   33°17'
Difference   1°30'   1°39'

Therefore it delayed [its effect] through a whole year for which there was no corresponding revolution and through half of the one following that did correspond. But in truth, such an effect was from such a cause.

In the year 1572, on the 10th day of November, he was made captive, and he suffered many losses in wealth and possessions, and other evils in connection with cures and bodily afflictions. And these things sprang from the direction of Mars, ruler of the 12th and the Ascendant, in the 2nd, to Mercury, ruler of the 8th and the 10th, in its exile and fall on the cusp of the 4th. And these causes are very evident.

Oblique Ascension of Mercury in the
circle of position of Mars   347°14'   347°17'
Oblique Ascension of Mars   308°13'   308°31'
Difference   39°01'   38°46'
Converted time of the accident   39°16'

Finally, on 3 May 1577, by the force of the wind, he fell into some water with great danger of drowning. Which effect happened from the direction of Saturn, in exile in a water sign and in the 8th house, to the opposition of the Sun, also in exile in an air sign and a domicile of Saturn, as is evident per se.

[Oblique] Descension of the opposition of
the Sun in the circle of position of Saturn   162°19'   162°15'
Oblique Descension of Saturn   118°44'   118°51'
Difference   43°35'   43°24'
Converted time of the accident   43°37'

What, I ask, can be wished for in this nativity that is more in agreement with the effects of the causes as far as the kind—indeed the type and time of the ten accidents above? Or, having seen this, would ab Hemminga, Pico, and de Angelis have dared, or would it not have shamed them to write against astrology and to rage furiously against it? Do I not demonstrate with these [accidents] a thousand times more evidently the truth of this divine science than they were able to show its falsity with all their books? But we may conclude with the axiom we have used—nothing is more unjust than an ignorant man.[208]

Chapt. 5. *In which We Propose and Resolve Objections of no small Import.*

Having explained the objections of others, some occur to us that are a little more subtle, nor so easy to resolve as the former—at least not by every astrologer—but which are clearly resolved by the doctrine we have given down to this point.

And so, first I object that the ecliptic coincides with the horizon at an elevation of the pole of 66°30' or with some other circle of position above that latitude. And let the Sun in the former case be situated in the Ascendant. The question is whether the Sun and the Ascendant are two [separate] significators or one? And if they are one, for what [subjects] and in what way should it be directed? [But] if they are two, how should they be distinguished, and for what should each be directed?

I reply that the Sun and the Ascendant in this case are two distinct significators. Namely, there is the Ascendant, viewed with regard to its celestial state, which is the presence of the Sun and its aspects falling on the ortive part of the horizon. For the Ascendant must be directed as a significator, as it is thus disposed, according to the principles we have given above, namely that every significator should be directed by reason of its own state and determination in the figure. And in addition there is the Sun, since it is in the Ascendant with its own aspects; for the Sun must be directed by reason of its own determination and state on account of the same cause. And it is plain that these things should be considered separately because the Sun will be the ruler of the 5th by our universal method of erecting a celestial figure, and consequently the significator of children; and in consequence it must be directed, not only for the native, whom it signifies, but also for his children, because the Ascendant per se is incapable of doing this. And the reasoning is the same in the rest.

I object secondly: Let 2, 3, 4, or all of the planets be partilely conjoined in the same point or degree of the ecliptic. Which of them will be the significator or promittor in directions?

I reply that the place of the conjunction must be directed as the significator for any planetary conjunction, having regard to the determination and celestial state to which state that conjunction belongs; observing, however, with which significator the promittor will better agree for the effect or the subject represented by the significator. And it must be understood that either the promittor is singular,

---

208 But Sixtus ab Hemminga would not have been satisified, since he wanted the calculated times of events to match experience fairly closely, and these do not. The average deviation from Morin's figures is 31' or six months; and the average deviation of the recalculated figures is 39' or 7 3/4 months.

such as one planet or one aspect, or it is multiple, such as two planets partilel conjoined or sextiles or squares of the abovesaid planets. For it will always b necessary to see which of the conjoined promittors agrees more with the give significator. Therefore, if the significator is singular or solitary, such as th Midheaven or the Sun, and the promittor is multiple, such as 2, 3, 4, or all of th planets partilely conjoined, or also many aspects, it is plain that the one that is mor appropriate will be the promittor—namely, the one that agrees better with th significator for the subject that it represents.

I object thirdly: The termini of the directions are only mere points observe in the *caelum*. For in the direction of the Ascendant as significator, not any part o the *caelum* is directed, but only the point that is on the Ascendant. Similarly, in th direction of the Sun as significator, not any part of the *caelum* is directed, but onl that point which with respect to us corresponds to the center of the Sun. But ther is no force in the point. Therefore there is also no force in the directions of suc significators.

I reply. The point that is the Ascendant is not seen as a point formally, but a the beginning of the part of the *caelum* that is in the first house and is determinec to life. Moreover, the virtue of that whole part [of the *caelum*] is in it—more indeed, when it is closer to the Ascendant, and consequently greatest in the Ascendant itself, according to the common axiom *on account of that, every single one is such, and that one is more.* But as for the Sun, the point corresponding tc its center is not always directed as a point formally, but as the middle of that par of the *caelum* that the Sun hides for us with its own visible diameter and determines for us; in which whole part, in fact, the force is solar, but it is greatest in the center. Whence, of the planets conjoined to the sun, those that are nearer the Sun share the conjunction's force more efficaciously; and for this reason, partile conjunctions are valued above the rest. But most efficaciously of all—the one that is centrally conjoined to the Sun is said to be "in the heart of the Sun,"[209] and it is thought by the old astrologers to be another Sun as it were, because then it assumes the nature of the Sun, the greatest of all. Moreover, that which is said here about significators, should also be deemed to have been said about promittors, whether they are planets or aspects, in which also the whole diameter of the aspecting planet and its center must be understood.

I object fourthly: Very many directions, and notable ones too, occur with absolutely no effects proper to them—at least in the year in which they fall. Therefore, the doctrine of directions is either fickle or at least very lame—that doctrine in which all astrologers place particularly great trust and about which they boast.

I reply that directions alone do nothing without the agreement of annual revolutions, or at least monthly revolutions with transits in agreement on account

209 The *cazimi* of the Arab astrologers.

of the causes that will be explained in the next book.[210] Therefore, since a direction and a revolution in agreement do not always occur together, it is no wonder that a direction may sometimes be frustrated in its effect, or may be retarded for one or two years, or may be advanced by the same number of years, when a revolution in agreement occurs. But this confirms the doctrine of directions rather than refutes it. Besides, if no direction were to be frustrated in the effect proper to itself, fatal necessity would be instituted by the stars; but with the force of human prudence and freedom [of will] many things may be done and avoided that are contrary to the celestial influences, which makes this science only conjectural. And let these things suffice that we have said thus far about directions for the praise and glory of the Omnipotent God, Who created and wisely arranged the *caelum*, the stars, and the earth.

End of Book 22.

---

210 Book 23. The Revolutions of Nativities.

APPENDIX 1

1. Jerome Cardan on the Latitude of Aspects.

Seven Segments of Astronomical Aphorisms

Segment I

29. And it is convenient for you to have an instrument similar to a planisphere, big enough to be divided into 3,600 [parts], with which you will make directions without effort, both direct and converse. And in the same manner for genitures you will put in a big table all the fixed [stars] of the zodiac and the rest of the big ones outside [the zodiac] in their own exact places, and in the outer margin [there should be space] for entering the degrees and minutes of latitude.

30. It is also very likely that any planet may be directed by the line in which it moves, such as the Sun in the ecliptic and all the rest in their circles of latitude. And thus we may know the fixed [stars] to which they move bodily, for the direction of the place is always by the degrees of the ecliptic.

31. When, therefore, it is done thus, it is also appropriate for all the rays to be taken in the same way in that circle; and thereby only the oppositions agree with the method of Bianchini; therefore, the maximum latitudes of the planets ought to be known and the places where the circle of latitude cuts the ecliptic at that time—from which to find the radiations and directions by tables of the *primum mobile* or with an instrument.

32. Moreover, the maximum latitude should not be taken simply,[1] but [rather] that [latitude] which is then the maximum when the planet moves in that circle.

Maximum Latitudes of the Planets

	Saturn	Jupiter	Mars	Venus	Mercury	Moon
South	3°05'	2°08'	7°07'	7°22'	4°13'	5°00'
North	3°02'	2°04'	4°21'	7°23'	4°05'	5°00'

33. It is, therefore, manifest that astrology depends upon a comprehensive knowledge of the [celestial] motions and upon natural philosophy; and since the majority have neither, and prior to this no one [had] both, it is no wonder that our predecessors added infamy to the art.

---

1 That is, the maximum values given in the table should not be used in every case, but rather the value discovered from the motion at a particular time.

34. It is for this reason that just as astrology is very beautiful, so it is also very laborious and difficult.

The Judgments of Genitures

Chapt. 7. *How Aspects and Conjunctions ought to be Taken.*

The opposition aspect is [made] to the opposite sign under the same degree of longitude and in the same number of degrees of latitude but in the opposite part [of the sphere], just as in the 19th Geniture[2] the opposition of the Moon is in 11°42' Virgo with latitude 4N20, and the opposition ray of Venus is in 23°03' Aries with latitude 0S52.

First Table of Oppositions	Ari Lib	Tau Sco	Gem Sag	Can Cap	Leo Aqu	Vir Pis

And the square aspect is 90° of the ecliptic before and behind, and in the ecliptic itself without latitude, just as the square aspect of the Moon in the same geniture is in 11°42' Sagittarius without latitude, and it is called *dexter* because it precedes, and the other square is in 11°42' without latitude, and it is called *sinister* because it follows the order of the signs; and both of them lack latitude.

Second Table of Signs in Square Aspect					
Ari Cap Can	Tau Aqu Leo	Gem Pis Vir	Can Ari Lib	Leo Tau Sco	Vir Gem Sag
Lib Can Cap	Sco Leo Aqu	Sag Vir Psc	Cap Lib Ari	Aqu Sco Tau	Pis Sag Gem

And the trine is [obtained] by adding 120°, with the exception of a few minutes, which we will describe in the table below; the *dexter* [trine] is the preceding one, and the *sinister* [trine] the one following the order of the signs; and in each one the latitude is half of the planet's latitude but in the opposite part [of the sphere]. For example, the Moon's trine: the dexter trine is in 11°37' Scorpio with latitude 2N20, and the sinister trine is in 11°37' Cancer with latitude 2N20, which is half of the Moon's latitude in the opposite part [of the sphere].

---

2 Cardan's own horoscope (C 468B): No. 19 in his *Examples of One Hundred Genitures.*

Third Table of Signs in Trine Aspect	Ari Leo Sag	Tau Vir Cap	Gem Lib Aqu	Can Sco Pis

By these tables and those that follow, without any computation, you can obtain the place of the aspect in its sign, subtracting for the trine the minutes in the last table for the latitude of the planet; and putting with the opposition aspect, as was said, all the degrees [and minutes] of latitude, but in the opposite part [of the sphere]; and for the square, without latitude; and for the trine, half of the latitude, but in the opposite part [of the sphere], as was said.

But for the sextile you will take the corresponding degree in the sinister sextile sign according to the order of the signs or in the dexter sextile sign preceding, adding the minutes contained in the table following; and for the degrees [and minutes] of latitude of the star, you will take half of the star's latitude—in the northern part [of the sphere] if it is north or in the southern if it is south.

Fourth Table of Signs in Sextile Aspect					
Ari Aqu Gem	Tau Pis Can	Gem Ari Leo	Can Tau Vir	Leo Gem Lib	Vir Can Sco
Lib Leo Sag	Sco Vir Cap	Sag Lib Aqu	Cap Sco Pis	Aqu Sag Ari	Pis Cap Tau

You will do the same without the table, having added or subtracted 60° from the ecliptic [longitude] and also the minutes from the table according to the degrees [and mintues] of the latitude.

Example: the sinister sextile of the Moon falls in 11°47' Taurus, having added 5' from the preceding table, which corresponds to the Moon's latitude of 4°30', and the latitude of the aspect will be 2N20, i.e., half of the Moon's latitude in the same part [of the sphere], but the dexter sextile of the Moon will be in 11°47' Capricorn with latitude 2N20.

And you should know that the forces of aspects are just like the work of bending [the arm of] a catapult, for the conjunction or the aspect of 2° is ten times that which is made from a distance of 10°; and that which is made from the same degree is ten times that which is made from a a distance of 2°; and that which is made from 6' is ten times that which is made from a distance of around 1°, from which the greatest events [result].

Fifth Table of Addition for the Sextile and Subtraction for the Trine	
Latitude of the Planet	Distance to be subtr. or added
0°30'	0'
1 00	0
1 30	1
2 00	1
2 30	1
3 00	2
3 30	3
4 00	4
4 30	5
5 00	6
5 30	7
6 00	8
6 30	10
7 00	11
7 30	13
8 00	15

Translator's Comment

In the example, if the Moon's latitude is 4S20, then the latitude of its sextiles should be 2S10 and the latitude of its trines 2N10; and in the next to last paragraph the Moon's latitude is mistakenly given as 4°30'.

Aside from this, this method is straightforward. It assumes that the position of a planet in longitude and latitude defines the point of maximum deviation of the aspect circle from the ecliptic. Obviously then the aspect circle has an inclination to the ecliptic equal to the planet's latitude, and it intersects the ecliptic at the two points that are 90° from the planet. These are the squares. They coincide with the nodes of the aspect circle upon the ecliptic; consequently, the two squares have zero latitude. The opposition, of course, marks the point of maximum deviation from the ecliptic, but in the opposite direction; so that, if the planet has south latitude, its opposition has north latitude, and vice versa. In the case of the sextiles and the trines, they are all 30° from the squares, which mark the nodes; consequently, they have latitude equal to exactly half that of the planet—in the same direction in the case of the sextiles, but in the opposite direction in the case of the trines.

Mathematically, the latitude of any point on the aspect circle is represented by the formula

$$\sin b = \sin i \, \cos A$$

where b is the latitude of the aspect, i is the inclination of the aspect circle, and A is the aspect angle.

For the sextile, the angle is $60°$; and the cosine of these angles is 0.5 or 1/2. For the square, the angle is $90°$; and the cosine of these angles is zero. For the trine, the angle is $120°$; and the cosine of these angles is -0.5 or -1/2. The semisextile and the quincunx would be represented by $30°$ and $150°$ angles respectively; their cosines have the approximate value 0.866—positive for the semisextiles and negative for the quincunxes.

Table 5, which gives the correction to the longitude of the aspect, can be calculated approximately from the formula

$$D = 3438'(\text{abs}[\tan^2(i/2) \, \sin 2A])$$

and[3], since it is only intended for sextiles and trines, the angle $2A = 120°$ for the sextile and $240°$ for the trine. The sines of these angles have the values +0.866 and -0.866 respectively. Consequently, the numbers in the table can be calculated from the approximate formula

$$D = 2977'(\tan^2 (i/2))$$

But Cardan's rule for applying them is only correct for sinister aspects. For dexter aspects, it must be reversed: subtract the correction for a sextile and add it for a trine. He apparently forgot that his correction is properly applicable to the ecliptic arc from the planet to the aspect. Applying it directly to the uncorrected or nominal position of the aspect itself is permissible, but it must be done in such a way that the corrected aspects are equidistant from the planet. Thus, if 5' is added to the sinister sextile (as he has done in his example), it should be subtracted from the dexter sextile. And if 5' is subtracted from the sinister trine (as he has done), it should be added to the dexter trine.

Having corrected this blunder, we can compare Cardan's method of aspect correction with Morin's. Cardan's method is simple and logical. It begins with two assumptions: 1) that the point in precise opposition to a planet must be $180°$ greater in longitude and must also have the same latitude but in the opposite

---

3   The number of minutes in a radian is 3438. Multiplying this value by the cosine of $30°$ gives 2977'.

direction; and 2) that the planet is located at a point of maximum latitude in the aspect circle. If these premises are accepted, then the rest follows naturally.

Morin's method accepts the first premise but not the second. Instead, he teaches us how to select either a previous or a subsequent maximum latitude and directs us to take that for the inclination of the aspect circle. The planet's original position can be anywhere on that circle (unlike Cardan's concept, which assumes the planet to be at the point of maximum latitude). Thus, except for the opposition, the two methods will almost always produce different results.

Which of these two methods is preferable, or whether either of them has any merit, is unknown. It would have to be decided by experimentation. And the question is further complicated by the uncertainty about the proper method of house division and the proper method of calculating primary directions.

APPENDIX 2

J. B. Morin on the Mundane Position of Aspects.

Astrologia Gallica

Book 16, Section 1

Chapt. 9. *In what Great Circle the Real Aspects of the Planets should be Conceived according to the Truth of the Matter.*

Nature herself and the true principles of astrology must be consulted about this matter. In fact they will furnish another method to follow, which I have found after lengthy mental exertions.

It is conceded by all that the true places of the planets are to be looked at in the *primum mobile*, and it is certain that their bodies influence us from their own true places with respect to us, or as they appear to us in the *caelum* itself, and not from any other [place]. Therefore, from those same places they will determine the *caelum* with respect to the Earth or the native himself, both by reason of their own bodily position, and by reason of the aspects through which they also act. Moreover, these [aspects] must be counted from the true place of a planet, as Regiomontanus and Bianchini[1] have done. Not to be sure in various fictitious circles, such as Regiomontanus proposed, nor in the same and also fictious one that Bianchini proposed, but in the same real [circle], or at least in the real path of the planet as it appears to us as it moves in the *primum caelum*; the discovery of which excercised my mental abilities acutely for many years because I could see that the matter itself was one of the greatest importance to astrology—and the astrologers acknowledge this—and yet it was unknown to Kepler, Regiomontanus, and Ptolemy himself, all of whom discussed the correction of aspects, although they were distinguished astrologers, and Ptolemy was the chief prince of astrology.

Moreover, after numerous and time-consuming speculations on this matter, at last I considered the path of each planet to be twofold, that is, a true or absolute path, and the one that is apparent to us. The true path is that which the planet

---

1   Giovanni Bianchini (fl. 1450-1500) was a professor of astronomy at the University of Ferrara and the author of astronomical tables. He was well known in his own time and also in the 16th century (he is cited by Gaurico, Cardan, Naibod, and Junctinus). Thorndike, HMES V, 565, cites a passage from Cardan's book *On the Subtility of Things*, XVI (1663 ed.: vol. III, 607), in which Cardan says that Regiomontanus's tables of directions were based on those of Bianchini. Thorndike also notes (HMES VI, 120) that Naibod discusses Bianchini's aspect theory in his *Description of the Elements of Astrology*.

describes absolutely in space about its own bodily center which is represented as being joined to the *primum mobile*, and it is called the orbit or *excentric* of the planet. Moreover, this apparent [path] is in the *primum mobile*, under which the planet itself is observed to move with respect to the Earth or to us. Moreover, on the Sun the true orbit continued to the *primum mobile* coincides with its appearance to us, because the true orbit of the Sun is arranged around the Earth,[2] and the Sun and the Earth are always in the same plane of the ecliptic. And therefore the circle of the ecliptic is the same one in which the Sun always moves with respect to us, and consequently it influences us both through its own body and also through its aspects, exactly defined in it, as experience testifies.

But according to Copernicus and Tycho, Saturn, Jupiter, Mars, Venus, and Mercury have true orbits that are not arranged about the Earth, and consequently they appear from our point of view to move on the *caelum* in lines that are not circular, as will be plain to anyone if he traces their paths in longitude and latitude through the whole zodiac on a celestial globe. Yet, because the orbits of Saturn, Jupiter and Mars enclose that of the Earth, these depart less from a circular line; and these same planets in their own revolution become north or south of the ecliptic only once [in a year]; but Venus and Mercury, beyond the true orbits of which the Earth is placed, will describe for us apparently in the *caelum* lines that are more irregular and tortuous around the ecliptic, and especially Mercury, which, in traversing the zodiac [in the course of a year] becomes five or six times north and then south in latitude.[3] Moreover, all the astrologers, educated by experience, agree that aspects should be taken in the actual celestial circle in which the true place of the planet is, in which its aspects are defined by proper quantities. And they further agree that a planet acts with respect to us not only by reason of its own true location but also by reason of all its aspects defined in the same great circle, although the orbits of Venus and Mercury do not go around that of the Earth, in fact because the true place of a planet in the *caelum* will determine eleven others in the same great circle for the places of its own aspects, as we said in Chapt. 4. And the whole difficulty consists of designating that circle which at least goes along with the real path of the planet as it appears to us in the *primum caelum*.

And in the first place it is certain that that circle is not the ecliptic, for, in the case of Saturn, Jupiter, Mars, Venus, and Mercury, the latitude of the body of the planet, if it has any, must be observed in directions, and [also the latitude of] its opposition, as Ptolemy enjoins and as experience compels. But no valid reason can be put forward why the body of the planet and its opposition are beyond the ecliptic but the rest of the aspects are in the ecliptic, as Ptolemy himself held; for thus not all the aspects would be in the ecliptic, and either the circle of aspects

---

2   Morin, following Tycho Brahe, refused to accept the entire Copernican theory.

3   Morin is calling attention to the fact that the superior planets generally stay on one side of the ecliptic for a substantial length of time before crossing to the other side. But the inferior planets, particularly Mercury, switch back and forth much oftener.

would not be an exact circle or two circles would have to be admitted—one for the body [of the planet] and its opposition, and the other, namely the ecliptic, for the rest of the aspects of the same planet, which is absurd.

And in the second place it is also certain that that circle is not the true orbit of the planet, [as seen] from the Sun, projected onto the *primum caelum*. Because that orbit, although it is a circle inclined to the ecliptic, is however inclined at a constant angle, which is 2°32' for Saturn, 1°20' for Jupiter, 1°50' for Mars, 3°22' for Venus, and 6°54' for Mercury.[4] But the true latitudes of Saturn, Jupiter, Mars, Venus, and Mercury frequently exceed these inclinations,[5] and Mars can have up to 7 degrees of latitude; for the [geocentric latitudes] can be taken between the ecliptic and the true orbit. Therefore, it is necessary that the inclination of the circle that we seek be either the latitude of the planet at the moment for which the aspects are required or the maximum latitude nearest following or preceding that moment, in which the planet itself is descending from the ascending; or else, on the contrary, the maximum and final latitude which the planet can attain while it is situated in the northern or southern part [of the *caelum*], for every other method departs more from the true path of the planet in the *caelum*, as will be evident from the following objections.

But now the first method is that of Bianchini, who makes the instantaneous latitude of the planet to be the measure of the inclination of the circle of aspects to the ecliptic. For example, let the ecliptic be ABEC, the planet Mars D, which had no latitude in point A on the ecliptic, and let Mars then be made [to have] north [latitude] and its path to be indicated by the points ADF. And in addition, from the circle of latitude of Mars Fig. 1. through its place D, let the circle DEG be drawn[6] for the circle of aspects, and in this way in fact the square of Mars will fall at point E on the ecliptic; but it is evident to the eye that Mars does not in any way move along this circle; otherwise, from D to E it would necessarily move to the ecliptic, when, on the contrary, it necessarily moves away from it on its own apparent path ADF on the celestial sphere. Therefore, Bianchini's circle must be rejected as being foreign to nature.

The second mode coincides with the third for Mars, Venus, and Mercury, for these planets never become descending after having been ascending, or vice versa,[7] except when they have attained the maximum latitude that they can have when they are north or south in latitude, but necessarily they increase in latitude up to that

---

4   These inclinations are a tribute to Kepler's reduction of Tycho Brahe's careful observations. For the epoch 1600.0, the modern mean elements are 2°30' for Saturn, 1°20' for Jupiter, 1°51' for Mars, 3°23' for Venus, and 7°00' for Mercury.

5   Because the minimum distance between the Earth and a planet is less than the mean distance of a planet from the sun.

6   The text has DFG by mistake.

7   The terms *ascending* and descending refer to the planet's motion in latitude—*ascending* when it is moving from south to north and *descending* when it is moving from north to south. Morin means that they never retrograde in latitude.

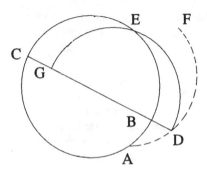

Figure 1.

maximum as is also evident in the ephemerides. Moreover, Saturn and Jupiter, although they do not necessarily increase in latitude up to the maximum, but are often seen (especially Saturn) to retrograde in latitude, nevertheless, when returning, do proceed to the maximum latitude north or south which they can attain in their own revolution. And consequently, if, for the circle of aspects, that circle is put, whose inclination to the ecliptic is the maximum north or south latitude (as the planet is in the north or south part [of the *caelum*]) which the planet itself can attain, then that circle before [all] the rest, coinciding as it does with the apparent path of the planet in the *caelum*, which is not circular, must be considered to be the true and most natural of all the circles of aspects.

Besides, both of the orbits of Saturn, Jupiter, Mars, Venus, and Mercury that are seen in the *caelum*, i.e., the apparent [path as seen] from the Earth and the true [orbit as seen] from the Sun, projected [upon the *caelum*], are such that, whenever a planet in its own true orbit, also projected upon the *caelum*, is free from latitude according to Kepler's opinion, and it is in its own node in that orbit, then that same planet is also free from latitude in its own apparent orbit and in the circle of aspects assumed by us, and it is in the nodes of the latter. But these [two sets of] nodes are in different places, that also differ by many degrees; just as the excentric place of the planet and its apparent place in the *caelum* differ in the ecliptic. For example, on 23 April 1647 at Paris noon Venus is found in *The Rudolphine Tables* to be in 19°49' Taurus in true (or apparent) motion, without any latitude; therefore, it is in the intersection of the apparent orbit and the ecliptic, and it is [moving to the] north. Moreover, at that same time the north node of Venus in its own true orbit with mean motion is 13°37' Gemini; and consequently the difference between the two is 23°48'. Besides, the motion of the nodes in each orbit differs greatly. For in the true orbit the nodes move uniformly and very slowly, but in the apparent orbit they move irregularly and much more rapidly. Finally, the inclination of the true orbit to the ecliptic is invariable as was said above, but the inclination of the apparent orbit is variable. For its maximum north latitude is not the same in each revolution of the planet, nor the maximum south latitude, nor the north as compared to the south, but these latitudes are different as often as the planet crosses from the northern part [of the *caelum*] to the southern part. And the transfer of these planets from the Sun and the parallax of the orbit causes all this with respect to the Earth.[8]

With this behind us, it would now be appropriate to show how this circle can be drawn in the *primum mobile* for Saturn, Jupiter, Mars, Venus, and Mercury, and how their aspects can be defined in it.

First then, the maximum latitude that the planet can attain in the northern part or the southern part [of the *caelum*] in which it is situated, is taken for the inclination to the ecliptic of the circle of aspects at the given time.

Second, from that inclination and from the true latitude of that same planet at that same time, the place [of the planet] between the intersections of that same circle and the ecliptic at the same time is found by the following method.

In the year 1647, at the month, day, and hour mentioned above, Venus was in 19°49' Taurus without any latitude, consequently in its apparent node. Thereafter, it is noted [in the ephemeris] that it attained a maximum north latitude of 1°47'.[9] This latitude then is taken for the inclination of the circle of aspects to the ecliptic, which is [the arc] AEC in the figure below, and the circle of aspects coinciding with the apparent path of Venus is ADB, and their intersection or the north node is A, from which Venus is conceived to be moved, necessarily with its latitude increasing, until it reaches B with a maximum north latitude of 1°47'. Moreover, let Venus be at point D of that circle, with north latitude DE of 1°10', which it attains on 22 May at Paris noon in 25°15' Gemini. Now, from the given BC and DE may be found first the arc of the ecliptic AE by saying as the tangent of BC is to the tangent of DE, so is the total sine AC to the sine of AE; and AE is found to be 40°52'.[10] Which, subtracted from the place of Venus in the ecliptic, 2 signs 25°15', leaves 1 sign 14°24', i.e., 14°24' Taurus for the place of the north node A, in which the intersection of the circle of aspects [with the ecliptic] occurs at that time. This place must be noted, and also its opposite 14°24' Scorpio for the south node.

---

8 Morin refers to the transfer from heliocentric to geocentric coordinates, which transforms the simple latitudinal motion of Mercury and Venus into a complex one with rapid variations in (apparent) orbital inclination and position of the nodes.

9 Towards the end of June 1647.

10 This procedure yields a value (actually 40°51') for the arc AE that is only formally correct. That is, it assumes that the values of the two latitudes that are used to determine it are absolutely exact. For example, let us repeat the calculation with DE = 1°11' instead of 1°10'. We get AE = 41°34' instead of 40°51'. Thus a change of 1' of arc in the intermediate latitude causes a change of 43' in the arc AE. Unfortunately, if the latitudes are only given to the nearest minute of arc, the calculated arc from the planet to its apparent node will be subject to considerable error.

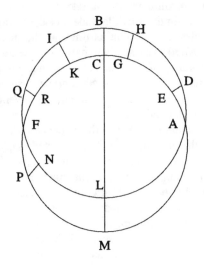

Figure 2.

After this, AD is found by saying as the sine of BC is to the sine of DE, so the radius or the sine of AB is to the sine of AD, 40°52', which is the arc of the circle of aspects corresponding to the arc of the ecliptic AE, marking the place of Venus in that circle and its distance from the node A.[11]

Now from this same point D, the place of Venus in the circle of aspects or the apparent orbit, which is 40°52' from the node A, are to be counted all its exact aspects in that same circle, namely by giving 30° to the dodectile, 60° to the sextile, 90° to the square, etc. And let the sinister dodectile be at H, for which the longitude and latitude is required. So, having added AD, 40°52', to DH, 30°, it makes 70°52' for AH. And therefore let it be done: as the whole sine AB is to the sine of AH, 70°52', so the sine of BC, 1°47', is to the sine of GH, 1°41', which will be the north ascending latitude of that dodectile terminating at the point G in the ecliptic; and since that point is known, or the arc of the ecliptic AG, let it be that as the tangent of BC is to the tangent of GH, so the total sine AC is to the sine of AG, 70°44', or 2 signs 10°44'. And if to this is added the place of the node A, 1 sign 14°24', it

---

11 Note that the arc AD in the circle of aspects has the same value in this example as the arc AE in the ecliptic. This is because the inclination (1°47') is small. The difference can amount in extreme cases to 17' of arc. Also, note that in the next numerical example Morin forgets that he found AD = AE when the arc in question was 40°52' and derives an erroneous difference for an arc of 70°52', although the maximum difference must occur at 45°.

will make 3 signs 25°08' or 25°08' Cancer for the true place of that dodectile in the ecliptic.[12]

For finding the sinister square of Venus, 90° are added to the same [value of] D, i.e., 40°52', and it will make 130°52' for the arc ADI, which, subtracted from the semi-circle ABF, leaves 49°08' for FI; and so let it be made as the total sine of FB is to the sine of FI, so the sine of BC is to the sine of IK; and it will make 1°21' for IK, the north descending latitude of the square itself, which terminates in the ecliptic at the point K; and since that point is known, or the arc of the ecliptic FK, let it be that as the tangent of BC is to the tangent of IK, so the total sine FC is to the sine of FK; and it will make 49°12' for FK, or 1 sign 19°12', which, subtracted from the place of the south node F, 7 signs 14°24', will leave 5 signs 25°09', i.e. 25°09' Scorpio for the true place of that square in the ecliptic.

The sinister quincunx will be found [thus]: if 60° is added to the place of the square I, it will terminate at the point N; and so if from the 60° are taken away 49°08' for [the arc] FI, 10°55' will be left for [the arc] FN. And therefore let it be made: as the total sine of FL is to the sine of FN, so is the sine of ML or BC to the sine of N; and it will make 0°20' for NP, the south descending latitude of the quincunx itself, which terminates in the ecliptic at the point P; and since arc FP is known, let it be that as the tangent of LM is to the tangent of NP, so the total sine FM is to the sine of FP, 10°46', which, if it is added to the place of the node F at 12°24' Scorpio, it will make 25°10' Scorpio for the place of that quincunx. And so with all the others for Saturn, Jupiter, Mars, and Mercury. Moreover, having found the sinister aspects as above, the dexter aspects are diametrically opposed to them, with equal latitudes but of the opposite denomination, viz. the sinister dodectile is opposed to the dexter quincunx, the sinister sextile to the dexter trine, the sinister square to the dexter square, the sinister trine to the dexter sextile, and the sinister quincunx to the dexter dodectile; and consequently it is only necessary to find the sinister [aspects] or the dexter. Moreover, we shall give an excellent table in Book 22, with the aid of which these aspects and their own longitudes and latitudes can very easily be found, for the present method is only suitable for learned persons and those fond of theory.

---

12 This method of calculation, while formally correct, is impractical because the aspect arc is made to depend on the ratios of the sines and tangents of two small angles. And unless these angles are calculated to seconds of arc, the aspect arcs cannot be depended on to the nearest minute of arc. For example, Morin calculates the ratio of the tangents of 1°41' and 1°47' and gets for the arcsine of that ratio 70°44'. If we change 1°41' to 1°42' and repeat the calculation, we get 72°25'. Thus, a change of 1' of arc in the latitude produces a change of 1°41' in the longitude of the aspect. This procedure is obviously unsatisfactory. It seems odd that Morin, who was the Regius Mathematician of France, did not notice this. (Actually, the difference between the arcs AG and AH is only about 31" of arc, which should have been apparent from the fact that he found above that AE = AD when AE is 40°52'.)

179

But since for finding the true place of any aspect in the ecliptic, the arc of th ecliptic first found must be added to or subtracted from the true place of the nod that is nearest to the true place of the planet in the ecliptic, it may be known whethe this node is the ascending node or the descending node of the planet as follow: When the true latitude of the planet is north and subsequently increases, the plane is departing from its own true north node and is going toward the northern limit; i it decreases, the planet is departing from the northern limit and is going toward th descending node. And when the true latitude of the planet is south and increase thereafter, the planet is departing from its descending node and is going toward i southern limit; if it decreases, it is departing from the limit and going toward th ascending node. And this is always true for Mars, Venus, Mercury, and the Moor but not for Saturn and Jupiter. And so in general if a planet in the northern part [o the *caelum*] has not yet attained its maximum north latitude, it precedes th ascending node; if it has already passed [its maximum north latitude], it follow the descending node.[13] And think the same about a planet in the southern part [o the *caelum*]. Moreover, when it precedes the ascending node or the descendin; node, take away the arc first found (which is the distance of the planet from th node in the ecliptic) from the planet itself, and the remainder will be the place o the node in the ecliptic. But if it follows the ascending node or the descendin; node, add that same distance to the place of the planet to get the node.

But some things can be objected to in this doctrine, from the resolution o: which it may be established more firmly. And first, that the planet does not move in the assumed circle of aspects, as the Sun in the ecliptic circle for the aspects o the Sun; therefore, this circle is also fictitious, as are the circles of Bianchini anc Regiomontanus.

I reply: There is no other circle that coincides more closely with the apparent path of the planet, especially for Saturn, Jupiter, and Mars, from whose paths the circles of Bianchini and Regiomontanus absolutely diverge; and consequently the circle assumed by us ought to be chosen in preference to the rest as being more natural and real, seeing that the apparent path of the planet in the *caelum* is not circular, but the aspects are put in an exact circle by the astrologers, forced by experience.

It may be objected in the second place that through this method the true node of the planet in the *caelum* appears not only to run through more degrees in a year but even more signs, although the mean motion of that same node, at least for Saturn, Jupiter, Mars, Venus, and Mercury, is not even 2' in any year. Therefore, that apparent motion is fictitious.

But I reply. It is not fabricated, but it also really happens. For example, on 23 April 1647 Venus lacking any latitude is in 19°49' Taurus, and its own true north node according to *The Rudolphine Tables*; and on 13 August it is in 3°05' Libra, in

---

13 To precede in the zodiac is to be further advanced in the counterclockwise direction. For
example, Taurus precedes Aries. To follow is the reverse.

s own true south node; and consequently its true north node at that time ought to
e in 3°05' Aries; and so, from the day 23 April to 13 August it had moved backward
sign 16°44'. Moreover, on 4 December of that same year this same Venus is again
acking in latitude in 8°02' Sagittarius, in its own north node, although that same
iode had previously been in 19°49' Taurus; and so from 23 April to 4 December it
iad moved backward 5 signs 11°47'. And in short, in the figure above, Venus's
notion in longitude from its own true ascending node A up to C, where its latitude
s a maximum, is less than a quadrant or 90° just as much as the true node A itself
ias gone back apparently in the preceding direction because of the transfer [of the
coordinates] of these planets from the Sun and the phase of the Earth. Nor is that
only true of this quadrant AC, but also of the arcs AE and AG, when the true motion
of Venus in longitude is less than the quantity of these same arcs.

It may be objected in the third place that the inclination of the apparent
planetary path in the sky is never the same, but is continually varied, otherwise it
would be a perfect circle; therefore, the maximum apparent latitude cannnot be
taken for the constant inclination to the ecliptic of the circle of aspects while the
planet is moving from its own node to that maximum latitude, or from the latter to
the former.

But I reply that since the abovesaid circle of aspects and the apparent path of
the planet in the *caelum* have this in common: that through each line the planet
proceeds from its own true node to the abovesaid maximum latitude, or recedes
therefrom, the difference in longitude and latitude of the aspects arising from this
variation is for the most part insensible, at least in the same northern or southern
semicircle through which the planet runs, and which alone is considered, because
the other [line] from its determination is continuous with it, namely they make one
single perfect circle.

It may be objected in the fourth place that this method cannot always be used
for Saturn, Jupiter, Mars, Venus, and Mercury. For when the planet is lacking in
latitude, being in its own true node, what will its circle of aspects be then? Perhaps
the ecliptic? But the planet does not move in the ecliptic. Perhaps another circle?
But what will its inclination to the ecliptic be? And will it be the maximum north
latitude, or will it be the maximum south latitude, differing between themselves by
several degrees?

I reply that although the planet is truly in its own node, lacking any latitude,
yet it is certain that it truly moves with respect to us in its own apparent orbit,
inclined to the ecliptic. And consequently, that will always be the circle of aspects
which goes according to that apparent path. Moreover, its inclination will be the
maximum latitude from which the planet has departed, and it has decreased up to
that very node in which the planet's latitude has ceased [altogether], and not the
maximum latitude [next] following, to which it is going, because it has not yet
entered upon that. And this objection can be made for any other circle of aspects
going with the apparent path of the planet in the *caelum*, whatever inclination is
taken for it from the north part [of the *caelum*] or the south.

It may be objected in the fifth place that it seems more probable that the circle of aspects ought to be traced through the true place of the planet and the nodes of its own true orbit, reduced to the ecliptic of the *primum caelum* through the phase of the Earth. For thus, from the given true place of the planet with its longitude and latitude and also from the true place of its node, an inclination of the circle of aspects will be given that is appropriate and conformable to whatever time was assumed. That indeed seems to be more conformable to reason than to take the maximum apparent latitude of the planet for the constant inclination of the circle of aspects as long as the planet moves from its own node to that maximum latitude or from the latter to the former.

I reply that it does indeed seem more probable at first glance, and I myself was deluded by this method until I discovered that the inclination to the ecliptic of the circle of aspects of Mars could amount to as much as $12°$, which deviates too much from the maximum latitude of Mars, which never exceeds $8°$. And the true places of Venus and Mercury in the ecliptic sometimes (that is, when they are traversing the inferior parts of their own true orbits) coincide with the true places of their nodes, and yet [placed] thus Venus and Mercury possess a latitude of several degrees even, which cannot happen, or their latitudes are made equal to their distances from their true nodes, which would call for a $90°$ inclination to the ecliptic of the circle of aspects, and this deviates much more from the true latitude of Venus and Mercury. Therefore, if the circles differ too much from the motion in the apparent paths of the planets in the *caelum*, and consequently then the only thing left for us is to take the circle we have explained, which follows that motion more than the others and never exceeds the maximum latitude of the planet, although for Saturn and Jupiter either method can be employed indiscriminately without any great error.

But as for the Moon in its orbit around the earth, it also admits a double orbit, that is a true orbit that it describes truly with the center of its own body around the earth, which orbit is called the *mean excentric orbit*[14] by Kepler, inclined to the ecliptic at a constant angle of $5°$, then the apparent orbit, in which it is seen from our point of view to move projected upon the *primum mobile*, and it undergoes monthly anomalies by means of which its longitude and latitude are varied.[15] And this apparent orbit is called the *monthly excentric* [orbit], librating about the mean

---

14 In Latin *excentricus solutus*. That is, the excentric orbit "freed [from minor variations]" that yields the "unperturbed" or elliptical position of the Moon. Morin does not actually use the Latin word *medius* 'mean', but by (modern) definition a *mean orbit* is one "freed from perturbations."

15 Morin refers here to the variation of the Moon's inclination. Tycho Brahe introduced terms into the lunar tables that had the effect of causing the inclination of the Moon's orbit to oscillate back and forth by as much as $9'30''$ on either side of its mean value of $5°08'$. This also caused the Moon's nodes to oscillate back and forth by as much as $1°46'$ on either side of their mean position. The variation of the nodes is something like

[orbit] and inclined to it by a variable angle because of the libration, but not exceeding 19' according to Tycho and Kepler. Moreover, the true place of the Moon in longitude and latitude with respect to the center of the earth is always taken in this orbit, also the true place of its north node, and these are put into the ephemerides.

But since the inclination of the apparent orbit or of the lunar path in the *caelum* is continually varied by this libration, it results that the path itself is not a perfect circle, as happens in the case of Saturn, Jupiter, Mars, Venus, and Mercury, but somewhat different from a circle, although [the difference is] nearly imperceptible. And consequently the maximum latitude that the Moon can attain in the northern part [of the *caelum*] or the southern, through which it moves, can be taken much more accurately for the inclination of the circle of aspects, which is nearly the same as the librational orbit. And the places of the aspects can be projected from the true place of the Moon, as is done for Saturn, Jupiter, Mars, Venus, and Mercury. And so, for all these planets there will be one and the same method, which recommends it still more, and whose verity will begin to shine forth particularly in the Moon's aspects, because their circle and the Moon's apparent orbit nearly coincide.

Indeed, since the place of the north node is given in the ephemerides of the Moon for every single day, it will be a shorter method for the Moon if from the places of the Moon and the nearest node, calculated for the same moment, the preceding is taken away from the following, and the distance of the Moon from its node will remain. Then let it be: as the sine of that distance is to the total sine, so is the tangent of the true latitude of the Moon to the tangent of the maximum latitude, or the inclination to the ecliptic of the apparent lunar orbit at that time, which inclination will be the measure of the angle A in the figure above, a quantity that is variable in individual revolutions of the Moon because of the libration, but without any sensible error for the aspects; and finally (with the Moon placed at point D) let it be as the sine of BC is to the sine of DE, so the total sine is to the sine of AD, and the place of the Moon in the apparent orbit will be had at point D, or [its place] in the circle of aspects, from which the aspects will be projected, as is done for Saturn, Jupiter, Mars, Venus, and Mercury. And this method differs hardly at all from the one given above for the correction of the Moon's aspects.

With everything we have said above thus established by reason and approved by experience, at length by chance I fell upon Cardan's *Aphorisms* 30,31, and 32 of the first section,[16] which I had previously read many times but could not

---

the so-called "true node" given in some modern astrological ephemerides. The combination of the variation of the inclination and the nodes gives rise to variations in the Moon's latitude. In addition to these motions, the Moon's longitude in the ephemerides of Morin's time contained three variations or "anomalies" that caused it to vary by as much as 7° from its mean elliptic position. But Morin is mainly concerned here with the variation of the latitude, the inclination, and the nodes.

16 *Seven Segments of Astronomical Aphorisms*, Seg. I, Aphs. 30-32 (1563 ed., p. 31). See App. I.

understand on account of his brevity of speech and the ambiguity of the words in this rather difficult matter. I began to suspect that Cardan had scented the circle of aspects that I had set forth, although he says some things that are foreign to this circle. But in the rest he explains his own intention so badly, that what he really had in mind is unknown. Moreover, whether he really scented [my method] and disclosed it, the reader, experienced from what has already been said, may judge.

And so, in *Aphor.* 30 he says: "It is also very likely that any planet may be directed by the line in which it moves, such as the Sun in the ecliptic and all the rest in their circles of latitude. And thus we may know[17] the fixed [stars] to which they move bodily. For the direction of the place is always by the degrees of the ecliptic."

Here, when he says "It is very likely" it is plain that he does not assert this, but he is in doubt about it. When he says "that any planet may be directed by the line in which it moves" that line can be understood as well by the true orbit as by that which we have called the apparent orbit, and he did not make any distinction. Besides, the circle that we have assumed is neither of these lines, and the apparent orbit is not the circle. When he says "and all the rest in their circles of latitude" he has confused [both] himself and the reader's understanding. For if any particular planet ought to be directed by the line in which it moves, how should all the rest of the planets? And then he says "these are to be directed in their circles of latitude." It is established in astronomy that the circle of latitude of a planet is that which descends from the pole of the ecliptic through the center of the planet at right angles to the ecliptic. And this is not the circle we have set forth above. Finally, when he says "And thus we may know the fixed [stars] to which they move bodily. For the direction of the place is always by the degrees of the ecliptic" he gave a nod to the twofold direction of a planet; one bodily in the line in which it moves, or (as he says) in its circle of latitude, and the other through its place in the ecliptic, which he wants to be directed by the degrees of the ecliptic. But this direction is contrary to the intention of Ptolemy, who wishes the latitude of a planet to be used in the method of directions;[18] and, directing by the horary times, he directs by the degrees of the equator; and this is also contrary to reason, for a planet ought not to be directed from a place in which it is certainly not present; and certainly it is not in the ecliptic, but is only reduced to the ecliptic if it has latitude. Moreover, in the other direction there is nothing different from the methods of Bianchini and Regiomontanus for directions to the fixed [stars], for every fixed [star] of the same declination with the planet being directed can come to it according to these methods.

---

17 The Latin text has *inveniemus* 'we may find' by mistake for Cardan's *sciemus* 'we may know', but Morin cites it correctly below.
18 This is false. Ptolemy says nothing about using the latitude of the planets in directions. His instructions and examples are for what we would call zodiacal primaries by the Placidus method.

Aphorism 31 says "When, therefore, it is done thus, it is also appropriate for all the rays to be taken in the same way in that circle." And this is certainly true, if it means that all the rays are taken in the circle we have set forth as they are taken for the Sun in the ecliptic. And when he goes on to say "and thereby those opposed to the Sun agree with the method of Bianchini" he has again confused [both] himself and the reader's understanding. For what else can be understood by those opposed to the Sun than Saturn, Jupiter, and Mars, which are seen by us [at times] to be opposed to the Sun, but not Venus and Mercury? Now in our method for aspects neither Saturn, Jupiter, and Mars, nor Venus and Mercury agree with Bianchini's method, in which the aspects always fall in the ecliptic, as is also the case in Regiomontanus's method.[19] But [on the other hand] if it is only to be understood as "about the opposite aspect of these planets" then he has added "to the Sun" in vain, for in both Ptolemy's and Regiomontanus's methods the opposite aspect falls in the same point of the *caelum* as with Bianchini's and our own methods.

And when he says subsequently "the maximum latitudes of the planets ought to be known" it means which they can have simply from the northern part [of the *caelum*] or the southern and which Cardan himself gives, although not exactly. Namely, 3°05' for Saturn, 2°08' for Jupiter, 7°07' for Mars, 7°22' for Venus, and 4°05' for Mercury.[20] And when he continues "And to know the places where the circle of latitude cuts the ecliptic at that time" this certainly ought to mean the circle set forth by me, but this is not a circle of latitude, as is said above. And when he proceeds "from which to find the radiations" it is doubtful whether the radiations or aspects are to be taken in the ecliptic from the point where it is cut by the circle of the planet *proprie dicto* or whether they are to be taken in the circle set forth by us, and counting from the point in which the circle itself cuts the ecliptic, but neither of which is to be done in our method. But they are to be counted in the circle set forth by us beginning from the body of the planet, although from the point where the ecliptic is cut or we may use the node recognized by us for finding or determining the longitudes of the several aspects in the ecliptic, as was made plain above.

Finally, Aphorism 32 says "Moreover, the maximum latitude should not be taken simply, but [rather] that [latitude] which is then the maximum when the planet moves in that circle." Now Cardan seems to favor our [position] entirely. For, for the inclination to the ecliptic of the circle of aspects, I take the maximum latitude that the planet can have or has had in the northern or southern semicircle through

---

19 Morin has been led astray by the typesetter's error in capitalizing the Latin word *soli* 'only', so that it reads *Soli* 'to the Sun. The translation should read '...only the oppositions agree with Bianchini'. See this Aphorism in Appendix 1.

20 Cardan, *op. cit.*, gives the maximum northern and southern latitude for each planet in two successive rows of figures. Morin has taken the top row (south latitude) for all the planets except Mercury, for which he has unaccountably given the northern maximum. (The southern maximum given by Cardan is 4°13'.) Cardan's figures are of course based upon the ephemerides of his day that were less accurate than those available to Morin.

which it moves, either in the northern or southern part [of the *caelum*] in which it is situated.

If anyone then wants to deny that Cardan in these three aphorisms understood the method given by me, that may be permitted him on account of that which was said above in the explanation of these aphorisms. But if anyone asserts the opposite, at least our method will be confirmed from the fact that [by means] of it I myself have explained the intricate and confused intention of Cardan, which neither I nor anyone else had done hitherto.

But nevertheless it is certain that Cardan himself did not explain how to reduce this method to practice, perhaps intimidated by the difficulty of the matter, nor did he ever make use of it, but instead [he used] the method of Bianchini which he recommends and openly teaches in his *Book on the Judgment of Genitures*, Chapt. 7.[21] And no astrologer from Cardan's time down to ours has taught or employed our [method]; however, Origanus, Argol, and other more recent [astrologers] who have discussed the correction of aspects have read and reread the aphorisms cited above, just as I too did; and before [I arrived at] my own conception, I understood nothing in them, nor did I think about them, nor did I venture to affirm until now what Cardan had in mind in them. Whatever then, with everything considered, we were able [to do] in a matter of such moment and one so difficult, one thing only seemed to be left to be desired in our astrology; this the kindly reader may receive with a grateful spirit, or, with me also applauding, he may propound something better. But we warn [the reader] that this thing must be used with the very best ephemerides, in which the true longitudes and especially the latitudes of the planets are given correctly, if the astronomy fundamentally restored by us at last, once it has supplied such ephemerides, in which at the beginning of each year, at least for Saturn, Jupiter, and Mars, are put their maximum latitudes in the northern or southern semicircle through which they move, and at what time it has gone ahead or it is going to come after, lest searching for these things be too tedious, especially in the case of Saturn, which in the same semicircle is ascending in latitude around twelve times and descending as many in the space of about 15 years. Moreover, how much it matters to have ephemerides or exact tables for this procedure, he will sufficiently infer who notices that the latitudes of Saturn, Jupiter, Mars, Venus, and

---

21 This chapter is on p. 444 of the 1563 ed. Cardan does not mention Bianchini (or anyone else), but explains that the oppositions and squares fall in the same degree and minute as the planet itself, but the sextiles and trines must be corrected by a table that he gives in Col. 1. The table proceeds at intervals of 30' from 0°30' to 8°00', and the correction ranges from 0' to 15'. Cardan says to add the correction to sextiles and subtract it from trines. For the latitudes of the aspects, he says the opposition has the same latitude but the direction is reversed, the squares have zero latitude, the sextiles have half the planet's latitude, and the trines have half the planet's latitude with the direction reversed. See Appendix 1 for a translation of the entire chapter.

Mercury in the *Prutenic Tables*, the *Lansbergian Tables*, and the *Rudolphine Tables* frequently differ among themselves by 1°.[22]

Translator's Comment

Morin's method of finding the appropriate maximum latitude for a planet in a particular instance seems to be this:

1. If the planet is decreasing in latitude, find the previous maximum.
2. If the planet is increasing in latitude, find the subsequent maximum.
3. In the case of the slower planets, take the maximum obtained from Rule 1 or Rule 2 even though the maximum so obtained is only a "yearly maximum."
4. For the Moon, use the nodes given in the ephemeris, and determine the inclination from the Moon's latitude and its distance from the nearest node, as explained above.
5. Having determined the appropriate inclination to use and the distance of the planet from the nearest node, add multiples of 30° to the planet's "excentric arc" to obtain the excentric location of the aspects.
6. Convert the excentric positions of the aspects into ecliptic longitude and latitude by following the rules given above or by using Morin's tables.

This method is somewhat similar in concept to Cardan's, in that it postulates an "aspect circle" whose inclination and nodes must be determined for each particular case. But Cardan always locates the planet at either the northern or southern limit (the point of maximum latitude), while Morin's method permits the planet to be anywhere in the circle. Consequently, the derived corrections to the aspect longitudes (other than that of the opposition) and the determined latitudes of the aspects will nearly always be different.

---

22 The *Prutenic Tables* (1551) were prepared by Erasmus Reinhold (1511-1553), the *Lansbergian Tables* (1632) by Philip van Lansberge (1561-1632), and the *Rudolphine Tables* (1627) by Johann Kepler (1571-1630). Of these, Kepler's tables were the most accurate. Morin also issued his own version of the *Rudolphine Tables* in 1650, and it is probably these to which he refers under that title. The solar and planetary positions given by these tables are usually accurate to within a few minutes of arc, although the solar positions have a sinusoidal error with a maximum of 7 or 8 minutes of arc, which, in the worst case can be multiplied several times in the position of Mercury or Venus. The Moon positions can be off by 15' or more, since only the three largest perturbations of its true longitude had been determined (empirically) by Kepler and his predecessors, and twenty or more are required to ensure a maximum error of no more than 1'. This sizable error in the Moon positions would tend to vitiate Morin's efforts to apply his aspect correction.

Both methods seem to be developments of the earlier idea (Bianchini's?) of assigning the planet's latitude (with reversed direction) to its opposition. And behind the whole thing is the doctrine of the *projection of rays*, much discussed by the Arabs, which contains the basic idea that the arcs of aspects must be adjusted for latitude under certain circumstances.

In view of the fact that the maximum errors in the Moon's longitude given by the best tables of Morin's time are equal to or greater than the maximum aspect longitude correction given by his theory, it seems doubtful that Morin's "experience" with his method is entitled to as much weight as he gives it.[23] And since the errors in both the lunar and planetary longitudes were much larger in Cardan's time, it is virtually certain that he could not have proved the validity of his method. (And in fact he does not claim to have done so.) Thus, we are left with an interesting subject for modern research.

---

23 The change of mundane position caused by the assignment of latitude to an aspect will ordinarily be greater than that caused by the shift in longitude, especially in higher latitudes, but the maximum ephemeris error can still cause a shift of half a degree in the mundane position, with a consequent error in timing of 6 months. Also, like virtually all astrologers before and since, Morin ignores the effect of parallax upon the Moon's position.

APPENDIX 3

The Solar Eclipse of 8 April 1652

The solar eclipse mentioned in Sect. 2, Chapt. 3, was only partial in France. According to my calculations the path of totality passed through the Irish Sea, cut across southern Scotland, and ran nearly parallel to the coast of Norway, perhaps touching land here and there, as in the Lofoten Islands. This is somewhat further south and east than the path indicated on Oppolzer's chart 136.[1]

In England, Nicholas Culpeper and William Lilly both published mundane predictions based upon this eclipse.[2] And Morin refers to it in the Preface of the *Astrologia Gallica*, where he mentions "...the great eclipse of the Sun in this year 1652 in the 19th degree of Aries, with Saturn, ruler of the eighth house, rising at Paris in the 22nd degree of Cancer, which the Moon rules; which eclipse, aside from the political changes [it signified], was followed by so great a mortality in France, that in Paris the dead and those sick with malignant fevers are believed to number more than 100,000, without an epidemic..."[3]

This eclipse was observed by Agarrat and Morin, with an unnamed assistant, at the Orleans Palace in Paris. It was also observed in Paris by Ismael Boulliau (1605-1694) and at Digne by Pierre Gassendi (1592-1655).[4] Gassendi's record of his observations was published in volume 4 of his Opera[5] and reprinted by Simon Newcomb in his *Researches on the Motion of the Moon, Part I* (Washington, 1878), pp. 86-87.[6]

---

1   Theodor, Ritter von Oppolzer, *Canon of Eclipses* (New York,1962) [repr. of the *Canon der Finsternisse* (Vienna, 1887),with a translation of the Introduction by Owen Gingerich].

2   Nicholas Culpeper, *Catastrophe Magnatum* (London, 1652) and William Lilly, *Annus Tenebrosus* (London, 1651). Some of their predictions must either have missed the mark or else seemed unlikely of early fulfillment, as they provoked an anonymous rejoinder entitled *Black Monday turn'd White, or the Astrologers Knavery Epitomized...* (London, 1652), a 4-page diatribe against Culpeper and Lilly, which was published a few days after the eclipse (which fell on a Monday).

3   This passage was noted by Lynn Thorndike, HMES 7, p. 487, n. 58.

4   Gassendi also reports the observation made by an unidentified aristocrat at Avignon. He recorded the beginning of the eclipse at 9:33 (vs. calc. 9:34), the middle at 10:50 (vs. calc. max.10:44), and the end at 11:53 (vs. calc. 11:58).

5   Pierre Gassendi, *Opera omnia* (Lyons, 1658) 6 vols. folio.

6   Newcomb also reprints (*op. cit.*, pp. 92-94) the observation records of Johann Hevel (1611-1687) of Dantzig (now Gdansk), who used a sundial and a clock in addition to taking solar altitudes. His results were the best of all: for the beginning he reports 11:00 AM (vs. calc. 11:01) and for the end 1:19 PM (vs. calc. 1:20).

The observation records of Agarrat and Morin and of Boulliau seem to have perished, so Morin's account in the *Astrologia Gallica* and Gassendi's report are all that remain. Gassendi's report of his results and those of the other observers are as follows:

	Gassendi	Boulliau	Agarrat & Morin
Beginning	9:43	9:12:47	9:30
Middle	10:51	10:25:19	10:45
End	11:58	11:42:14	12:12
Magnitude (digits)	9;24	10;20	10;20

Gassendi's report of Boulliau's and Agarrat and Morin's times does not agree very well with Morin's own account, which says the eclipse "began at precisely 9:30 AM, and left off at precisely noon" and "[Boulliau] put the end of the eclipse at 11:50." I don't know what to make of Boulliau's times as reported by Gassendi. They are 10 or 15 minutes too early if they are referred to the meridian of Paris, and Gassendi says nothing to the contrary.

I have calculated the local circumstances of the eclipse at Paris and Digne for comparison with the observed times.

Paris 48N50 2E20 (Local Apparent Time)

	Calculated	Morin (AG)	Boulliau
Beginning	9:29	9:30	9:12:47
Maximum	10:40	10:45*	10:25:19
End	11:53	12:00	11:42:14
Magnitude (digits)	10;24	10;20	10;20

*as reported by Gassendi (not given in the AG)

Digne 44N07 6E16 (Local Apparent Time)

	Calculated	Gassendi
Beginning	9:42	9:43
Maximum	10:52	10:51
End	12:05	11:58
Magnitude	8;51	9;24

It is a pity that Boulliau's times are affected by some unknown constant difference from Local Apparent Time on the Paris meridian, since they appear to have been made with a clock. Also, Gassendi's and Morin's reports of Boulliau's time for the end of the eclipse disagree for some reason.

Considering only Agarrat and Morin's and Gassendi's times, we note that their observations of the beginning of the eclipse are within one minute of the calculated time; but Agarrat and Morin observed the end of the eclipse 7 minutes late, while Gassendi observed it 7 minutes early. Their errors in the ending time are almost certainly due to their having determined the time from altitudes of the Sun. Since the calculated end of the eclipse was near noon, it was impossible to determine the time with any accuracy by observing the solar altitude.

Gassendi also employed a sundial, for he says "Since the times exhibited here were deduced from altitudes of the Sun, I should not fail to mention that a sundial showed the beginning about two minutes earlier and the end two or three minutes later." And he would have been better off if he had used the times from the sundial, since he would still have been only a minute off at the beginning, but his error in timing the ending would have been reduced from 7 minutes to 4 or 5.

In the case of the magnitude of the eclipse, Agarrat and Morin and Boulliau were very close to the calculated figure, while Gassendi differed by 4 or 5 percent.

Finally, a biographical note: Gassendi's report contains the phrase ...*observationes duas Parisiis...alteram a nostro Bullialdo, alteram a meo quondam Agarrato, ac Morino...* 'two observations at Paris...one by our friend Boulliau, another by my former friend Agarrat, and Morin'. It is known that Gassendi and Morin were constantly sparring with each other, but we might wonder whether Gassendi had some other reason for relegating his friendship with Agarrat to the past or whether he merely resented his having joined with Morin in this instance.

APPENDIX 4

Some Horoscopes Mentioned in the Text

Morin's horoscope is from the *Astrologia Gallica*, p. 397. Cardan's chart is from his *Book of Twelve Genitures (Opera omnia* V, p. 517). The other charts are originally from Junctinus's *Mirror of Astrology*. However, not having access to a copy of that book at this writing, I have cited them from Alan Leo's *Notable Nativities*. Like all charts drawn prior to the availability of Kepler's *Rudolphine Tables*, the planetary positions are often in error. The errors are smallest for the Sun (usually no more than 1 degree), somewhat larger for the Moon, Jupiter, and Saturn (usually within 2 or 3 degrees), variable for Venus and Mars (usually within 1 or 2 degrees, but occasionally 3 or 4 degrees), and very variable for Mercury (sometimes fairly close, but sometimes in error by 10 degrees or more). There are also occasional errors in the house cusps.

I have not recalculated the charts because Morin cited them as he found them in the *Mirror of Astrology*. However, I have noted a few discrepancies. In the case of the birth places, dates, and times, I have furnished most of the information myself, since it is not always given in *Notable Nativities*. In particular, I have established the birth times from the cusps of the charts in *Notable Nativities*, so they may differ by a few minutes from the times given in the *Mirror of Astrology*. The times are of course local apparent time.

Junctinus copied some or perhaps most of these charts from his predecessors, Jerome Cardan and Luca Gaurico, whose published collections antedated his by a generation. Most of them are probably approximately correct, but, since their ultimate origins have not been investigated, they should not be taken as being absolutely certain.

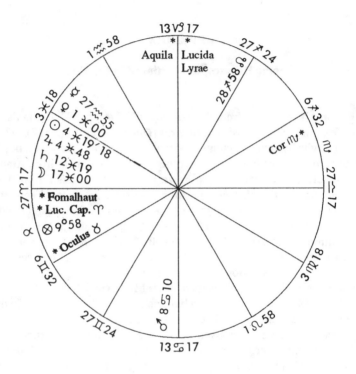

Jean Baptiste Morin, M.D.
Villefranche, Rhone 46N00 4E43
23 Feb 1583 8:33 AM
6 Nov 1656
Paris

Note: Morin thought the latitude of Villefranche was 45N25, and the house cusps shown above are calculated for that latitude.

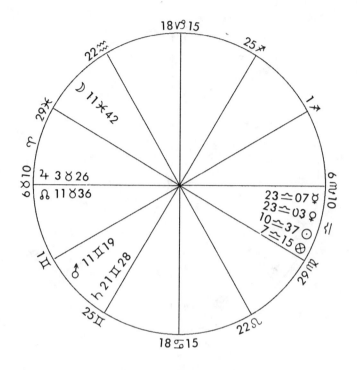

Jerome Cardan, M.D.
Pavia 45N12 9E11
24 Sep 1501 6:40 PM
21 Sep 1576
Rome

Note: Cardan's chart has Milan for the birthplace, but he was actually born at Pavia (20 miles south of Milan). The printed chart has several typographical errors, which I have corrected. Calculation yields the following more precise longitudes: Moon 10°40' Pisces, Mercury 26°27' Libra, Jupiter 2°40' Taurus, and Saturn 19°20' Gemini. The other planets are fairly close. The chart has Alchabitius cusps, which Cardan favored in this one instance. (He thought the Regiomontanan house positions did not suit his life.)

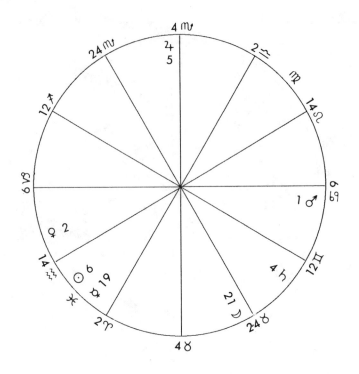

Pietro II de' Medici
Governor of Florence
Florence
16 Feb 1471-2 3:33 AM
28 Dec 1503   drowned
Garigliano River

[NN 468]

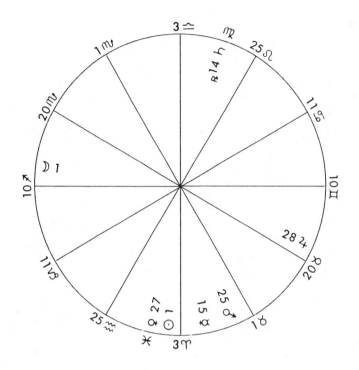

Giuliano II de' Medici
Duke of Nemours
Florence
13 Mar 1478-9 0:06 AM
17 Mar 1516   sickness
Fiesole

[NN 481]

197

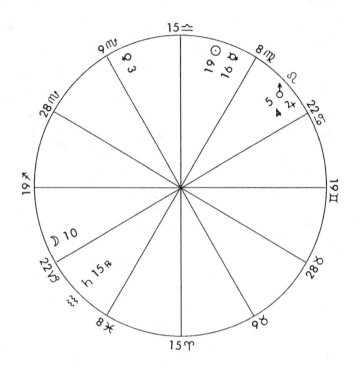

Lorenzo II de' Medici
Duke of Urbino
Florence
1 Sep 1492 1:36 PM
4 May 1519 sickness
Florence

[NN 499]

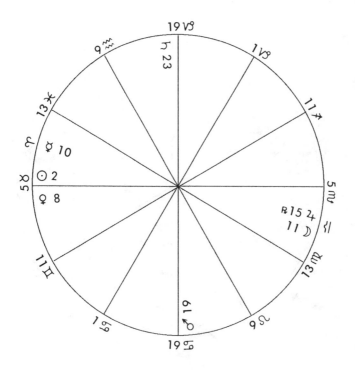

Catherine de' Medici
Queen of France
Florence
13 Apr 1519 5:22 AM
5 Jan 1589
Blois

[NN 538]

Note: This is Junctinus's chart. However, Luca Gaurico, who was court astrologer to Catherine, gives her birth time as 4:38 AM in his *Tractatus astrologicus* (Venice, 1552). His chart is NN 537; it has 17 Aries rising instead of 5 Taurus.

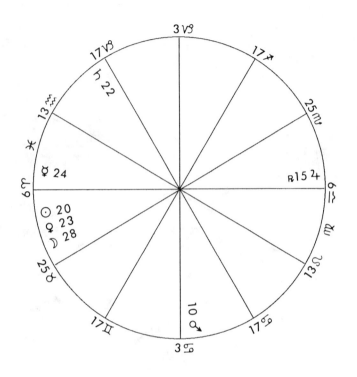

Henry II
King of France
St. Germain-en-Laye
31 Mar 1518-9 5:04 AM
10 Jul 1559 eye injury
Paris

[NN 535]

Note: Another source says he was born at 7 PM, but Junctinus probably took this chart from Luca Gaurico, *op. cit.*, who gives 5 AM for the birth time. Gaurico should have known the correct birth time.

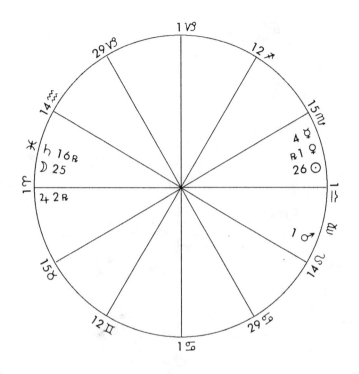

Ottavio Farnese
Duke of Parma & Piacenza
Rome (?)
9 Oct 1524 4:23 PM
18 Sep 1586
Parma (?)

[NN 546]

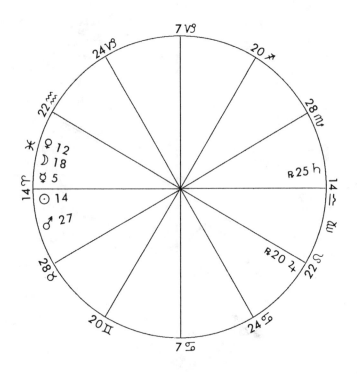

Francis I de' Medici
Grand Duke of Tuscany
Florence (?)
25 Mar 1541 5:39 AM
19 Oct 1587 sickness
Florence

[NN 558]

APPENDIX 5

Regiomontanus Primary Direction Formulae

Primary directions in the Regiomontanus system amount to bringing Point 2 to the same Circle of Position as Point 1 by adding an appropriate arc (the Arc of Direction) to the RAMC. This arc can be calculated as follows:

1. Calculate the elevation of the pole above the Circle of Position of Point 1 in the latitude of the place.
2. Calculate the Oblique Ascension of P1 under the Pole of P1.
3. Calculate the Oblique Ascension of Point 2 under the Pole of P1.
4. Then the Arc of Direction = OA2-OA1.

If the latitude of the planets is taken into account, the directions are called *mundane* or *in mundo*; but if the latitude is neglected, the directions are called *zodiacal* or *in zodiaco*. Morin favored mundane directions, while some of his predecessors favored zodiacal directions.

Most of the 16th and 17th century astrologers used Regiomontanus's tables (or a similar set by a later author) to make their calculations, but with the current availability of electronic calculators and computers, the following trigonometrical formulae may be found convenient.

Notation:		
RA	=	Right Ascension
D	=	Declination
L	=	Zodiacal Longitude (from 0 Aries)
B	=	Zodiacal Latitude
F	=	Latitude of the Place
RAMC	=	Right Ascension of the Midheaven
MD	=	Meridian Distance (in RA)
		(+ on the left and - on the right)
CP	=	Circle of Position
A	=	an auxiliary angle
G	=	another auxiliary angle
H	=	another auxiliary angle
P	=	Pole (polar elevation)
AD	=	Ascensional Difference
OA	=	Oblique Ascension
OD	=	Oblique Descension
Arc	=	Arc of Direction (in RA)

If a numerical suffix is added to any of these quantities, it refers to Point 1 or Point 2. Thus, MD1 = Meridian Distance of Point 1.

For each pair of points, calculate the following:

$$
\begin{aligned}
\text{MD} &= \text{RA - RAMC} \\
\text{G} &= \arctan(\tan \text{D1}/\cos \text{MD1}) \\
\text{H} &= \text{F - G} \\
\text{A} &= \arctan(\cos \text{H}/(\tan \text{MD1} \cos \text{G})) \\
\text{P} &= \arcsin(\sin \text{F} \cos \text{A}) \\
\text{CP} &= \arctan(\cos \text{F}/\tan \text{A}) \\
\text{AD1} &= \arcsin(\tan \text{D1} \tan \text{P}) \\
\text{AD2} &= \arcsin(\tan \text{D2} \tan \text{P})
\end{aligned}
$$

Then, when Point 1 is in the eastern (left) half of the chart:

$$
\begin{aligned}
\text{OA1} &= \text{RA1 - AD1} \\
\text{OA2} &= \text{RA2 - AD2} \\
\text{Arc} &= \text{OA2 - OA1}
\end{aligned}
$$

else, when Point 1 is in the western (right) half of the chart:

$$
\begin{aligned}
\text{OD1} &= \text{RA1 + AD1} \\
\text{OD2} &= \text{RA2 + AD2} \\
\text{Arc} &= \text{OA2 - OA1}
\end{aligned}
$$

The calculation can be verified by adding the Arc to the RAMC, recalculating MD2, and calculating CP2 for the Latitude of the Place. The calculated value of CP2 should be equal to the value of CP1. That is, with the RAMC increased by the Arc of Direction, the Circle of Position of Point 2 should be exactly equal to the original Circle of Position of Point 1.

An alternative to calculating directions in the right half of the chart is to calculate the directions of the opposite points in the left half of the chart. This method was often used by the 16th and 17th century astrologers. If this is done, it is important to find the RA and D of the oppositions by taking the Longitude + 180° of each point and reversing the direction of the Zodiacal Latitude. For example, if Saturn should be in the right half of the chart at 8°21' Libra and 2N36, then its opposition in the left half of the chart should be taken to be 8°21' Aries and 2S36.

If Point 1 is the MC, then the Arc of Direction is simply equal to the difference in RA of Point 2 and the MC: Arc = RA2 - RAMC. This follows naturally from the definition of a Regiomontanan direction: Point 1 in this case is the RAMC; if we bring Point 2 to the (progressed) RAMC, then RA2 - RAMC must equal the Arc of Direction. Or, by the formulae above, the Pole of Point 1 is 0°; hence, the

OA's of Points 1 and 2 are the same as their RA's, so OA2 - OA1 = RA2 - RA1 = RA2 - RAMC.

If Point 1 is the Ascendant, then the Arc of Direction is equal to the difference in OA of Point 2 and the ASC: Arc = OA2 - OA1 = OA2 -RAMC -90°, where the OA's are taken for the Latitude of the Place. This follows from the definition and the formulae, for when Point 1 is the Ascendant, it is on the horizon, and its Circle of Position is 90° from the RAMC; consequently, its Pole is the same as the Latitude of the Place.

If Point 1 is an intermediate cusp, then its Longitude is the zodiacal longitude of the cusp with zero Zodiacal Latitude. Its Circle of Position will of course be a multiple of 30°.

Example

As an example, we may calculate the direction of Mars to the conjunction of Jupiter *in mundo* in the chart of Sixtus ab Hemminga in Book 22, Sect. V, Chapt 4. With the longitudes and latitudes of the planets given by Morin, we have:

RAMC 165°24'   Latitude 53N00   Obliquity 23°30'

Planet	RA	Decl.	MD
Jupiter	263°14'	-22°53'	+97°50'
Mars	288°37'	-23°09'	-

with Jupiter as Point 1 and Mars as Point 2, we calculate:

$$G = 72°06'$$
$$H = -19°06'$$
$$A = -22°56'$$
$$P = 47°21'$$
$$CP = 125°07'$$
$$AD1 = -27°16'$$
$$AD2 = -27°39'$$

and from these quantities

$$OA2 = 316°16'$$
$$OA1 = 290°30'$$
$$Arc = 25°46'$$

This arc agrees with that previously calculated by computer for verification of Morin's figures. Morin, however, derived the value 26°45', which may be explained as a combination of errors. First, he seems to have rounded off the calculated value of the Pole from 47°21' to 47°00'. This would alter the values of OA2 and OA1 to 315°54' and 290°09' without affecting their difference by much. His published values are 316°52' and 290°06'. Thus we can infer that he actually derived 315°52' and 290°06' with a difference of 25°46'. This is virtually the same as the difference 25°45' from our own calculation (with the rounded value of the Pole). But he inadvertently wrote down the degrees of the first angle as 316 instead of 315, thereby increasing the difference to 26°45'.

ADDENDA

ASTROLOGIA GALLICA

BOOK TWO

Chapt. 3. *How Many Years Passed between the Creation of the World and the Incarnation of Christ; and from then to this Year 1648 according to the Method of Numeration used by the Church.*

Although it was sufficiently demonstrated in Book 1 that this world could not have [existed] eternally, the same thing can also be demonstrated in another way. Since the Sun is in individual points of the ecliptic at a particular time, let it be supposed that it was at the beginning of Aries from eternity. Therefore, it was not in a degree of Aries from eternity. Second: and since when one day had passed it came to the 2nd degree of Aries, then it was very true to assert that the world had existed for only one day; therefore it is false to say that it had existed from eternity, which is contrary to the hypothesis. Moreover, if anyone says that the world was possible from eternity and that with the possible having been made actual, nothing absurd follows; and the world therefore could have existed from eternity, this reasoning is convicted of manifest falsity by the fact that the thousandth circulation of the *primum mobile* was possible from eternity; and yet it could not have been an actuality from eternity because the thousandth circulation could not have been an actuality unless 999 [circulations] had gone before; in addition to which, the world would have been simultaneously an actuality and a potentiality, which cannot be the case.

Furthermore, with regard to the number of years that have passed since the creation of the world, there are great controversies among both the old and the modern chronologists and theologians which it is not our purpose to discuss here. For us, therefore, it suffices to set forth compendiously that according to the Oriental Greek churches 5508 years ought to be reckoned from the foundation of the world to the Birth of Christ. According to the Western Latin Churches 5199. Among the Jews and Rabbis 3761. But according to historical truth and the more outstanding chronologists, Origanus in the first part of his *Introduction,*[1] Chapt. 1,

---

1   David Origanus (1558-1628), *Astrologia naturalis sive tractatus de effectibus astrorum...* (Marseilles, 1645).

will reckon neither more nor less than 3949 years. And Gallisard[2] in his brief *Chronography* puts 3964 years among the Hebrews and [The Venerable] Bede from the creation of the world to the Nativity of Christ. But Longomontanus, Book 1, Theor. Chapt. 3, puts 3966. And Kepler in his *Rudolphine Tables*, Chapt. 33, counts 3993 years, although from the motion of the solar apogee assumed by him they ought to be reckoned as 3968, as it will appear below. Thus to be sure these astronomers differing little among themselves deduce their own numbers from the motion of the solar apogee, which according to the reformation of astronomy made by Tycho Brahe moves about one minute and two seconds a year in the ecliptic. For the astronomers think it very agreeable to reason, and I think it most concordant with Divine Wisdom on account of the causes that will be given at the end of Chapt. 4 that the solar apogee was placed by God at the beginning of the world at the intersection of the equatorial and ecliptical circles, i.e., in the Midheaven, whose extremes are the poles of the ecliptic and the equator, for this intersection is referred to both poles. From which supposition it follows that this apogee was in the beginning of Aries; otherwise, if it had been in the beginning of Libra, 14420 years would have been reckoned according to the motion of the solar apogee from the creation of the world to the Birth of Christ. For from *The Rudolphine Tables*[3] the apogee was at the Birth of Christ in $8°20'44''$ Gemini, i.e., the 246044'' that the apogee had moved from the founding of the World to the Birth of Christ divided by the 62'' of the annual motion of that apogee from Tycho's observations will make 3968 years from the creation of the world to the Birthday of Christ, i.e., about 4000 years up to the Passion of Christ and the preaching of the Gospel. Which calculation, since it agrees very well with historical truth and the Sacred Scriptures, makes it certain that the rest ought to be rejected and that we should depend upon this consensus of astronomy, history, and the Sacred Scriptures, although there is some doubt about the true year.

Moreover, there is a still greater and more acrimonious controversy among chronologers about how the years from the Birth of Christ ought to be numbered, as one can see in Kepler's *Book on the Natal Year of Christ* and in his *Chronical Eclogues*, and the matter is very involved, requiring much reading, learning, and prudence in conjecture, in order to arrive at anything that should be held for certain about it. Wherefore, relinquishing to others this task, which has already tormented many men learned in this matter, we shall only take note here of two things. First,...

If, therefore, from the founding of the world to Christ 3968 Julian years elapsed; and from Christ down to this year 1648 years, there will be 5616 years from the founding of the world down to the present.

---

2   Pierre Gallisart (fl. 1577), a Dominican of the convent of Arles, was a schoolmaster and
    writer on religious subjects.
3   Johann Kepler, *Tabulae Rudolphinae* (Ulm, 1627).

BOOK THIRTEEN

TABLE OF THE UNIVERSAL RULERSHIPS OF THE PLANETS

The Seven Planets are the Primary and Universal Causes of Physical Generation in the Family of Nature as a Whole. They are allotted an affinity with those things of a particular nature placed below, either from their own essence or because of analogy, and on this account they are said to rule them.

Parts of Heaven

Saturn: Capricorn, Aquarius.
Jupiter: Sagittarius, Pisces.
Mars: Aries, Scorpio.
The Sun: Leo.
Venus: Taurus, Libra.
Mercury: Gemini, Virgo.
The Moon: Cancer.

Elements

Saturn: earth.
Jupiter: air, fire.
Mars: fire.
The Sun: aether, fire.
Venus: air.
Mercury: earth.
The Moon: water.

Elemental Qualities

Saturn: Intense cold, dryness, density, opacity, heaviness.
Jupiter: Moderation, with an excess of lightness, heat, and dryness.
Mars: Heat and dryness in intensity.
The Sun: Vital heat, rarity, lightness.
Venus: Moderation, with a little moistness.
Mercury: Cold and dryness in some degree.
The Moon: Cold, wetness, liquidity, density, and heaviness.

Colours[1]

Saturn: Black, dark, earth-colored, swarthy.
Jupiter: Blue.
Mars: Red.
The Sun: Yellow.
Venus: Green.
Mercury: Variegated.
The Moon: White, pale.

Odours

Saturn: Foul, narcotic.
Jupiter: Sweet.
Mars: Sharp.
The Sun: Fragrant, aromatic.
Venus: Delightfully sweet.
Mercury: Mixed.
The Moon: Dull, imperceptible.

Flavours

Saturn: Sour, astringent.
Jupiter: Sweet.
Mars: Bitter.
The Sun: Salted just right.
Venus: Rich.
Mercury: Acid.
The Moon: Flat, watery.

Parts of the Year

Saturn: Fall.
Jupiter: Spring.
Mars: Summer.
The Sun: Summer.
Venus: Spring.
Mercury: Fall.
The Moon: Winter.

---

1 The printed text mistakenly has *Odores* 'Odours'.

Weather Conditions and Effects in the Air

Saturn: Intense and frightful cold, and sometimes pestilence. Heavy, black clouds, dark rainstorms, snows, frosts, destructive winds, violent winds.

Jupiter: Mildness, healthy condition, moderate winds, fair weather, clouds turning from white to red.

Mars: Intemperate, hot, dry, very hot, pestiferous, wasting, fair weather, or red clouds, tawny, green, thunder, flashing, cloud-to-cloud lightning, thunderbolts, hail. Comets with tails, glowing impressions,[2] tornadoes, tempestuous, harmful, destructive winds.

The Sun: Heat, dryness, fair weather and sometimes very hot, tawny clouds or turning tawny from red, moderate winds, dry and healthy.

Venus: Mildness, health, fair weather, dew, fog, mist, clouds completely white, light and healthy rain, moderate and somewhat humid winds.

Mercury: Dryness, sudden winds, strong, gusty, shifting; violent, damaging winds; variegated clouds, thunder, flashing, thunderbolts.

The Moon: Humidity and cold from itself.

In Waters and in the Sea

Saturn: Overflowings, floods, corruption, destruction or scarcity of fish, violent winds and raging storms, difficult voyages, shipwreck.

Jupiter: Moderate and useful increases in waters, abundance of fish, tranquility, or moderate winds, favourable and profitable passages of ships.

Mars: Drying up of waters, corruption, destruction of fish, violent winds, sudden shipwrecks, invasions of pirates.

The Sun: Droughts and decreases.

Venus: Useful increases and overflows, good health, great abundance of fish, easy, secure, and fortunate voyages.

Mercury: Violent winds and sudden storms, increases when it is matutine, decreases when vespertine, plots of pirates.

The Moon: Increases, ebbing and flowing.

On the Earth

Saturn: Sterility of fruits and corruption of useful plants by malign air, cold, frost, rain storms, hail, floods, caterpillars, locusts; destruction of useful animals, appearance of harmful ones; earthquake, collapse of buildings and cities.

Jupiter: Abundance and health of plants, fruits, and useful animals, and the suppression of injurious ones, or those spawned from rotten material.[3]

---

2 Probably the glowing trains of meteors.

3 Maggots, etc.

Mars: Scarcity and unhealthiness of plants, fruits, and animals useful to ma
from intemperate heat and dryness or from the poisonous quality of the ai
generation of venomous creatures, fires, earthquakes.

The Sun: Four parts of the year, but especially the summer per se; drought
forest fires; the rest according to the characteristics of the ruler and the aspects.

Venus: The same as Jupiter, but with more fertility.

Mercury: Great earthquakes, but a diversity of other events, instability, an
often, with Saturn or Mars, destruction of plants and animals.

The Moon: Putrefaction, but in accordance with its relation to the Sun an
the other planets, whose configurations with the Moon ought to be carefull
noticed, since the Moon is closest to the earth.

Minerals

Saturn: lead, black stones, dark-colored, field-stones.

Jupiter: Tin, sapphire, amethyst.

Mars: Iron, lodestone, jasper, bloodstone, reddish [stones].[4]

The Sun: Gold, carbuncle, hyacinth,[5] chrysolite.

Venus: Copper, emerald, turquoise, coral, pearl.

Mercury: Quicksilver, chalcedony, carnelian, *alecterius*.[6]

The Moon: Silver, crystal, beryl, diamond, pearl.

Plants

Saturn: The oak, medlar, quince,[7] rue, hellebore, narcotic [plants], and th
rest of the thick substances, and those growing slowly.

Jupiter: The laurel, sandalwood, cinnamon, sugar, balsam, frankincense.

Mars: Pepper, ginger, mustard, radish, scammony, colocynth,[8] garlic, every
thing bitter, and hot poisonous [plants].

The Sun: The palm, rosemary, heliotrope, crocus, grain, and spices.

Venus: The date palm, olive, pine, lily, rose, pea.

Mercury: The hazel, yarrow.

The Moon: Gourds, cucumbers, pumpkins, lettuce.

---

4 The Latin has *rubinus* 'reddish'.

5 A hyacinth-colored precious or semiprecious stone, either a variety of amethyst or
sapphire. Cf. Pliny, *Natural History*, xxxvii. 40 (Sect. 122).

6 I cannot identify this mineral or stone, unless the reference is to the *alectoria* or "cock's
stone" mentioned by Pliny, N.H., xxxvii. 54 (Sect. 144).

7 Reading *cydonius* 'quince' instead of *citonius* [unidentified].

8 The *Cucumis colocynthis* of Linnaeus, a wild cucumber used as a purgative. See Pliny,
N.H., xx. 8 (Sect. 14).

Animals

Saturn: The camel, bear, goat, ass, cat, owl, bat, tortoise, mouse, beetle, and others that walk slowly, and those that roam about at night, toad.

Jupiter: The elephant, deer, bull, stag, peacock, falcon.

Mars: The horse, wolf, boar, dog, ostrich, kite, hawk, venomous serpents, scorpion, spider.

The Sun: The lion, eagle, falcon, cock.

Venus: The nanny goat, sheep, pheasant, partridge, dove, turtledove, sparrow.

Mercury: The fox, ape, serpent, parrot, spider, bee, ant.

The Moon: The hare, swan, nightingale, frogs, fish, juicy snails, shellfish, crabs, slugs.

The Humours

Saturn: Melancholy, black bile.

Jupiter: Moisture, blood, semen.

Mars: Yellow, vitelline, aeruginous, [or] porraceous bile.[9]

The Sun: Vital spirit, bilious blood.

Venus: Phlegmatic blood, semen.

Mercury: Animal spirit.

The Moon: Phlegm, serum.

Parts of the Body

Saturn: The bones, teeth, cartilage, right ear, spleen, bladder.

Jupiter: The liver, veins, lungs, diaphragm, sides, muscles.

Mars: The gall bladder, left ear, pudenda, kidneys.

The Sun: The heart, arteries, right eye, and the right side in men, but the left one in women.

Venus: The throat, breasts, belly, buttocks, womb, kidneys, genitalia.

Mercury: The legs and feet, arms, hands, fingers, tongue, nerves, ligaments.

The Moon: The brain, left eye, the left side in men, but the right one in women. Intestines, stomach, vulva, membranes.

The Faculties

Saturn: The retentive.

Jupiter: The digestive[10] and vegetal.

---

9 Vitelline means yellowish, aeruginous bluish-green, and porraceous greenish.

10 Literally, *coctrix* 'cooking'.

Mars: The expulsive.

The Sun: The vital, attractive.

Venus: The generative.

Mercury: The mental, rational.

The Moon: The expulsive, vegetal, mental.

The Senses

Saturn: Hearing on the right.

Jupiter: Touch, smell.

Mars: Hearing on the left.

The Sun: Sight on the right in a man, especially by day; on the left in a woman.

Venus: Taste, smell, touch, the pleasures [arising] from these senses.

Mercury: Taste, hearing.

The Moon: Sight on the right in women; on the left in men.

Parts of the Mind

Saturn: Memory.

Jupiter: Judgment, the concupiscible appetite.

Mars: The irascible appetite.

The Sun: The universal appetite for good.

Venus: The concupiscible appetite.

Mercury: Common sense, imagination, ingenuity, reason, or the rational appetite.

The Moon: Apprehension, the universal appetite.

The Natural Laws of Men and their Relations amongst themselves by Analogy

Saturn: Great-grandfather, grandfather and father, then also a servant, a hidden enemy.

Jupiter: The master, children.

Mars: The husband in women's charts, elder brothers, open enemies.

The Sun: The father and the husband in women's charts.

Venus: The wife and the mother by day, sisters, daughters, lovers, concubines.

Mercury: Younger brothers, servants.

The Moon: The mother and the wife especially by night, widows, pregnant women.[11]

---

11 Or, less likely, 'pregnant widows'.

Corporature

About which there can be no universal determination. For even though in general and everywhere on earth Martial types are drier and more slender, Jovial and Venus types, moister, juicier, fairer-skinned, and more beautiful, Saturnians uglier and darker, etc., still the particular conformations of parts and colors do not always correspond equally to the natures of the planets, but there is a [particular] character of body native to each place on earth, as is obvious from the Ethiopians, the Tartars, and the Peruvians, who differ greatly among themselves in body, hair, and shape of face, but the Ethiopian in France begets an Ethiopian. Therefore, consider the region and the parents; and understand that the things given here [are mainly applicable] to the white men of Asia, Europe, etc.

Saturn Oriental: Cold, moist, moderate flesh, moderate in stature, a long face, large dark eyes, occasionally spotted, uneven teeth, an ugly and grim appearance, face and body rather dark in color, tawny,[12] honey-colored,[13] pallid, dark hair, thickset, rugged, crooked feet.

———Occidental: Cold, dry, thin, short in stature, dark eyes, dark plain hair, scanty on the head and in the beard, the rest of the body hairless.

Jupiter Oriental: Moderately hot and moist, fleshy, round cheeks, moderate and elegant and majestic in stature, white in color, inclining to yellow or rose, eyes rather large [and] dark, handsome, with a mark in the right foot.

———Occidental: Somewhat moister in temperament, moderate in stature, bald, with a mark in the left foot, which rarely fails.

Mars Oriental: Hot, dry, less fleshy, decently tall and well proportioned, in color from white to red, with bluish eyes, much hair between curly and straight, with hairiness of body.

———Occidental: Drier, moderate in stature, with a big head, a round and freckled face, or with a mark on his forehead, small eyes, large nostrils, long teeth; red in color, red-haired, rigid, with a hairless body, and a long and military stride.

The Sun: Hot and not so dry, moderate in stature, a large head; a round, white, and shining face, eyes large and splendid and yellow in color, long hair but growing bald, a somewhat harsh voice.

Venus: Hot and moist, moderate in stature, plump, and the face especially full and delicate, white with a blush of red, beautiful, lovable, hair somewhat curly, tawny, or rather dark, tawny-colored eyes, handsome, happy, glancing charmingly, thin eyebrows and lips, narrow chest, full legs. And these features are more apparent when Venus is oriental.

Mercury Oriental: Somewhat hotter, moderate in stature and well proportioned, with good color, or honey-colored, small eyes, moderate, yellowish hair.

---

12 Reading *fulvus* 'tawny' rather than *fulcus* [no such word].
13 Latin *mellinus*.

———Occidental: Somewhat dry, thin, slim, with small teeth and fingers, scanty beard, a thin voice, small, quick steps, a very sharp mentality.

The Moon: Moist, tall stature, a beautiful face, white in color, gray eyes, fine hair, a becoming beard.

Note

Judge cautiously and carefully on the form of the body, for this part of judgment often fails, since it is not yet well understood. But through experience it can be perfected, namely by having looked at the planets in the first house and their lords and the lord of the Ascendant, along with the forms of the natives.

Character and Talents

Saturn well-placed.[14] Very talented, investigators of secret things, prudent, outstanding in counsel, secretive, rather solitary, suspicious and jealous, dissembling, hardworking, long-suffering, persevering, overcoming, violent, thrifty, eager for wealth, great accumulators, striving for dominion, fit for governorships, useful and dear to princes.

But badly disposed. Sad, melancholy, abject, repulsive, austere, shameless, sluggish, timid, nervous, envious, outstanding ineptitude in crime, wretched, complaining, or taciturn, those who hate association and light, very solitary, paupers, or trading in evil arts, very suspicious and jealous, liars, spiteful, fraudulent, plotters, traitors, and those who frequently suffer judicial punishment for their crimes.

Jupiter well-placed. Straightforward, upright, religious, just, faithful, courteous, merciful, clean, modest, cheerful, obliging, easy to talk to, moderately serious, frank, dutiful, prudent, sensible, strong in counsel, obliging, generous, illustrious, great, in giving justice, in making laws, fit for magistracy, for first place, and for kingdom, fond of and partial to his own and his own things, truthful.

Badly disposed. Character in one way or another like the previous, but artificial and inclining to faults, as superstition in place of piety and religion,[15] silliness instead of courtesy, timidity instead of modesty, pretense instead of fidelity, prodigality instead of generosity, pride and arrogance instead of greatness, of course in accordance with the way of the planet by which it is afflicted by connection[16] or by rulership.

Mars well-placed. Brave, strong, spirited, noble, bold, arrogant, boastful, despising the praise of another, and full of contempt for other men, irascible, prone

---

14 The Latin reads *bene affecto* 'well affected', which means "well placed by sign and house and well aspected." "Badly placed" is of course the reverse.

15 Reading *pro pietate* instead of *proprietate*

16 That is, by aspect.

o strike and wound, eager for revenge, obeying no one, unable to endure servitude and injuries, eager for dominance, craving battles and conflicts, arrogant tyrants, reckless and scornful of danger, active, ready, in a hurry, self-confident, spurning wealth, generous, lucky, well-suited for commanding soldiers, ill-suited for ruling citizens, scornful of God or not concerned.

Badly placed. Unscrupulous, unjust, pitiless, arrogant, quarrelsome, seditious, loud-mouthed, reckless, mad, truculent, aggressive in challenging, cruel, assassins, murderers, tyrants, drunkards, destroying their own property and that of others, incendiaries, robbers, thieves, pirates, neglecting their own people.

The Sun well-placed. Upright, just, honest, faithful, clean, sensible, in one way or another irascible, great, very eager for honours and much honoured, illustrious, grand, distinguished, famous, cultivators of friendships, but not overly fond of wife and children.

Badly placed. Silly, spiteful, less observant of honour, artificial, and degenerate from the things said above in accordance with the nature of the planet making it unfortunate by rulership or unfavourable connection.

Venus well-placed. Endowed with good character, charming, upright, and worshiping God religiously, merciful, peace-making, cheerful, sociable, fond of cleanliness and decoration, devoted to dancing, singing, music, and dining, elegant and charming in their actions, playful, and inclined towards all delights and pleasures, fortunate and cautious in love affairs and friendships, kind especially towards his own [people], unable to endure hard work, quarrels, anger, and misfortune, and easily reconciled.

Badly placed. Timid, idle, suitors, and bothersome in love affairs or friendships, imprudently and unfortunately jealous, womanizers, addicted to indecent desires, disreputable, and with many expenditures on account of women, mischances, bothersome to the wretched and bad; unless Venus herself rules most of the principal places of the geniture and is in an important angle.

Mercury well-placed. Endowed with outstanding character, excelling in shrewdness of intellect, easily capable [of learning] the sciences and arts of all kinds, but especially mathematics, readily conjecturing and reasoning; learning many things without a teacher, and finding unknown things first, finely differing and discussing, quick, wary, prudent, composed in behavior, readily adapting himself to any person, situation, or time, and therefore sociable and fit for getting things done.

Badly placed. Unstable, foolish, forgetful, addicted to mental wanderings, talkative, boastful, dull-witted, insolent, liars, stubborn, flatterers,[17] dissemblers, crafty, deceivers, treacherous, spiteful, perjurers, plotters, slanderers, given to falsifications of writing, testimony, or money, disreputable, pimps, rudely embroiling themselves in matters of every sort, giving dangerous advice, and boldly undertaking crimes.

17 And "yes-men."

The Moon well-placed. Fine mental ability, famous, honoured, well composed in behavior, honest, frank, honourable.

Badly placed. Dull in mental ability, timid, common, untruthful, vagabonds, artificial, and of no name, or servants, or fools.

Professions, or Characters Speaking to them

Saturn well-placed. Great theologians, philosophers, treasurers, mine superintendents.

Moderately placed. Farmers, excavators, miners, potters, builders, leather workers,[18] monks, hermits.

Badly placed. Practitioners of magic, fortunetellers, sorcerers, those who clean out cesspools and sewers, beggars, [and] executioners.

Jupiter well-placed. Advisers, senators, judges, presidents, executive secretaries,[19] high priests, generals of sacred orders, or provincials,[20] abbots, bishops, cardinals, popes, governors of provinces or cities.

Badly placed. Schoolmasters and athletic directors.

Mars well-placed. Knights, commanders-in-chief of armies, generals, and colonels,[21] hunters, lawyers, physicians, blacksmiths, founders,[22] [and] cooks.

Badly placed. Butchers, leather-workers, pirates, bandits, cattle-rustlers,[23] [and] executioners.

The Sun well-placed. The Pope, emperors, kings, princes, governors, magnates, and all administrators with royal honours or dignities.

Venus well-placed. Spice-merchants, perfumers, druggists, painters, jewelers, musicians, tavern keepers, soothsayers, members of sacred orders.

---

18 The Latin word *coriarii* 'tanners' or 'curriers' designates those who work with raw hides rather than artisans who turn finished leather into consumer products.

19 Not copyists and routine office workers, who are under Mercury (see below).

20 *Generals* and *provincials* are the superiors and division superintendents of Catholic religious orders such as the Benedictines. The leader of the Salvation Army also holds the title *General*.

21 The Latin has *Capitanei exercituum, Duces atque Praefecti*. The ranks mentioned in the translation are arbitrary. Certainly, military officials of higher rank than captain are meant. (Cf. the Spanish *capitán general*.)

22 That is, those who make castings in a foundry.

23 The Latin text has *Lictores* where I have translated 'cattle-rustlers'. Lictors were official attendants who walked before the high magistrates of Rome carrying an axe. This word is certainly wrong here. The Latin version of Ptolemy's *Tetrabiblos*, iv. 4, printed by Cardan has the following (Textus XVI, p. 324, col. 2) *...carnifices...raptores, latrones, abactores...* 'executioners...robbers, bandits, cattle-rustlers...' I think what Morin wrote was *abactores* 'cattle-rustlers'. My second choice would be *luctatores* 'wrestlers', which appears a few lines up in the same text.

Badly placed. Whores, seductresses, enchantresses, painted ladies,[24] beggar-women.

Mercury well-placed. Mathematicians, geometers, astronomers, astrologers, philosophers, orators, copyists, secretaries, poets, painters, merchants. All ingenious craftsmen, and inventors of new arts.

Badly placed. Pimps, thieves, counterfeiters, forgers, and sellers of fake goods.

The Moon well-placed. Queens, widows, couriers, sailors, fishermen, hunters, commoners.

Accidents of Fate

Saturn well-placed. High positions, governorships, authority, discovery of treasures, great wealth.

Badly placed. Fall from honour and high position, low status, poverty, servitude, bad luck with projects and actions, secret enemies, disgrace, imprisonment, exile, punishment, a sorrowful end.

Jupiter well-placed. Independence, riches, honours, high position, friends, servants, fortunate marriages, or high positions in the Church, fame, glory, an abundance of children, and from them happiness, profits. And, to sum it up, Jupiter well-placed bestows good luck in undertakings and in all things, and happy outcomes.

Badly placed. It denies these things, or lessens them, or gives merely the appearance of them, or makes them unfortunate.

Mars well-placed. Friendships with and cultivation of military men, fortunate in duels, positions of command in war, victories in battles when storming cities or attacking fleets of ships, spoils, [and] triumphs.

Badly placed. Enmities, lawsuits, fights, duels, battles and military assaults unluckily undertaken, losses of personal property and high position, robberies, squandering, destruction, plots, attacks, thefts, homicides, illicit intercourse, imprisonment, and frequently a violent death.

The Sun well-placed. Glory, fame, splendid status, honoured appointments, public offices, high royal or ecclesiastical positions, in both cases, i.e., secular and ecclesiastical, with honour and outstanding respect, powerful friends, a name famous from death.[25]

---

24 The Latin word *fucatrices* is not in my lexicon. If it is not simply a misprint, it would seem to be derived from *fucatus* 'counterfeit' or 'artificial'. I suppose it refers to women who wear heavy makeup, but if the derived sense of *fucatus* is taken, it could be translated as 'deceivers'. And if *fucatrices* is a misprint, perhaps Morin wrote *fututrices*, a coarse word that could be translated as 'sluts'.
25 This could mean 'from the manner of death' or 'from [the time of] death', i.e., 'after death'.

Badly placed. It gives powerful enemies, and it renders unfortunate the things mentioned above, or else it denies them [altogether], and it portends misfortune in all things undertaken for himself.

Venus well-placed. Good will from everyone, profits, happy successes in love affairs, happy marriages, fortunate and numerous offspring; high positions and exceptional good fortune in undertakings and actions.

Badly placed. It lessens, renders unfortunate, or even denies the things mentioned above.

Mercury well-placed. Successful business activities, profitable missions, fortunate contracts, outstanding and successful inventions, high positions, professions, and honour and profit from these, many and useful friends.

Badly placed. It corresponds to the opposite [of the preceding], then [it indicates] useless occupation in curious, arcane [activities], expenses and misfortunes, deceptions, falsifications, inconstant position in life[26] due to various unexpected events, and liable [to experience] an uncertain demise.

The Moon well-placed. A renowned name, wealth, happiness, honourable and lucrative missions, possessions of watery lands, many offspring, happy marriages, high positions and also royal positions, highly placed friends in both spheres.

Badly placed. It lessens, renders unfortunate, or even denies [altogether] the things mentioned above, and it gives a life of change, hardship, and liable [to experience] various unexpected events.

Ages

Saturn: Decrepitude extending to the end of life.
Jupiter: Old age to the 68th year.
Mars: Virility to the 56th year.
The Sun: Youth to the 42nd year.
Venus: Adolescence to the 21st year.
Mercury: Boyhood to the 14th year.
The Moon: Infancy to the 4th year.

---

26 The text seems to be falsely punctuated here. I have read *falsificationes, vitae status inconstans* as above, instead of *falsificationes vitae, status inconstans* 'falsicications of life, inconstant position'.

Sicknesses[27]

Saturn: Of the parts of the body which Saturn itself rules. Then quartan ague,[28] scabies,[29] leprosy,[30] wasting diseases, melancholy,[31] paralysis, the black jaundice,[32] dropsy, arthritis, cancer, cough, asthma, tuberculosis, and other serious catarrhs, deafness, toothache, lethargy,[33] apoplexy, hernia.

Jupiter: Of the parts over which it presides. Then chronic fever, variola, exanthema, angina, back pains,[34] inflammation of the liver, pleurisy, inflammation of the lungs,[35] spasms; then sicknesses [arising] from winds, stench and inflammation, phlegm.[36]

---

27 Morin was a medical doctor, so his list of the diseases peculiar to each planet should be reasonably reliable. However, medical terminology has changed considerably in the three centuries since he wrote. Consequently, it is not always possible to equate the names of the diseases and conditions he mentions with their present day names. And of course the reader must bear in mind that the real cause of most diseases or conditions was unknown to Morin and his contemporaries. The medicine of his time classified diseases according to their symptoms, thereby confounding different ailments that displayed similar symptoms but arose from different causes.

28 Probably the malariae form of malaria. (Most of the medical notes that follow are from the introduction to W.H.S. Jones's translation of Books XX-XXIII of Pliny's *Natural History* [Loeb Classical Library, Pliny, N.H., vol. 6]).

29 In Latin, *scabies*, but this term is now narrowed to mean an itchy skin eruption caused by the itch insect. The older usage was broader and referred to any ruddy hardening of the skin accompanied by itch.

30 Not necessarily true leprosy, but any scaly condition of the skin resembling leprosy and accompanied by itch.

31 Melancholy refers to a state of mental lassitude, which can have either a physical or psychological cause. It is one of the manifestations of chronic malaria in certain patients.

32 Probably the name used for a long-standing case of *yellow* jaundice, in which the skin has taken on a dark green or dark brown hue.

33 Probably *coma* is meant, rather than sluggishness, although, from an astrological point of view, Saturn would rule both.

34 Disregarding the comma in *passiones, spinae dorsi.*

35 Latin *peripneumonia*, probably the disease we call pneumonia.

36 In Morin's time, two hundred years before the adoption of the germ theory of disease, it was believed that various diseases were caused by winds or bad smells (from swamps, sewers and cesspools, or rotting garbage). Malaria (from the Italian *mala aria* 'bad air'), a disease caused by a protozoal parasite, is a case in point.

Mars: Of the parts over which it presides. Then acute, burning fevers, plague,[37] yellow jaundice, convulsions, hemorrhage, dysentery, carbuncles, anthrax, erysipelas, gangrene,[38] wounds, especially in the face, tertian fever.[39]

The Sun: Of the parts over which it presides. Then ephemeral fevers, spasm, fainting, catarrhs, sicknesses of the eyes.

Venus: Of the parts over which it presides. Then venereal disease, gonorrhea, sicknesses of the womb and the genitals, priapism, weaknesses of the belly arising from cold or moisture, and from that, diarrhea, inflammation.

Mercury: Of the parts over which it presides. Then intermittent and recurrent fevers, madness, frenzy, delirium, insanity, epilepsy, convulsion, stammering, catarrhs, cough, abundance of spittle.

The Moon: Of the parts over which it presides. Then quottidian fevers,[40] epilepsy, apoplexy, silliness, catarrhs, colic, vomiting, fluxes from the belly, excessive menstruation, dropsy, stroke, phlegm.

Death

Saturn well-placed. A natural death from the sicknesses over which Saturn itself presides.

Badly placed. Sudden or violent death from the collapse [of buildings], from a fall, a precipitous fall, drowning, shipwreck, suffocation, incarceration, hanging, lead shot; or with infamy, as by an executioner.

Jupiter well-placed. A natural death from the sicknesses over which it presides.

Badly placed. A violent death from drowning, from war, a duel, or by order of a prince.

Mars well-placed. A natural death from the sicknesses over which it presides.

Badly placed. A violent death from wounds [made] by iron, from fire, or catapults; from decapitation, mutilation of [bodily] members, being torn to pieces, strangulation, hanging, bites of animals, especially vevemous ones, mangling or letting of blood by unskilled surgeons and physicians, [or] by being burnt up.

The Sun well-placed. A natural death from the milder sicknesses over which it presides, such as fevers.

Badly placed. Sudden death from plague, [or] stroke; or a violent [death] from a public order of a prince, or in battle, or by being burnt up.

Venus well-placed. A natural death from the sicknesses over which it presides.

---

37 Probably the bubonic plague or "black death." But the term would have also have been applied to outbreaks of typhus or malignant malaria.
38 In the Latin, *ulcera phagedenica & serpentia*. These are eruptions on the skin that are round and putrefying or streaked.
39 An attack of chills and fever that recurs every other day, as in vivax malaria.
40 Daily attacks of chills and fever.

Badly placed. A violent or premature death from poison, medicine, intoxication, an excess of intercourse or of women, or because of lust.

Mercury well-placed. Death from those sicknesses over which it presides, and a natural one.

Badly placed. An unexpected and very violent death, by murder, poison, magic, or on account of counterfeiting, perjury, forgery, or misapplication of the law.

The Moon well-placed. A natural death from those sicknesses over which it presides.

Badly placed. A violent death from the excessive [administration of] laxatives, from drowning, or murder, generally public or judicial.

Particular Places on the Earth

Saturn: Subterranean [places], pits, sewers, latrines, prisons, cemeteries, lonely [places], hermitages, deserted [places].

Jupiter: High [places], and lofty churches, palaces, [places] especially intended for judicial purposes.[41]

Mars: Foundries and machine shops, fortified places.

The Sun: Courts of kings and princes, auditoriums, churches, *places* of cities.[42]

Venus: Parks, greens, groves, gardens, banquet-houses, theatres, whorehouses.

Mercury: Markets, academies, colleges.

The Moon: Forests, seas, rivers, pools, and places dedicated to public gatherings.

Days of the Week

Saturn: The Sabbath.
Jupiter: Thursday.
Mars: Tuesday.
The Sun: The Lord's Day.
Venus: Friday.
Mercury: Wednesday.
The Moon: Monday.

---

41 Or, less likely, 'High and lofty palaces of the Church, especially intended for judicial purposes.'

42 That is, a large open area in a city—*place* in French, *piazza* in Italian, *plaza* in Spanish, sometimes *square* in English.

BOOK FIFTEEN

Chapt. 6. *The Triplicities of the Planets, or the Trigons and the Trigon Rulers According to the Opinions of the Old [Astrologers].*

Nothing in universal astrology has so disturbed my thinking as the fact that the majority of the old astrologers, and especially the Arabs, the Greeks, and the Latins have judged all sublunar effects chiefly from the trigons and their rulers and not from the exaltations or their rulers, despite the fact that the Arabs, the Greeks, and the Latins disagree very much among themselves about the rulers of the trigons and thereby they have furnished those who hate astrology with no small opportunity to impugn and deride [it].

But, so that this doctrine may be more clearly set forth, assume from Book 14, Sect. 1, Chapt. 5, that there are four triplicities of signs in the zodiac, namely the fiery [triplicity] of Aries, Leo, and Sagittarius; the earthy of Taurus, Virgo, and Capricorn; the airy of Gemini, Libra, and Aquarius; and the watery of Cancer, Scorpio, and Pisces. And about this all astrologers agree; and the signs of the same trigon have among themselves the same nature and temperament, against Cardan's commentary on the *Quadripartite*, Book 1, Chapt. 16, as we have shown in Book 14, Sect. 1, Chapt. 5.

But as for the rulers of the trigons, Ptolemy, *Quadripartite*, Book 1, Chapt. 16, puts the Sun in charge of the fiery trigon by day and Jupiter by night; Mars in charge of the watery trigon both by day and night, with which, however, he associates the Moon by day and Venus by night; Saturn in charge of the airy trigon by day and Mercury by night; and finally Venus in charge of the earthy trigon by day and the Moon by night. Moreover Cardan holds in his commentary that Ptolemy took account of the sex and condition[1] of the signs and planets in this distribution.

But this [distribution] suffers from many defects. First, because it puts three rulers in charge of the watery trigon, but only two in charge of the rest. Second, because in the watery trigon he excludes the Moon from the principal rulership although it is suitable by sex and condition, and in that same trigon it is the most powerful by domicile because it is the ruler of a cardinal sign; but it admits Mars, which is in its fall in Cancer and contrary by sex according to Ptolemy himself, then too by condition, because the reason why Ptolemy made it nocturnal by condition is evidently absurd [as we have shown] in Book 13, Sect. [2], Chapt. 2.

---

1 The term *condition* refers to the sect, i.e.., nocturnal or diurnal.

Third, because in the fiery trigon it rejects Mars, which is more powerful in it than the others by domicile (since it is the one in charge of an equinoctial sign) and similar by sex and condition, then too it is more fiery than the others; and yet it would have this trigon to be mixed of Africus [the southwest wind], according to the domicile of Mars who stirs up the African winds, and western [winds], whereby it is self-contradictory. Fourth, because it would have the same Trigon be northerly on account of the southern sign Sagittarius which Jupiter rules, although Jupiter's rulership in this trigon is less than the rulership of the Sun or of Mars; for the Sun is allotted a domicile and an exaltation in this trigon, and Mars a domicile in a cardinal and primary sign. Therefore it is established from what has been said above that this distribution is not consistent and is not natural but is only based upon a false foundation of condition and sex as is demonstrated by [its treatment of] Mars.

Moreover, the Arabs along with Julius Firmicus, John of Seville, and others of that same faction appoint three rulers in each trigon.[2] Namely, in the fiery trigon the Sun by day and Jupiter by night with Saturn as a partner both by day and by night, which is of course utterly absurd, since Saturn by nature is contrary to this trigon and is rendered very unfortunate in it. In the watery trigon Venus by day, Mars by night, and the Moon continuously, for the foundation of the Arabs is also similarity of sex and condition as above; and consequently in the case of Mars they follow Ptolemy's error, or he follows theirs. In the airy trigon Saturn by day, Mercury by night, and Jupiter continuously, which again is most absurd, since Jupiter in this trigon is allotted neither a domicile nor an exaltation, but on the contrary an exile. Finally, in the earthy trigon Venus by day, the Moon by night, and Mars continuously on account of a false opinion of its condition, with Mercury excluded because of its sex and common condition (as they maintain), which is the strongest of all in this trigon. And Cardan, most absurdly of all puts five rulers in charge in his *Book of the Judgments of Genitures*, Chapt. 27, namely Venus and Mercury by day, the Moon and Mars by night, and Saturn both by day and by night. But the celebrated astrologer Schöner dissents from the Arabs in the trigons somewhat only in the fiery [trigon] and the earthy, for in the fiery [trigon] he puts Mars in charge by day and by night, or continuously; and in the earthy [trigon] he puts the Moon in charge by day, Venus by night, and Saturn continuously.

Besides which Ptolemy makes those planets diurnal rulers of the trigons which rule the fixed signs of the trigons because according to Cardan's commentary those signs are pure, sincere, and strongest. Schöner chose those which are exalted in the trigons. But the Arabs observe no order here, from which it is plain how much confusion there has been up to now among astrologers with regard to these trigon rulers, which I shall put below with their authors for the sake of easier reference.

---

2   This is in fact, although unknown to Morin, the standard scheme of Greek astrology going back at least to Dorotheus of Sidon (first century).

	Ptolemy		Arabs			Schöner		
	Day	Night	Day	Night	Partner	Day	Night	Partner
ri Leo Sag	Sun	Jupiter	Sun	Jupiter	Saturn	Sun	Jupiter	Mars
an Sco Psc	Moon	Venus Mars	Venus	Mars	Moon	Venus	Mars	Moon
ib Aqu Gem	Saturn	Mercury	Saturn	Mercury	Jupiter	Saturn	Merc	Jupiter
ap Tau Vir	Venus	Moon	Venus	Moon	Mars	Moon	Venus	Saturn

Chapt. 7. *Trigons and Trigonocrators According to Our Opinion.*

First we may state something about this matter by means of which the errors introduced with regard to these rulers of the trigons may be averted: it seems to be necessary to suppose here from the practice or observation of astrologers that if a great conjunction or eclipse of the Sun should happen in any sign of the zodiac, judgment would be made in either case principally from the nature and state of the planet which rules the place of the eclipse or the conjunction. And similarly if at any birth Aries is in the Ascendant or the Midheaven, judgment will be made about the accidents pertaining to the Ascendant or the Midheaven from the nature and state of Mars which is the the ruler of Aries, but not primarily and per se from the nature and state of a planet which lacks rulership in these places, and much less from the nature and state of a planet which happens to be in exile in these same places. And the reason for this practice is because, as is more fully set forth elsewhere, the signs and their rulers are determined to the subjects of the houses in which they are and which they rule; and the effects of the signs are changed in accordance with the diverse state of their own rulers, which, consequently, it is necessary to take special notice of for judgment and not indiscriminately [to notice] just any planet—for example, Saturn for the effects of Aries, Leo, or Sagittarius as the Arabs do. Otherwise astrology would have no certain foundation, and consequently no certainty, which is inconsistent with the reality of its practice.

Nevertheless, since not only do the signs of the same trigon agree with each other in nature, as we said above against Cardan, but also the planets that are rulers of those signs agree with each other, either in important things or in predominant nature, which indeed is present in them both elementally and influentially, or in less important things which are present only influentially; consequently, on account of this consensus whatever happens in any or through any sign pertains to some extent to the whole trigon of that sign and to the planets that are rulers of those signs; whence it occurs that both the rulers and the signs are moved to act or to exert an influence together. Nor indeed should anyone be surprised since in fact it seems more marvelous that on the same guitar or even on different musical instruments when one string is touched, another string untouched but in unison should also move by its own motion, but one not in unison should not move; of which effect the reason must be ascribed solely to the identity of the nature of the

sound, as the Reverend Father Marin Mersenne proves in Book 4, Prop. 27 of h
book on *Harmonics*.[3]

Moreover, that the planets that rule the signs of the same trigon harmoni:
among themselves by their important or less important nature is shown th
individually. For Mars, the Sun, and Jupiter rule the fiery signs Aries, Leo, ar
Sagittarius; of these, the Sun is totally of the nature of fire, but Mars and Jupit
are principally of the same nature, as was shown in Chapt. 3 above; and cons
quently they harmonize in a fiery nature. The Moon, Mars, and Jupiter presi
over the watery signs Cancer, Scorpio, and Pisces; of these, the Moon is totally
the nature of water, but Mars and Jupiter are less principally of the same natu
from the third chapter. Venus, Saturn, and Mercury rule the airy signs Libr
Aquarius, and Gemini; all of which [planets] are of an airy nature—Venus indee
principally, but Saturn and Mercury less principally. Finally, Saturn, Venus, ar
Mercury preside over the earthy signs Capricorn, Taurus, and Virgo, [these plane
being] of the same earthy nature among themselves; Saturn indeed and Mercur
principally, and Venus less principally from the same third chapter, so that conse
quently in the signs of the zodiac constituting the trigons and in their rulers th
greatest consensus is perceived, nor is it fictitious, but entirely natural, so that th
matter itself neither should nor can be conceived otherwise without introducin
confusion and falsehood throughout.

And here it should be noted incidentally that Jupiter and Mars are so formall
determined to a fiery nature and a watery one that they cannot be determined to a
airy or earthy one by any formal or intrinsic reason; whence it is plain which plane
are more powerful and should be carefully observed in the individual trigons an
how absurdly Saturn was given command over the fiery trigon by the Arabs, an
Venus over the watery, Jupiter over the airy, and the Moon over the earthy one.

But, with these things already brought up and understood, now I say that thre
rulers or trigonocrators are in charge of each trigon, namely those planets whicl
preside by rulership over the individual signs of the trigon; and consequently th
rulers or trigonocrators of the fiery trigon are Mars, Sun, and Jupiter; of the water
trigon, the Moon, Mars, and Jupiter; of the airy trigon, Venus, Saturn, and Mercury
and of the earthy trigon, Saturn, Venus, and Mercury. And the reasons are plai
from what is said above, [so that] they need not be repeated here superfluously
since they have [already] been sufficiently explained by us. Therefore the whole
difficulty consists of determining which of the planets in which trigon, other thing
being equal, should be preferred to the others for the rulership; or which will be the
first ruler, which the second, and which the third, with which the Arabs are so mucl

---

3 Marin Mersenne (1588-1648) conducted a voluminous correspondence with the scientist
of his day and studied the frequencies and velocity of sound. Apparently the reference
is to his *Préludes de l'harmonie universelle* (1634) or perhaps to his eariler work *Traite
de l'harmonie universelle* (1627).

ccupied; or which will be first by day, which by night, and which at both times ut less principally according to Ptolemy and the others.

Moreover this prerogative of rulership can be defined in three self-consistent vays. First, that the planet that is ruler of the cardinal sign as the principal sign of he whole trigon be first by day principally or primarily, the ruler of the fixed sign principally by night, and the ruler of the common sign by day and by night less principally or secondarily. And yet this order is plainly repugnant to the nature, ex, and condition of the luminaries, for the Sun's whole nature is fiery, masculine, and diurnal; consequently it would be absurd for it to be principally dominant at ight and not by day in the fiery trigon, which is also masculine and diurnal. And he Moon by its whole nature is watery, feminine, and nocturnal; and consequently t would be absurd for it to be principally dominant by day and not by night. Therefore, this order, which would be attended by these absurdities, must be rejected.

Second, that the planet that is ruler of the fixed sign should be first by day, the ruler of the movable or cardinal sign by night, and the ruler of the common sign at both times, which method by reason of the diurnal rulership agrees with Ptolemy. But it seems to go wrong in that Jupiter and Mercury never rule principally but always and only less principally according to this order; still, it is more rational than all the preceding methods.

Third, that a planet which is more powerful than the others in a trigon, namely by domicile and exaltation and is without debility may be put first by day primarily; and this one must be especially noticed in judging by triplicities; but the one which is ruler of the cardinal sign should be first by night and primarily; and finally, the one that is left, by day and by night secondarily, as they are here appointed by us. Take special note that the diurnal trigonocrators are mutually contrary in their domiciles: namely, the Sun and Saturn mutually, and Jupiter and Mercury mutually; it is the same with the nocturnal trigonocrators, namely Mars and Venus mutually, and the Moon and Saturn mutually. And the same with the partners, namely Jupiter and Mercury mutually, likewise Mars and Venus mutually, and in the same order.[4]

		Day	Night	Partner
Eastern	Ari Leo Sag	Sun	Mars	Jupiter
Northern	Can Sco Pis	Jupiter	Moon	Mars
Western	Lib Aqu Gem	Saturn	Venus	Mercury
Southern	Cap Tau Vir	Mercury	Saturn	Venus

In which the Sun and the Moon especially are disposed in the best way, and the Moon much more reasonably than by Ptolemy, the Arabs, or Schöner.

---

4   That is, the Sun's domicile, Leo, is opposed to Saturn's domicile, Aquarius; Jupiter's domiciles, Sagittarius and Pisces, are opposed to Mercury's domiciles, Gemini and Virgo, etc.

In addition, moreover, the [planet] that is more powerful in the trigon always precedes the weaker, as is plain in the fiery trigon with Jupiter, which is only ruler of the common sign, and consequently it is put last as a partner of the diurnal and nocturnal rulers. Similarly in the watery trigon: even though Mars is ruler of the fixed sign, yet because it is in its fall in Cancer, it is put in the last place. In the airy trigon Mercury follows the abovesaid rationale of Jupiter; and in the earthy trigon Venus follows the rationale of Mars; and there is no planet that does not ever rule principally either by day or by night. On which account this order, besides the fact that it is particularly conformable to nature and reason, also agrees particularly well with itself; and to sum it up it is the most perfect of all [the schemes] that have been thought up, wherein in addition it is perceived that each trigonocrator is at least allotted a domicile in its own trigon, but not among the Arabs who most absurdly put Saturn in the fiery trigon by day and by night when it is in its exile and its fall in it. And consequently in the case of a planet staying in any sign in whose trigon it does not have a domicile, it may rightly be said to be peregrine, namely because it is peregrine in a trigon alien to its own nature and in which it lacks any dignity, except that it is exalted in the sign that it occupies, for there it cannot be said to be peregrine, for the rulers of the trigons are established by reason of domicile rather than exaltation; that is, the trigonocrators must agree with the trigons by nature, moreover they agree per se by reason of domicile as is plain but not by reason of exaltation, otherwise Mars exalted in Capricorn would be of an earthy nature, which however is not inherent in it either principally or less principally; therefore in every case the trigonocrators are established optimally.

Chapt. 8. *To Which Regions of the World the Trigons Pertain; and Consequently Which Regions of the World the Trigonocrators Principally Rule.*

Ptolemy and the Arabs differ about this matter too, for the former, in *Quadripartite* i. 16, attributes the fiery trigon especially to the North, on account of Jupiter, which rules the Austral sign Sagittarius, so that all the same it may take on a mixture of the West and the Aphric[5] on account of Mars, which he nevertheless expels from rulership of the trigon; from which it is sufficiently plain how poorly these things hang together. For he says that Jupiter stirs up the Boreal winds and Mars the west winds; from which it does not follow that the fiery trigon, in which it has less power, is northern. For this might perchance happen on account of another trigon in which it would be more powerful, such as the watery [trigon]. But consequently he attributes the watery trigon to the West with a mixture of the South; the earthy [trigon] to Auster or the South, with a mixture of the East or Subsolanus; and the airy [trigon] to the East with a mixture of the Boreal. But in the case of the planets he puts Jupiter in charge of the North, Mars the West, Venus

---

5 The name of the southwest wind.

the South, and Saturn the East—on account of (he says) its familiarity with the Sun. But the Arabs want the fiery trigon to be Eastern, which they put Jupiter in charge of; the watery trigon they attribute to the North, which they put Mars in charge of; the airy trigon to the West, which they want Saturn to be in charge of; and the earthy trigon to the South, which they put Venus in charge of. But here again no logic can be discovered in the rulers of the trigons, nor is there any any consistent order. And in fact in the fiery triplicity, Jupiter is the ruler of the common sign without any infortune;[6] in the watery [trigon], Mars is the ruler of the fixed sign, with dejection or depression;[7] in the airy [trigon], Saturn is the ruler of the fixed sign, with exaltation;[8] and in the earthy [trigon], Venus is ruler of the fixed sign, with fall or depression.[9] Nor can it be said that in this matter the Arabs have looked at the sex and condition of the trigons and planets, since Mars from its sex and condition disagrees with the watery trigon, as has already been said above. Therefore, since those things which are arranged by nature are self-consistent and conformable to reason, it seems that it must be acknowledged that here too Ptolemy and the Arabs have wandered away from the truth; and those things that they have predicted from the trigons and their rulers have happened either by chance or from other causes. Wherefore, in order that this difficulty may be resolved, nature itself must again be consulted. And it will indicate to us that the four cardinal signs, Aries, Cancer, Libra, and Capricorn, the primary [signs] of the trigons, are distributed to the four regions or corners of the world by their own position: and in the case of Cancer in the North and Capricorn in the South there is no difficulty; but only in the case of Aries and Libra, which of them will claim the East for itself, since both of them begin at the equator or middle of the world. But the [direction of] rising, that is the nobler cardinal point is [rightly] due to Aries. [This] may be proved first because heat, the active quality, predominates in Aries; but in Libra humidity, the passive quality; and the active is nobler than the passive. Second, because Aries is subject to the rulership of a masculine planet [and] Libra to a feminine. Third, because Aries is in a nobler and commanding part of the world, namely the North, as has been shown previously, while Libra is in an ignoble and obedient part. Fourth, because the rising is dry, as is Aries, and the setting is moist, as is Libra. From these causes, therefore, Aries belongs to the rising and Libra to the setting. Therefore, the fiery trigon will be Oriental, the watery Northern, the airy Occidental, and the earthy Southern; and this is in complete agreement with our division of the zodiac in Book 14, Sect. 5, Chapt. 5, where we have said that the active qualities, heat and cold, are dominant in the Boreal part of the world through Aries and Cancer, namely in the rising and the North, and the passive qualities in the Austral part through Libra and Capricorn in the setting and the

---

6   He means that Jupiter is not debilitated in any sign of the triplicity.

7   In Cancer, where it is in its fall.

8   In Libra.

9   In Virgo.

231

South. And consequently the trigonocrators we have put above will preside over those same regions of the world in which their trigons fall. And hence the reason is now apparent why Jupiter excites the Boreal winds, namely because it is the principal and most powerful ruler of the Boreal trigon, [just as] the Sun is of the Oriental, Mercury of the Southern, and Saturn of the Occidental.

You will object. The same part of the earth is simultaneously oriental and occidental, and there is no place on the terrestrial sphere that may be particularly assigned to the east or to the west. Therefore, the fiery trigon does not preside over the east or the airy trigon over the west.

I reply that of course there is no part that is simply and absolutely eastern or western, but only when compared to another: as Germany is east of France, but west of Hungary; and it can also be said that Germany is north of Italy and south of Denmark. And therefore the divisions of the zodiac into two parts, north and south, then into 4 trigons for the 4 corners of the world, insofar as they are referred to the earth, are in fact universal, so that nothing can be concluded from them for particular places on the earth; for example, if there is an eclipse in the northern half of the zodiac, then it will primarily pertain to the peoples of the north, but to which particular [nation] cannot be specified from this alone. Similarly, if there is an eclipse in the fiery trigon, its effect will be allotted to those lands of the earth which will be eastern with respect to others; and it may perhaps signify eastern lands actively and western ones passively; as when the king of Spain subjugated America to the west of himself. But it cannot be specified from this alone which are the eastern places and which are the western ones. And since the East contains the space of the *caelum* or the earth from the rising of the Sun in the beginning of Cancer to the rising of the Sun in the beginning of Capricorn, if an eclipse should occur in Aries or Leo, it may in fact be said that the eastern part of the earth that is signified is in the north part, but this signification is more general still than to be able to designate the very location in particular. But the celestial figure erected for any particular location at [the time of] mid-eclipse, if it has the degree of the eclipse in the eastern part of the figure, will show by its eastern place that it signifies a part of the earth that is between its place in the figure and the ninetieth degree to the east; and the distance of the place of the eclipse from the meridian will more particularly designate the very place according to terrestrial longitude, but not according to latitude. And for this reason it will be necessary in addition to take into account other things that are discussed in Book 20, Sect. 1, Chapts. 4 and 5. And a more precise conjecture will have to be be elicited from them. But if the eclipse occurs in Sagittarius, an eastern place on earth will be signified in the southern part [of the earth]. And if the ruler of the eclipse is in the fiery trigon, the signification of an eastern place will be more certain; [but] if in another trigon, the signification of the place will be a mixture of the two trigons, or [it will be] of several places, as, if the eclipse is in the fiery [trigon] and its ruler is in the watery [trigon], a place between the rising and the North will be signified; but if the ruler is in the airy trigon, which presides over the setting, since the same place cannot e both oriental and occidental with respect to the same [point], then of necessity at least two places will be signified, of which one will be to the east of the other.

Furthermore, what was said above is understood for the disposition of the air, such as winds, as well as for mutations of kingdoms. Moreover, in individual genethliacal figures, if a fire sign is in the ninth house, it will signify a journey to the East; if an earth sign [is there, one] to the South; if another [element], to another region. But if the rulers of the signs are both in a water sign, then on the contrary the journey will mainly be made to the North. And the reasoning is the same with the rest. And these things appear plainly in my geniture, where Sagittarius and Capricorn are in the ninth. And their rulers are conjoined in Pisces and the twelfth house. And of my own accord I have traveled in Provence to the South, Paris to the North, and in Hungary to the East with respect to Villefranche, the place of my nativity; and this by my own decision, impelled by the stars.

Chapt. 9. *Some Things about these Trigons that should be Especially Noted.*

Since we have defined the rulers and regions of the trigons above, now we may mention some things about them that are particularly worthy of note.

First. The Sun is the most powerful of all in the fiery trigon, namely by house and exaltation. In the watery [trigon], Jupiter [is the most powerful] for the same reason; in the airy [trigon], Saturn; and in the earthy [trigon], Mercury. Also, since these planets experience no debility in these particular triplicities, for this reason special account must be taken of them in judging by triplicities. And these 4 planets are opposed when they are in their own houses, namely the Sun and Saturn to each other, and Jupiter and Mercury to each other; whence it is plain that these are most appropriate to great changes of sublunary things, but especially to changes in the air. Moreover, because Mars rules Aries and Scorpio, fire and water signs, and is exalted in the earth sign Capricorn, it has a strong propensity towards rains, chain lightning, thunder, thunderbolts, and thunderclaps, for fire, water, and earth concur in these things; in addition to the fact that Mars itself is principally of a fiery nature and less principally of a watery one.

Second. The northern equinoctial sign, namely Aries, belongs to the Sun and Mars, and this is especially fitting for the northern [peoples], who in empire, glory, and arms are superior to the southern [peoples]. The southern equinoctial belongs to Venus and Saturn, which agrees with the southern [peoples], who are lustful, ugly, indolent, and servile. The northern solstice belongs to the Moon and Jupiter, which precisely suits the northern peoples on account of their fame, religion, justice, and mutability, for which they are remarkable. But the southern [solstice belongs] to Saturn and Mars; from which [arise] impiety and moral depravity, common among the southern peoples. And further, the northern peoples are principally affected and governed by the luminaries and then by Jupiter and Mars;

but the southern peoples principally by Mercury and Saturn, and by Mars; whic'
is to be understood as a generality and one particularly worthy of note.

Third. The particular rulership of the trigonocrators ought to be defined i
accordance with the following rules:

1. The one that is in the trigon should be preferred to the one that is absent

2. The one that is above the earth should be preferred to the one that is unde
the earth.

3. The diurnal one should be preferred by day if it is above the earth, and th
nocturnal one by night.

4. The diurnal one can be secondary or less principally [preferred] by night
and the nocturnal one by day, if they are above the earth.

5. When two planets are conjoined in the same sign of their own trigon, the
ruler of that sign should be preferred for the trigon rulership of that sign.

6. In the case of an eclipse, or of any significator, the ruler of the sign of the
eclipse or of the significator should be preferred, especially if it is above the earth
and in its own trigon, and if it aspects its own place.

7. The partner in the rulership, or the one which rules both by day and by
night, will dominate primarily when it is above the earth and the one which attains
the domination only by day or by night is under the earth.[10]

But of these rules, this one is unique and fundamental: that the stronger is
always to be preferred to the weaker. Furthermore, whatever may be understood
from the instruction of the Arabs about these trigonocrators, with regard to universal
constitutions, and also with regard to the genethliacal nativities of men, for making
judgments in a special way here and there, we shall explain in its own place.,[11]
Here it may suffice to warn [the reader] in passing that it was entirely erroneous.

Chapt. 10. *The Faces or Persons or* Almugea *of the Planets.*

This dignity of the planets is wrongly reckoned by Ptolemy, *Quadripartite*
i. 20, and his commentators, among the essential [dignities], as will appear
below. And it only concerns the five lesser planets, or those which are secondary
with respect to the Sun and the Moon.

---

10 That is, if the day ruler is under the earth by day, but the "partner" is above the earth,
then the "partner" predominates over the day ruler; and similarly for the night ruler.

11 Apparently a reference to Book 21, Sect. 2, Chapt. 7, where he discusses the technique
of using triplicity rulers given in Albohali's book, *The Judgments of Nativities.* Morin
was of course unaware that this was a standard technique of classical Greek astrology.
Despite Albohali's references to Dorotheus, the fact that the technique does not appear
in the *Tetrabiblos* made it appear to Morin to be an Arabian invention. He would most
likely have dismissed it anyway, but believing that it was of Arabian origin made it easier
for him to do so.

A planet is said to have its own face or to play its part with respect to the Sun or the Moon when it is as far distant from the Sun, when vespertine or occidental to it, or from the Moon, when matutine [or oriental] to it, as the domicile of the planet following Leo (the domicile of the Sun) is distant from the beginning of Leo, or as the domicile of the planet preceding Cancer (the domicile of the Moon) is distant from the beginning of Cancer. For example, if Venus is occidental to the Sun and is distant from it by 60 degrees, which is the amount by which the beginnings of Leo and Libra are distant from each other, Venus is said to have its own face with respect to the Sun, or by the Arabs to be in *Almugea*[12] with the Sun. But, if oriental and matutine to the Moon,[13] it is distant from it by 60 degrees, which is the amount by which the beginnings of Taurus and Cancer are distant from each other, it is said to be in *Almugea* with the Moon. And the reasoning is the same with the rest.

Having stated this, I say first: This is not an essential dignity. For the essential dignities of the planets are immutable, and they do not pass from one part of the zodiac to another, as was set forth above about the domiciles, exaltations, and trigons. But this [particular] dignity can happen to a planet in different signs of the zodiac, as can simple orientality or occidentality with respect to the Sun and the Moon. Therefore it is not an essential [dignity].

I say second: By postulating this dignity I have destroyed the simple orientality of a planet with respect to the Sun, and yet Ptolemy himself and all the astrologers correctly attribute great powers to planets that are oriental to the Sun. For in the case of Mars in *Almugea* with the Sun, i.e., occidental to the Sun, and that same Mars oriental to the Sun, let Ptolemy say which prevails and which is inferior. Besides, why don't Ptolemy and the others make the *Almugea* of the Sun oriental and that of the Moon occidental? For this would have seemed more reasonable too from Ptolemy's teaching, which holds that planets oriental to the Sun and occidental to the Moon are fortified.[14]

Finally, no mention or observation is made among astrologers of the strengths or effects of this dignity, and it is always with some aspect of a lesser planet with a luminary, with which aspect its own force really coincides, as is said in its own place; wherefore, I suspect that it has been taken from some figments of the Arabs.[15] And therefore we here put an end to the essential dignities of the planets.

---

12 The text has Almugara in error. The word *almugea* is a Latin corruption of the Arabic *al-muwajaha* 'facing', a translation of the Greek astrological term *idioprosopia* 'being in its proper face'.

13 Reading *Lunae* 'to the Moon' rather than *Luna* 'the Moon'

14 The reason is that the solar signs of the planets are those occidental to the Sun, while the lunar signs are oriental. The best that can be said for Almugea is that it provides a dignity for a planet whose position of orientality or occidentality to the Moon or Sun would otherwise not provide one.

15 Not so, because as Morin has just said, it is mentioned by Ptolemy (*Tetrabiblos*, i. 23). And, unknown to Morin, it is also mentioned by Vettius Valens (*Anthology*, ii. 5, 10, 12, and 14; vii. 2), so it is of Greek origin.

Chapt. 11. *The Thrones, Seats, or Chariots of the Planets.*

This dignity is not simple, but mixed or composed of several essential dignities, for Ptolemy, in the place cited above, along with the rest of the astrologers, holds that a planet may be said to be in its own seat when it is in a sign in which it is allotted several essential dignities; and they think this correctly. For the [planet] that is strong in any sign from several essential dignities will obtain the highest authority; whence not unreasonably when occupying that sign it is said to be situated in its own seat as it were. Moreover, since we admit only three essential dignities, viz. domicile, exaltation, and trigon, it is obvious when and where a planet may be said to be in its own chariot. And it may have such dignities in any place in the figure, such as the Ascendant, the Midheaven, the Sun's position, etc. For if the Ascendant is in Aries, the Sun in the Ascendant will be strong by exaltation and trigon at the same time. And so with the rest.

Therefore, if the Sun is in Sagittarius, it will only be in its trigon; but if it is in Aries or Leo, it will be in its seat; because, besides the trigon, it has its domicile in Leo and its exaltation in Aries. If Mars is in Scorpio or Aries, it will be in its throne, and the reasoning is the same with the rest. But from this it is plain that any planet, when it is in its own domicile, is in its own throne, for it can be in its own trigon and not in its own domicile or exaltation, as is the case with Saturn in Gemini, but, when it comes to its own domicile in Aquarius, it is certain that it ascends one degree in dignity, and it rides in its own chariot, namely because aside from its own domicile it [also] has the authority of rulership in the whole triplicity. Moreover, the *pit* [of a planet] is opposed to its throne, and it is a great debility for a planet, consisting [as it does] of several others. As if Mercury were in Pisces, where it experiences both its exile and its fall.

Chapt. 12. *The Joys of the Planets.*

The *joy* of a planet is not an essential dignity of its own; it is neither simple nor mixed, and it only applies to Saturn, Jupiter, Mars, Venus, and Mercury, each of which is allotted two domiciles in the zodiac; of which that one of its domiciles is called its *joy* which corresponds more closely to its ruler, either by reason of its principal nature, or by reason of its sex, or by reason of its more tempered effect or influx.

And in fact from the first mode Saturn's joy will be Capricorn; for this is a cold sign and one that corresponds to Saturn's principal nature, which is cold and dry (which [qualities] are inherent in it both elementally and influentially, as has been shown elsewhere), [more] than Aquarius, a hot and humid sign; and so with the rest. By the second mode, the joy of Mars will be Aries and not Scorpio, as the astrologers falsely suppose, for Mars is of the masculine sex, but Scorpio is feminine. Finally, by the third mode, Aquarius will be the joy of Saturn and Scorpio the joy of Mars, if to be sure the cold and dry influx of Saturn may be tempered more than in Capricorn; and the hot and dry influx of Mars may be tempered more in Scorpio than in Aries. But because the third mode is only something we have invented, it is not natural to the planets themselves, which, like other physical causes, rejoice mostly in that place where they encounter the greatest similitude of nature, in accordance with the principle that everything rejoices in something like itself. Therefore, the joy of a planet will be properly defined in accordance with the first two modes: where they agree in the same sign, that will be the greatest joy of its own ruler; elsewhere, nature will be preferred to sex. For these reasons, therefore, the joy of Saturn will be in Capricorn, that of Jupiter in Sagittarius, that of Mars in Aries, that of Venus in Libra, and that of Mercury in Virgo.

Chapt. 13. *The Terms, Novenas, Decans, Dodecatemories, etc. of the Planets in the Several Signs of the Zodiac. Then, the Light, Smoky, Pitted, and Empty Degrees of the Signs, their Monomoiriai, etc.*

So far, whole signs of the zodiac have been distributed to the planets in accordance with their commonly received essential dignities; and there is then a division of the zodiac into 12 equal parts; then, superimposed upon these is a natural distribution, or at least one depending upon a natural foundation, as is seen in Books 14 and 17. But for the terms, the novenas, the decans, etc., individual signs are subdivided into various parts, which are again distributed to individual planets for smaller superimposed dignities, which those who introduced them also hold to be essential [dignities]. But this is my opinion about these [subdivisions]

The Devil, the worst enemy of mankind, with the blindness of mind introduced into the human race by sin, little by little called those men away from the true recognition and worship of God and at length cast the greater part [of them] into the abyss of idolatry, so that they granted the honours due to God alone not only to the Sun, the Moon, and the rest of the celestial bodies, but also to the commonest animals, then to the dead works of their own hands, viz. to idols—indeed even to the demons themselves. And, lest man, by nature desirous of learning, might rise up again to the recognition of the true God by means of the sciences, either those accepted by tradition from Adam, or those cultivated by the vivacity and inclination of the intellect, and especially the celestial [sciences], which above all others provide confirmation of God and His infinite goodness, wisdom, and providence, the wicked demons, either by their own inspiration or by the depraved natural light of men subject to themselves, have polluted the celestial sciences among themselves with very many falsities, figments, and superstitions, so that the truth of these things, overwhelmed by falsehoods, is ineffective [in directing] them to the necessary knowledge of God; and among others, obscured by such false additions, it has fallen into contempt and derision by another most wicked design of the Devil.

From such sources as this, then, there have come forth in astrology the terms, the novenas, the bright degrees, the smoky degrees, the monomoiriai, etc., which are nothing other than mere symbols of the ineptitude, stupidity, and insanity of men who were ignorant of the principles of this divine science, which [follies] the wiser astrologers have always disdained.[16] Moreover, the haters of astrology have made [of them] a most useful tool for themselves [with which] to disparage, defame, and destroy the science.

But what any of these dignities is, and by what reasoning the signs are subdivided for the individual planets, it is not even pleasing to explain here; these madnesses are not worth our time; they may be left to the stupid and the ignorant. But I say this in general against their vanity: there is no sublunar accident concerning which from the abovesaid dignities there cannot be at the same time a true affirmation and negation: namely it can be true by the terms and false by the decans or the novenas, etc., on account of the various divisions of the signs and the distributions of the planets fighting against each other, as is seen in the authors. To this I add that these divisions of the signs and distributions of the planets repose on no natural foundation and are only fictitious. And this is plainly proved because the division of each sign into 30 degrees is not natural but only assumed for convenience in calculation; and the dignities mentioned above are based upon the hypothesis of this division; therefore they are only fictitious. And this will be more clearly exposed by their tables of dignities. For among the Arabs Saturn has his terms in Taurus from the 21st degree to the 27th, his decan from the 20th to the 30th, his novena [from 0] to 6 2/3 degrees,[17] and his dodecatemory from 7 1/2 degrees up to 10; and so with the other [planets].

Nevertheless, all the modern astrologers will still object that in fact the novenas, the decans, and all the rest ought to be thrown out of the true science of Astrology. But the terms are wrongly rejected by me, since they are approved of and retained by Ptolemy and all astrologers generally.

But I reply that I not only marvel that the philosophers, especially the Christian philosophers, should employ this nonsense of novenas, decans, monomoiriai,[18] pitted degrees, etc., and have made them principles or bases of their

---

16 Perhaps a slap at Placidus, who says in Thesis 56 of his *Primum Mobile* "The dignity of the planets in the signs and their parts, which are called the bounds and terminations, have a real and natural foundation...they are highly deserving of admiration." (John Cooper's translation) But in any case a distinct departure from most other astrological writers, including Ptolemy.

17 The ninths were assigned rulers by equating them to the signs of the zodiac beginning with Aries. Their planetary rulers are then the planets ruling the signs. The first two ninths of Taurus are equated to Capricorn and Aquarius; hence their ruler is Saturn. See the table in John of Seville, *Epitome of All Astrology* (Nürnberg: Montanus and Neuber, 1548), between Chapts. 12 and 13.

18 Single degree rulers. See, for example, the table in Paul of Alexandria, *Introduction to Astrology*, Chapt. 33.

adgments, thinking with Julius Firmicus Maternus that great powers are inherent in them and great mysteries not to be revealed to the common crowd,[19] but also that they have so far retained the terms of the planets by unanimous consent, since their worthlessness can be proved very evidently from Ptolemy alone, even though he would not (*Quadripartite*, iii. 14) have the Anareta kill when it comes to the Apheta in directions if it is posited in the term of a benefic planet; and thus he attributes no small force to these terms.

For Ptolemy, Book 1, Chapts. 18 and 19, explains three systems of terms or a threefold partition of the individual signs for these terms, i.e., an Egyptian, a Chaldean, and one from a certain old MS, the first two of which systems he rejected and followed [instead] the last, in which Saturn, Jupiter, Mars, Venus, and Mercury are distributed among the individual signs divided into 5 parts. For example, in Aries Jupiter has according to the Chaldeans the first 6 degrees of that sign, Venus the 6 following, Mercury the 8 following, Mars the 5 following, and Saturn the last 5. But in the Ptolemaic system Jupiter has the first 6, Venus the 8 following, Mercury 7, Mars 5, and Saturn the last 4. And so with the [other] individual signs, having excluded the Sun and the Moon. Moreover, Ptolemy offers some reasons for this diverse division and distribution, both for the systems he discarded and for the one that he follows, but which in truth are mere figments as devoid of any natural basis as are the novenas, the decans, etc., which are similarly divided up and established, so that just as Cardan ingenuously confessed in his *Commentary* that he had found the greatest confusion in these various systems of terms, with which he was not content, he wanted too to think up a method of his own for himself in which each sign is distributed to the 7 planets, and he gave both his reasons for it and a table in his *Book on the Judgments of Genitures*[20] And I once, adding figments to figments, thought up another system of terms, with reasons even more plausible than those of Ptolemy and Cardan; but what are these other than outstanding foolishness. And so both the terms and the rest of the things mentioned above may be cast out of our astrology.

And this reason is brought forward by us as to why the terms were employed hitherto by Ptolemy and the rest of the astrologers. Of course Ptolemy, *Quadripartite*, Book 4, Chapt. 11, wanted only 5 significators to be directed in a genethliacal figure for all the native's accidents, viz. the Ascendant for health and travel, the Part of Fortune for wealth, the Moon for the mind, habits, and association, the Sun for dignity and fame, and the Midheaven for the rest of the actions of life and the procreation of children. And since the bodies and the aspects of the planets coming to these significators would not satisfy all the accidents, either on account of the paucity of significators or the lack of promittors coming to them, they supposed that besides the bodies and the aspects there were still other promittors in the nature of things, and they could conceive of no others than these terms which they

---

19 *Mathesis*, iv. 22
20 *Opera Omnia*, vol. 5, pp. 455-456 (the table on p. 456)..

themselves had invented, and by the introduction of which they were rarely lacking promittors from the occourse of which in directions some reason might be had for the [observed] effects or the accidents of the native. And it is very common in Junctinus and the rest of the astrologers for a man to die even a violent death from the direction of the Ascendant or the aphetic luminary to the term of Saturn or Mars or to attain a great dignity from the direction of the Sun to the term of Jupiter or Venus, etc. And since it seems to me very absurd to ascribe such effects to such meager and controversial causes, which had in the same way been imputed to novenas, decans, and dodecatemories, only by a careful examination of the directions and by unceasing effort did I discover that those terms are fictitious causes and not only the significators that are directed, but also their aspects must be multiplied from the nature of the thing, and thus the true causes of all the native's accidents are ascertained, but of these [I shall speak] more fully in their own place namely when it is a question of directions.[21] And what has been said hitherto about the essential dignities and debilities of the planets should suffice; and it may be noted that every planet that is posited outside of its own domicile, exaltation, or triplicity is said by us to be peregrine, and peregrinity also is twofold: a simple kind without any essential debility, as the Sun in Capricorn; and another mixed with an essential debility, as the Sun in Aquarius, and this latter kind is worse.

---

21 In Book 22.

BOOK SEVENTEEN

SECTION 1

Chapt. 3. *The Special Division of the whole* Caelum *into Twelve Astrological Houses with respect to the Person being Born.*

Truly, since some astrologer of the foremost wisdom, whoever he was, older than the rest that followed him, understood that the *caelum* was made and was movable for the sake of man rather than for the sake of other living or inanimate things, and that many things were made to suit man himself on account of his more divine nature—things that would hardly be suitable for more ignoble natures; therefore, for the sake of man himself he reasonably decreed that the whole circuit of the *caelum* should be divided into twelve parts, which he called houses, by great circles brought down from some point of the *caelum* and cutting another great circle of the *caelum* into that many equal parts, as will be explained in its own place. And, placing the first house in the east, he handed down to posterity that it rules the life of man and that from it conjectural knowledge can be had and judgment made about his life; and that the second house, which follows next according to the motion of the planets, rules over wealth; the third, brothers; the fourth, parents; and so on with the rest. And in the house diagram below these are arranged in order and named.[1]

And this division of the *caelum* and this designation of the houses has endured uncorrupted from him down to us, although Ptolemy and the others who followed him may seem to differ from that old tradition and to pervert the division in many places, as when they make their principal judgment about children not from the 5th house but from the one opposite it, the 11th, and about servants and animals not from the 6th but from the one opposite it, the 12th—which apparent error we shall correct below, notwithstanding the division of the *caelum* instituted variously by different astrologers.

[The lower half of p. 385 of the *Astrologia Gallica* contains a large square chart. Rather than reproduce it in tiny type on this small page, I shall describe its contents.]

Outside the chart, Morin places two catchwords at each angle: (Ascendant) Birth, Life; (Midheaven) Vigor, Action; (Descendant) Decline, Marriage; and (Imum Caeli) Suffering, Burial.

---

1 I have appended a table rather than the diagram mentioned.

The house rulerships are as follows:

1. Life, temperament, state of health, moral nature, mental qualities.
2. Wealth, gold, goods of the acquired estate.
3. Brothers, relations.
4. Parents, successions.
5. Children, bodily pleasures.
6. Servants, subordinates, domestic animals.
7. Marriage, open enemies, lawsuits.
8. Death.
9. Religion, journeys.
10. Action, profession, dignity, fame.
11. Friends.
12. Sickness, imprisonment, exile, secret enemies, hardships.

[The chapter continues with philosophical arguments and answers to critics.]

Chapt. 6. *Things to be Particularly Noted about the Significations of the Houses.*

....For example, almost all astrologers, in company with Ptolemy, have supposed that sickness belongs to the 6th house per se, although it [actually] belongs to the 12th house per se, which is the essential house of bodily afflictions and especially of sickness in accordance with the division mentioned above, and the 6th house per se is that of servants and animals; but besides the essential signification of the houses, they have this property in addition: that each of them signifies the same thing, only weaker, as the one that it opposes, on account of that opposition and because both of them are included in the same half circles that result from the division. And so the 6th house, by accident or secondarily, signifies sickness, imprisonment, and secret enemies by reason of the opposition; and in turn the 12th house carries the signification of servants and animals. Similarly, the 7th will, by accident, be the significator of sickness and death because it is opposed to the 1st, which is the significator of health and life per se; and in turn by accident it will signify marriage. And for the same reason astrologers judge from time to time about religion from the 3rd, about wealth from the 8th, about the parents—and especially about the mother—from the 10th, about children from the 11th, although they would not think these houses to be the genuine cause of the truth of their judgments, as one can infer from their books, and especially from Ptolemy; but they are of course deceived in this, because the essential signification of each house has not become known to them, since it can only become known through the higher Cabbala, although Hermes, convinced by experience, offers something similar in

242

Aphorism 42,[2] when he says that the ruler of the 2nd will have the same force for impediting as the ruler of the 8th, and similarly that the ruler of the 6th will have the same force as the ruler of the 12th. But they err seriously who judge about things neither from their proper houses nor from the opposite houses, but rather from those that are completely alien to the signification, such as when someone wants to judge about wealth or brothers or the spouse or children from the 11th without any more valid reason than because Jupiter, Mercury, the Moon, or Venus is in the 11th. But here in addition one detects the error of Ptolemy and his following, who judge about individual matters almost entirely from the angles of the figure and the luminaries, and from the relationship of the other planets to the angles and the luminaries. For the angle of the 1st house, for example, is the angle of life, but it is the native's life in three ways—in itself, in God, and in his own children, and yet they deny that judgment can be rendered about all of these from the angle of the 1st house alone. And so with the rest of the angles.

---

2 Hermes, *Centiloquy*, Aph. 42. The Lord of the second house has the same strength in hurting as the Lord of the eighth; the Lord of the sixth the same with the Lord of the twelfth. --Translated by Henry Coley in his *Clavis Astrologiae Elimata* (London: Tooke & Sawbridge, 1676. 2nd ed.), p. 333.

BOOK EIGHTEEN

Chapt. 7. *The Extrinsic Strength of the Planets arising from their Reception in the Signs of the Zodiac.*

Every planet outside of its own domicile is said to be received by another, namely by domicile, exaltation, or triplicity. As, if Jupiter is in Libra, it will be said to be received by domicile by Venus, by exaltation by Saturn, and by triplicity by Venus, Saturn, and Mercury. Moreover, there is reception *with presence* and *with absence*. *With presence* is when the receiving planet is in the same sign with the received planet, as if Venus is in Libra with Jupiter. *With absence* is when the receiving and the received planet are in different signs. In either case it is very important to notice whether the planet is received by a friend or by an enemy; then whether it is received in signs concordant with itself by exaltation or by triplicity, or whether it is received in contrary signs. For if the Moon in Cancer receives Jupiter, a friend to herself and exalted in Cancer, it will be an excellent and most efficacious reception *with presence*. But if Mars in Scorpio receives Venus, the reception will be completely bad, and it will greatly distort the influence of Venus.

Moreover, a reception *with absence* is either mutual or not mutual. A mutual reception is if Jupiter receives Venus in any of her dignities, and she receives him reciprocally, which can happen in two ways. First, if they receive each other mutually in the same dignities, as both by domicile or both by exaltation. Just as, if Jupiter is in Libra and Venus is in Sagittarius. And this reception is the strongest per se for doing good or doing evil. And indeed for doing good if neither planet is made unfortunate in the sign that it occupies by being in its exile or fall, but on the contrary the other one of the two is made fortunate by being in its domicile or exaltation; as, if Mars is in Leo, and the Sun in Aries where it is exalted; and consequently in such a reception Mars is very powerful; or, if the Moon is in Pisces, and Jupiter is in Cancer where it is also exalted. But for doing evil, if either of the planets is made unfortunate in the sign that it occupies by being in its exile or fall, as, if the Sun is in Aquarius and Saturn in Leo, or the Sun in Libra and Saturn in Aries, or Mars in Cancer and Jupiter in Capricorn. From which mutual [configurations] of extreme strength, others of medium strength easily become known. Namely, those in which either neither planet is made fortunate or unfortunate in the sign that it occupies, or else only one of the two.

But a second kind of mutual reception occurs if the planets receive each other in dissimilar dignities, as, if Jupiter receives Venus by domicile, but she receives him by exaltation or triplicity. And this reception is much weaker than the first. And it will also be benefic or malefic accordingly as one of the received planets or the other of them is favourably or unfavourably posited by reason of domicile or exaltation or their opposites.

Finally, every reception *with absence* is either with a benefic or a malefic aspect of the receiving planets or with none. And with a benefic, it is benefic; with a malefic, it is malefic; with none, it is neither. On which account, with the Sun posited in Aries and Mars in Leo, or with the Moon in Pisces and Jupiter in Cancer with a trine aspect [in each case] the reception will be excellent and benefic. But with the Sun posited in Aquarius and Saturn in Leo, or with Mars in Cancer and Jupiter in Capricorn, with an opposite aspect the reception will be unfortunate and very bad.

It could be said that Saturn in Leo opposed to the Sun in Aquarius, combines its [influence] with the Sun by opposition with respect to us, and for this reason since it is in Leo the Sun's state is less unfortunate than if Saturn had been in Cancer and the Sun in Capricorn. And consequently, that opposition with mutual reception by domicile lessens the evil of the opposition; and the same reasoning applies to the opposition of the Sun in Libra and Saturn in Aries, and to the square of Mars in Cancer and the Moon in Aries. But it could be said in rejoinder that Saturn does not act on the Sun but on us; and the influence on Saturn from Leo is the worst with regard to us, just as is the influence upon the Sun from Aquarius, when moreover to these is added the opposition of the Sun and Saturn, which is also evil with regard to us, the malignity of that influence is more increased than decreased. Moreover, when Mercury is posited in Pisces and Jupiter in Gemini with a square aspect, that reception will be of medium strength and misfortune; but when Mars is posited in Taurus and the Moon in Capricorn with a trine aspect, the reception will be of medium strength and good fortune. From which examples it is now easy to render judgment on the rest, and to distinguish which of the receiving planets may be stronger for doing good or doing evil. And in fact a considerable part of the science of [astrological] judgments depends upon these [combinations].

Someone may say that these things are contrary to the doctrine of the old [astrologers], those namely who maintain that every mutual reception—at least by domicile or exaltation—is benefic; and he will contend that this is proved in various genitures, as in that of the most illustrious François de Bonne, Constable of France,[1] who had Mars in Taurus ruler of the Sun, and Venus in Aries ruler of the Part of Fortune. But he was always most fortunate in his wars, and step by step he achieved the highest honour in the army, which none of the common astrologers would fail to refer to the mutual reception of Venus and Mars by domicile, although both planets were in exile and without any aspect of the ruler.

But nevertheless, the doctrine we have proposed is true, and the common opinion is false; nor does the proposed example stand in the way. For the good fortune of that man in the wars and his promotion to the highest dignity had causes other than the mutual reception of Venus and Mars.

---

1 He was born at Saint-Bonnet, Dauphiné (*now* in the Dept. of Hautes-Alpes) 1 April 1543 with 30 Gemini rising and became the Duke of Lesdiguières in 1611 and Constable of France in 1622.

For in the first place, Mercury ruler of the Ascendant was in Taurus, besieged ⸱ Venus and Mars, which signified a fortunate propensity for arms, especially ᵑce Mars ruled the 7th by exaltation. The 7th house, which has 30 Sagittarius on ᵉ cusp, is empty and is largely occupied by the sign Capricorn, which is the ᵗaltation of Mars. [Hence it indicated] both singular prudence in arms and also ᵢlitary honours because of Mars's rulership of the Sun. Second, the Sun was ᵗalted in the 11th and conjunct Venus, which indicated kings as friends and ᵉnefactors. Third, the Moon ruler of the 1st[2] was in the 10th under the rulership ᵗ Jupiter, which was also the ruler of the cusp of the 7th, which is [the house] of ᵃrs, mutually and almost partilely applying to the trine of Saturn ruler of the 7th[3] ᵃ the domicile of Mars, which signified that the native would be raised to the ᵢghest military honours because of wars, and that there would be a fortunate ᵤtcome of wars undertaken because Jupiter was itself the ruler of the 7th and the ᴼth in the domicile of and in partile opposition to Venus, which rules the ᵢidheaven by exaltation and is conjoined to the Sun exalted in the 11th. And these ᵣe the genuine, powerful, and numerous causes of the outstanding good fortune ᵗat this native attained. Moreover, that mutual reception of Venus and Mars rulers ᵗf the 5th and the 11th in the 11th with Mercury ruler of the Ascendant and their ᵖpositions to Saturn and Jupiter rulers of the 7th, which is also [the house] of the ᵖouse, very powerfully signified a propensity to venereal pleasures and marriages ᴼ persons of lower rank because each planet is in its own exile, and Jupiter and ᵃturn are also in domiciles of Venus and Mars [respectively] in the 5th house; and ᵗese affairs were open and well-known on account of the Sun's being with Venus ᵃnd in opposition to Jupiter. And so, such mutual receptions are unfavourable and ᵐust be distinguished from the causes of fortunate things, with which they may ᴼccasionally be found mixed together, lest there be attributed to them some ᵒrtunate occurrence which is not from them.

And the truth of the doctrine we have proposed will be proved from very many ᵍenitures. For I know three noble women; and in the geniture of the first of them ᵗhe Sun and the Moon were rulers of the 1st, and the Moon was in Taurus with Mars ᵢn the 11th, and the Sun was in Scorpio with Venus in the 5th.[4] It can scarcely be ᵖut into words how greatly she was inflamed with a desire for luxury from that ᵐutual reception of Venus and Mars in signs where each planet is in exile, and in ᵗhose houses of the figure, and with the luminaries dominant as rulers of the 1st. ᴵn the geniture of the second, Jupiter was in the 7th and in Gemini, and Mercury ᵂas in the 3rd and in Pisces.[5] She was twice married unhappily and had lawsuits ᵂith relatives. In the geniture of the third, Venus was the ruler of the Ascendant in

---

2   The 1st house, which has 30 Gemini on the cusp, is empty and is largely occupied by the sign Cancer; hence, Morin assigns the Moon as its principal ruler.

3   Again, because the 7th house is largely occupied by the sign Capricorn.

4   An unidentified lady, perhaps born on 16 November 1595.

5   This lady was born in one of the years 1586, 1598, 1610, or 1622.

Aries and in the 12th, and Mars ruler of the 12th in Taurus and in the 1st, whic configuration occasioned many sicknesses to her. But who will now say that the [mutual] receptions were beneficial?

Again, in the nativity of the very noble Joan. De Giam D. De Rispe,[6] Venu ruler of the Midheaven was in Aries with the Sun ruler of the Ascendant, and Ma was in Taurus in sextile with the Moon and Jupiter and also in partile trine wit Saturn ruler of the 7th, which is [the house] of wars, and therefore he should hav been fortunate in martial endeavours and actions according to the common astro ogy; when, in fact, he was unfortunate in war and finally perished miserably in duel, wounded in the head by a bullet, from which he died on the spot. For Ma was with Caput Algol[7] partilely square the Ascendant, and Saturn ruler of the 7t was opposed to the Moon and square the Sun ruler of the Ascendant, nor did th things mentioned above help,[8] nor even Jupiter in Pisces in the 8th. [And we ma add] to these that in the nativity of Mr. Des Hayes[9] Jupiter was in the 7th degre of Gemini in the 8th with Mars ruler of the Ascendant, and Mercury was in Pisce and the 4th, and the Moon was in the 7th with the Head of Medusa and th Pleiades[10] square the Sun ruler of the 10th in exile in the 4th. And this man ha his head struck off by order of the King; nor did the mutual reception of Mercur and Jupiter in the 8th help, because both of them were in exile and there was mutual square between them.

There is no need here for further examples. They occur elsewhere, bein noted *passim*. Moreover, the logic of the doctrine we have proposed is [as follows] since Venus in Aries is a bad influence, and Mars in Taurus is also bad, or Venu in Scorpio and Mars in Taurus also with an opposition aspect, therefore the tota influence that is combined from these cannot be favourable to the native receiving it. It could perhaps be said that this is the same as if Mars were in Aries or Scorpic and Venus in Taurus, but this is false. For, from the principles of astrology, which are fully supported by experience, Venus in Taurus effects one thing, and Venus in Aries or Scorpio effects another; and similarly Mars; and also the direction of the Midheaven to Venus in Taurus effects one thing, and to Venus in Scorpio another for the latter direction will scarcely bring about anything good, but the former wil bring about much good, as is consistent with experiences. Therefore, in the case of mutual receptions, what is said above must be carefully noted.

---

6 Unknown to the translator. But from the horoscope details given next his birth can be dated to 4 April 1607 at about 1:30 PM.

7 The star Algol or Beta Persei at about 20°42' Taurus.

8 That is, the mutual reception of Venus and Mars.

9 Louis des Hayes, who is mentioned again in Book 21, Sect. 2, Chapt. 2, was executed in 1642 for plotting against Cardinal Richelieu. From the horoscope elements given, his birth can be dated to 12 February 1598 at about 11:30 PM.

10 The Head of Medusa is another name for Algol, which was at 20°34' Taurus. Alcyone or Eta Tauri, the brightest star of the Pleiades, was at 24°23' Taurus.

BOOK TWENTY

SECTION 3

The Various Universal Modes by which the Celestial Bodies act on Sublunar Things

Chapt. 7. *The Action of the Constellations and of the Fixed [Stars] on these Inferior Things; and the Dependence in Action of some of these on the Twelfths and the Planets.*

In the preceding chapter it was said that the firmament does not determine the *caelum* influentially per se or through its own substance, but only by that first and simple determination by which any physical thing that acts determines the first physical cause; nor does it also act influentially on sublunar things, but only with a simple virtue of its own that is formal to itself and unknown to us. But about the firmament, insofar as it is filled with constellations and fixed [stars], plainly the contrary will have to be asserted.

As a matter of fact, through a constellation and a fixed [star] it influentially determines the particular part of the *primum mobile* with respect to which that constellation or fixed [star] is subjected to the earth. Not indeed with a perpetual determination like that which was made by the Sun at the beginning of the world, but temporary and transitory, like that which is made by the transits of planets under the signs—i.e., it determines transitorily its part [of the *caelum* to acting in accordance with the force and influence of that constellation or fixed [star]; and it does not act on inferior things in accordance with the influence of these; and this is proved by the most evident and frequent experience, not only in universal charts or configurations of the *caelum* in annual revolutions of the world[1] and lunations, but especially in particular figures of nativities, where it is very clear, so that to have any doubt about it would be to testify to one's own ignorant stupidity. For it is evident that the point of the *caelum* under which a fixed [star] was at the time of a geniture retains the force and nature of that fixed [star] with respect to the native as long as he lives, even if he should live a thousand years. And for that reason the old astrologers, also educated by experience, were quite right in their judgments of the principal fixed [stars], which they call *royal [stars]*, observing the fixed [stars] in the Ascendant or posited in the 1st house, or coascending with the ruler of the Ascendant at the place of the genethliacal figure, or being in the same circle of position with that ruler, for life, mental qualities, and the moral nature. And

---

1 In modern terms, Aries Ingresses.

observing the fixed [stars] posited in the Midheaven or the 11th house, or culmina-
ing with the ruler of the Midheaven, or allotted the same circle of position with th.
ruler, for actions and dignities; and thus with the other houses. And similarly i
directions they observe the fixed [stars] located in the same circle of position wit
a significator, to which when the promittor comes by direction it also comes to tl
star, whence a greater effect follows than from the significator alone, then thos
that are borne with the promittor to the circle of position of the significator itsel
and from which they properly judge. Indeed, they will perceive that the directior
of significators to the principal fixed [stars] seen by themselves, then the transi
of the former over these, yield notable effects. Others, too, inspect the princip:
fixed [stars] that have a strong position with respect to the Sun both in univers:
and particular configurations, in accordance with Ptolemy's nine modes, which w
have reduced to three, viz. when the Sun and a star are on the circle of the horizo-
or together on the meridian, or when one of these stars is on the horizon, and anoth
is on the meridian, or on the contrary, provided that a star before sunrise or aft
its setting is visible in its rising, setting, or in the meridian circle, for if it is not see
thus because of hindrance from the solar rays, it will be of much less virtue. An
these things must especially be understood about the fixed [stars] that are locate
in the zodiac, with which the planets can be conjoined corporally, then of thos
which are directly overhead in the region of the chart; those to be sure which ar
more efficacious than the rest, especially when those fixed [stars] occupy the angle
of the chart, from which in directing any [such] angle as a significator it is greatl
strengthened, i.e., it is allotted a greater effect, whether for good or evil, accordin,
as the star was benefic or malefic, as will be explained more fully in its own plac
and confirmed with examples.

Furthermore, it must be noted that of the fixed stars in the firmament som
are arranged in asterisms or figures, which are commonly called *constellations*, an
some of these figures are very distinct, so that they naturally seem to be or t
comprise one particular nature, which is perceived in contrast with the others: [suc]
as] the head of starry Aries, the head of Taurus, the Pleiades, Gemini, Leo, Scorpio
Sagittarius, Ursa Major and Minor, Cassiopeia, Perseus, Corona Borealis, Lyra
Cygnus, Delphinus, Aquila, Orion, Canis Major, Corona Australis, Grus, Trian-
gulum Australe, Crux, and others, which at the first glance arrest the eyes and th
mind, and divide the firmament as it were into regions different in nature and mor
notable than the rest, in which it is undeniable that there is a special virtue. But th
rest are more confused and only invented by the judgment of men in contrast wit
the others. They are: Cancer, Virgo, Capricorn, Aquarius, Pisces, Cepheus, Her
cules, Coma Berenices, Balaena, Lupus, and others, in which perhaps many natura
figures have been combined into one artificial figure. In addition to which
however, many stars are still scattered here and there in the sky, which have no

been able to be collected conveniently into figures by the imagination of men, and for that reason they have called these stars *unformed*.[2]

Besides, Astrology has suffered no small damage from the fact that the old astrologers confused the constellations of the zodiac with the *twelfths* of the zodiac,[3] supposing that there is no distinction between them, on account of the to them unknown *primum mobile*, under which the fixed [stars] move, thus they ought to be [so] called only with respect to their own *caelum*; but with respect to the *primum mobile* [they ought to be called] *erratic*, just like the planets. And they have judged about astrological effects from these constellations, which they have put together from the fixed [stars] scattered along the zodiac, when the first star of Aries was situated in the point of the vernal equinox, which for that reason has been called down to the present time the Beginning of Aries. [And this occurred] about 400 years before the birth of Our Lord Jesus Christ, which Gallissard's *Chronology*,[4] along with that of the Hebrews, Bede, Longomontanus, Kepler, and other astronomers suppose to have occurred around the year A.M. 3964,[5] at which time lived Herodotus, Socrates, Anaxagoras, Melissus, Plato, Aristotle, and other men of great name, who brooded over the founding of the sciences and handing them down to posterity, and at which time also I think the science of astrology that has come down to us was founded. Moreover, the proper natures of the twelfths have

---

2   A term used by Hipparchus and his successors to designate stars that lay *between* the constellations and did not belong to any of them. Modern astronomers have eliminated this situation by expanding the constellations to fill all the available space, so that every star is in some constellation.

3   That is, the *signs* or 30-degree sections of the tropical zodiac. Morin calls them *dodecatemoria*, but we cannot call them *dodecatemories* in English because that word is used for the twelfths of the *signs*.

4   Pierre Gallissart (fl. 1577), a Dominican of the Convent of Arles, was a schoolmaster and writer on religious subjects.

5   That is, these chronologists put the creation of the world 3964 years before the birth of Jesus, which Morin assigns to 25 December 0 Astronomical (or 1 B.C. according to the usual historical reckoning). See Book 2, Chapts. 3 (translated above) and 4, where Morin rehearses the opinions of the principal authorities known to his time. He himself estimates the creation of the world to have taken place 3968 years before the birth of Christ, since according to Tycho Brahe's determination of the motion of the solar apogee (adopted by Kepler for *The Rudolphine Tables*) the apogee would have been at 0 Aries at that time, and Morin evidently felt that God would not have created the world and set the astronomical machine in motion with the apogee at some odd location.

It is interesting to note that a century and a half later the Marquis de La Place (1749-1827) in his *Mécanique Céleste* VI.x. Art. 31 (Bowditch's translation, vol. 3, p. 266) made a similar observation: *the time when the longitude of the sun's apogee, counted from the moveable equinox, was nothing, precedes, about sixty-nine years, the epoch usually assumed for the creation of the world* [the year 4004 B.C., in this case]. (Laplace's value of the motion of the solar apogee was slightly smaller than Tycho's.)

been attributed to these constellations by these astronomers, and so they have confused the powers of these [constellations] as well as of those [twelfths] in turn; and although a little after, Tymocharis, and following him, Hipparchus, who flourished around 300 years before Christ,[6] and finally Ptolemy, strenuous observers of the fixed [stars], detected the abovesaid error, having discovered the motion of the fixed [stars] in the following direction,[7] from which they distinguished the starry signs from the twelfths,[8] compelled nevertheless by nature to concede 30 degrees of the zodiac to each individual twelfth, although the starry signs were very unequal in this respect,[9] they then established the twelfths associated by trine aspect to be of the same elementary nature,[10] although this did not necessarily agree with the starry signs.[11]

However, this was unknown to or ignored by those who came later, so that in their judgments they continued the errors of the old [astrologers], namely attributing to the starry signs the force of the twelfths on effects, or, on the contrary, attributing the force of the starry signs to the twelfths, saying that the twelfth of Aries signified sheep, that of Taurus cattle, that of Gemini humans, etc., because of the names Aries, Taurus, Gemini, etc., given to those constellations by the more ancient masters of astrology, who also from the conceded truth of an appellation proved by experience were unaware whether such a proper truth should belong to the constellation or to the twelfth,[12] namely because they disregarded the twelfths, even though the elements of the triplicities of the signs similar to nature received by them through the Cabala,[13] but not conformable to the constellations, evidently makes known that the first astrologers (from whom emanated the Cabala, thereafter neglected or corrupted) had a true understanding of the *primum mobile* and the twelfths.

But among the moderns I cannot fail to marvel at Cardan, who has a great name as a philosopher, astrologer, and physician, and who in his *Commentary on the Quadripartite*, Book 4, the chapter on Professions,[14] thinks that "The twelfths have acquired a certain force on account of the similarity of the place to the figures (*i.e., the starry signs*) which underlay them at the time of the great conjunction in

---

6 Timocharis flourished in the early third century and Hipparchus in the middle and latter part of the second century B.C.

7 The precession of the equinoxes.

8 That is, the constellation Aries from the mathematical Aries, etc.

9 A fact deliberately ignored by Cyril Fagan and the other modern "siderealists."

10 The triplicities.

11 Aquarius, for example, was classified as an air sign, although it represents a man carrying water and pouring it out of a large pot.

12 Since the constellations at that time approximately coincided with the signs to which they had assigned the same names.

13 The system of triplicities with its four elements seems rather to reflect the influence of Greek philosophy.

14 Cardan, *Opera Omnia*, vol. 5, p. 326, col. 2.

the heads of Aries and Libra of the eighth and ninth spheres (*He thought this was the* primum mobile.) at the time of Christ. For aside from the fact that such a conjunction was fictitious, just like its origin, viz. the motion of trepidation of the eighth sphere,[15] as we have explained elsewhere, a huge absurdity results: namely, that either before this conjunction the twelfths were lacking in virtue, although Cardan already acknowledges them to be powerful, or that the starry signs by their own transit of the twelfths have formally conferred their own powers on them. But this would be absurd, as we have shown in Chapt. 5 in the case of the planets' transit of the twelfths; thus, by the same reasons, it would [also] be absurd in the case of the starry signs' transit [of the twelfths].

Furthermore, from the confusion of the starry signs with the twelfths it has resulted that those things that seem to be naturally derived from the constellations as well as the strengths of the individual fixed [stars] have hitherto in greater part remained unknown, for the understanding of which however from the beginning it was necessary to be free from great contention of the mind. And now we are usually compelled to frame our judgments from these twelfths and from the planets, just as if there were no fixed [stars] or as if they were of no virtue, with only a few of the brighter ones excepted, whose force cannot escape notice because of its sudden and notable effects, and I do not see how such a defect can be restored in this [age of] decline of the world; for if any fixed [star] has its own proper virtue that is influential upon inferior things (which cannot be denied), who will deny that when they join with the signs and the planets in the same effect they alter the significations of these or their effects? I certainly confess this freely, and I marvel at how those things which are predicted to occur from the signs and planets alone, without any consideration of the fixed [stars], may also often happen so fortunately,[16] and it should not seem to be so marvelous if they did not come to pass, especially because the fixed [stars] move not unlike the planets in the twelfths, and consequently even their aspects to the planets may seem to be admissible.

But to this the reply can be made that every fixed [star] has its own inherent influential force, but only the greater [stars] have the capacity of producing visible effects, either in the air or in men. Which is proved from the fact that for any man there are directions of the significators to the fixed [stars] in individual years, indeed in months or weeks, on account of the countless multitude of them, then in individual hours transits of the planets to them; however, no great or visible effects are produced except from the occourse of the planets and their aspects or from the more notable fixed [stars]. Moreover, there are no effects just from the transits of the planets over the places of the fixed [stars], or at least none are observed in genitures; and therefore I would not deny that the minor fixed [stars], such as those

---

15 The so-called Trepidation of the Equinoxes, a supposed backwards and forwards movement of the equinoxes first mentioned by Theon of Alexandria in the fourth century.

16 Morin means that astrologers are lucky to have their predictions come to pass when they have ignored the influences of the fixed stars.

of the fourth, fifth, or sixth magnitude do nothing at all, although I should think that not even the far smaller satellites of Jupiter are devoid of powers towards us. [17] Whence I think it should be concluded that in astrology men can at least discern and predict the more conspicuous things, but that demons, being by nature most perspicacious in all these things, can also discern and predict lesser things. Also, it can be said that the lesser stars, if not individually at least collectively, produce notable effects, as is plain in the case of the Pleiades.

And, having expounded these things, I now judge that the title of this chapter has been satisfied in accordance with the principles of this science as established by us and based upon experience. When any fixed [star] or constellation is moving in any twelfth, it plainly determines that twelfth in the same way as a planet passing through the same sign, and it does not change its own proper nature or its virtue, nor does it receive anything formally from the sign in which it acts, as was said in the case of the planets, but it determines the sign for many [more] years than any planet, since a fixed star stays in a sign 2,118 years according to the *Rudolphine Tables*, but Saturn, the slowest of the planets, stays only two and a half years. Therefore, through all that time the sign may act with the conjoined powers of that constellation or fixed [star], whence it is no wonder that it has seemed to some astrologers, and especially to Cardan, *The Judgments of Genitures*, Book 4, Chapt. 22, "...[that] now the powers of the twelfths are different from what they once were," [18] namely because when a starry sign passes from one twelfth into another, it alters considerably the proper effects of that [twelfth] because of its own new concurrence in action with that [twelfth], just as happens with the planets. And consequently in any twelfth these three things must be looked for: the nature or virtue of the twelfth, the nature of the constellation, and the nature of the planet if there is one present corporally or by aspect. And from these three, judgment must be made. Because, even though Alexander de Angelis, *Against the Astrologers*, Book 4, Chapt. 8, thinks it impossible on account of the variety of causes and cries out in his fashion against astrology, yet he must be pardoned for his ignorance, for indeed he had no experience in this science, nor did he know how to erect a

---

17 This sentence seems to mean that Morin feels obliged to *say* on the basis of experience that the minor fixed stars do not do anything in nativities, although he *thinks* that they, and even the satellites of Jupiter, do have some small power.

18 The *Judgments of Genitures* is not divided into books. Nor does the 22nd chapter contain the exact words Morin quotes. However, Cardan does say (*Opera Omnia* [1663 ed.], vol. 5, p. 451, col. 1) "For the fixed [stars] or the erratic [stars] or the parts of the *caelum* do not signify exactly the same things as they did in Roman times...and the zodiac has another nature, for the fierce and violent stars that were formerly in Leo are now in Virgo, whence both signs are more moderate." By which he means that the departure of those active stars from Leo has reduced its penchant for violent action, while their arrival in Virgo has invigorated a previously mild sign. This agrees with Morin's dictum that the fixed stars determine the signs.

oroscope, as is revealed by his book.[19] For if he had not devoted himself to eradicating astrology instead of to discovering its truth by experiments, he would have recognized that we also in these present times experience the same forces from the individual twelfths as were attributed to them by Ptolemy and the older astrologers from the Cabala or from observation, even though they are now occupied by other constellations than they once were—not because they have no effect, but because in their concourse the twelfths (which are parts of the prime physical cause) as well as the planets (the principal governors of the world) prevail over the fixed [stars] and the constellations; and consequently these [fixed stars] only produce sudden and fleeting effects, but not lasting ones unless they are supported by the planets, as is generally known among astrologers.[20]

Besides, a constellation or a fixed [star] depends upon the twelfth that it occupies, and the planet to which it is conjoined, only so much as [it would] upon a companion in action, just as two men hauling the same boat; for a fixed [star] is like another planet, and vice versa, and the planets are not rulers of the fixed [stars], because these are said to be of the nature of Saturn, Jupiter, Mars, Venus, etc., just as the fixed [stars] do not preside over the twelfths; for a fixed [star] is not said to be of the nature of Mars because it has accidentally been determined to the nature of Mars, but because it is essentially similar in nature to Mars; nevertheless, Mars is the ruler of the fixed [stars] that are moving in Aries no less that it is of Saturn moving in Aries, for this is proper. And so the fixed [stars] in their action depend upon the planet whose sign they occupy, but the planets never depend upon the fixed [stars] in the same way. But if the twelfths are viewed as parts of the *primum mobile*, then a constellation and the fixed [stars] are subordinate to those on which they depend, as an inferior cause or secondary cause is to a superior or primary cause. And from what is said above the majority of the difficulties raised from time to time by those who hate astrology and those who are ignorant of it have been clearly resolved.

---

19 Alessandro Angeli (1562-1620), *In astrologos conjectores libri quinque*. (Rome: B. Zannetti, 1615). According to Lynn Thorndike, HMES 6, pp. 202-4, he was director of the Jesuit college at Rome. His book seems to have been first published in 1604 and again in 1615 (both at Rome and Lyons). Thorndike says "...de Angelis gives an elaborate rehearsal of past arguments against astrology, but there is little or nothing new said." He also notes Angeli's acceptance of "...the statement that a child weaned on goat's milk, after it had grown up, would leap like a goat and eat such plants as goats are wont to crop." Which perhaps shows that Angeli understood nutrition about as well as he did astrology.

20 Here, and in what follows, Morin addresses the naive charge frequently leveled against astrologers that the signs of the zodiac no longer correspond with the constellations bearing the same names.

BOOK TWENTY-THREE

Chapt. 18. *The Universal Laws of Judgments on Solar and Lunar Revolutions of Nativities.*

Although from what was said in all of Book 21 about the determinations of the celestial bodies and then especially what was said in Chapts. 6 and 7 of the present book, it should be plain enough how revolutions should be judged, at least in a general way; nevertheless, because the universal laws of judgments are common to genitures and revolutions, the doctrine of revolutions also possesses some laws of its own, both universal and particular; therefore, it seems to us that the universal laws ought to be given here, lest anything should be lacking in a theoretical doctrine of such importance; and we shall give the particular laws in our [book] *Astrological Prediction*, if God grants us the time to compose it.[1] Therefore, the principle ones of the universal laws follow, from which the lesser principal laws can easily be discovered by a skillful astrologer.

1. In a revolution, nothing should be predicted—at least nothing significant—unless it is signified by the radix or by its directions at the time of the revolution. For if the Sun in the 10th of the radix is directed to the trine of Jupiter well disposed (which is a distinguished and fortunate direction per se), but in the revolution of the year indicated by the direction, the Sun is in the 12th square Saturn or Mars without any fortunate aspect of Jupiter, which is also badly afflicted, the direction will produce nothing, and only ineffective attempts for honours will occur along with impediments, and perhaps also misfortune in connection with honours; and so with the rest. But generally one ought to look in every revolution, both of the Sun and of the Moon, how the planets on that day are related to the places of the geniture. For, if favourably related [they indicate] good, if unfavourably related, evil in the affected type of accident of life, wealth, honours, etc., having taken into account the determination of the planets themselves, both radical and revolutional.

2. Similarity of signification of a revolution with the geniture brings forth the things signified in the geniture. But dissimilarity suppresses or retards them, or fulfills them in a minimal fashion or corrupts them. And therefore whatever is performed by a revolution must certainly be presignified in the nativity. But whatever is presignified in the nativity for any particular year, is not performed by the revolution of that year in the absence of similarity to the thing predicted, which actuates the potential of the geniture and its directions in the things signified. Therefore Cardan rightly warns that nothing should ever be pronounced about

---

1   This work was unfortunately never written, as Morin died not long after finishing the *Astrologia Gallica*.

radical directions without having inspected the revolution of the year indicated by the direction—but in fact also the one immediately preceding or following; otherwise, even the best astrologer will be deceived.

3. The more the figure of the revolution, whether solar or lunar, is similar to the radical position of the signs and planets, the more efficaciously it will bring forth the significations of the geniture, whether good or evil, and especially those that will be signified by a similar direction. For that similarity is not always favourable and a promise of some great good, as Origanus and many others suppose, but it only signifies the same things as the figure of the geniture, whether good or evil. Otherwise the planets would not act in accordance with their determinations; and a malefic influx in a nativity would be corrected by one similarly malefic, or it would be completely changed, which is inconsistent with experience and nature. But this greater similarity (at least in the position of the signs) can be acquired or vitiated by the native's travelling to appropriate places of the earth for the time of the revolution, and especially for that of the Sun, as was already said in Chapt. 4. And this is a secret of the science that should by no means be despised. And in particular those revolutions should be watched for in which the same degree of the ecliptic is found in the Ascendant as was in the Ascendant of the radix; for then each planet rules the same houses in the revolution as it ruled in the radix, which does not usually happen without [producing] some notable effect signified by the nativity, since the force of signification of the signs will also be doubled, at least in the place of the nativity and thereabouts.

4. A thing strongly signified by the nativity or by a radical direction can be reduced to actuality or perfected by a weak solar revolution of the same signification; and therefore much more readily by a strong one. But it will not be perfected by a weak lunar revolution. And vice versa, a thing weakly signified by the nativity or one of its directions can be brought forth into actuality by a strong solar revolution of the same signification, but hardly by a strong lunar revolution. But a thing weakly signified in the nativity will hardly be brought into actuality by a weak solar revolution of the same signification, and it will not be done at all by a weak lunar revolution, because a strong resistance of secondary fate, i.e., a strong contrary disposition (if it is present) of sublunar causes passively or actively joining in an effect, wards off a weak celestial influx. Therefore, in all things signified in a particular year the disposition of the secondary fate must be carefully attended to. And the natives must be questioned about those things, so that where their undertakings, actions, and experiences lie may be discovered; and from this [information] a more sagacious prediction can be made after having considered the virtue of the revolution.

5. When the Ascendants of the radix and the revolution are opposed, it is evil and disturbing, and worse still when the degrees [themselves] are opposed, especially in the case of a solar revolution. For, since the revolution either brings forth or inhibits the effect of the nativity, and it can only bring it forth from a similarity of the figures, it is plain that this contrariety of position, both of the Sun and of the

ole *caelum*, will inhibit the radical influx and prevent it from bursting forth into tion, but especially into good action, and will only bring forward ineffective forts in connection with the good things signified by the directions in that year, th many contrarieties, damages, anxieties, sicknesses, and dangers to life. And e reason is because the signs are then determined to significations contrary to the dix. For just as bad changes and harm happen in the Great World, or in universal ture, when the sign Leo of solar nature is determined to the contrary saturnine ture by Saturn's movement into Leo, and Saturn's virtue is also corrupted there, also when the planets and signs in revolutions, and especially in transits, are termined to significations contrary to their radical ones, or the planets themselves e disposed in a contrary manner, bad changes and misfortunes must be expected the Microcosm, or the native. But if Jupiter or Venus is in the 1st [house] of the volution, without rulership in the 8th or 12th of the radix or the revolution, the ril things in the essential significations of the 1st house indicated by this con- ariety will be removed or mitigated, and some happiness and joy will also happen connection with marriage, lawsuits, and contracts, especially if the 7th of the dix is well disposed and the directions are in accord—namely because each house f the radix can [also] signify for its opposite. But if any evil is signified by the eniture and its directions in that year, especially in connection with sicknesses, wsuits, and open enemies, and the 7th of the radix is badly disposed, and there e bad planets in the 1st of the revolution, those evils will happen in that year. And e same thing should be thought in the case of opposed signs culminating[2] in the dix and the revolution, and also in the case of the other cusps.

6. If the Ascendant of the revolution is trine the radical Ascendant, it is good or the significations of the 1st house; if it is square, it is evil. But one must not ronounce about the good or evil of the significations of the first house simply from ese [aspect indications] alone, but the state of both Ascendants and also the state f the planets in the revolution must be looked at, and especially the state of the ulers of the Ascendants of the radix and the revolution, along with the direction f the radical Ascendant and its ruler. And one must think about the Midheaven's f the radix and the revolution in the same way.

7. The sign ascending in the revolution, in which some planet is posited in he radix, and especially the place of that planet on the Ascendant of the revolution, ffects the native in the things signified by the 1st [house] according to the nature, tate, and determination of that planet in the radix and the revolution. And the same hing is true of the Midheaven of the revolution and the other cusps. And if in the olar revolution the Ascendant is the place of the radical Saturn, or of Mars in the 3th, or of the ruler of the 8th, [the native] will have to be on guard against death in hat month in which the Ascendant of the lunar revolution is the same, or in that quarter in which it is the same, and with the rest in agreement.

---

2   That is, on the cusp of the 10th house.

8. Each sign's effect signified by the geniture happens in connection with th
significations of the house of the figure that that sign occupies in the revolution
especially if the radical directions are in agreement. And thus the sign of the 1
[house] of the radix in the 12th or the 8th of the revolution threatens sicknesse
imprisonment, enemies, death, or dangers to life if the radix and its directions agree
in the 11th it presages friends; in the 10th, undertakings, actions, dignities, etc. Th
sign of the 2nd of the radix in the 7th of the revolution [indicates] wealth from
marriage, lawsuits, and contracts, or expenses and losses in connection with these
same things in accordance with the state of the 7th and its ruler, both in the radi
and in the revolution. For the signification of good or evil state of the 7th of th
revolution does not overturn the signification of the state of the 7th of the radix c
act against it [as was explained] in Chapt. 7. And the reasoning is the same in th
rest.

9. Any planet in the revolution can act in accordance with the nature of th
house that it occupied in the radix, yet it acts more evidently according to the natur
of the house that it occupies in the revolution, whether it is a solar or a luna
revolution. This is proved from the Sun itself, which in all its own revolutions i
in the same house of the radix, although it will vary its effects in individua
years—indeed, that which is radically signified by the Sun from the house of th
[natal] figure will be specified and determined to the signification of the house tha
the Sun occupies in the revolution; and it will be proved similarly by the Moon i
its revolutions. Therefore, if Mars from the 2nd [house] of the radix comes to th
5th of the revolution, it will signify prodigality or outlays for pleasure in that yea
But on the contrary, if Jupiter from the 5th of the radix comes to the 2nd of th
revolution, it will presage increases in wealth from children or lovers[3] or game
and pleasures. But although the same thing could be said of the ruler of the 2nd o
the radix in the 5th of the revolution or the reverse, yet, because the presence of a
planet is stronger than its rulership when absent, if in the nativity the ruler of th
2nd is in the 5th, but in the revolution it is in the 12th, one will have to say that [th
native] will become sick as result of pleasures, or that he will be incarcerate
because of them or from outlays on them,[4] and thus the significations of the three
houses 2, 5, and 12 are combined. But it is not always necessary to combine th
significations of all the houses. And the reasoning is the same in the rest
Nevertheless, it must be noted that in revolutions the determinations of the planet
by reason of bodily position and rulership in the figure of the revolution must be
combined in accordance with the doctrine of Book 21, Sect. 2, but always with
respect to the determinations of the same planets in the radical figure also thus
combined. And this is to combine the radical combinations with those of the
revolution, because whoever does this more sagaciously will judge more certainly

---

3 Reading *amasiis* 'lovers' instead of *amesiis*.
4 That is, from going into debt from expenditures on pleasures.

10. In the case of any planet in the figure of the revolution, one must first turn his attention to which house of the radix it falls in, and after that to which house of the revolution. For the radical figure precedes the figure of the revolution in time, in virtue, and in universality. And therefore one must first look at how these planets are related to the figure of the radix, rather than how they are related to the figure of the revolution. And this is proved by the fact that if Saturn is the *anareta* in the radix and in the revolution it comes to the Ascendant of the radix, it threatens the native with danger to his life no matter in which house of the revolution that Ascendant is. But that house can decree the *type* of danger, e.g., if the Ascendant comes to the 5th of the revolution, the danger will be from pleasures or from their cause, because there it takes a new determination to pleasures. But if the radical Ascendant and Saturn in it comes to the 8th of the revolution, sudden or violent death is signified or some great unforeseen danger to life on account of the doubled anaretic force of Saturn and the doubled aphetic force of the subordinated Ascendant. And consequently, the following things must be looked at for each planet in the revolution. First, what is its nature. Second, what is its celestial state in the radix. Third, what is it determined to in the radix by body and by rulership. Fourth, which house of the radical figure does its [position] in the revolution fall into. Fifth, what is its celestial state in the revolution. Sixth, what is it determined to in the revolution by body and by rulership. Seventh, how can the radical and revolutional determinations be combined with regard to their conformity, contrariety, or dissimilarities. For the greatest secret of revolutions lies in these [considerations] before [all] the rest.

11. Any planet will fulfill its own radical significations in any year mainly in accordance with the house that it occupies in the revolution. And therefore one must judge about its effects from each of its determinations—the radical, namely, and the revolutional—arising from its celestial and terrestrial state in each figure. And it must be seen from what and into what it may be changed from the radix to the revolution by reason of sign, house, ruler, and configuration. Noting that its radical determination is specified [as to type] and determined by its signification in the revolution. And therefore the ruler of the 1st [house] of the radix, or the planet that is in the 1st of the radix, if it comes to the 5th of the revolution, and especially Venus,[5] will incline to pleasures; if it comes to the 10th, and especially Jupiter, it will cause ambition for honours; and the reasoning is the same with the others.

12. A planet migrating from one house of the radix to another house of the revolution does not have a simple and absolute influx on its significations as it does in the radix, but a mixed one and dependent upon the significations of its radical

---

5 That is, 'and especially [if it is] Venus'. However, only the planet's symbol is given in the Latin text, so it could also be translated 'and especially to Venus', but I incline to the former interpretation. (And similarly for Jupiter in the latter part of the sentence.)

house. And one must always look in both places, insofar as it pertains or refe
primarily and per se to the native and not to other persons. And therefore Schön
and others are mistaken when they assert that a planet migrating from the 11th
the radix to the 8th of the revolution signifies the death of the native's friends. F
the 8th house in the native's particular, or radical, figure is not the house of dea
of the native's friends or for everybody in general, but it is only the house of dea
of the native himself, as we have explained elsewhere. And consequently such
planet is determined to the native's death, and it will rather signify death for hi
or danger to his life from a friend. But in universal constitutions[6] the 8th house
the house of death in general. And it will be better to say that if a planet in the 11[
of the radix comes in a revolution to the 6th of the radix, which is the 8th from th
11th of the radix, some friend of the native will die, especially if that planet is evil
disposed in the revolution. In this regard, a planet migrating from the 11th of th
radix into the 8th of the revolution does not signify the same thing as a plan
migrating from the 8th of the radix into the 11th of the revolution. For the form
signifies that a friend concurs per se in the native's death, especially if it is a malefi
planet, but the latter signifies that it happens to a friend that accidentally and witho
any intent he is the cause of the native's death. But it can also signify escape fro
death through the favour or assistance of a friend. Similarly, a planet from the 11
of the radix coming to the 7th of the revolution turns a friend into an open enem
or it stirs up lawsuits because of friends or it gives a spouse through the efforts o
friends, or it settles lawsuits. But a planet from the 7th of the radix coming to th
11th of the revolution turns an open enemy into a friend, or it settles lawsuits wit
the aid of a friend. But the nature of the planet must always be noted, and in thes
examples how it is related to each Ascendant, and especially to the radica
Ascendant. Furthermore, that which is said here about a planet in the 7th can als
be said about the ruler of the 7th.

    13. A planet in a revolution is returned either only to the sign or only to th
house that it occupied in the figure of the radix, or to both of them at the same time
or to neither. If it is only returned to the sign, it will produce an effect signified by
the radix in accordance with the house that it occupies in the revolution. If only to
a similar house, it will produce its own radical effect from the house by reason o
the sign and its ruler in the revolution, also by reason of the radical house that tha
sign occupied, and both of these cases are strong on account of the doubled force
of the planet, either from the sign or from the house. But if it comes to the sign
and house at the same time, this case is the strongest of all and will very often
produce effects from unexpected sources, which makes the influx even more
admirable. But if a planet returns to neither [sign nor house], it must be seen
whether it returns to its own opposition by sign or by house, which is very bad, but
less so if it only returns to the opposition of the latter. And if it comes to its own
trine, it will bring forth its own fortunate radical significations; but if to its own

---

6 The charts erected in mundane astrology.

square, the reverse. And the nature and celestial and terrestrial state of the planet must be taken into account in each figure. But if the planet does not come to any of its own radical aspects, it will generally be weak in regard to its own radical significations, although it can do something else.

14. A planet in the revolution coming to the radical place of another combines the radical significations of both planets, and these are specified or determined by the signification of the house of the revolution in which the place [of the planets] is. However, it must be noted which of these planets is in the stronger place there, then whether they are friends or enemies by nature and by radical determination, i.e., whether they presage similar or contrary things in the radix. But a planet in a revolution coming to the radical aspect of another, whether good or evil, is affected—being made fortunate or unfortunate—in those things that it signifies in the revolution by reason of both of its determinations, viz. the radical and the revolutional, by that aspect in accordance with its type and the nature of the aspecting planet and the latter's radical determination. And consequently, if the ruler of the radical Ascendant comes in the revolution to the 12th house in square to Saturn ruler of the 8th of the radix, a lethal sickness or one with danger to life will be portended by this. And if Venus [comes] from the 7th of the radix to the 5th of the revolution in trine to Jupiter ruler of the Ascendant of the radix, [the birth of] children from his wife will be signified for a married native. And thus with other [combinations].

15. If a planet in the radix that is in evil aspect to another comes in the revolution to the evil radical aspect of that same planet, and there is no reception between them by house or by exaltation, it will be very evil, but less so if there is reception; but if it comes to a good radical aspect of the same planet without reception, it signifies no good from this, [but] with reception, a little good, in which one can hardly trust. But if a planet in the radix in benefic aspect to another comes in the revolution to a malefic radical aspect of the same planet with mutual reception, a great good [accomplished] by contrary means is signified if the determination is to good; [but] if there is no reception, evil will happen, no matter what the determination of the planets is.

16. If planets conjoined in the radix are conjoined anew in the figure of the revolution or similarly configured, they will bring forth the radical effects, whether good or evil, that are signified by their radical connection, [but] in accordance with the significations of the house of the revolution that they occupy. [But] if they are configured dissimilarly, i.e., if they are in trine in the nativity and they aspect each other by square or opposition in the revolution, or the other way around, and if there is no reception by house or exaltation between them, the change to a trine will produce nothing, but the change to a square will produce harm. But if there is reception between them, especially mutual reception, the change to a trine will be potent for good, and the change to a square will hardly produce any harm.

17. If the celestial state of a planet is the same in the geniture and the revolution, as if in each figure it is in its own domicile or exaltation, or it is direct,

swift, oriental of the Sun, occidental of the Moon, free from the rays,[7] in fortunate aspect with other planets, diurnal by day above the earth, etc., it will be very effective in bestowing its own radical significations in that year, especially if its direction and determination in the revolution are in agreement. But if the state is entirely contrary, it is very evil and disturbing for those same significations, especially if the change should be made from a benefic state in the radix to a malefic state in the revolution. But [if it is] partly similar and partly contrary, it insinuates that [the effect] must be declared according to the part that prevails.

18. A planet determined to the same signification in both the radix and the revolution will undoubtedly produce it in that year if its direction is in agreement or there is something else of similar or concordant signification. [But] without a direction, it will either do nothing or little.

19. If two planets are determined to the same thing[8] or something similar in the radix, and in the revolution they come together or are in concordant aspect and in concordant places of the figure, they will also produce their effect for certain in that year, as [was said] above.

20. For any planet, it must be seen in both the radix and the revolution whether it is subject to the same ruler or to different rulers. For if the latter happens, the prediction about its effects will be more obscure and confused; and one will have to pay attention to whether the different rulers are mutually friendly or inimical by their nature, connection, and determination in the revolution, and one must judge according to that.

21. In solar revolutions, one must chiefly look at the Sun itself and those things that it signified in the radix, for because its virtue is greater than that of the others, it will always do something in each year in accordance with its own radical determination, even without any new solar directions. This is plain in my case, as I have the Sun in the 12th with Jupiter, the Moon, and Saturn, and I have always had great opposition in all my undertakings, either by magnates, or by the lords whom I served, or by public affairs, such as wars, the plague, new laws, the state of the royal court, or such like. And the same thing must be said about the Moon in lunar revolutions. And one will have to be fearful when Saturn by its own proper motion transits the Moon's sign or the opposite sign in lunar revolutions because of the conjunction or opposition of Saturn, especially if it is partile, also on the day of the revolution. And if Saturn is the significator of sickness or death and the Moon is the significator of life, one will have to be very fearful of sicknesses or death in that month, especially if there is a concordant radical direction. And the reasoning is the same with the rest. Besides, in solar and lunar revolutions, those things that concur with the radical directions of the luminaries must be more diligently attended to than the rest; for if they agree in their signification, they will undoubtedly produce their effect.

---

7 That is, not *under the Sunbeams*.
8 Reading *ad idem* 'to the same thing' instead of *ad diem* 'to the day'.

22. Whoever has many planets in the same house of his geniture will experience many things throughout his whole life in connection with the things signified by that house. Because each year those planets act in the revolution in accordance with their radical determination; and therefore, whether [instigated] by one of them or by another, something of the things signified by that house will always happen. This is plain in my case, as I have Venus, the Sun, Jupiter, Saturn, and the Moon in the 12th, and there is never lacking a year in which there are not some things from among those signified by that house that must be endured or overcome.

23. In a solar revolution, see how the significator and the promittor of the new direction are related to each other, especially in the case of a strong direction that falls in that year or close by and has not yet produced its effect. For if the significator is in the place of the promittor or comes to its good or evil aspect (according to the goodness or malice of that direction), and the promittor is there by body or by concordant aspect, it will complete the effect of the direction in that year. But if the promittor is absent by body or by ray, the direction will be less effective. But it will also be very effective if the planet that is the promittor in the revolution is in its own radical place, and the significator is concordant in its ray with the direction; then, if each of them returns to its own radical place without an aspect, one must also see first whether they are allotted a determination in the revolution that is similar to their radical determination or its direction.

24. In the case of the ruler of the year, or of the solar revolution, one must generally judge from its nature, then from its state, both celestial and terrestrial, in each figure. But in particular, the ruler of the year benefic and strong in each chart will in general bring forth the fortunate things signified for that year, but especially those that it signifies by reason of each figure and its own direction. In this regard it mitigates the evils of the revolution, especially if it sees the significators of evil in the revolution by a friendly ray, or if it rules them. But the ruler of the year in each chart malefic by nature or by determination and unfortunate will bring forth all the misfortunes of that year, but especially those that it signified by reason of its own determination in each figure; and it will impede all the good things in the revolution, especially if it sees the significators of good things by a hostile ray. And the same judgment must be made about the ruler of the month, or the ruler of the lunar revolution.

25. If the ruler of the revolution, either solar or lunar, is combust, it threatens evil in those things that it signifies in both charts, and in hidden things, either in being acted upon or in suffering, and especially from [the action of] magnates.

26. If the ruler of the revolution, either solar or lunar, is also the ruler of the geniture, it will be very strong either for good or for evil. The same thing must be said about the ruler of the lunar revolution if it is also the ruler of the solar revolution.

27. If the ruler of the revolution comes to the place or the radical aspect of another planet, it will have to be judged by Law 14 [above], but the influx of the ruler of the revolution will be more effective.

28. In every revolution, one must pay particular individual attention both to the rulers of the Ascendant and the rulers of the Midheaven, then to the Sun and the Moon, namely by taking note of the nature and determination of the individual rulers in each figure, to what radical places they return, and what their state is in the revolution, and especially which planet they apply to, and how, and what they are determined to.

29. If any house of the radical figure that signifies good is well disposed and is also well disposed in the revolution, and not [affected] by planets determined in the radix to a contrary signification, the significations of that house will be advantageous in that year; but if it is evilly disposed in the revolution, especially by planets determined in the radix to a contrary signification, and they are malefics, the significations of that house will be evil. But on the contrary, if a house of the radical figure that signifies evil is also evilly disposed in the revolution, the evil significations of that house will happen; but if it is well disposed, the evils will not happen, or they will be mitigated.

30. The agreement or disagreement of two revolutions of the Sun following one after the other must be noted not only universally but particularly, both as regards [the charts] themselves and also the radical directions. For universally, a bad [revolution] succeeding universally to another bad one certainly threatens misfortune universally. But particularly, one indicative of sickness succeeding another one indicative of sickness certainly portends sicknesses, especially if the directions are in agreement. For what one could not do, or could only begin, the other one will perfect. And the reasoning is the same in the case of other particular significations.

31. One must not judge any revolution without having inspected the radical figure and its directions for the year of the revolution. However, in every revolution pay careful attention to that which it principally signifies, for it will principally bring that forth if it is signified strongly. And the greater part of the contents of the above laws are made plain in the examples given previously.

Chapt. 19. *Compendiously Embracing General Things that must be Looked at in Revolutions, with a Directory of Judgment.*

H ere we have compressed into a few words those things that are said at greater length in the chapters above.

Therefore, note first: Whether in the figure of the revolution, either of the Sun or of the Moon, the *caelum* is disposed as it is in the radix, and whether the Ascendants are opposed or in trine or square, and into which houses of the revolution the signs of the houses of the radix are removed.

Second. Note whether the cusps of the revolutional figure are the places or radical aspects of the planets, then of which [planets] by nature, determination, and state, also to which rulers they are subject by nature and to what kind of rulers they are subject by state and determination in the revolution.

Third. For each planet in the revolution, note which house of the radix it is in and especially which houses it rules. Then, note what it presages from these positions and from its own celestial state in the radix.

Fourth. Note whether it has returned to its own radical place or to any aspect of it. And to the place or aspect of any other radical planet, and how these are related among themselves by connection and determination in each figure.

Fifth. Note from which house of the radix it departs and to which house of the revolution it comes and which it rules, and in which house of the revolution its radical house is located and and how it is disposed in the revolution.

Sixth. Note to which ruler it is subject and how it is related to it, both in the radix and in the revolution.

Seventh. Note whether its celestial state in the revolution is the same as its state in the radix or contrary to it and how much or in what respects.

Eighth. Note whether it is allotted the same determination in the revolution as it has in the radix or one similar to it. And this should particularly be noted in the case of significators and promittors of directions completed within the current year.

Ninth. Note whether the same house in each figure, such as the 10th or the 8th, presages the same things or at least something related, or whether they presage contrary things.

Tenth. Note whether the directions favour or are contrary to the things signified by the revolution, both in their kind and type.

Eleventh. Gather the significations of each planet from its nature and its celestial state and determination in the figure of the radix and keep this collection [of information], made accurately and once for all, for [use in] judging the individual revolutions. And do the same with the figure of the annual revolution. Then, see in what respects the radical and revolutional significations agree and disagree among themselves and with the significations of the direction of the planet if any new direction is completed then; and judge about the effects of that planet in the revolution in accordance with the combination of these significators; and take this for a secret [of astrology].

Twelfth. From those directions agreeing in the same kind or type of effect in both the radical figure and in the annual revolution, select the one in the revolution that agrees and is most concordant with the radical direction; and at its time inspect the revolution of the Moon, and if it is also in agreement, the effect will happen in that month, and on that day on which that lunar revolution revolution supplies a concordant direction, especially [when accompanied] by a concordant transit. But perhaps it will be safer to erect all the individual lunar revolutions of the year, so that the more concordant one can be selected, especially if an effect of great importance is expected.

And from these considerations it is plain that astrological judgment is very difficult, especially when the types of effects and their accurate times are to be described. And for this purpose not only is an outstanding perspicuity and sagacity of intellect required, but also good luck, which God alone, or a Good Spirit, or the natal stars bestow by some impulse of nature. But it is also plain that the solar revolution must be judged first, rather than erecting [all] the lunar revolutions, since only those that are conformable to the solar revolution are investigated, so far as this is conformable to the radical signification and its direction. For if the solar revolution does not agree with the signification of the radix and its direction, the lunar revolutions will hardly produce anything at all, unless the effect is strongly signified by the radix and its direction and a similar lunar revolution, i.e., one which also signifies the same thing strongly.

Chapt. 20. *A Caution of no Small Importance that Must be Observed in Judging Revolutions.*

Lest the mind of the astrologer be terrified by the multitude of directions established both in solar revolutions for the Ascendant, the Midheaven, and all the planets to the places of the radical figure and of the solar revolution, and in lunar revolutions to the places of the radix and to those of the revolutions, both of the Sun and of the Moon itself, it must be known that the greater part of these produces no effect or at least no significant effect in a [particular] year, but only some of them. For the number of significant effects that can happen in a year is not so many as the number of directions that can occur from the solar and lunar revolutions (as I shall omit the revolutions of the other planets that are only satellites of the Sun to their own radical places, which I think are useless or superfluous, and at least of minor efficacy and less universal in signification than the revolutions of the Sun and the Moon), and they cannot produce great or significant events; perhaps they serve to produce the daily minor [events] to which we pay little attention; and this is much more certain than the fictitious planetary hours from which some falsely think they can predict daily accidents,[9] even down to the hour. So that, if all the abovesaid directions are set up and the days on which they fall are sought out, all the things, both significant and trivial, may be known that are going to happen throughout the whole year from [the action of] the astrological influences, unless [some] secondary fate or human will should oppose them. For since it is established by certain experience that significant effects are produced by the greater and more powerful causes, why can't the trivial effects be produced by minor and weaker causes in accordance with their own determination in the figure? Certainly

---

9 Accidents in the astrological sense, i.e., *occurrences.*

no valid reason can be offered in opposition. And therefore, if anyone has calculated all these directions from the beginning of a year and has arranged the days of the year on which the individual directions fall in order and according to their succession, he will have for almost every day, or at least very often, the means whereby he may marvel at the stupendous forces of the stars. But these minutiae are in fact concealed from men, but not from Demons.

And because the Director does not concern himself with details, as it is commonly said, nor do men consult astrologers on account of them, but only for accidents of major importance, whether unexpected or undertaken deliberately, relating to life, dignities, marriage, journeys, etc., the astrologer should therefore see in a particular year which effects are signified by the radical directions in that year that are more significant in type or in kind, and whether the solar revolution confirms that signification. For when he has done this he will arrive at the effects for that year. And therefore in a solar revolution one should see which directions are more concordant in type or kind with accidents of a certain sort, for effects of that sort are produced by these. As, if a sickness is signified by a direction of the radical Ascendant to the square of Mars, the directions of the Ascendant of the revolution to the body or the bad aspects of Mars, in the radix as well as in the revolution, should be made, or also those to Saturn or to the Sun and the Moon, especially if they are in bad houses of the radix or the revolution, or if they rule them. For the Ascendant of the revolution is determined to the life of the native in that year as the Ascendant of the radical figure is for his whole time of life; and among these directions, let the stronger one be selected, i.e., the one that is more concordant and closer to the terminus of the radical direction, for the principal effect will be produced by this one. And so, having found the day of the year on which that idrection falls, one should see whether it falls in [the period of] a concordant lunar revolution. For when this is the case the effect will be produced in that month by a concordant direction of the lunar revolution, and especially by a direction of its Ascendant, especially when a concordant transit occurs [at the same time]. And the same thing will have to be done for the rest of the effects of greater importance signified by the radix and its directions, and in this way the immense labor of [calculating] all the directions will be avoided, to which the recognition of particular effects [otherwise] compels us.

But vice versa, if on some day anything unusual or new should happen, first having noted its type, by means of which it is referred to one of the twelve houses of the figure, and having made the directions in the solar revolution and the lunar revolution appropriate to that time, one will detect by what cause it was produced, which by the way the transits do not furnish.

But if anyone wants to know on what day the *caelum* may influence him in some way in connection with his health or his life, he will find this out as follows. First, let him direct the radical Ascendant and its ruler for that day, i.e., let him see where their direction comes to on that day. Second, let him direct similarly the Ascendant of the annual revolution and its ruler for that day. Third, let him direct similarly the Ascendant of the lunar revolution in whose [period] that day falls and its ruler; and the places to which the directions of the revolution come should be looked at, not just in the figures of the revolutions but particularly in the figure of the radix. Fourth, one should look in the ephemerides to see which transits the planets may make in the figures of the revolutions, and especially in the figure of the radix. And according to these [precepts] he will judge far more certainly than he has been accustomed to do hitherto. Noting, however, that planets in the 1st, 8th, and 12th and those that are the rulers of these houses also signify by accident in connection with health and life; therefore, their directions must be inspected as said above if you want nothing to be lacking [that would lead] to a more certain judgment. And the same thing will have to be done for [predicting] actions and dignities by directions of the Midheaven and its rulers in the the figures of the radix and the revolutions, etc. to a day on which the native wants to to undertake something outstanding or difficult.

However, two things must be noted here. First, that sometimes an effect that is also noteworthy happens without any radical direction, by the solar revolution concordant to that effect and powerful and its concordant direction to the places of the radix and of the solar revolution, with a lunar revolution concordant with them, and its direction, along with appropriate transits, not opposing but rather agreeing with the radical figure.

Second, not all the abovesaid causes must be subordinated to themselves for a particular effect, even a significant one, viz. the radix, its concordant direction, a solar revolution and its concordant directions, a lunar revolution and its concordant directions, nor concordant transits. But some of the subordinated causes will suffice with a radical figure that signifies the effect at least in kind. Thus in fact nothing (at least influentially) happens that is alien to the radical figure, but transits—as actual causes of the effects—are very effective in producing them. But what has already been said about this is sufficient.

BOOK TWENTY-FOUR

Chapt. 12. *Whether the Planets act upon the Native through their Syzygies outside of the Places of the Geniture through which their Transits are Customarily Made; and How and When.*

The planets, when transiting through the places of the geniture, not only produce effects upon the native or upon things pertaining to him in accordance with their own radical determination, as was said above, but they also act through their mutual syzygies[1] outside of those places, or in vacant houses of the figure—not, however, outside of their determination, but within it. For example, on the day when the ruler of the Ascendant and the ruler of the 8th are conjoined—even in empty houses of the figure—some sickness or danger to life will happen. And similarly, on the day when the rulers of the Ascendant and the Midheaven are conjoined or when they are in trine aspect some piece of good fortune will happen to the native in connection with his undertakings, actions, or honours.

And yet, effects do not always result from these syzygies, but only when they make good a lack of transits, i.e., if two things are perceived in them that render them efficacious. The first of which is that the planets constituting the syzygy are badly configured and disposed to an evil effect by directions and by the presignification of revolutions, or favourably for good.[2] Second, that the syzygies are made in a house or houses concordant with the effect of the radical figure. Thus in fact the planets act through their syzygies in accordance with the house or houses of the radical figure in which the syzygy falls and in accordance with the nature or quality of the syzygy. And the effect of a syzygy happens on the very day of the syzygy, and often at the very hour, that is if the planets constituting the syzygy are found at this time to have been rotated by the diurnal motion into a concordant position with respect to the horizon, i.e., in concordant houses of a celestial figure that is erected for that time. Moreover, the reason why and how such syzygies are effective is this: the bodies of the planets are the causes of the celestial places in the figure of the radix, since those places are determined by the planets whose places they are said to be. And the planets themselves were also determined in the radix to this or that kind of accident with respect to the native in accordance with their own bodily position and rulership. And they retain their own force upon the native from such determination, and they continue to carry this efficacy for the native as long as he lives, as we said in Chapt. 4. Therefore, it results from this that

---

1 That is, their conjunctions.
2 The Latin text has *& fauste pro bono* 'and favourably for good', but *&* must be a typographical error for *aut* 'or'.

when the rulers of the Ascendant and the 8th come together by syzygies—even outside the radical places—they nevertheless act upon the native himself in accordance with the syzygy and its radical determination, for it is proper that both of them concur for the effect.

Chapt. 13. *Aphorisms or the Principal Laws of Transits.*

One who is strong in the theory of astrology can compose innumerable particular aphorisms because particulars depend on universals already known from theory. Therefore we shall only put here some principal universal aphorisms, from the knowledge of which, other aphorisms both universal and particular pertaining to transits may easily be deduced. Let it be then:

First. The transits of Saturn, Jupiter, and Mars are more efficacious than the transits of the other planets. For these, being slower than the others, stay longer in the places they transit; especially if they are stationary; and consequently from these places they make a more efficacious actual impression on the native. And hence it follows that the Moon's transits (at least the solitary ones) have the least virtue of all; otherwise their effects would be the most frequent, contrary to experience; but those of Saturn are the greatest of all, especially the stationary or retrograde ones.

2. The effect of any transit arises from the actual combination of the radical significators of the transiting planet and of the place through which it is transiting, having taken into account the natures and analogies of the planets.

3. The transits of the planets other than to the places of the geniture, namely the twelve cusps, the seven planets, the Part of Fortune, and their aspects and antiscions, have no efficacy for the native. For as the essence of the native depends upon these places, so also do all his changes. And yet, the syzygies of the planets in empty houses of the figure are efficacious, as we said in Chapt. 12.

4. The bodily place of the transiting planet must be noted in transits, for Mars transiting over the cusp of the 7th in opposition to the Ascendant more certainly portends lawsuits by reason of its bodily position than sickness by reason of its opposition to the Ascendant.

5. The celestial state of the transiting planet at the time of the transit must be noted in every transit—namely, whether it is in accordance with or contrary to the effect signified by the transit. For the energy of the transiting planet is increased or decreased by this. And its radical latitude must also be noted and that of the transit.

6. During an effect caused by directions and transits of the stars, the motion of the Moon and of those planets that are judged to be the cause of the effect must be carefully observed, and how in the radical figure they may move by transit from place to place of similar or dissimilar signification; then too, how by their own motion they apply by syzygies to the luminaries and planets of similar or dissimilar

signification, either by nature or by determination. For from this the success and end [result] of the effects can be discovered.

7. The transits of the Moon through the places of a figure erected for the beginning of a sickness, but especially through its own square and opposition, are of great virtue, as is established by experience; and it will be set forth when in *Astrological Prediction* (if God gives us [the length of] life to do this) we will treat of the use of astrology in medicine.[3] Why then, in a figure erected for the beginning of any other thing, will the transits of the Moon (and the other planets that signify the thing) through the places of that figure not be efficacious at any time in its duration? And this is certainly useful in the doctrine of elections; but if the figure of the geniture is at hand, its transits will have to be especially taken into account.

8. Since all the planets act in accordance with their own radical determination and their proper nature both by direction and by transit, but in a nativity they are determined to some thing, such as life, or to its opposite, such as sicknesses and death, or neither to life nor to death, but to some other thing, such as dignities; therefore, in directions and in transits, a promittor planet, determined to life and benefic and well aspected, coming to the significators of life, but especially to the Ascendant, strengthens life, [but] determined to the contrary, is harmful to life, or destroys it; but, if it is determined to neither of these, it neither helps nor hinders, or it does nothing (at least nothing significant) in connection with life. Similarly, a planet transiting through the Midheaven, appropriate to honours by its nature and radical determination, will confer honours; but determined to the contrary, such as prison, exile, or death—especially when it is malefic by nature and badly aspected or unfriendly to the Midheaven—will destroy them, or it will do much harm to them, or it will prevent them from happening; but if it is determined to neither of these, it will cause nothing (at least nothing significant) in connection with honours, actions, or undertakings, although it can occasion something trivial to occur in connection with them in accordance with its own nature or radical determination— indeed, to confer or destroy a dignity is a greater effect than to introduce some trivial good or evil occurrence into an [existing] dignity. But major effects are from major causes, and minor effects from minor causes that are not determined to anything. And the same reasoning applies to other things.

9. In transits, not otherwise than in directions, the more ways a planet coming to the Midheaven is determined to honours and is in better state, both in the radix as well as at the time of the direction and especially at the time of the transit, the more efficaciously and abundantly it will bring good fortune to the native in his undertakings and actions. Just as, if the Sun or Jupiter is the ruler of the Midheaven in the radix, and at an age concordant with dignities it is directed as promittor to the Midheaven, [and] on the day of the year in which the direction is completed, it—well aspected—will transit that same Midheaven bodily or by an appropriate aspect, especially with a concordant revolution, it will cause some notable good

---

3 Another reference to the *Astrological Prediction* that Morin had in mind to write.

fortune in dignities or undertakings, since it is determined to honours in several ways—namely by nature or analogy, rulership, direction, and by a transit concordant with a fortunate state. But, on the contrary, the more ways a planet transiting the Midheaven is determined against honours, the more efficaciously it will bring bad fortune to the native in connection with honours and undertakings, as for example Saturn in the 12th of the radix, inimical to the Midheaven because it occupies the sign Leo, coming by direction and transit to that same Midheaven, badly aspected in the radix and also at the time of the direction and transit. And the same reasoning applies to the rest of the significations.

10. If two planets, the same or related in their signification, either by analogy, as the Sun and Jupiter for honours, or Saturn and Mars for sicknesses, or by radical determination, or both, transit at the same time by body or by concordant aspect through the same place of the same or related signification as just mentioned, then their signification and virtue will be doubled in their effect and consequently in the magnitude of that same effect. But the conjunction of the transiting planets in that place is stronger than their aspects. Especially if it is the conjunction of the luminaries, or of one of them with another planet. And this aphorism is clear from many experiences. And therefore the conjunction of the Sun and the Moon in the degrees of the malefics in the natal figure or the degrees opposite them should be carefully noted, especially when both the luminaries or one of them rules the 1st; but a malefic, in whose degree there is a conjunction, is a significator of sicknesses or death, or is inimical to the Ascendant; for such conjunctions certainly signify sicknesses or death with a concordant direction; and the effect will begin on the very day of the conjunction, as I have often experienced. Similarly, the conjunction of the rulers of the Ascendant [and] the 8th of the radix in the 8th of the radix, and especially on the place of a planet that is in the 8th with a lethal direction, is lethal at the time of that conjunction. And in sum, the conjunction of two or more planets in the place of another planet must be carefully noted, and one must see what these planets are determined to, so that a correct judgment can be made about the event; and this can be applied similarly to conjunctions made in the places of good or evil aspects.

11. The simultaneous transit of two planets, related in their signification as mentioned above, through different places, with the planets themselves mutually related by nature or by radical signification (just as the places of the ruler of the Midheaven and the ruler of the 2nd house are said to be mutually related by signification, or the places of the ruler of the 12th house and the 8th house), strengthen themselves in turn for a more intense effect. For two concordant transits are stronger than one.

12. If there is a cluster of planets in any house, a planet transiting through that cluster will act in accordance with its own nature and determination and with that of each of the planets [in the cluster] when it transits through their individual places, and from the succession of transits the success of producing an accident may be discovered, or what other accidents will accompany it.

13. Luminaries joined by body or concordant aspect to a transiting planet still increase the force of the transit even though they are alien to the transit's analogous or radical signification. How much more then will they increase it when they are related?

14. When transits are being made to places in the radix, the states of those same places in the current revolutions should be noticed. For if the radical place of Saturn is in the 8th, and Saturn is in the 12th of a revolution, especially when it is badly aspected and badly configured in its own radical place, on the day that the ruler of the Ascendant transits that radical place either some sickness or some danger to the life will happen; but especially if at the time of the transit Mars or Saturn or either of the luminaries makes a bad aspect to that place. And not only should the state of a place through which a transit is being made be noted, but also the state of the transiting planet. For if Mars, transiting the Ascendant of the radix, is in the 8th or 12th of a revolution and badly afflicted, its transit across the Ascendant will be very bad.

15. The transit of planets conjoined over the degree of a direction of the radix, even an empty degree, i.e., one that is not the place of a radical planet or cusp, will not be lacking in effect; indeed, there will be a notable effect if the transit is of the luminaries conjoined, and especially with an eclipse.

16. The actual virtue of a lunar transit lasts for six hours before and after the partile transit, but in the case of the other planets, for one day before and after, by the common agreement of astrologers that esteems partile aspects much more than platic. And yet whenever a planet by its own orb of virtue rules the place through which a transit is said to be made, it has a force efficacious to produce the effect of the transit, especially the swifter planets, such as the Moon, which effect is often produced quicker or slower than the limits given above; but a single transit by itself is not equal to [producing] an effect—it would demand the necessary concourse of other causes also having an influence upon the action, which happens quicker or slower. And it must be noted that the future effect depends upon a transit, not only with regard to its actual time, but also with regard to its own nature, mode, and circumstances; for a transit produces all these things, and consequently they can also be foreseen from a transit. Moreover, when one bad transit is followed immediately by another one through the same place in a short interval of time, during a concordant radical direction and solar revolution, as for example if the transit of Saturn ruler of the 12th across the Ascendant is followed by the transit of Mars ruler of the 8th across that same Ascendant by body or by square or opposition, it will be lethal. And you will judge similarly about the rest of the significations.

17. If a benefic planet is in the Midheaven of the radix or is its ruler, and, in a concordant radical direction or solar or lunar revolution [indicative] of honours, that same benefic transits the Ascendant of the radix or the place of its ruler, especially if it is well-disposed and powerfully configured with the ruler of the Ascendant by syzygy, then the native will have good fortune in dignities or undertakings.

275

Chapt. 14. *How, from What has been Explained so far, Future Events can be Predicted from the Stars with Regard to the Type, the Year, Day, and Hour.*

In this chapter we shall repeat in a very brief compendium what was said about this subject in Books 22, 23, and 24.

First, therefore, one must have the figure of the nativity exactly rectified, with the true places of the planets, especially of the Sun and the Moon.

2. From Book 22, Sect. 1, Chapt. 9; Sect. 2, Chapt. 3; and Sect. 3, Chapts. 3 and 4, the year of the completed direction of one of its significators to any promittor may be found.

3. From the same book, Sect. 4, Chapts. 2 and 3, the kind of future accident signified by any direction may be deduced.

4. From Book 23, Chapts. 4 and 5, the figure of the solar revolution can be erected for the year found above. Then, from Chapt. 12, one can determine from the agreement or disagreement with the radical figure, the direction, and the annual revolution of the Sun, whether or not any effect may be expected from these three in that year, especially of the kind discovered above.

5. Having made the hypothesis that an effect is to be expected and having deduced its kind as discovered above, one must establish directions of the concordant significators in the annual revolution, [as explained] in Book 23, Chapt. 15, both to the places of that revolution and especially to those of the radix that are concordant with the effect that is signified; and from these it will be plain on what day of the year that effect may probably be expected.

6. In accordance with Book 23, Chapt. 9, erect the lunar revolutions that immediately precede the times indicated by the concordant directions in the solar revolution. And if one of these revolutions agrees closely with the signified effect, establish the directions of the significators that are concordant with it to concordant promittors, but especially to the places concordant in the radix. For in fact those times of the directions that coincide to the day in both revolutions promise the effect for that day. And a direction in a lunar revolution will also indicate the hour, as was seen in Book 23, Chapt. 16, in events for which the hour is given. And this will be more certain, the more directions there are that are concordant with the effect in each revolution that agree on the same time.

7. But if concordant transits of the planets occur at this same time, from [what is said in] Chapts. 5, 7, 8 and 9 of this book, there can scarcely be any doubt about the effect signified on the indicated day; and further, the hour can be discovered from the transits and the position of the planets with respect to the horizon, [as is explained] in Chapt. 11. And this procedure for predicting future events is the most natural and genuine of all, and the most certain.

But perhaps the following procedure will seem briefer and more pleasing to some. If a solar revolution agrees with a radical direction, look at each day of a lunar revolution[4] to see how the celestial state of the Moon and the planets compares with the radical figure and the radical direction. And on that day on which the state is found to be most concordant with the direction, erect a figure of the lunar revolution; for if the times of the concordant directions in both the solar and lunar revoutions coincide to the day, [the effect] will be on that day and in that hour, as was set forth above.

You will object: This procedure for discovering the state of a whole year and the true time of the effects is not only very tedious, but also one very much abounding in confusion. For besides the radical directions, there are now established revolutionary directions, both annual and monthly—and of the angles as well as of the individual planets—not only through the individual places of the radix, but also through those of the revolution, scattered through the whole zodiac. And since there are ten significators, the Ascendant, the Midheaven, the Part of Fortune, and the seven planets, and four principal aspects of these, the opposition, trine, square, and sextile, of which the trine, square, and sextile are duplicated on the right and the left; therefore each significator in a revolution can be directed to 56 places of the aspects alone for the seven planets in a single figure; and consequently 560 directions for the ten significators, just to the aspects of planets; to which, if the 63 directions of these ten significators to the bodies of the planets are added, there will be 623 directions to be established in a single figure, such as a solar revolution. And since the directions of a solar revolution should be established for these ten significators both for the places of the radix as well as for the solar revolution, then by doubling 623 there will be 1,246 directions to be calculated for a solar revolution; therefore, in each lunar revolution there will be 1,869 directions by reason of the solar revolution itself and the radical figure; and consequently, for twelve lunar revolutions in a year, [the total comes to] 22,428 directions;[5] and by adding to this 1,246 for the Sun, it becomes 23,674 directions[6] for the solar and lunar revolutions, determined to their day, and not even judged, so that with the associated transits, which are also very numerous, the state of the whole year might become known. But if from so great and so confused a task some Demon is able to extricate himself, there is no human, who could do it. And consequently this doctrine is either not true or it must be confessed that judiciary astrology is incomprehensible by a human, and should therefore be given up.

But I reply firstly: A wolf always seems bigger than he really is, and astrology is indeed the most difficult of the physical sciences, in accordance with that common saying *Those things that are beautiful are difficult.* But on this account it should not be set aside by man, but rather pursued by a more eager skill.

I reply secondly: In the old or common astrology, which admits annual, diurnal, and monthly progressions, along with the solar and lunar revolutions

---

4 That is, each day on which a lunar revolution will occur.
5 The text has erroneously 22028.
6 The text has 232[7]4, having added 1246 to 22028.

handed down by Cardan, scarcely fewer operations occur if the individual [factors] in the higher sense are minutely examined and considered. And the revolutions are to be individually or absolutely judged, without respect to the nativity, as Cardan himself did in his *Book of Revolutions*, and especially with the terms of the planets admitted.[7]

I reply thirdly: In solar and lunar revolutions, not [all of] the aforesaid ten significators are to be directed, but only the important ones, namely the Ascendant, the Midheaven, the Sun in solar revolutions, and the Moon in lunar revolutions. And even this is not always necessary, but [only] after it has been perceived from a radical direction falling in the year, and from a concordant solar revolution, that some new effect, especially one that is notably good or evil, is to be expected. If the significator of the direction is a cusp, such as the Ascendant, then the Ascendant of the revolution will also have to be directed. If it is a planet, the same planet will have to be directed in the revolution. However, it will always be useful to direct the abovesaid four significators in revolutions of both the Sun and the Moon, viz., the Ascendant, Midheaven, the Sun, and the Moon on account of the native's great dependency on them in being, acting, and being acted upon, whether a new radical direction is completed in that year or not; for there is not a year without a new radical direction, nor is there a year for the native without action or being acted upon. Besides, the previously completed direction of a radical significator to some promittor lasts in its virtue up to the occourse of another promittor, unless the latter is distant from the former by more degrees. Moreover, it will also be useful to direct the same planet in either the solar or lunar revolution, for it may also be the one that is alloted a determination concordant with the signification of the radical direction. As, if a sickness or dignity is signified, it will be useful to direct the planet which is found in the 12th house or the 10th of the revolution, especially if it was also in the 12th or the 10th of the radix, or if it was the ruler of the same house. Furthermore, the significator that will be directed in revolutions for an accident that is only signified by the nativity, or also by a new or recently elapsed radical direction, should not be directed to all the places of the nativity or the revolution, but only to those, i.e., to those promittors which, from their own nature and determination in the nativity or in the revolution, will be stronger and more concordant with the same accident, whether good or evil is going to be produced. And when, on the days that are indicated by those same directions for years and months, concordant transits occur, the effects will burst forth on those very days. And an astrologer skilled in the concordance of causes and effects will only need a few directions for the state of the whole year, i.e., for recognizing the principal changes emanating from the stars for the native in that year.

---

7 Taking the terms into account would at least double the amount of work, for not only would the condition of the ruler of a significator's sign have to be considered, but also the condition of the ruler of the significator's term. Thus, Cardan's procedure would be even more tedious than Morin's, since the latter ignores the terms.

But since it is certain that no effect, from the stars at least, ever happens without the actual concourse of concordant transits, or at least very rarely from syzygies, as was explained in Chapt. 12, it will be briefer to note down from the ephemerides those transits of the planets through the places of the geniture that are more concordant with the accident signified, whether good or evil. Then, to consider whether from the solar revolution any concordant direction may fall upon any of the days indicated by the transits; and this without conjecturing, from the comparison of the distance of the promittor from the significator, with the distance of the day indicated from the first day of the revolution, before the matter is defined by calculation, and by not taking in a solar revolution a significator and promittor that are 300[8] degrees apart for a transit that is made on the 60th day from the beginning of the solar revolution. Which being supposed, if in a lunar revolution that closely precedes the same day of the transit any concordant direction also falls at the same time, then there can be no doubt about the effect. And this is a secret of the science, evident nevertheless in the figures explained in this book and in Book 24, by means of which a confident and sagacious astrologer may come upon his object through the densest forest of directions by [following] the right path.

But lest the tyros in this new doctrine be deterred from seeking out the truth that is so much wished for, we shall set forth here for their benefit two of the abovesaid procedures in a systematic method.

First. Direct the principal significators of the annual revolution: the Ascendant, the Midheaven, the Sun, the Moon, and the planet that has completed any important radical direction in that year, and then their rulers if it seems needful; and dispose the individual arcs of direction according to the order of their ascensions in the first column of a Table constructed for that year, which may rightly be termed a *speculum* for that year.

Second. See on what numbered day from the beginning of the revolution of the year each month begins and at what hour, or what is the distance in time from the beginning of the revolution to the beginning of each month. And you will put the names of the months with that same number of days and hours [for each] across from the abovesaid arcs with the approximate same number [of days], as the number [of days] for each month, in the second column of the same Table; and so it will be plain which directions of the year fall in the individual months.

Third. Having erected the revolutions for the whole year, arrange their times similarly in the third column of the abovesaid Table, i.e., the month, day, and hour of the beginning of the revolution; and thus similarly it will be plain which directions of the year fall in the individual lunar revolutions.

Fourth. When this has been done, each annual direction of each significator may be taken, with a concordant radical direction; i.e., its arc may be taken in the first column of the Table and it may be reduced to time by the first and second Table

---

8   The Latin text actually has *;00* (a semi-colon followed by two zeros). I have put 300 because a 3 looks something like a semicolon.

of Directions for solar revolutions[9] in Book 23, Chapt. 15 (unless you prefer from the beginning to reduce the arcs of the individual annual directions to days, hours, and minutes of the annual revolution, which individual times arranged in order will be understood to have been measured from the beginning of the annual revolution), and if the number of the time is the same as the number of the beginning of any month, that direction will fall at the beginning of that month; but if it is different, subtract from it the nearest smaller number of the beginning of a month taken from Column 2, and the difference will be number of days and hours of that month in which the annual direction will be completed.

Fifth. From the time found thus, subtract the nearest time of the beginning of a lunar revolution from Column 3. And the difference of these two times will give the arc of the equator from the second and third Table of Directions for lunar revolutions;[10] and this added to the right ascension or the oblique ascension of the Midheaven or the Ascendant or the Sun or the Moon in the figure of the lunar revolution will show in Regiomontanus's *Tables of Ascension* where the monthly direction of any one of these significators extends to. Therefore, if a direction conforming to the annual direction is then completed, and finally a concordant transit of the planets is also made, the effect signified by the radical direction will happen at that time or [on that very] day; and this can also happen from a transit concordant with a single direction of a concordant annual or monthly revolution; in fact it can happen from the transit alone with a radical direction and a concordant solar or lunar revolution, especially if the transit is important and strong. But the more causes there are in agreement, the more certainly and efficaciously will the effect be produced. The same thing will be done if it is desired for individual annual directions whether a new radical direction is completed in the same year or not. And thus the state of the year will be perfectly plain if the right judgment is made about the individual [directions].

There is another and shorter kind of procedure without [the use of] the preceding table. Having taken from the ephemerides the day of a transit that is in accordance with an efficacious radical signification of the geniture, i.e., with a concordant radical signification of the geniture, count the number of completed days from the beginning of the annual revolution to that same day, and turn that into degrees of the equator by means of the second and third table of directions for

---

9 These tables are on p. 653 of the *Astrologia Gallica* and are constructed by setting 360 degrees of arc equal to 365.25 days. The reader with a pocket calculator can turn arc into days by multiplying arc by 1.014583, and days into arc by dividing days by that same constant (or by multiplying days by 0.9856263). (The fundamental equation should be 360 degrees = 365.2422 days, but the difference is slight.)

10 These tables are on p. 657 of the *Astrologia Gallica* and are constructed by setting 360 degrees of arc equal to 27.325 days. The reader with a pocket calculator can turn arc into days by multiplying arc by 0.0759028, and days into arc by dividing days by that same constant (or by multiplying days by 13.17475). (The fundamental equation should be 360 degrees = 27.32158 days, but the difference is slight.)

solar revolutions; and add that arc to the right ascension or the oblique ascension of the concordant significator, chosen in the figure of the solar revolution; and look up their sum in the tables of right ascension or oblique ascension; and it will then be plain whether that significator pertains to the concordant promittor in the natal horoscope or the solar revolution. For if that is the case, there is a great probability of a future effect on that very day. But for greater certainty, count the time similarly from the beginning of the monthly revolution most nearly preceding the day taken above to the day itself; and turn that into degrees of the equator with the second and third table of directions for lunar revolutions. And add that arc to the right ascension or oblique ascension of the concordant significator, chosen in the figure of the lunar revolution; and look up their sum in the tables of ascensions as before; and it will then be plain also whether that significator pertains to a concordant promittor in the natal horoscope or the lunar revolution. And if that is the case, there is a great probability of a future effect on that very day.

But if there are many days of transits that suit these requirements, it will be necessary to judge which is the stronger. For even though the effect from a strongly signified radical direction may happen on one particular day, not on several, yet in this most difficult science to hit the target with the first shot is very difficult for the human intellect, but not impossible; and continual excercise in this procedure is required to achieve this, along with an uncommon shrewdness of intellect that is able to discern which of the whole year's transits is the more suitable and powerful to actuate the potential of a radical direction, so that [needless] labor may be reduced.

Besides, I don't think there is any need to caution [the reader] that if the significators to be directed are placed in the descending half of the *caelum*,[11] the equatorial arcs about which we spoke above will have to be added to the OD's of their significators for their directions, or (which is easier) the place diametrically opposite to the significator will have to be directed by its ascensions, and the place diametrically opposed to the direction will be obtained, for we have supposed that this is sufficiently known from the doctrine of directions.

Only we should therefore caution [the reader] that since the doctrine we have set forth up to now for directions, revolutions, and transits is natural and uniform in both natal horoscopes and their revolutions, then it is also true, as is very plainly shown by the examples given in Book 23. And he will have to rely on this alone and not spare the labor [of making] the lunar revolutions for the whole year, especially when a new radical direction is completed in that year or it is alloted a determination in the radix that is of particular importance. For he will always produce the revolutions of the Moon and consider its directions either for any annual direction or for any concordant transit.[12] And from this it is plain that

---

11 The right side of the chart.

12 That is, he will select the appropriate one of the lunar revolutions and consider its directions.

particular events and their exact times cannot be predicted by an astrologer without great labor; because in fact particular effects depend not only upon universal but also upon particular causes, to which one must descend in order to obtain these same particular effects.

You will object secondly: That the native's future accidents cannot be predicted from the doctrine set forth by us above. So in fact the radical figure and its directions do not act without both the solar and lunar revolutions and the transits of the planets through the places of those three figures according to what was said above, and also the revolutions must be erected for the place in which the native is located at the time of each revolution, either of the Sun or of the Moon, in accordance with Book 23, Chapts. 4 and 9; and this [future] place cannnot be known from the natal chart. Indeed, it can scarcely be known even one year before the time of each solar revolution; therefore, astrology is unusable and worthless for predicting the future.

I reply first: That this objection only applies to those natives who travel some distance away, not to those who remain at their natal place, among whom are especially women,[13] or close to that place.

I reply secondly: From the nativity and the radical directions it can be known whether the native is going to travel and at what time, prior to which the revolutions erected for the natal place will be usable.

I reply thirdly: Some journeys are long, and others are short. Those which do not exceed 50 Gallic leagues from the natal place will scarcely make any noticeable change in the influx of revolutions erected for the natal place unless a difference of Ascendants is produced that exceeds 2 degrees.[14] And for those revolutions beginning with the native further distant, especially when a difference of sign is involved, they must be erected for the place where he is, and thus the things that are going to happen to him in that year may be known in advance. And it must be noted that a solar revolution, erected for the place where the native is, is valid for that whole year, however much he may travel during it, for he carries along with him the influx newly impressed at the beginning of that revolution, not otherwise than through the whole course of life he carries along the influx received at birth just as it was impressed upon him; but the lunar revolutions will be erected for the

---

13 In Morin's time women generally stayed at home and did not travel nearly so much as men.

14 A Gallic league was about 2.5 statute miles; hence 50 leagues would be 125 miles. In the latitude of Paris a degree of longitude is equal to about 49.6 miles, so in the worst case—when the native was due east or west of his birthplace at the time of the revolution—the RAMC would be increased or decreased by 2°30' or so. Again in the worst case—with 0 Capricorn on the Midheaven—such a change in the RAMC would alter the longitude of the Ascendant by 5.°4. To keep it down to the 2-degree maximum that Morin mentions, the maximum E or W distance from the birthplace would have to be restricted to 46 miles or 18 1/2 Gallic leagues. But in an average case this distance would be increased to about 100 miles or 40 Gallic leagues.

place in which the native is at the time. For just as the solar revolutions are related to the nativity that they actuate, so the lunar revolutions are to the solar revolution, which they actuate similarly. And hence astrology cannot be said to be unusable and worthless. Especially since the native can conjecture in individual years, and much more so in individual months, where he will be at the time of the next solar or lunar revolution. But whoever would do otherwise and would deliver an opinion about the native's individual accidents throughout the whole course of his life just from his nativity and its directions, or even with the addition of revolutions erected only for the place of the nativity, that one will certainly be deceived in many things, and more or less on account of the discrepancy of the revolutional figures in the different places [where the native may be]. For the stars do not make their influx upon the native except where he is. But let what has already been said about this suffice.

Leovitius, Cyprian 149 n. 187, 156
Lesdiquières, François de Bonne, Duke of 246
Libert, J. 110 n. 129
Liliputians 100 n. 119
Lilly, William 3, 72, 189
Linnaeus, Carl 212 n. 8
Little, Lucy xi n. 2
Loeb, James 221 n. 28
Longomontanus, Christian Severin 78, 208, 251
Louis XIII, King of France 53 n. 62
Louis XIV, King of France 53, 55
Luther, Martin 6
Magini, Giovanni Antonio 30, 36, 81, 83, 84, 88
Maginus *see Magini.*
Malatesta, G.B. 15 n. 16
Mammon 103
Manilius, Marcus 141 n. 173
Mantua, Charles I Gonzaga, Duke of 51 n. 57
Margherita *see Parma and Piacenza.*
Marie, Princess 53
Marie de' Medici, Queen Mother of France 53
Marie Louise of Gonzaga, Queen of Poland 51, 52
Masha'allah *see Messahala.*
Matthew, St. 103 n. 122
Medici, Catherine de' *see Catherine.*
Medici, Cosimo I de' *see Tuscany.*
Medici, Francesco I de' *see Tuscany*
Medici, Giuliano II de' *see Nemours.*
Medici, Lorenzo II de' *see Urbino.*
Medici, Lorenzo de' (Il Magnifico) 133 n. 157, 134 n. 160
Medici, Pietro II de' 133, 134 n. 159-160, 196
Melissus 251
Mersenne, Marin 228
Messahalla 30
Micheria, Clara 122
Mirandola, Giovanni II Pico, Lord of 2, 67, 70, 125, 139-145, 149, 152, 162, 163 n. 208
Modern Astrologers 186, 203, 252
Mohammed 6
Montanus & Neuber 238 n. 17
Morin, J.B. xi,xii,xiii,1, 3, 15 n. 16, 30 n. 25, 33 n. 33, 34 n. 35, 38 n. 45, 39 n. 46, 45 n. 52, 48 n. 53, 52, 58 n. 79-81, 59 n. 83, 62 n. 85, 63 n. 86, 64 n. 91, 69 n. 94, 85 n. 106, 87 n. 109, 99 n. 117, 100 n. 119, 104 n. 124, 106 n. 125, 110 n. 129, 120 n. 141-143, 121 n. 144, 122 n. 147-148, 133 n. 154-155 n. 158, 140 n. 170, 141 n. 173, 142 n. 176, 144 n. 178, 151 n. 191, 152 n. 196, 159 n. 206-207, 163 n. 208, 171-173, 174 n. 2-3, 175 n. 7, 178 n. 11, 179 n. 12, 182

This edition of
Astrologia Gallica, Book Twenty-Two,
was word-processed using Sprint,
a product of Borland International.
The document was reproduced
in Postscript mode
using Xerox Ventura Publisher,
a product of Xerox Corporation.

Other Books About Morin's Astrological Methods

The Morinus System of Horoscope Interpretation
Astrologia Gallica—Book Twenty One
Translated from the Latin by Richard S. Baldwin

A scholarly translation of Book 21 of the *Astrologia Gallica*, the book that contains the essence of Morin's method of interpreting natal horoscopes. The method rests on two fundamental principles: (1) the "determination" of a planet towards expressing its active potential in a certain facet of life; and (2) the use of accidental significators rather than universal significators.

This book assumes that the reader has a working knowledge of traditional astrology and is addressed to advanced students of astrology or to professional astrologers who would like to learn Morin's method. Beginning students should read *Cornerstones of Astrology* first and then this translation of Book 21.

In either case, this translation of Book 21 should be read before reading the translation of Book 22, since Morin assumed that the books of the *Astrologia Gallica* would be read in sequence.

Cornerstones of Astrology—Synthesis
By Friedrich Schwickert and Adolf Weiss
Translated from the Spanish version

A restatement of the Morin method by two Austrian astrologers. This book covers the same ground as Baldwin's translation of Book 21 of the *Astrologia Gallica*. It is essentially a paraphrase of the technical parts of Book 21 amplified by numerous examples from more than 20 modern horoscopes. The authors have also added their own statement of the influences of the signs and planets.

This book is suitable for those who are just beginning the study of astrology as well as for advanced students or professionals who would like to learn the essentials of natal chart interpretation by Morin's method. However, since it is essentially a paraphrase of Book 21, the student would profit by reading Morin's own words in Baldwin's translation of Book 21 after he has finished *Cornerstones*.

These books and others are available from:
American Federation of Astrologers, Inc.
PO Box 22040
6535 S. Rural Road
Tempe, AZ 85285-2040